THEORY OF ECONOMIC GROWTH

This book begins by formulating the neo-classical growth theory in a simple activity-analysis form. Then a number of major operations (involving the transplantation of material from Cambridge, Oxford, Massachusetts, California and Osaka) are performed on the existing theory to obtain the author's own model. An examination of the model reveals the existence of various equilibrium growth paths. These are then further studied from the normative and the stability points of view. Necessary conditions for the simultaneous optimum growth of population and capital, as well as those for Turnpike and Consumption Turnpike Theorems, are clarified; and the Harrodian avalanche is shown to be possible.

THEORY OF ECONOMIC GROWTH

BY

MICHIO MORISHIMA

CLARENDON PRESS · OXFORD

Oxford University Press, Ely House, London W.1

GLASGOW NEW YORK TORONTO MELBOURNE WELLINGTON
CAPE TOWN SALISBURY IBADAN NAIROBI DAR ES SALAAM LUSAKA
ADDIS ABABA BOMBAY CALCUTTA MADRAS KARACHI LAHORE
DACCA KUALA LUMPUR SINGAPORE HONG KONG TOKYO

First published 1969
Reprinted lithographically (*with corrections*) 1970

Printed by photo-lithography and made in Great Britain at the Pitman Press, Bath

PREFACE

In this book I intend to discuss economic growth within the framework of the theory of general equilibrium. In doing so I hope, on the one hand, to resolve much of the controversy on growth which is due to differences of assumptions made by various authors and, on the other, to make a contribution to the theory of dynamic economics.

The general theory of static equilibrium was nearing completion as early as 1874, but, in spite of our keen desire and constant effort, it is taking a long time to obtain its dynamic counterpart. It seems to me that this is mainly due to the lack of an established concept of 'dynamic' or 'moving' equilibrium. It is true that a number of definitions of dynamic equilibrium have been presented. But we have not yet been provided with a generally accepted one which can serve as the core of the theory. Such rigorous and systematic discussions as are usual in demonstrating the existence and optimality of the static equilibrium have seldom been made for a dynamic equilibrium. Moreover, possible motions of the whole system have not been scrutinized in their relation to the path of moving equilibrium; that is to say, no one has solved the problem of stability of motion in the complete, disaggregated system of dynamic equilibrium.

On the other hand, in the aggregative theory of economic growth, there are the concepts of dynamic equilibrium such as the Harrodian, the von Neumann, the balanced-growth, the Pasinetti or the anti-Pasinetti, the Golden equilibrium, and so forth. But unfortunately the theory is fogged with the aggregate concepts such as the aggregate production function, the quantity of capital, and the marginal productivities of labour and capital, all of which have recently been attacked by Joan Robinson and N. Kaldor. We would not be surprised if a seminar attended by both neoclassical and non-neoclassical economists were in a state of disorder five minutes from the start.

In such circumstances one naturally looks for a theory of general equilibrium of capital accumulation, both to avoid further unnecessary controversies and for the development of economic theory itself. The original idea of general equilibrium of capital accumulation is developed in Part V of Léon Walras' *Elements d'economie politique pure*, but the work has to be regarded as unfinished, particularly because no notion of the growth equilibrium is found in his theory. I graft J. von Neumann on Walras to grow a new kind of the theory of general equilibrium. The von Neumann Revolution thus brought about in dynamic economics might be comparable with the Keynesian Revolution in static economics. It makes a drastic change in the method of analysis and establishes a new norm of assessment of different growth patterns. A number of paths discovered by our predecessors (e.g. the Hicks-Malinvaud path of temporary equilibrium, the Hicks-Malinvaud path of perfect equilibrium over time, the Dorfman-Samuelson-Solow efficient path and the Ramsey optimal path) are all reviewed in the light of the new norm. A great avalanche conjectured by Harrod is seen to be possible especially in the present-day economy where the price mechanism does not work so completely as neoclassical economists assumed. I hope these discussions performed in this book will confirm the usefulness of the general equilibrium approach to growth.

Evidently, no scientific achievements can be produced by a single or a few persons. Many of the contemporary, active economists will probably be able to recognize their own contributions in various parts of the book. However, complete identification is impossible; so I reluctantly confine myself to making a few personal acknowledgements.

I started to write this book in a grand room in the historic tower of All Souls College, Oxford, when I was the 1963–64 Senior Visiting Fellow of the college. At that time Sir John Hicks was writing *Capital and Growth* in his room of the same college. We often talked about Tinbergen's difference-differential equation, choice of technique, von Neumann, Turnpike, and so on. It is no wonder my 'Capital and Growth' is so similar, in topics and even in style, to his now highly celebrated book! It was indeed an exciting experience to run a race with the champion. It will never be forgotten—especially since I began studying economics with his *Value and Capital* and was solaced by reading it in the gun room of Ohmura air base of the Imperial Navy when I was called up for active service in the war.

After Oxford, further work was pursued in Stanford, Osaka, and Colchester. I benefitted by discussing parts of the book with colleagues in these universities; in particular, the valuable comments which I received from Professor K. J. Arrow, Mr. K. Kuga, and Professor L. W. McKenzie, of Rochester, have to be acknowledged. A part of this book was also read as my Presidential Address at the First World Congress of the Econometric Society, which was held in Rome in 1965. It is still fresh in my memory that Professor Joan Robinson sent me comments from Peking, Delhi, and Cambridge after she visited Osaka on her way back from Australia.

Finally, I am indebted to the editors of *Econometrica* and *Quarterly Journal of Economics* for permission to reproduce parts of my previously published articles and to Mrs. Antoinette Dowden, University of Essex, who corrected my 93% English. Her work on this book was much more than stylistic, and I am very grateful to her also for removing a number of slips and errors from my pages.

M. M.

February, 1969

NOTE TO THE SECOND IMPRESSION

An addition and certain changes have been made in this impression. The new member, an Appendix, offers an elementary proof of the existence of a balanced-growth equilibrium in the original von Neumann system. The changes are in relation to views previously attributed to Sir Roy Harrod. He points out that, while some of these views have been attributed to him in other writings, authority cannot be found for them in his own works.

Furthermore, the word 'knife-edge' used in Chapter IV should be understood as synonymous with instability and not as implying extreme instability. In fact, A. B. Atkinson (*Review of Economic Studies*, 1969) has shown that the instability in the Harrod system is moderate only.

Finally, I would like to express my sincere appreciation of the kindness and assistance which Sir Roy Harrod offered me in correcting some bibliographical slips in the previous impression of this book.

M. M.

July, 1970

CONTENTS

PART I
THE PROTOTYPE

PART II
THE VON NEUMANN REVOLUTION

PART III

AFTER THE REVOLUTION

PART I

THE PROTOTYPE

I

WALRAS-TYPE MODEL OF MATCH-BOX SIZE

1. In this book we are concerned with the theory of economic growth as a branch of economic dynamics. We abstain from discussing practical problems, such as programmes for advancement of underdeveloped countries, the growth race between capitalist and socialist countries, the Ikeda–Shimomura programme for doubling income, and so on. Instead, our interest is confined to developing a dynamic theory from the formal theory of general equilibrium.

Léon Walras, the sun of one of the planetary systems in the universe of economics, developed a general equilibrium model of capital formation and credit, after he had explored models of exchange and production. But he was primarily concerned with momentary equilibrium to be established in a system with given stocks of capital goods that are shared among a given number of individuals. He did not discuss the working of the model through time, though his *Eléments* contains a part entitled 'Conditions and Consequences of Economic Progress', which was written with the clear intention of investigating the working of the economy in the course of time.[1] His analysis in that Part was fragmentary and did not go far beyond the confines of literal discussion. It is true that after Walras a number of attempts have been made to extend his theory towards dynamic economics; but it seems to me that they have not yielded a conclusive solution, so that I feel there is still room in the literature for adding a new formulation.

Given this aim, no one will blame us if we ignore such factors as public spending, foreign trade, technical improvement, and monetary policies, in spite of the well recognized fact that they usually play most important roles in determining the actual rate of economic growth. We deal in this book with an economy that is isolated from foreign countries and is provided with knowledge of industrial arts that does not change throughout the time horizon we are concerned with. In the first half of the book, decisions regarding investment are made by private enterprises either in the neo-classical or in the Keynesian manner, while in the second half the planning authorities are responsible for directing firms so that they invest the society's savings in such a way that the economy will progress along a

[1] Léon Walras, *Elements of Pure Economics*, translated by W. Jaffé (Homewood, Illinois: Irwin, 1954), pp. 377–92.

path of efficient or optimal growth. In this economy the wage bargain is made in terms of money. If the wage rate is fixed, prices are determined so as to cover the costs of production and the normal profits; it is clear that the real wage is governed by the relation of prices to the money wage rate.

In equilibrium, the rate of profit must equal the prevailing rate of interest with the addition of a risk premium. If the difference between the two rates is greater than the risk premium, there will be Wicksellian cumulative inflation. We can eliminate monetary effects on the 'real' growth if and only if the rate of profit and the rate of interest stand in the right relationship to each other. We assume, throughout the book, (*a*) that in the neo-classical case the monetary authorities adjust, with no time lag, the money rate of interest to the rate of profit determined, simultaneously with other variables, by the whole system of conditions, and (*b*) that in the Keynesian case, the causality is reversed; that is to say, the rate of profit (the marginal efficiency of capital) is harmonized with the rate of interest fixed by the monetary authorities. Accordingly, in either case the equilibrium condition is established between the rate of profit and the rate of interest, and there would be no monetary effects on the real side of the economy. In this book we shall disregard risk elements entirely, so that there can be no discrepancy between the rate of profit and the rate of interest.

Taking the Classical Dichotomy into real and monetary economies for granted, many economists have developed mathematical models of 'real' growth. They are, for the most part, on the line connecting the names of Keynes, Harrod, Domar, and Solow, using the aggregate production function and the aggregate investment and savings functions as the key concepts. There are, however, remarkable contrasts between their conclusions, in particular between those about the stability of the growth equilibrium. If we assume a Keynes-type economy having an investment function independent of saving decisions in which full employment is not secured by movements along the production function, then the Harrodian instability property of the equilibrium growth path is seen to follow (Harrod). On the other hand, if we make the two neo-classical assumptions, that capital can be substituted for labour in producing the output and that all savings are automatically invested, it is highly likely that the economy will be subject to a long-run tendency for the full-employment-full-capacity growth path starting from a historically given capital stock and labour force to approximate to the growth equilibrium where the stock of capital and the labour force grow at a common constant rate (Solow).

Apart from differences in investment functions assumed, differences in production functions are of great importance. If a number of production processes are available to industries, substitution between capital and labour is possible within each industry by making a shift in the method of production. However, this substitution is subject to limitation in varying degrees, since the production techniques available to the same industry are likely to be similar, so that the capital-labour ratio cannot change continuously over a wide range. It is clear that we would obtain an aggregate production function that is more or less of the proportional or 'limitational' type (i.e. with fixed coefficients of production), when relative outputs of various industries are assumed to remain constant. On the other hand, perfect substitution assumed by the neo-classical economists requires as its basis not only intra-industrial (weak) substitution but also big inter-industrial differences in capital- and labour-input coefficients. It follows that a *one*-sector model with a neo-classical aggregate production function cannot offer a complete and ultimate explanation of substitution between capital and labour. This is so because an increase in the aggregate capital-intensity may simply reflect the fact that a more capital-intensive industry (let us say, the consumption-good industry) has become relatively more important in its contribution to the aggregate output; the greater the aggregate capital-intensity, the greater may be the output of the consumption-good industry in comparison with other outputs. Thus, to different aggregate capital-intensities there may correspond different compositions of the aggregate output. But a one-sector model is not concerned with relative outputs of various industries at all. The problem of choosing techniques of production can therefore be treated appropriately only in multi-sectoral models.

A multi-sectoral model, even if it were of a match-box size, would be too complicated for us to be able to investigate its structure and working without using mathematics. We devote the present section and the following to examining a Walrasian model on the smallest possible scale in the hope that it will serve as a 'vaccine' to protect the reader from 'General Equilibrium shocks'. We assume that the economy we shall be concerned with consists of many firms which are classified into two industries: the consumption-good industry and the capital-good industry. We also assume (like Walras and Leontief) that there is no possibility of joint production; the consumption-good industry only produces the consumption goods and the capital-good industry only the capital goods. At first sight, this assumption looks very natural and admissible, but, as will be seen later in Chapter VI, it is so undesirable as to be purged away sooner or later at an appropriate stage of development of the Theory of Capital and Growth. It was, in fact, one of the victims of the von Neumann Revolution; but the present chapter describes the economy in the age when it was still on the throne.

2. It is assumed that a finite number of discrete manufacturing processes (or 'activities') are available to each industry, i.e., μ processes to the consumption-good industry and m to the capital-good industry. Throughout Part I, for the sake of simplicity, we make both μ and $m = 2$, but this does not deprive the ensuing argument of its generality at all.

Let α_1 and λ_1 be the capital- and labour-input coefficients of the first process of the consumption-good industry, and α_2 and λ_2 those of the second process; similarly, let a_i and l_i be the capital- and labour-input coefficients of the ith process of the capital-good industry ($i = 1, 2$).[1] There is no *a priori* justification for the assumption that all coefficients α_ι, λ_ι, a_i, l_i are *positive*; they are merely non-negative. In a highly aggregated model like our present two-sector one, however, they are all very likely to be positive; and it is convenient to assume throughout Part I (except when we are concerned with the general multi-sectoral model) that they are in fact positive in all possible manufacturing processes. It is also assumed, for simplicity, that the capital good does not suffer wear and tear. This is a quite unreal assumption for which the sole excuse is that it serves as a useful way of controlling traffic at a crossroads to stop the traffic on one street before that on the other starts.

Let π be the price of the consumption good, p the price of the capital good, q the price of the capital service (i.e., the earnings of a physical unit of the capital good), and w the wage rate. Each activity is evaluated at given q and w, and each industry chooses the cheapest of the technologically admissible processes. Competition among the firms will ensure that they obtain no supernormal profits. In equilibrium we have

price of the consumption good $\leqq$ cost of any process available to the consumption good industry,
price of the capital good $\leqq$ cost of any process available to the capital good industry.

As the cost per unit of output is the sum of the capital-input coefficient multiplied by the price of the capital service and the labour-input coefficient multiplied by the wage rate, the above price-cost inequalities may symbolically be written as[2]

$$\pi \leqq q\alpha_\iota + w\lambda_\iota, \qquad \iota = 1, 2, \tag{1}$$

$$p \leqq qa_i + wl_i, \qquad i = 1, 2. \tag{2}$$

An alternative justification of the price-cost inequalities may be as follows: an owner of a unit of the capital good could earn 'quasi-rent' of the amount $(\pi - w\lambda_\iota)/\alpha_\iota$ from the ιth process of the consumption-good industry, or $(p - wl_i)/a_i$ from the ith process of the capital-good industry. He will choose processes so that the aggregate amount of quasi-rents

[1] We follow Sir John Hicks in denoting prices and quantities of the consumption-good sector by Greek letters and those of the capital-good sector by the corresponding Latin letters. See J. R. Hicks, *Capital and Growth* (Oxford: Clarendon Press, 1965).

[2] In this book, an equation introduced in Chapter X and numbered i is described simply as equation (i) when it is referred to in some places in that chapter, but as equation (x. i) when it is referred back to in later chapters.

which he can expect to earn is maximized. Let q be the largest among $(\pi - w\lambda_\iota)/\alpha_\iota$, $\iota = 1, 2$ and $(p - wl_i)/a_i$, $i = 1, 2$; we then get the inequalities.

If (1) holds with strict inequality for some processes, those processes are not used in equilibrium; so that the positive production of the consumption good requires that (1) should hold with equality for at least one process. Similarly, the price of the capital good is as high as the minimum cost of production so long as some amount of the capital good is produced; processes that do not give the minimum cost would not be adopted, i.e. each of them is associated with the zero level of operation.

Let us classify citizens into two classes: capitalists and workers. Write K and L for the stock of the capital good and the number of the workers available at the point of time under discussion. In a state of equilibrium fully utilizing capital and labour, workers receive an income of the amount wL, while the income from owning capital is qK. The total income is the sum of these and is divided into consumption and savings. Since we are neglecting depreciation, we need not bother with double definitions of income and savings in terms of 'net' and 'gross'.

There are plenty of econometric studies of the consumption behaviour of various social groups, many of which have shown significant differences in the propensity to consume from one group to another, e.g. among farmers, business owners, and non-farm, nonbusiness units. We, however, assume as a first approximation a uniform society where capitalists and workers are homogeneous in their consumption-savings decisions. As workers also save, the stock of capital in the economy is owned not only by capitalists but also by those workers who have shares in the firms. We define (*ex ante*) savings as that part of the total income which is left after the intended consumption $\pi\gamma$ (γ being the demand for the consumption good) is deducted, and we assume that savings are a constant fraction of the total income. Let the quantity of the capital good that can be bought by spending the whole amount of the current savings be denoted by s; the total savings may then be written as ps. Let b be the constant that represents the community's average propensity to save. It follows from the definition of savings that the intended consumption $\pi\gamma$ is also a constant proportion of the total income. Thus we have

$$\pi\gamma = \beta(qK + wL), \tag{3}$$

$$ps = b(qK + wL), \tag{4}$$

where $\beta = 1 - b$, a constant representing the community's average propensity to consume.

The 'uniclass' consumption and savings functions, (3) and (4) obey the following two important rules. First, it follows immediately from the definitional relationship that the sum of consumption and savings is identically equal to the total income, i.e.

$$\pi\gamma + ps = qK + wL. \tag{5}$$

This is an identity in the prices, π, p, q, w, and is commonly referred to as Walras' law. It holds for all non-negative values of the prices so long as, either the price of the consumption good π or the price of the capital good p is positive, and the prices of factors, q and w, are not both zero. It is obvious that citizens are free from Walras' law when they can buy any good in any amount they want, so that all situations such that $\pi = p = 0$ and $q+w > 0$ should be excluded from the domain of the law.

Secondly, a recent development of demand theory has confirmed that individual demand functions derived from a regular utility function by the maximization procedure fulfil the (weak) axiom of revealed preference (or the Wald–Samuelson inequality): if at a certain set of prices P a consumer chooses a commodity basket A in spite of the fact that he could buy another one, say B, then the former would be found to be more expensive than the latter at those prices P' at which the latter is actually bought. This relationship is reasonable enough as far as a rational individual is concerned, because otherwise the consumer could buy A at P' as well, and the purchase of B would prove his preference of it to A. Indeed, the relationship that A is revealed to be superior to B at P if reversed at P' is a contradiction to the law of consistent preferences.

The community's demand functions, on the other hand, are not required to satisfy the axiom unless the members of the community have similar tastes. Changes in prices normally affect the distribution of income, which in turn affects the relative importance of each individual in the formation of the market demand. Consider an economy in which workers have a greater propensity to consume than capitalists, as in the Joan Robinson–Kaldor–Pasinetti world. It is possible that workers dominate capitalists at P and conversely at P', and the case is in fact obtained if w/q is very large at P and very small at P'. Suppose commodity baskets $A = (\gamma, s)$ and $B = (\gamma', s')$ are equally expensive at P and at P'; suppose also that workers prefer A to B and capitalists B to A. Then the market demand would more or less be of the type A at P and of B at P', so that 'inconsistent' preferences may consistently be revealed in the community. Thus the axiom of revealed preference would probably be violated in the market if consumers have dissimilar tastes, as we have confirmed by using the example of the consumption and savings functions of the Robinson–Kaldor–Pasinetti type. In the 'uniclass' Economy consisting of citizens with similar tastes for goods, however, a change in the distribution of income due to a price change will not have any effect on consumption and savings; the consumption and savings functions in such a community will, therefore, naturally be expected to satisfy the axiom.

In the present application the axiom may be stated as follows: Let $P = (\pi, p, q, w)$ and $P' = (\pi', p', q', w')$ be two price sets with which different consumption-savings plans (γ, s) and (γ', s'), respectively, are associated. Suppose (γ', s') is not more expensive than (γ, s) at P; then

(γ, s) would be more expensive than (γ', s'), if they are evaluated at P'. That is to say, the inequality, $\pi\gamma'+ps' \leqq \pi\gamma+ps$, implies the strict inequality, $\pi'\gamma'+p's' < \pi'\gamma+p's$.

It is evident that the axiom is established if we can show that the two inequalities

$$\pi\gamma'+ps' \leqq \pi\gamma+ps \quad \text{and} \quad \pi'\gamma'+p's' \geqq \pi'\gamma+p's$$

contradict each other. Suppose first $p/\pi \neq p'/\pi'$. We have, from (3) and (4),

$$\gamma = \beta(qK+wL)/\pi, \qquad s = b(qK+wL)/p,$$
$$\gamma' = \beta(q'K+w'L)/\pi', \qquad s' = b(q'K+w'L)/p'.$$

Substituting these into the above inequalities and eliminating the incomes $qK+wL$ and $q'K+w'L$, we finally obtain

$$\left(\frac{\pi}{\pi'}\beta+\frac{p}{p'}b\right)\left(\frac{\pi'}{\pi}\beta+\frac{p'}{p}b\right) \leqq (\beta+b)^2.$$

In this expression the inequality sign is found to be in the wrong sense as $\beta+b = 1$ and $p/\pi \neq p'/\pi'$. Therefore, the second inequality of the axiom follows if the first holds. Next, suppose $p/\pi = p'/\pi'$; it is clear that $(\gamma, s) \neq (\gamma', s')$ if and only if the real income is different in the two situations. On the other hand, when $p/\pi = p'/\pi'$, the first inequality of the axiom implies that the real income in the second price situation P' does not exceed the real income in the first P. This real-income inequality is strengthened by the condition $(\gamma, s) \neq (\gamma', s')$ and becomes a strict one; hence the second inequality of the axiom follows directly. Thus, the consumption and savings functions that we assume do satisfy the weak axiom of revealed preference.[4]

[1] Consider, for the sake of simplicity, an economy consisting of one capitalist and one worker. Let K_c be the part of capital owned by the Capitalist and K_w by the Worker. The Capitalist's consumption and savings functions,

$$\pi\gamma_c = \beta qK_c \quad \text{and} \quad ps_c = bqK_c,$$

are generated from the utility function $u = U_c(\gamma_c{}^\beta s_c{}^b)$, where U_c is any increasing function of $\gamma_c{}^\beta s_c{}^b$; similarly, those of the Worker,

$$\pi\gamma_w = \beta(qK_w+wL) \quad \text{and} \quad ps_w = b(qK_w+wL),$$

from $u = U_w(\gamma_w{}^\beta s_w{}^b)$. It is seen that each individual's consumption and savings functions satisfy the weak axiom of revealed preference, and his utility function is of the Cobb–Douglas type. In the case of the propensities β and b being common to both persons, we might regard the aggregate functions (3) and (4) as if they were generated from an 'aggregate utility function', $u = U(\gamma^\beta s^b)$.

Perhaps McKenzie was the first to see that the uniclass consumption and savings functions (or Graham's demand functions) do satisfy the weak axiom. See L. McKenzie, 'On equilibrium in Graham's model of world trade and other competitive systems', *Econometrica*, Vol. XXII (1954), pp. 147–61.

In summary, the community's consumption-savings plan (γ, s) of the 'uniclass' type fulfils:

(i) Walras' law (in the domain D consisting of all $(\pi, p, q, w) \geqq 0$, not in the coordinate plane $\pi = p = 0$, $q+w > 0$), and
(ii) the weak axiom of revealed preference.

Furthermore, it is seen that

(iii) γ and s are non-negative for all values of π, p, q, w in D,
(iv) γ and s remain unchanged when all prices change proportionately, and
(v) the income elasticities of γ and s are unity.

As will be seen below, these properties of the consumption and savings functions play essential parts in establishing the stability of the long-run equilibrium as well as guaranteeing the existence and Pareto optimality of the short-run equilibrium. The whole argument in Part I, although it is presented in terms of the 'uniclass' consumption and savings functions, can be applied *mutatis mutandis* to any system with more general non-linear consumption and savings functions, provided that they are endowed with properties (i)–(v). All the assumptions other than (v) are natural and require no comment, while (v) is a restrictive condition which, I hope, will gain entrance into our system, as a first approximation to reality, as it is conventionally assumed by many writers.

It is obvious that no more goods can be consumed than are produced; and the *ex post* consumption of any good must equal the *ex ante* demand for that good in a state of short-run equilibrium, similarly for the capital good. We have, therefore, the following inequalities as equilibrium conditions for the consumption good and the capital good respectively:

demand for the consumption good $\leqq$ its total output,

demand for the capital good $\leqq$ its total output.

Symbolically,

$$\gamma \leqq \sum_{\iota} \xi_{\iota}, \tag{6}$$

$$d \leqq \sum_{i} x_{i}, \tag{7}$$

where ξ_{ι} is the output of the consumption good produced by the ιth activity ($\iota = 1, 2$), x_i the output of the capital good produced by the ith activity ($i = 1, 2$), and d the demand for the newly produced capital good of firms or real investment. When (6) holds with strict inequality, the consumption good will be a free good and its price must be zero; similarly, strict inequality (7) implies the price of the newly produced capital good is reduced to zero. It is seen below that d must equal the real savings s in the state of equilibrium.

As a historical datum, the total stock of the capital good K has been distributed among various firms; for each of which we have an inequality stating that the amount of the capital good used cannot exceed the available stock. We assume, however, that the capital stocks are freely transferable from one firm to another, in order that a large number of inequalities may be replaced by the one implying no overall deficiency of the stock of capital. It is evident that this is an unwelcome assumption, but it immensely simplifies matters. We shall use it until it is liquidated in the von Neumann Revolution. On the other hand, there would be no very strong objection to assuming that labour is freely transferable from one firm to another. We thus have two aggregate inequalities:

utilization of the capital good $\leqq$ its availability,

employment of labour $\leqq$ its availability.

These conditions simply state that no more factors can be used than are available in the economy and may be written as:

$$\sum_{\iota} a_{\iota}\xi_{\iota} + \sum_{i} a_i x_i \leqq K, \tag{8}$$

$$\sum_{\iota} \lambda_{\iota}\xi_{\iota} + \sum_{i} l_i x_i \leqq L. \tag{9}$$

In neo-classical equilibrium, the Rule of Free Goods is also applied to factor markets: the price of capital services q is zero if (8) is a strict inequality, while the wage rate w is zero if (9) is a strict inequality.

In equilibrium, if it is non-trivial, one of the prices should be positive. If prices of all factors q and w vanish, the prices of products π and p will also vanish (see (1) and (2)); therefore, either q or w must be positive. As the production coefficients are assumed positive, the minimum costs (and hence π and p) are necessarily positive. This means that the consumption and the newly produced capital goods are not free, so that (6) and (7) hold as equalities. On the other hand, the Rule of Free Goods requires

$$qK + wL = \Big(\sum_{\iota} \alpha_{\iota}\xi_{\iota} + \sum_{i} a_i x_i\Big)q + \Big(\sum_{\iota} \lambda_{\iota}\xi_{\iota} + \sum_{i} l_i x_i\Big)w$$

because q (or w) is zero when (8) (or (9)) is an inequality, while the Rule of Profitability requires

$$\sum_{\iota} (\alpha_{\iota} q + \lambda_{\iota} w)\xi_{\iota} + \sum_{i} (a_i q + l_i w)x_i = \pi \sum_{\iota} \xi_{\iota} + p \sum_{i} x_i$$

because ξ_{ι} (or x_i) is zero when (1) (or (2)) is an inequality for the ιth (or the ith) process; we have, therefore, *in equilibrium*,

$$qK + wL = \pi \sum_{\iota} \xi_{\iota} + p \sum_{i} x_i = \pi\gamma + pd.$$

In view of Walras' law, we obtain $d = s$ (investment = savings) as an equilibrium condition.

3. Is there a state that satisfies all the short-run equilibrium conditions? We can give several rigorous proofs, the most natural one being marshalled in terms of excess demand for factors. Let us define the excess demand for capital services and for labour as

$$E_K = \sum_{\iota} \alpha_{\iota}\xi_{\iota} + \sum_{i} a_i x_i - K \qquad \text{and} \qquad E_L = \sum_{\iota} \lambda_{\iota}\xi_{\iota} + \sum_{i} l_i x_i - L,$$

respectively. They are *prima facie* functions of the activity levels of the industries, ξ_1, ξ_2, x_1 and x_2. However they may be reduced to functions depending only on the wage-rate by the following substitution procedure.

With given factor prices, we can compare all available processes with each other. If each industry has a unique process that gives the minimum cost—let it be the first process of each industry—then $\xi_2 = 0$ and $x_2 = 0$, so that we should have $\xi_1 = \gamma$ and $x_1 = s$ in equilibrium. We have, therefore,

$$E_K = \alpha_1\gamma + a_1 s - K \qquad \text{and} \qquad E_L = \lambda_1\gamma + l_1 s - L.$$

But when the two processes of the consumption-good industry are tied, ξ_2 need no longer be zero; ξ_1 and ξ_2 might be any non-negative numbers such that $\xi_1 + \xi_2 = \gamma$. A similar situation may of course happen in the capital-good industry. As will be observed in the next chapter, such singularities can only occur at some critical factor prices; and we have at most a *finite* number of critical sets of (normalized) prices.

Let us normalize prices so as to make the sum of q and w unity. It is evident that this procedure enables us to treat one of them, say q, as a function (the complement) of the other.

In view of the price-cost inequalities, we can also eliminate the prices of the products from the list of independent variables. We therefore find that, with given K and L, the normalized wage-rate w is the sole independent variable of the consumption and savings functions.

When $w = 0$, the excess demand for capital services E_K is necessarily zero, because we have the identity

$$qE_K + wE_L = 0$$

in w, holding when the rule of profitability and the rule of free goods (for the products) prevail.[1] Hence, if the excess demand for labour is zero or negative at $w = 0$, the demand-supply conditions for capital and labour, (8) and (9), are obviously fulfilled; we have an equilibrium at $w = 0$.

Suppose now that the zero wage rate does not give an equilibrium. Since $E_L > 0$ at $w = 0$ and E_L is a continuous function of w, we do not

[1] Walras' law implies this identity when each industry chooses only those processes which give minimum costs, and the tied processes are operated at the intensities ξ_{ι} and x_i such that $\sum_{\iota} \xi_{\iota} = \gamma$ and $\sum_{i} x_i = s$.

have any equilibrium in a small neighbourhood of $w = 0$. If $E_L = 0$ at some w, then E_K is also zero by virtue of the identity above, so that an equilibrium is established. We suppose, however, that E_L remains positive until w reaches a singular point.

At any singular point, either the consumption-good industry or the capital-good industry (or both) has tied processes, which may be worked at any intensity so long as they yield the total output, $\sum_{\iota} \xi_{\iota}$ or $\sum_{i} x_i$, in the amount that is exactly equal to the demand, γ or s; there correspond many values of E_K and E_L to the singular normalized wage-rate. It can easily be seen that collections of such E_Ks and E_Ls constitute *convex* sets, S_K and S_L, respectively.[1] It is also seen that the multi-valued correspondences $w \rightarrow S_K(w)$ and $w \rightarrow S_L(w)$ are *upper semicontinuous* at any singular point.[2] Since E_L is supposed to be positive before the normalized wage-rate reaches the first singular point $\bar{w}$, it follows from the upper semicontinuity at $\bar{w}$ that the set $S_L(\bar{w})$ contains a non-negative element, $E_L(\bar{w}) \geqq 0$. Hence, if it has a non-positive element, $E_L(\bar{w}) \leqq 0$, also, it is clear that it contains an element such that $E_L(\bar{w}) = 0$. In view of Walras' law we at once find that the set $S_K(\bar{w})$ contains $E_K(\bar{w}) = 0$. Therefore, $\bar{w}$ gives an equilibrium.

Let us suppose that all sets $S_L(\bar{w})$, $S_L(\bar{\bar{w}})$, etc. associated with singular points, $\bar{w}$, $\bar{\bar{w}}$, etc. consist of positive elements only, and that E_L remains positive (hence E_K remains negative) throughout the whole range of w starting from $w = 0$ until it arrives at 1. The continuity implies that at the terminus we have $E_K \leqq 0$ as the limit of a sequence of negative numbers and $E_L \geqq 0$ as the limit of a sequence of positive numbers (or if $w = 1$ is a singular point, it follows from the upper semicontinuity at $w = 1$ that the sets $S_K\,(w = 1)$ and $S_L\,(w = 1)$ contain elements, $E_K \leqq 0$ and $E_L \geqq 0$, respectively). As $q = 0$ at the terminus, Walras' law requires that $E_L = 0$. Hence we find that $E_K \leqq 0$ and $E_L = 0$ at $w = 1$; that is to say, the terminus should be an equilibrium point if there is no equilibrium at all on the way.

In the rest of this chapter, solutions to inequalities (1)–(9) obtained by the above procedure are denoted by π^0, p^0, q^0, w^0, ξ^0, x^0. Since a proportional change in prices does not affect γ and s, it can easily be verified that $\theta\pi^0$, θp^0, θq^0, θw^0, ξ^0, x^0 also fulfil the equilibrium conditions (1)–(9) for any positive number θ. We may normalize prices, as classical economists did, so as to make the price of the consumption good unity, i.e.

[1] A set is said to be *convex* if an average of any two elements of the set S with arbitrary non-negative weights is also an element of S, i.e. if $x \in S$ and $x \in S$ implies $\theta x + (1-\theta)x' \in S$ for any θ such that $0 \leqq \theta \leqq 1$.

[2] Let $\{x^i\}$ and $\{y^i\}$ be sequences of points with limits $\bar{x}$ and $\bar{y}$ respectively. A multi-valued correspondence $y \rightarrow S(y)$ is said to be *upper semicontinuous* at $\bar{y}$ if $x^i \in S(y^i)$ for all i implies $\bar{x} \in S(\bar{y})$.

$\theta\pi^0 = 1$. The corresponding w gives the real wage in terms of the consumption good. In the following, the equilibrium prices are always normalized in this way; hence $\pi^0 = 1$.

It will be convenient for use later to give the definitions of the terms 'reasonable' prices, 'admissible' prices, and 'feasible' activities now. We call prices fulfilling inequalities (1) and (2) *reasonable*[1] and activity levels fulfilling (8) and (9) *feasible*. Prices are called *admissible* if there are feasible activities that produce the exact amounts of the consumption and capital goods required by the consumption-savings plan that the citizens make at those prices. Using these terminologies we may say that an equilibrium is established when and only when the prices are reasonable and admissible, and the activities are feasible.

4. The axiom of revealed preference which has been shown to be fulfilled by the consumption and savings functions of the 'uniclass' type is irrelevant to the above proof of the existence of equilibrium. But, as we will soon realize, it is a powerful generator of the uniqueness of the equilibrium values of γ and s. Suppose that there are two sets of (normalized) equilibrium prices (π^0, p^0, q^0, w^0) and (π^1, p^1, q^1, w^1) to which there correspond *different* consumption-savings plans (γ^0, s^0) and (γ^1, s^1), respectively. We may assume, without loss of generality, that

$$\pi^0\gamma^1+p^0s^1 > \pi^0\gamma^0+p^0s^0;^{2}$$

in other words, when prices π^0, p^0, q^0, w^0 prevail, the consumption-savings plan (γ^1, s^1) *cannot* be carried out because of the shortage of income. Next, multiply (1) and (2), which hold for 'reasonable' π^0, p^0, q^0, w^0 by 'feasible' ξ_ι^1 and x_i^1 respectively, and add them up. We then get an inequality which holds for any reasonable prices and any feasible activity levels,

$$q^0K+w^0L \geqq \pi^0\sum_{\iota}\xi_\iota^1+p^0\sum_{i}x_i^1, \tag{10}$$

and states that no more outputs can be produced than the inputs consumed, provided that the outputs and inputs are evaluated at some reasonable prices. Now take ξ_ι^1 and x_i^1 as the equilibrium levels of activity associated with the second equilibrium. In any equilibrium, there is no excess demand for the consumption good and for the capital good, and the demand for the capital good (or investment) d must equal the savings s; we

[1] Reasonable prices correspond to the 'normal long-run supply prices' of Marshall, or the 'prices of production' of Marx.

[2] Otherwise we would have by the weak axiom of revealed preference

$$\pi^1\gamma^1+p^1s^1 < \pi^1\gamma^0+p^1s^0.$$

This reduces to the inequality in the text by the substitution of the superscript 0 for 1 and vice versa.

must therefore have $\sum_{\iota}\xi_{\iota}^1$ and $\sum_{i}x_i^1$ not less than γ^1 and s^1 respectively. It is at once seen from (10) that the consumption-savings plan (γ^1, s^1) *can* be carried out at the prices, π^0, p^0, q^0, w^0. This obvious contradiction to the inequality preceding (10) is due to the wrong supposition; hence (γ^0, s^0) = (γ^1, s^1). It is clear, however, that the equilibrium levels of activities, ξ_1^0, ξ_2^0, x_1^0, x_2^0, may not be unique, whereas the uniqueness of the growth rate s/K directly follows from the uniqueness of s.

As the consumption function is of the 'uniclass' type, the uniqueness of the real consumption implies that of the real national income, which in turn, together with the uniqueness of the savings s, implies a unique equilibrium price of the capital good (in terms of the consumption good). We also have a unique set of equilibrium factor prices, since the null hypothesis that there are multiple equilibrium values of q and w, say q^0, w^0 and q^1, w^1, is, as will be seen below, reduced to a contradiction. Suppose the processes chosen by an industry (either the consumption-good or the capital-good industry) at (q^0, w^0) are different from those at (q^1, w^1). Then ξ_{ι}^0 (or x_i^0) is positive for at least one process such that its cost at (q^1, w^1) exceeds the price of the output π^1 (or p^1); hence we have a strict inequality

$$\sum_{\iota}(\alpha_{\iota}q^1+\lambda_{\iota}w^1)\xi_{\iota}^0+\sum_{i}(a_iq^1+l_iw^1)x_i^0 > \pi^1\sum_{\iota}\xi_{\iota}^0+p^1\sum_{i}x_i^0.$$

It follows from the feasibility of (ξ_{ι}^0, x_i^0) that the left-hand side of the above inequality is not greater than q^1K+w^1L; while, in view of $\pi^0 = \pi^1 = 1$ and $p^0 = p^1$ (the uniqueness of the price of the capital good), the right-hand side is seen to be equal to q^0K+w^0L. Therefore, the inequality,

$$q^1K+w^1L > q^0K+w^0L,$$

is obtained, which evidently contradicts the uniqueness of the real income. This means that the null hypothesis should be rejected; hence the equilibrium prices are unique.

5. The equilibrium so far established with given K and L is now examined for the so-called Pareto optimality. A Pareto optimum is usually defined in terms of utilities or preferences as a state in which the satisfaction of any consumer cannot be raised without leaving someone else worse off than before. Given techniques of production, the factors of production restrict the products that can be produced in the economy. They may be distributed among the residents in various ways. A distribution of some feasible outputs is compared with a different distribution of the same outputs or with a different distribution of different (but still feasible) outputs. Each and every individual in the economy orders (or 'preorders', more exactly) all the possible distributions according to his preferences. An optimum is a state where no suitable change in production and distribution leads to better satisfaction of the preferences of an individual unless some others in the economy are sacrificed.

As many economists have observed in various models of a competitive economy, there is a two-way relationship between the (short-run) equilibrium and the (short-run) Pareto optimality;[1] that is to say, to any feasible state that is a Pareto optimum, there corresponds a certain initial distribution of the resources among the residents that makes that state an equilibrium; and conversely, an equilibrium that corresponds to a given initial distribution of the resources is necessarily a Pareto optimum. These two proposition are obtained on the basis of some regularity of the preferences of each individual. In the remainder of this chapter we are interested in establishing the latter proposition.

We begin by recalling some necessary definitions. As capital and labour are assumed to be freely transferable, we have no technical restriction on production other than the inequalities (8) and (9). We have called activity levels (ξ_ι^1, x_i^1) fulfilling those inequalities *feasible*. We have then called a price set (π^2, p^2, q^2, w^2) *admissible* if it is associated with a feasible set of activity levels (ξ_ι^2, x_i^2) producing the total outputs, $\sum_\iota \xi_\iota^2$ and $\sum_i x_i^2$, that equal the consumption γ^2 and the savings s^2 corresponding to that price set. We also call activities (ξ_ι^2, x_i^2) admissible.

Now let θ_j denote the amount of the consumption good that the jth individual consumes, and v_j the amount of the newly produced capital good that falls into his ownership. The total output is entirely distributed among individuals, so that we have, for any feasible activities (ξ_ι^1, x_i^1),

$$\sum_\iota \xi_\iota^1 = \sum \theta_j^1, \qquad \sum_i x_i^1 = \sum_j v_j^1, \tag{11}$$

where it is noted that the summations on the right-hand sides are taken over all individuals, while those on the left-hand sides are taken over all activities. Let L_j and K_j be the amount of labour and the stock of the capital good which are at the disposal of the jth individual before making any transaction. Finally, let (γ_j^2, s_j^2) be the set of consumption and savings which would actually be chosen by the jth individual as the most satisfactory one, when an admissible price set (π^2, p^2, q^2, w^2) prevailed. Obviously, from the definitions and admissibility, we have

$$\sum \gamma_j^2 = \gamma^2 = \sum_\iota \xi_\iota^2, \qquad \sum_j s_j^2 = s^2 = \sum_i x_i^2.$$

Suppose now that, for some admissible distribution (γ_j^2, s_j^2) associated with prices (π^2, p^2, q^2, w^2) there is a feasible state (θ_j^1, v_j^1) such that a change in distribution of goods from (γ_j^2, s_j^2) to (θ_j^1, v_j^1) will shift the

[1] See, for example, G. Debreu, *Theory of Value* (New York: John Wiley, 1959), pp. 90–7.

satisfaction of at least one person to a higher level, with no one feeling worse off than before. Then we should have:

$$w^2L_j+q^2K_j \leqq \pi^2\theta_j^1+p^2v_j^1, \qquad \text{for all } j, \tag{12}$$

with strict inequality for at least one individual j who to be consistent prefers (θ_j^1, v_j^1) to (γ_j^2, s_j^2). In fact, if the left-hand side of (12) were greater than the right-hand side for an individual who is indifferent between (θ_j^1, v_j^1) and (γ_j^2, s_j^2), he could save more by choosing the former instead of the latter. Similarly, if the left-hand side of (12) did not fall short of the right-hand side for an individual who prefers (θ_j^1, v_j^1) to (γ_j^2, s_j^2), he would choose (θ_j^1, v_j^1). In any case we have a contradiction to the fact that (γ_j^2, s_j^2) is chosen at (π^2, p^2, q^2, w^2). It is evident that the Pareto optimality of the given distribution (γ_j^2, s_j^2) rules out existence of a feasible and more preferable distribution (θ_j^1, v_j^1); we can, therefore, adjudicate (γ_j^2, s_j^2) to be optimal if we do not find any other feasible distribution yielding (12).

Let us now show that the short-run equilibrium characterized by the inequalities (1)–(9) is a Pareto optimum. We use the method of *reductio ad absurdum* and suppose the contrary. As the short-run equilibrium is an admissible state, we suppose that there is a feasible distribution (θ_j^1, v_j^1) such that

$$w^0L_j+q^0K_j \leqq \pi^0\theta_j^1+p^0v_j^1$$

holds for all j, with strict inequality for at least one j. Therefore,

$$w^0L+q^0K < \pi^0\sum_j\theta_j^1+p^0\sum_j v_j^1$$

for the whole economy. The feasibility of the distribution (θ_j^1, v_j^1) implies that with it are associated feasible activities ξ_ι^1 and x_i^1 fulfilling (11). We have already observed that the inequality (10) is satisfied by any feasible activities and equilibrium prices. Hence we get

$$w^0L+q^0K \geqq \pi^0\sum_\iota\xi_\iota^1+p^0\sum_i x_i^1.$$

In view of (11), we can at once see that the above two inequalities contradict each other. This absurdity is observed for any feasible distribution. Hence there is no feasible state which is preferable to the short-run equilibrium state; therefore, the latter is a Pareto optimum.

6. The discussion has hitherto proceeded on the assumption of perfect flexibility of investment decisions; it has, in fact, assumed that there are always enough opportunities to invest capital goods so that the aggregate amount of investment can be made to be as great as the aggregate savings. We have seen that investment equals savings in equilibrium; but up to this last part of the chapter, the demand for new capital goods or investment has not been put in a precise and definite functional form.

We are now reminded that the discussion has assumed investment decisions obeying the following rules: First, firms do not adopt unprofitable processes for the production of goods. Second, the total utilization of the capital good should not exceed its availability. We then have, at time t,

$$K(t) \geqq \sum_{\iota} \alpha_{\iota}\xi_{\iota}(t) + \sum_{i} a_i x_i(t),$$

while, at time $t+\Delta t$ very close to t,

$$K(t)+d(t)\,\Delta t \geqq \sum_{\iota} \alpha_{\iota}\xi_{\iota}(t+\Delta t) + \sum_{i} a_i x_i(t+\Delta t).$$

These two inequalities are reduced to equalities when the capital good is scarce and, therefore, the full utilization of the capital good continues to prevail. We would then obtain an investment function of the Acceleration Principle type,

$$d(t) = \sum_{\iota} \alpha_{\iota}\dot{\xi}_{\iota}(t) + \sum_{i} a_i \dot{x}_i(t),$$

provided that the same processes remain profitable. (The dot denotes, as usual, differentiation with respect to time.)

Since we have assumed, as the pricing rule, the Rule of Free Goods, the full utilization will be established unless the price of the capital service vanishes; so that the acceleration principle would be valid almost everywhere except at the 'singular' points at which an industry switches from one process of production to another. As has been seen, the Rule of Free Goods, together with the Rule of Profitability, means the short-run equilibrium is obtained at every point of time; except at the extreme points, where $q = 0$ or $w = 0$, both capital and labour will be fully employed, and investment will be equated to savings at the full-employment level.

Our final remark concerns the Rule of Profitability and the Rule of Free Goods. We have assumed that these rules become operative in the state of short-run equilibrium satisfying the conditions (1)–(9). This results, as has been seen, in an equality between investment and savings, although the original system of inequalities, in terms of which the short-run equilibrium is defined, does not take any explicit account of equality between investment and savings. As the converse (but alternative) way of approach, we might first define the short-run equilibrium as a state of affairs satisfying the investment-savings equation in addition to the other nine sets of conditions, (1)–(9), and could then show that the Rule of Profitability and the Rule of Free Goods would be obtained in that state. This is so because we have, from (1)–(9) and the non-negativity of variables,

$$\begin{aligned} \pi\gamma + pd &\leqq \pi\sum_{\iota}\xi_{\iota} + p\sum_{i}x_i \\ &\leqq \sum_{\iota}(\alpha_{\iota}q+\lambda_{\iota}w)\xi_{\iota} + \sum_{i}(a_i q + l_i w)x_i \\ &\leqq qK + wL = \pi\gamma + ps; \end{aligned}$$

at least one of these three weak inequalities should hold with strict inequality if either the Rule of Profitability or the Rule of Free Goods is not fulfilled; hence, we should have $d < s$—an obvious contradiction to the required equality of investment to savings. It is thus seen that, once conditions (1)–(9) have been imposed and accepted, the two Rules are equivalent to the aggregate condition, $d = s$.[1]

The working of such a system through time will be discussed in Chapter III. It is worth noticing that the path generated is a neo-classical one in which the full employment of labour and the full utilization of capital are realized almost all the time. Recent writers such as Meade, Solow, and Uzawa have been concerned with the approach of such paths to the long-run equilibrium of steady growth, the existence of which is the subject of the next chapter. The Keynesian mechanism of economic growth, on the other hand, completely differs from the neo-classical one and violates the Rule of Free Goods (competitive pricing) and, accordingly, always faces dangers which will land the economy into a state of secular stagnation with persistent unemployment. Chapter IV, which is the dual to the neo-classical Chapter III, will be devoted to discussing the *in*stability of such Keynesian paths.

[1] To avoid unnecessary confusion, a footnote may be helpful. It must be recalled that ps is a particular kind of *ex ante* savings which is defined as the difference between the full-employment income, $qK+wL$, and the corresponding *ex ante* consumption, πy. In the Keynesian underemployment equilibrium where the Rule of Free Goods does not prevail, investment is also equated with savings, but savings in this case are different from the *ex ante* savings in the above sense. They are the savings which are realized from the *actual* income, which is not necessarily at the full-employment level. Thus the regulation of the Rule of Profitability and the Rule of Free Goods is not equivalent with the equality between investment and savings in the Keynesian sense but with the one in the sense of classical (or neoclassical) economists.

II

POSSIBILITY OF PERSISTENT GROWTH EQUILIBRIUM

1. SO FAR we have seen that there is a short-run equilibrium corresponding to any given positive amounts of capital and labour. In the first half of this chapter, instead, the rate of real wages is exogenously fixed at some level, and the stock of capital and the number of workers are treated as variable. The equilibrium prices of the capital goods and the capital services, the activity levels of the two industries and the required amounts of capital and labour are found by solving inequalities (1)–(9) in the previous chapter with the real-wage rate specified at the given level. As will be recognized in the second half, this alternative line of argument, which may be referred to as the Growth Equilibrium method, will be more suitable for finding a long-run, steady growth equilibrium where outputs of all goods grow together at a rate equal to the growth rate of the labour force, all the prices remaining unchanged forever.

The argument proceeds in terms of the natural and the warranted rate of growth, the most fundamental concepts of growth economics originally due to Sir Roy Harrod. With no technological improvement the natural rate of growth may be equated to the rate of increase of the working population. On the other hand, to get the warranted rate, defined by Sir Roy as 'that over-all rate of advance which, if executed, will leave entrepreneurs in a state of mind in which they are prepared to carry on a similar advance',[1] some preliminary bulldozing is necessary; in fact, as is seen below, it is a concept that results from a combination of Samuelson's outer envelope of the factor-price frontiers and Kahn's inter-industrial multiplier.

We begin by elucidating the factor-price frontiers that give the correspondence between the real-wage rate and the rate of return on the capital good, where the latter is defined as the ratio of the rental (quasi-rent) that a unit of the capital good earns *per annum* to its price, $r = q/p$. Let us normalize prices in such a way that the price of the consumption good is unity; the normalized wage rate then gives the real-wage rate. As the price-cost inequalities contain three variables (i.e., the price of the capital good p, the price of capital service q and the real-wage rate w), two of them, say the first two, can be expressed as functions of the last. Hence we get a relationship between the rate of return of the capital good

[1] R. F. Harrod, *Towards a Dynamic Economics* (London: Macmillan, 1948), p. 82.

and the real-wage rate, which, as will be seen below, gives the rate of return as a decreasing function of the real-wage rate in an interval restricted by technology.

Let us consider the following pair of equations obtained by arbitrarily picking out processes ι and i among those available to the two industries:

$$\begin{aligned} 1 &= rp\alpha_\iota + w\lambda_\iota, \\ p &= rpa_i + wl_i. \end{aligned} \tag{1}$$

Eliminating p, we have

$$r = \frac{1-w\lambda_\iota}{a_i + w(\alpha_\iota l_i - \lambda_\iota a_i)}. \tag{2}$$

In this equation we may note that $\alpha_\iota l_i - \lambda_\iota a_i$ is positive if and only if the capital-good industry is less capital-intensive than the consumption-good industry (Uzawa's condition). Although it is very likely, at least in the present stage of technological development, that the consumption-good industry has some processes that are more capital-intensive than some processes of the capital-good industry, it is very unlikely that all processes of the consumption-good industry are more capital intensive than any of the processes available to the capital-good industry. It would be of great importance to observe that the existence of the long-run equilibrium and other principal properties of the system are established without imposing any conditions upon the relative factor-intensities between the two industries.

Measure the real-wage rate w along the horizontal axis and the rate of return along the vertical axis. The relationship (2) traces out a downward sloping curve (called a factor-price frontier (by Samuelson)) starting from $1/a_i$ and terminating at $1/\lambda_\iota$. (The sign of dr/dw derived from (2) is independent of the capital-intensity condition, i.e. the sign of $\alpha_\iota l_i - \lambda_\iota a_i$, and is always minus. But the sign of d^2r/dw^2 depends on the Uzawa condition; it is positive or negative according to whether it is fulfilled or not.) For each pair of processes we can draw a similar curve so that we obtain Fig. 1 for $(\mu = m = 2)$,[1] where we assume that $\frac{a_1}{l_1} < \frac{\alpha_2}{\lambda_2} < \frac{a_2}{l_2} < \frac{\alpha_1}{\lambda_1}$, and the processes are arranged so that $\lambda_1 \leqq \lambda_2$ and $a_1 \leqq a_2$. Note that Uzawa's condition holds for all process pairs except the pair consisting of the second processes of both industries.

We have 4 ($= \mu m$) possible pairs of processes. To each of them there corresponds a rate of return given by the formula (2); therefore, we have 4 (i.e., μm) possible rates of return. Among them the maximum gives the

[1] As before, μ and m are numbers of processes which are available to the consumption-good and the capital-good industry, respectively.

'reasonable' (or short-run equilibrium) rate of return corresponding to the given real-wage rate. It is seen that the relationship between them is traced out by the heavy kinky curve in Fig. 1 (that is called the 'outer envelope of factor-price frontiers' by Samuelson or the 'wage frontier' by Hicks[1]). We find that if a given real-wage rate w is less than the smallest

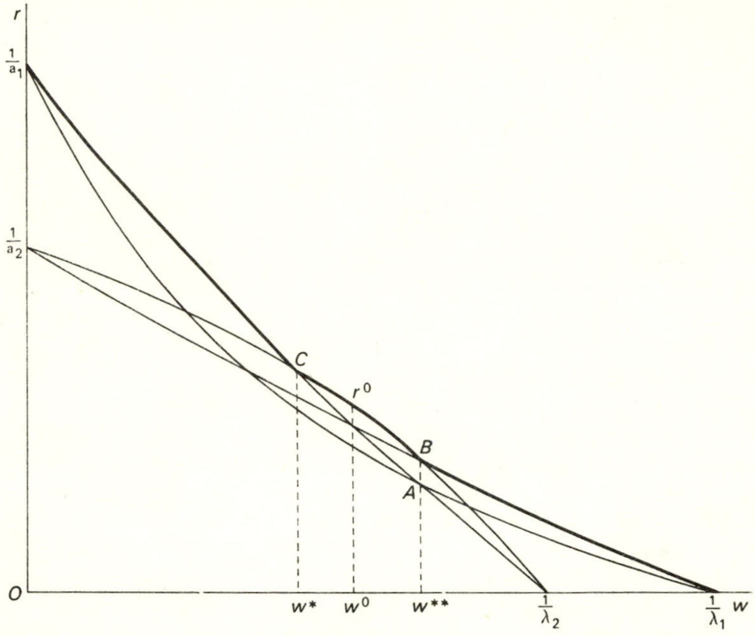

FIG. 1

singular rate w^*, then the consumption-good industry selects the second process (α_2, λ_2) while the capital-good industry selects the first process (a_1, l_1); if w is greater than w^* but less than the second singular rate w^{**}, both industries select the second processes (α_2, λ_2) and (a_2, l_2); if w is between w^{**} and the technologically attainable maximum $1/\lambda_1$, the consumption-good industry selects the first process (α_1, γ_1) and the capital-good industry the second process (a_2, l_2). We also find that at the first singular point w^* the capital-good industry may choose a mixture of the first and the second processes. The consumption-good industry is in a similar situation at the second singular point w^{**}.

[1] See P. A. Samuelson, 'Parable and realism in capital theory: the surrogate production function', *Review of Economic Studies*, Vol. XXIX (1962), pp. 193–206; J. R. Hicks, *op. cit.*, p. 150.

It is now shown that 'reasonableness' which is a necessary condition for equilibrium is established only on the outer envelope of factor-price frontiers.[1] Let r^0 be the greatest among the four (or μm) possible rates of return corresponding to a given real wage w^0, so that it is on the outer envelope. Let p^0 be the price of the capital good associated with r^0; and let (ι^0, i^0) be the particular set of processes that generates such r^0 and p^0. We have, of course,

$$\pi^0 = 1 = r^0p^0\alpha_{\iota^0}+w^0\lambda_{\iota^0},$$
$$p^0 = r^0p^0a_{i^0}+w^0l_{i^0}. \qquad (1^0)$$

Consider next another particular set of processes ι and i for which the price-cost equations (1) are satisfied by r^1 and p^1 when the wage rate is fixed at w^0. It is then seen that $r^0p^0 \geqq r^1p^1$, because otherwise (i.e., if the latter exceeds the former) a pair of processes ι and i^0 would yield a rate of return greater than r^0;[2] that is clearly a contradiction to the fact that r^0 lies on the outer envelope. Hence we have

$$1 \leqq r^0p^0\alpha_\iota+w^0\lambda_\iota$$

for any process ι. We also have

$$p^0 \leqq r^0p^0a_i+w^0l_i$$

for any process i, because if there were a process i not satisfying the above inequality, then the pair ι^0 and i would yield a rate of returns greater than r^0.[3] Therefore, no process pair which gives a rate of return greater than r^0 is found in the 'catalogue of techniques' available to the industries, provided the wage rate is fixed at w^0. This establishes the 'reasonableness' of r^0, p^0, and w^0.

[1] For the definition of reasonable prices, see above, Chapter I, p. 14.

[2] Consider the simultaneous equations:

$$\pi = 1 = rp\alpha_\iota + w^0\lambda_\iota$$
$$p = rpa_{i^0} + w^0l_{i^0}.$$

As stated above, we have $r\,p = r^1p^1$. If r^1p^1 is greater than r^0p^0, the right-hand side of the second equation is greater than the corresponding one of (1^0). As the wage rate is fixed, it follows that p on the left-hand side must increase less than the proportion, by which the capital cost increases from $r^0p^0a_{i^0}$ to $r^1p^1a_{i^0}$. This implies that the r determined by the above equations is greater than r^0 determined by (1^0).

[3] Comparing the first equation of

$$1 = rp\alpha_{\iota^0}+w^0\lambda_{\iota^0}$$
$$p = rpa_i+w^0l_i$$

with the first of (1^0), we obviously have $rp = r^0p^0$, so that the right-hand side of the second equation is less than p^0, by hypothesis. Thus, $p < p^0$; this means that the r determined by the above equations must be greater than r^0; a contradiction again.

2. It seems that a digression may be in order at this point.[1] Since each industry has two processes, there are four possible sets of processes available to the economy. The sets consist of: I, the first process of each industry; II, the first process of the consumption-good industry and the second process of the capital-good industry; III, the second process of the consumption-good industry and the first process of the capital-good industry; and IV, the second process of each industry. Fig. 1 shows that the economy will choose, as the most efficient set of techniques, set III at very low rates of real wages, set IV at higher rates, and set II at very high rates; set I is never adopted at any rate of real wages. As far as Fig. 1 is concerned, the sets of techniques are ordered in a monotonic way, so that there is no possibility of the so-called 'Ruth Cohen Curiosum' (Joan Robinson);[2] that is to say, a set of processes that has been adopted as the most efficient one at a low rate of real wages and replaced by another one at a higher rate is not re-adopted at any even higher rate.

We now ask two natural questions: (i) Can this monotonic property be regarded as a general law, or do we get it only in special cases such as those illustrated in Fig. 1? (ii) What modifications of the model will make the 'atavism' of technology possible? These questions are more or less related to each other; we shall be provided with the answer to the latter as soon as we are ready to give the correct answer to the former.

The first problem will be easily handled if we introduce the notion of the 'partial' envelope of factor-price frontiers. For convenience of analysis let us suppose, for a while, that one of the industries, say the capital-good industry, continues to use an arbitrary but specified technique of production, say the first process, independently of the market prices. Then we have two (or μ) factor-price frontiers, connecting $1/a_1$ on the vertical axis in Fig. 1 with $1/\lambda_1$ and $1/\lambda_2$ on the horizontal axis. The curve $\left(\frac{1}{a_1}\ CA\ \frac{1}{\lambda_1}\right)$ gives the partial envelope of those factor-price frontiers which would prevail when the capital-good industry sticks to the first process; the other partial envelope $\left(\frac{1}{a_2}\ CB\ \frac{1}{\lambda_1}\right)$ is obtained in the case of the capital-good industry sticking to the second process.

It is evident that at the point of kink A the factor-price frontiers constituting the partial envelope in question give the same rate of return; so that we have at A

$$\frac{1-w\lambda_1}{a_1+w(\alpha_1 l_1-\lambda_1 a_1)} = \frac{1-w\lambda_2}{a_1+w(\alpha_2 l_1-\lambda_2 a_1)}\ (=r).$$

[1] This section originally appeared in the November, 1966 issue of *The Quarterly Journal of Economics* in a slightly different form.

[2] Joan Robinson, *The Accumulation of Capital* (London: Macmillan, 1956), p. 109.

It is seen that this equation in w has only two solutions, one of which is always zero, and the other is

$$w = \frac{\alpha_2 - \alpha_1}{\alpha_2\lambda_1 - \alpha_1\lambda_2}, \tag{3}$$

which is positive and less than $1/\lambda_2$ if and only if $\alpha_1 > \alpha_2$ and $\lambda_1 < \lambda_2$.[1] This means that any two frontiers originating from the same point on the vertical axis can intersect at most once. Hence there is no possibility of the reappearance, on the partial envelope, of a method of production of the consumption-good industry that has been absent in an intervening part; in other words, processes of the consumption-good industry are *monotonically* ordered on the partial envelope. It is furthermore seen that the abscissa (3) of the singular point where the technique of the consumption-good industry is switched from the second process to the first is independent of that process of the capital-good industry which forms the partial envelope. From this fact we find that the processes of the consumption-good industry appear on every partial envelope in the same manner. As the envelope of factor-price frontiers is the envelope of partial envelopes, this find implies the impossibility of the 'coming back' of a technical method. Exactly the same argument ensures a monotonic arrangement of the processes of the capital-good industry.

From all that has so far been said we can easily see what factors are responsible for the non-atavistic theorem. It must be remembered that our two-sector model assumes *inter alia* (*a*) that each process yields its output without any time-lag, and (*b*) that all capital goods are 'malleable', so that they can be aggregated into a homogeneous metaphysical capital good. Since a process with a lapse of time from the initial input of factors of production to the final output of the product (i.e., the so-called roundabout method of production) may be decomposed into a number of instantaneous processes using heterogeneous capital goods by introducing as many fictitious intermediate goods and fictitious sectors as we require, it is seen that the assumption of homogeneous capital goods is more basic than the assumption of instantaneous production. As we shall see below, a counter-example to the non-coming-back law is obtained as soon as the heterogeneity of capital goods is allowed for.

Suppose there are two kinds of machines m_1 and m_2. The former can be produced by two alternative ways, while the latter can be produced in one way only. The production-coefficients are:

[1] The inequality $\alpha_1 > \alpha_2$ implies that the consumption-good industry will select the second process at very low wages; while it follows from $\lambda_2 > \lambda_1$ that it chooses the first at very high wages. It is clear that there is a 'watershed' wage rate w^{**} at which the consumption-good industry switches from the second process to the first.

	Process 1		Process 2		Process 3	
	Input	*Output*	*Input*	*Output*	*Input*	*Output*
Machine m_1	0·5	1	0	1	0·2	0
Machine m_2	0·1	0	1	0	0	1
Labour	0·5	0	0·2	0	1	0

It is not difficult to calculate that, at low wage rates, the second method is used to produce machine m_1; and that as wages rise, the system shifts over to the first method. One might be tempted to consider the latter as the more 'mechanized' or 'roundabout' method of production. But, as Joan Robinson, Ruth Cohen, and Piero Sraffa have insisted, the same calculation shows that this system (which is indecomposable) will shift back, at very high wage rates, to the technique used at the lowest wage rate.[1]

With the coefficients prescribed in this example, the industry producing m_1 will obviously prefer the second process to the first, when the wages or the rental of m_1 is very high; while it prefers the first to the second at very high rentals of the machine m_2. It is seen that when the wage rate is very low, the rental of m_1 is very high, so that the second process of the consumption-good industry is chosen at low rates of wages as well as at high rates; moreover, it is seen that for those wage rates belonging to the middle range, the rental of the m_2 is so high as to make the first process cheaper than the second. Thus the Curiosum is reasonable enough, so that the non-atavistic (or non-switching) theorem is shown to be definitely false for models with many capital goods.[2]

3. We now return to the main subject. It has been observed that, given the real-wage rate w^0, the industries choose processes such that they yield the maximum rate of return r^0; the equilibrium prices are obtained by solving the pair of equations (1) corresponding to the processes chosen. The remaining problem is to find the equilibrium levels of activities, (ξ_ι^0, x_i^0), as well as the required capital K^0 and labour L^0.

[1] Levhari has wrongly asserted the impossibility of the 'coming back' for the indecomposable case. See David Levhari, 'A nonsubstitution theorem and switching of techniques', *Quarterly Journal of Economics*, Vol. LXXIX (1965), pp. 98–105, particularly pp. 102–5. Although the falsity of the Non-Switching Theorem (which was first pointed out by Luigi Pasinetti in his paper delivered at the First World Congress of the Econometric Society, Rome, September 1965) does not impair the validity of the Nonsubstitution Theorem of the first half of Levhari's paper, he proves his Nonsubstitution Theorem under the unnecessarily restrictive assumption of indecomposable matrices. Not only is this logically unnecessary, but also it gratuitously rules out many cases which should not be neglected from the realistic point of view.

[2] Cf. the related papers in *Quarterly Journal of Economics*, November, 1966, also.

Since both capital and labour are indispensable for the production of the consumption and the capital goods, their costs of production are always positive, no matter whether either capital or labour is free. The consumption and the capital goods have, therefore, positive prices, so that by virtue of the rule of free goods, the demand for the consumption good γ must equal its supply $\sum_\iota \xi_\iota$, and savings s must equal investment $\sum_i x_i$; hence we get a variant of Kahn's multiplier[1]

$$\frac{\sum_\iota \xi_\iota}{\sum_i x_i} = p\,\frac{\beta}{b}, \tag{4}$$

in view of (I.3) and (I.4)—note that $\pi = 1$ by the normalization. Remembering that the price of the capital good, p, depends on the real-wage rate (the envelope of factor-price frontiers), we find that the real-wage rate is the ultimate determinant of the relative outputs of the two industries.

The required amount of capital is defined as the sum of the products of the capital coefficients and activity levels:

$$K = \sum_\iota \alpha_\iota \xi_\iota + \sum_i a_i x_i. \tag{5}$$

Similarly, for carrying out the production of (ξ_ι, x_i), labour is required in the amount,

$$L = \sum_\iota \lambda_\iota \xi_\iota + \sum_i l_i x_i. \tag{6}$$

It is evident that if $\xi_\iota{}^0$, $x_i{}^0$, K^0 and L^0 satisfy (4)–(6), then if these are multiplied by any positive number they will also satisfy the equations. We may, therefore, normalize the solutions by dividing both sides of the equations by $\sum_i x_i{}^0$; in particular, we have from (5)

$$\frac{\sum_i x_i{}^0}{K^0} = \frac{1}{\sum_\iota \alpha_\iota \eta_\iota{}^0 + \sum_i a_i z_i{}^0} = \frac{b}{\dfrac{p(\sum_\iota \alpha_\iota \xi_\iota{}^0 + \sum_i a_i x_i{}^0)}{\sum_\iota \xi_\iota{}^0 + p\sum_i x_i{}^0}}, \tag{7}$$

where $z_i{}^0 = x_i{}^0/\sum_j x_j{}^0$ and $\eta_\iota{}^0 = \xi_\iota{}^0/\sum_j x_j{}^0$, and the second equality follows since $b = p\sum_i x_i{}^0/(\sum_\iota \xi_\iota{}^0 + p\sum_i x_i{}^0)$, i.e. the average propensity to save equals, in equilibrium, investment divided by the real national

[1] Professor Kahn has been concerned with multiplier effect of a given increment of primary employment in the investment industry upon total employment. See R. F. Kahn, 'The relation of home investment to unemployment', *Economic Journal*, Vol. XLI (1931).

product. On the extreme right-hand side, the denominator gives the required capital per unit of output (Harrod's C_r) and the numerator the average propensity to save (his s); it is seen that the rate of growth of capital, $\sum_i x_i^0/K^0$, thus obtained gives the 'warranted rate of growth' of the economy in the Harrodian sense, i.e., s/C_r.[1] If the economy grows at this rate, all the equilibrium conditions other than the one in the labour market (I. 9) will be fulfilled. There is no reason, on the part of entrepreneurs, for changing the growth rate; it will persist if the supply of labour adapts itself to the demand for labour.

By the use of the diagram of factor-price frontiers and Kahn's inter-industrial multiplier, the warranted rate of growth can now be analysed effectively in the following way. If w^0 is a point other than the singular points, w^*, w^{**}, etc., the processes (ι, i) adopted by the two industries, as well as the prices and the rate of return, are uniquely determined. It follows, therefore, that z_i^0 is unity for the process i chosen by the capital-good industry and zero for all others; and that η_ι^0 for the process ι chosen by the consumption-good industry equals the relative outputs of the two industries given by Kahn's multiplier (4), and all the other η^0s vanish since the corresponding processes are not operated at that wage rate. We may then write (7) in the form,

$$\frac{\sum_i x_i^0}{K^0} = \frac{1}{\alpha_\iota p \dfrac{\beta}{b} + a_i}.$$

As p is a continuous function of w in the range where the same process set (ι, i) is chosen, the warranted rate of growth, denoted by $g(w)$, changes continuously as w changes in that range. In fact, it is seen that an increase in w gives rise to a decrease (or an increase) in $g(w)$ if the consumption-good industry is more (or less) capital-intensive than the capital-good industry.

At the singular points, the process sets chosen by the industries are not unique; they may be operated at any relative intensity such that

[1] If we assume the savings function of the Joan Robinson–Kaldor type, instead of the one adopted in the text, i.e. if we assume that workers do not save at all, then we get the equilibrium condition that investment equals the capitalists' average propensity to save times the profits they earn. The warranted rate of growth may in that case be put in the Kaldorian form; that is to say, it equals the capitalists' average propensity to save times the rate of profit on capital. In the intermediate case where workers and capitalists save at different rates, we are confronted with the so-called Pasinetti paradox discussed by Samuelson, Modigliani, and others. (See, for example, P.A. Samuelson and F. Modigliani, 'The Pasinetti paradox in neoclassical and more general models', *Review of Economic Studies*, Vol. XXXIII (1966) pp. 269–302.) This problem will be extensively discussed later in sections 5 and 6 below as well as Chapter VI.

$\sum_{\iota}\eta_{\iota}^{0} = p\beta/b$, and $\sum_{i} z_{i}^{0} = 1$. Hence the warranted rate of growth $\sum_{i} x_{i}^{0}/K^{0}$ and the capital-labour ratio K^{0}/L^{0} are not unique.[1]

Let us now concentrate our attention on the correspondence between $g(w)$ and w at the singular points, w^{*}, w^{**}, etc. We may continue to assume without loss of generality that each industry has two processes available to it. Let $(\eta_1^0, \eta_2^0, z_1^0, z_2^0)$ and $(\eta_1^1, \eta_2^1, z_1^1, z_2^1)$ be two different solutions associated with the same singular real-wage rate w^0. We at once find that another solution is obtained by taking a weighted sum of the two solutions above, such that the weights, θ^0 and θ^1, are non-negative and add up to one. Hence the set of all such possible solutions is convex and closed. In view of (7) we get

$$g^{\theta} = \frac{1}{\sum_{\iota}\alpha_{\iota}\eta_{\iota}^{\theta} + \sum_{i} a_i z_i^{\theta}} = \frac{1}{\dfrac{\theta^0}{g^0} + \dfrac{\theta^1}{g^1}} \tag{8}$$

where η_{ι}^{θ} and z_i^{θ} denote the composite solutions, and g^0 and g^1 are the rates of growth of the capital stock associated with the solutions (η_{ι}^0, z_i^0) and (η_{ι}^1, z_i^1) respectively. Equation (8) shows that g^{θ} is the harmonic mean of g^0 and g^1, so that it lies between them; it also shows that the set of the rates of growth is convex and closed.

Two further remarks on singularity are needed in order to draw the warranted-growth-rate curve.[2] First, two different processes κ and ν of the consumption-good industry that are chosen indifferently at a certain (singular) real-wage rate w^0 cannot *simultaneously* be chosen as equilibrium

[1] It is seen that a unique rate of growth of the capital stock is obtained, if and *only* if a unique short-run equilibrium pair of processes is associated with a given real-wage rate. Suppose that the consumption-good industry (say) has two processes κ and ν which are selected as the cheapest at prices π^0, p^0, q^0, w^0. Obviously,

$$\pi^0 = r^0 p^0 \alpha_{\kappa} + w^0 \lambda_{\kappa}, \qquad \pi^0 = r^0 p^0 \alpha_{\nu} + w^0 \lambda_{\nu};$$

it follows that $\lambda_{\kappa} = \lambda_{\nu}$ if and only if $\alpha_{\kappa} = \alpha_{\nu}$.

Next, let the nth process be the process of the capital-good industry that is cheapest at those prices. If the pairs of processes, (κ, n) and (ν, n), are operated with intensities (ξ_{κ}, x_n) and (ξ_{ν}, x_n') such that $\xi_{\kappa}/x_n' = \xi_{\nu}/x_n' = p\beta/b$, then we have from (7)

$$\alpha_{\kappa}\frac{\xi_{\kappa}}{x_n} + a_n = \frac{1}{g}, \qquad \alpha_{\nu}\frac{\xi_{\nu}}{x_n'} + a_n = \frac{1}{g'}.$$

We find $g = g'$ if and only if $\alpha_{\kappa} = \alpha_{\nu}$ (and hence if and only if $\kappa = \nu$).

Under the weak axiom of revealed preference it has been shown in Chapter I that there is one and only one rate of growth corresponding to *given* K and L (or given K/L); it is possible, however, that we have the same real-wage rate w for different values of K/L, so that the correspondence of the growth rate g to w is not in general unique (although it typically is so), but there may, in fact, be several singular points, w^{*}, w^{**}, . . . , to any of which there corresponds more than one value of the rate of growth.

[2] Throughout the following generalized discussion we allow both industries to have two or more processes.

processes at any other real-wage rate w^1. This is so, because otherwise we would have for the consumption-good industry

$$\begin{cases} r^0p^0\alpha_\kappa + w^0\lambda_\kappa = 1, \\ r^1p^1\alpha_\kappa + w^1\lambda_\kappa = 1, \end{cases} \qquad \begin{cases} r^0p^0\alpha_\nu + w^0\lambda_\nu = 1, \\ r^1p^1\alpha_\nu + w^1\lambda_\nu = 1. \end{cases}$$

If these two pairs of equations are regarded as equations determining α_κ, λ_κ, and α_ν, λ_ν respectively, we at once find that they give the same solutions; that is, $\alpha_\kappa = \alpha_\nu$ and $\lambda_\kappa = \lambda_\nu$, which contradicts the fact that κ and ν are different. A similar observation is made for the capital-good

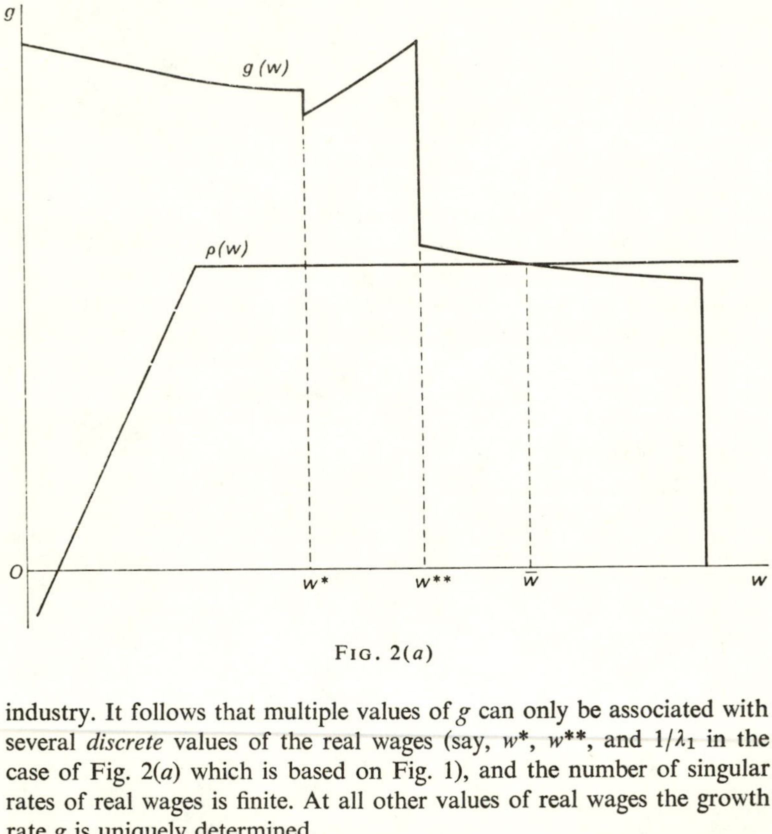

FIG. 2(*a*)

industry. It follows that multiple values of g can only be associated with several *discrete* values of the real wages (say, w^*, w^{**}, and $1/\lambda_1$ in the case of Fig. 2(*a*) which is based on Fig. 1), and the number of singular rates of real wages is finite. At all other values of real wages the growth rate g is uniquely determined.

Second, suppose multiple values of g are associated with a given real-wage rate, say w^*. At w^*, several processes κ, ν, . . . are selected as equilibrium processes of the consumption-good industry, and processes k, n, . . . as those of the capital-good industry. A number of pairs of the processes are possible; among them, let (κ, k) and (ν, n) be the pairs which generate the minimum and the maximum rates of growth, g_* and g^*, respectively.

Let σ be any equilibrium process of the consumption-good industry such that $\sigma \neq \kappa$. Consider two states of affairs in which the sets of processes, (κ, k) and (σ, k), are operated at intensities (ξ_κ, x_k) and (ξ_σ, x_k'), respectively, such that the relative intensities ξ_κ/x_k and ξ_σ/x_k' are both equal to Kahn's multiplier, $p^*\beta/b$, where p^* is the value of p corresponding to the real-wage rate w^*; we get

$$g_* = \frac{1}{\alpha_\kappa \dfrac{\xi_\kappa}{x_k} + a_k} \quad \text{and} \quad g = \frac{1}{\alpha_\sigma \dfrac{\xi_\sigma}{x_k'} + a_k}.$$

Since $g_* < g$, we have $\alpha_\kappa > \alpha_\sigma$. It follows from

$$\pi^* = q^*\alpha_\kappa + w^*\lambda_\kappa = q^*\alpha_\sigma + w^*\lambda_\sigma$$

that $\lambda_\kappa < \lambda_\sigma$. Hence it is seen that, when the real-wage rate is increased, the process σ is eliminated from the list of the equilibrium processes. Similarly, an increase in the real-wage rate eliminates any process j (other than k) from the list of the equilibrium processes.

Thus the only pair of processes which survives when the real-wage rate is increased is that which gives the minimum rate of growth g_* at w^*. This fact shows that at the singular point w^* the curve $g(w)$ in Fig. 2(*a*) extends to the right from the bottom of the vertical segments. A similar argument leads to the conclusion that it extends to the left from the top of them.

We have so far examined the correspondence between the warranted rate of growth and the real-wage rate at a point other than the maximum attainable real-wage rate. For the latter we have $q^0 = 0$; hence we have, instead of (7), an inequality requiring that the left-hand side of (7) should not exceed the right-hand side. This means that at the maximum real-wage rate the warranted rate of growth can fall to zero, but it cannot exceed a certain value, because the right-hand side of (7) is bounded above by a positive number, $1/\min_i (a_i)$.

We can now draw the complete curve showing the relationship between the warranted rate of growth and the real-wage rate. It has been shown that so long as there corresponds a unique pair of processes to a given wage rate w, g is uniquely determined and $g(w)$ generates a continuous curve in each interval of w in which we have a unique correspondence between g and w. At each end of the intervals where the cheapest process set is not unique, multiple rates of growth of the stock of capital are associated with w; and the consecutive curves are connected by a vertical segment. We thus have a staircase-like curve showing the correspondence between g and w as is illustrated by the curve $g(w)$ in Fig. 2(*a*).

4. Let us now give our attention to the other blade of the scissors. The rate of growth of population (that is equivalent to Harrod's natural rate of growth if there is no technological improvement) is often assumed constant (i.e. independent of the values of economic variables). We assume, however, throughout Part I, as a more plausible relationship, that the working population grows at a rate depending on the real-wage rate: The rate of growth of the labour force ρ is negative for very low levels of

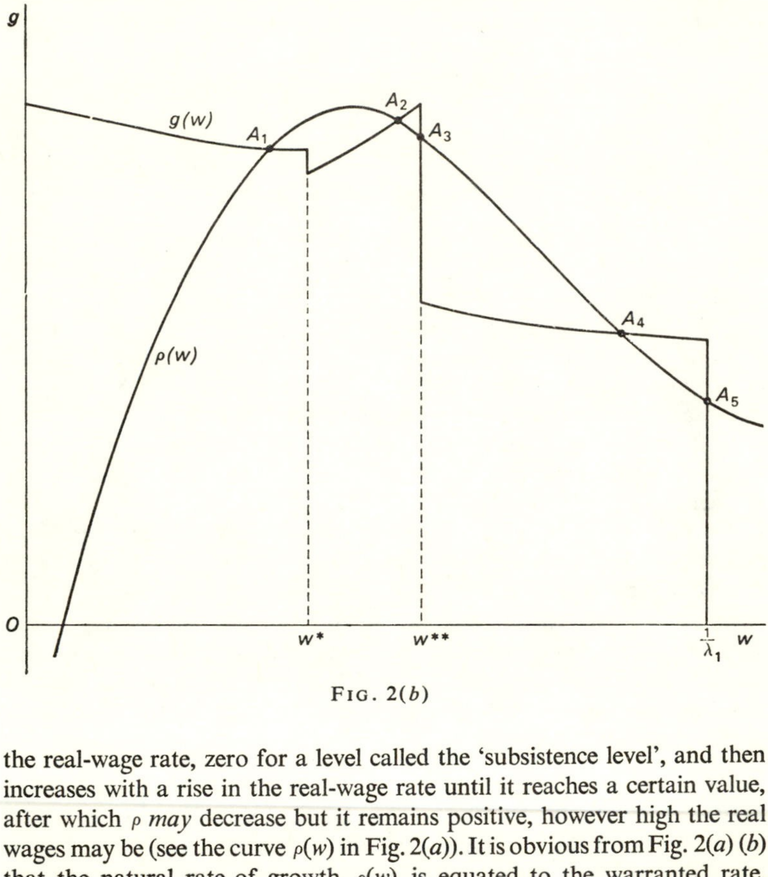

FIG. 2(*b*)

the real-wage rate, zero for a level called the 'subsistence level', and then increases with a rise in the real-wage rate until it reaches a certain value, after which ρ *may* decrease but it remains positive, however high the real wages may be (see the curve $\rho(w)$ in Fig. 2(*a*)). It is obvious from Fig. 2(*a*) (*b*) that the natural rate of growth, $\rho(w)$, is equated to the warranted rate, $g(w)$, at several (and at least one) points, at each of which the stock of capital and the labour force grow at the same rate.

Suppose $\bar{w}$ is a real-wage rate such that the stock of capital and labour increase by the same proportion (say $\bar{\rho}$). Let the short-run equilibrium values of π, p, q, ξ_i, x_i, K, and L associated with $\bar{w}$ be denoted by the corresponding letters with a bar; we have $\bar{\pi}$, $\bar{p}$, $\bar{q}$, $\bar{w}$, $\bar{\xi}_i$, $\bar{x}_i$, $\bar{K}$, and $\bar{L}$

satisfying inequalities (I. 1)–(I. 9). The prices are normalized, so that $\bar{\pi} = 1$. As the consumption-saving coefficients are invariable, a proportional increase in the capital stock and labour gives rise to an increase in the consumption and savings at the same rate, provided prices remain constant. Therefore, we can easily verify that so long as prices remain constant, a new equilibrium is established at $\{G(t)\bar{\xi}_\iota, G(t)\bar{x}_i, G(t)\bar{K}, G(t)\bar{L}\}$, where $G(t) = e^{\bar{\rho}t}$, and t stands for the point in time referred to. We can thus say that when the real-wage rate $\bar{w}$ prevails, the stock of capital, the labour force and the outputs of the two industries grow forever at the common rate $\bar{\rho}$, and prices remain unchanged. Such a state is referred to as a state of 'long-run' or Silvery Equilibrium, and $\bar{w}$ as the long-run or the Silvery real-wage rate.[1]

The discussion developed so far clarifies the mechanism which guarantees the existence of the long-run equilibrium. The long-run equilibrium condition in the labour market, or the Harrodian equality of the warranted rate of growth to the natural rate, determines the equilibrium wage rate, which in turn determines the relative prices, the rate of return, the relative activities (Kahn's inter-industrial output multiplier), the capital-labour and capital-output ratios, the distribution of income among workers and capitalists, and so on. But their absolute levels have yet to be determined. Apart from the level of prices which is determined by the supply and demand for money (the Quantity Theory of Money), we must clear up how the absolute level of activity is fixed.

It must be remembered that the (short-run) supply and demand condition for labour (I. 9) has so far played no part in the proof of the existence of the Silvery Equilibrium. The condition contains only one unknown, i.e., the absolute level of activities $\sum_i x_i$, since the demand for labour may be written as

$$\sum_\iota \lambda_\iota \xi_\iota + \sum_i l_i x_i = \left(\sum_\iota \lambda_\iota \eta_\iota + \sum_i l_i z_i\right) \sum_i x_i;$$

η_ι and z_i are determined when the wage rate is specified; the absolute level of activities may be determined such that the demand for labour is equal to the supply, L. It would be of some historical interest to find that the part in parentheses in the above expression is a kind of Kahn–Keynes employment multiplier; in fact, if the demand for labour is put in the form $k(\sum_i l_i x_i)$ with $k = 1 + \sum_\iota \lambda_\iota \eta_\iota / \sum_i l_i z_i$, k is exactly the Kahn–Keynes multiplier.

Finally, we pay attention to the fact that the following two tacit assumptions are responsible for the existence of the Silvery Growth Equilibrium: (1) the 'subsistence wage rate', at which the growth rate of the labour

[1] From the viewpoint of optimality, it will be seen later that a Silvery Equilibrium is a 'second-best' optimum. It is superseded by the Golden Equilibrium (which appears before the foot-lights later) but it is preferred to other states.

force vanishes, is lower than the technologically attainable maximum $1/\lambda_1$ of the real wage rate and (2), the society's savings are positive even if the wage rate is less than the subsistence level. It is true that we may imagine, as a logical possibility, a state of affairs such that the level of technology is so low that workers cannot continue to live even at the maximum attainable real-wage rate. However, from the realistic point of view it is a very unlikely state even in the earlier stages of development of technology as well as in the present stage. It is also true that workers will not save at all when they are paid wages less than the subsistence level; in that case, however, the rate of return of the capital good will be very high, so that there will be some positive amount of savings from the capitalists' income. The society's savings are, therefore, found to be positive at such low wages, although the uniformity of the consumption-savings decisions of workers and capitalists (which is, strictly speaking, one of the 'chessmen' of our proof) is not satisfied. Thus the two assumptions are plausible, and the existence argument is complete.

5. An approach Hicks devised for discussing the effects that changes in the saving ratio, technology, and the rate of growth of the labour force have on the distribution of income among capitalists and workers may be regarded as an alternative way of finding the growth-equilibrium solution.[1] The analysis proceeds in terms of the 'factor share of profits', the 'price-quantity curve' and the 'saving curve' (as Hicks has called them); and the equilibrium value of the first is given at the intersection of the last two.

Let us first draw the price-quantity curve of the share of profits on the plane with the rate of profits and the share of profits as the two coordinates. We have from the definition of f as the factor share of profits, rpK, in the total income, $rpK+wL$,

$$\frac{1}{f}-1=\left(\frac{1}{r}\right)\left(\frac{w}{p}\right)\left(\frac{L}{K}\right). \tag{9}$$

When the Rule of Profitability prevails, so that inequalities (I.1) and (I.2) are satisfied, both w and p are given as functions of the rate of profit r; they are derived from the outer envelope of the factor-price frontiers. The ratio of w to p is also a function of r. We have

$$\frac{w}{p}=\frac{1-a_i r}{l_i}, \tag{10}$$

when the ith process is the sole efficient process of production available to the capital-good industry. When the consumption-good and the capital-

[1] See J. R. Hicks, loc. cit., pp. 170–82.

good industry choose the ιth and the ith process from among the sets of processes they can use, the quantity equations (5) and (6) are reduced to

$$K = \alpha_\iota \xi_\iota + a_i x_i,$$
$$L = \lambda_\iota \xi_\iota + l_i x_i.$$

We then take into account the fact that the steady growth of the stock of capital at the natural rate $\rho(w)$ requires $x_i/K = \rho(w)$. Defining the relative capital-intensity of the two processes as

$$m_{\iota,i} = \left(\frac{\alpha_\iota}{\lambda_\iota}\right) \Big/ \left(\frac{a_i}{l_i}\right),$$

and putting[1]

$$M_{\iota,i} = \frac{1+(m_{\iota,i}-1)a_i \rho(w)}{m_{\iota,i}},$$

we can solve the above two equations to obtain

$$\frac{L}{K} = \frac{l_i}{a_i} M_{\iota,i}. \tag{11}$$

Hence we get from (9), (10), and (11) the following 'price-quantity' relationship giving the share of profits as a function of the rate of profits:

$$f = \frac{r a_i}{M_{\iota,i}+(1-M_{\iota,i}) r a_i}. \tag{12}$$

Hicks was concerned with the case of a constant natural rate of growth. In the present case, however, it depends on the rate of real-wages. By means of the factor-price frontiers, we may regard the real-wage rate as depending upon the rate of profits, so that $M_{\iota,i}$ (depending on the natural rate of growth) is given as a function of the rate of profits. It is seen that the price-quantity curve (12) bulges upwards or downwards according to whether $M_{\iota,i}$ is less than or greater than unity. Unless $\rho(w)$ takes on an extremely large value, $M_{\iota,i}$ is less than unity when the consumption-good industry is more capital intensive than the capital-good industry, and vice versa.

Relationship (12) is valid throughout the range where the processes ι and i are adopted. At either end-point where it ceases to be valid, f, which has so far been on the curve (12) goes on to another similar curve with either a different $M_{\iota,i}$ or a_i or both. At the end-points where the choice of techniques is 'singular' and at least one of the industries has two processes that are equally profitable, it is seen that the curves are connected vertically. On the basis of the factor-price frontiers illustrated in Fig. 1

[1] Note that $M_{\iota,i}$ is the reciprocal of Hicks' M.

the price-quantity curve may be drawn something like the curve OA in Fig. 3(a) where r^* and r^{**} are the 'singular' rates of profit corresponding to w^* and w^{**}, respectively.

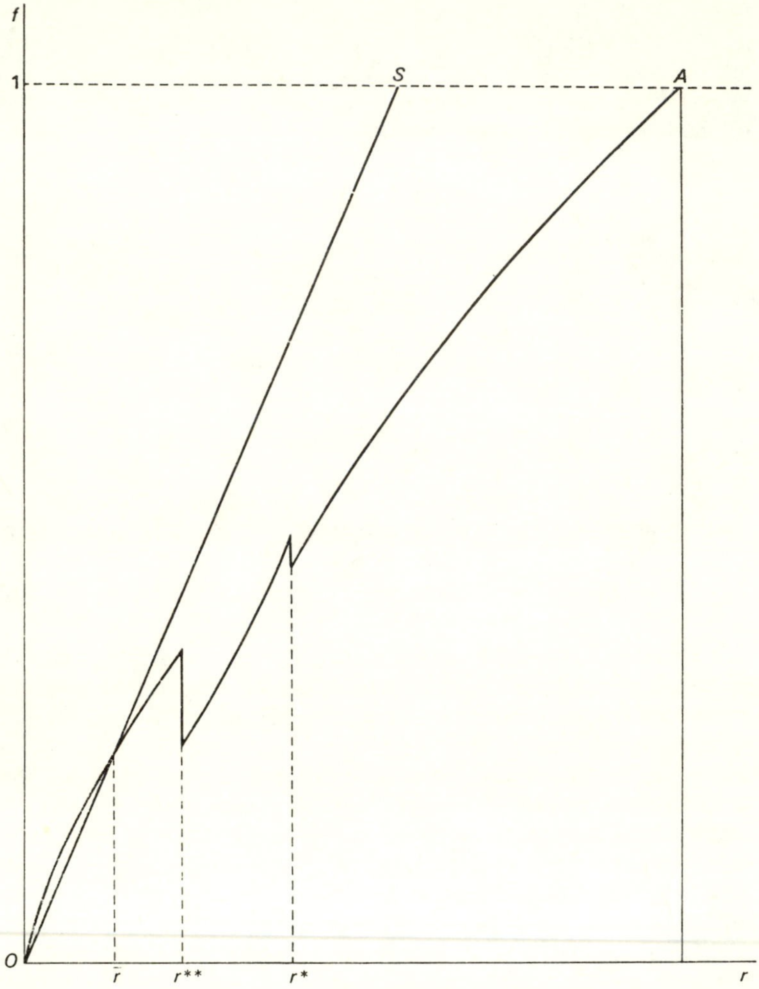

FIG. 3(a)

On the other hand, the 'saving curve' of the factor share of profits is derived from the investment-savings equation. Assuming that the stock of capital increases at the natural rate, and allowing the savings function to be of the 'uniclass' type, we may put the investment-savings equation in the form:

$$\rho(w)\, pK = b(rpK + wL),$$

where b is the average propensity to save. From this it at once follows that the 'saving curve' is of the form:

$$f = b\frac{r}{\rho(w)}.$$

As w is a decreasing function of r, we may regard f as a function of the sole, independent variable, r. When the natural rate does not respond to changes in the real-wage rate, the curve reduces to a straight line, as shown by the curve OS in Fig. 3(a). In all other cases when the natural rate of growth is flexible, it will in general be non-linear.

The share of profits determined by the savings curve thus obtained may be called the Kaldorian share of profits, although Kaldor himself has utilized the investment-savings equation for fixing the distribution between the capitalists and the workers on the assumption that the workers' average propensity to save is less than the capitalists'.[1] We may also refer to the share of profits determined by the price-quantity curve as the technical share of profits. The long-run equilibrium established at the intersection of these two curves may then be described as a state where the Kaldorian share of profits is equated to the technical share. This condition, which may be referred to as the Hicksian condition for the Silvery Equilibrium, might serve, in the theory of growth equilibrium, as a substitute for the famous Harrodian condition that the real-wage rate be determined at such a level that the warranted rate of growth is equated to the natural rate.

We have so far assumed that the savings function is of the 'uniclass' type. It is clearly a limiting case of a more general savings function with the workers' propensity to save, s_w, and the capitalists', s_c, which may be different from each other. Hicks was concerned with the case of the former being less than the latter. In such an economy, the distribution of *profits* between the capitalists and the workers emerges, in addition to the factor share of profits in the total income, as a variable to be fixed. The workers own capital, indirectly through loan of their past savings to the capitalists; profits are distributed in proportion to ownership of capital.

There are two kinds of Silvery Equilibria which are called the Pasinetti and the anti-Pasinetti equilibrium, respectively. A more detailed discussion of the so-called Pasinetti problem is left to sections 6 and 7 in Chapter VI; here we are content simply to use, without establishing them, some of the results obtained there. It will be observed there that if the total profits E are greater than $\frac{s_w}{s_c - s_w} W$ (W denotes total wages), the Silvery Equilibrium

[1] N. Kaldor, 'Alternative theories of distribution', *Review of Economic Studies*, Vol. XXIII (1955–6), pp. 83–100.

should be of the Pasinetti type, and the total income will be distributed between the workers and the capitalists according to the following formulae:

$$E_w = \frac{s_w}{s_c - s_w} W, \qquad \text{(VI.8)}$$

$$E_c = E - \frac{s_w}{s_c - s_w} W, \qquad \text{(VI.9)}$$

where E_w and E_c stand for profits which accrue to the workers and the capitalists, respectively.

When E is not greater than $\frac{s_w}{s_c - s_w} W$, we have a Silvery Equilibrium of the anti-Pasinetti type, where (as a result of the Samuelson-Modigliani counter-revolution[1]) capitalists cease to be capitalists and the entire stock of capital is owned by the workers; we should have

$$E_w = E, \qquad \text{and} \qquad E_c = 0.$$

It is clear from these observations that the workers' and the capitalists' *long-run* saving functions are of the following respective forms:

$$S_w = s_w \left\{ W + \min\left(\frac{s_w}{s_c - s_w} W, E \right) \right\}, \qquad (13)$$

$$S_c = s_c \left\{ \max\left(E - \frac{s_w}{s_c - s_w} W, 0 \right) \right\}, \qquad (14)$$

where S_w and S_c are the workers' and the capitalists' amounts of savings, and s_w and s_c their savings ratios, respectively. The investment-savings equation can now be put in the form:

$$\rho(w)\, pK = s_w \left\{ wL + \min\left(\frac{s_w}{s_c - s_w} wL, rpK \right) \right\} + s_c \left\{ \max\left(rpK - \frac{s_w}{s_c - s_w} wL, 0 \right) \right\}.$$

Multiplying by r and dividing by $\rho(w)(rpK + wL)$, we get the formula for the Kaldorian share of profits which implies: (i) that when r takes on the Pasinetti value such that $\rho(w) = s_c r$, the Kaldorian share of profits f can take on any value greater or equal to s_w/s_c, and (ii) that as long as r does not reach the Pasinetti value, f obeys the anti-Pasinetti formula: $f = s_w r / \rho(w)$.

1 See P. A. Samuelson and F. Modigliani, 'The Pasinetti paradox in neoclassical and more general models', *Review of Economic Studies*, Vol. XXXIII (1966), pp. 269–301.

The long-run saving curve is illustrated by the broken curve *ORS* shown in Fig. 3(*b*). It has at least one (possibly several) intersection with the price-quantity curve. The intersection, A_3 in Fig. 3(*b*), represents a Silvery Equilibrium of the Pasinetti type as it is located in the vertical segment of the savings curve, while other intersections on the sloping

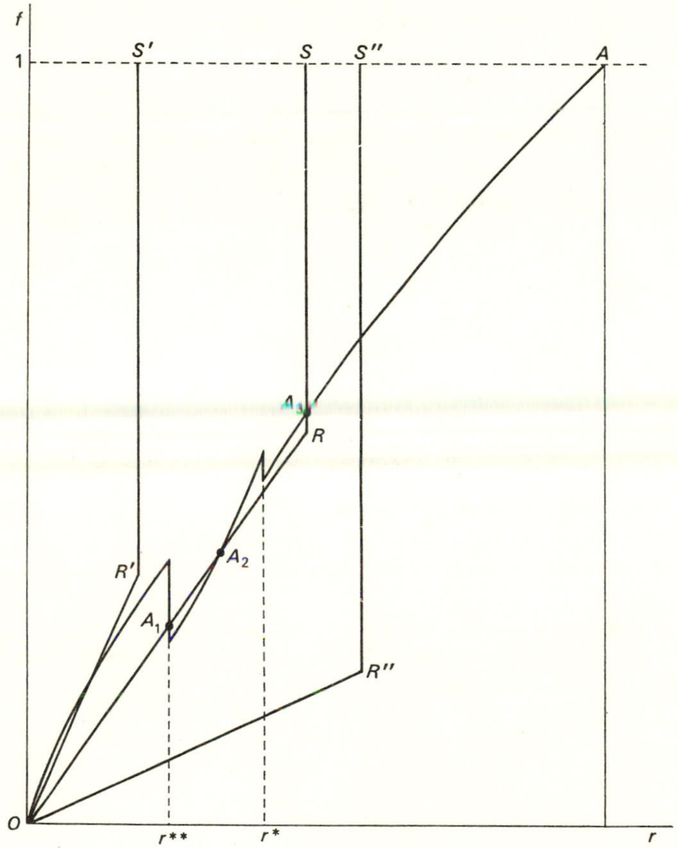

FIG. 3(*b*)

section of that curve, such as points A_1 and A_2 in Fig. 3(*b*), are of the anti-Pasinetti type. It would be of interest to note that there are possibilities of multiple Silvery Equilibria. If the workers' savings ratio s_w is quite high in comparison with the capitalists' s_c, then the corner *R* of the savings curve will lie above the price-quantity curve, and there will be no Silvery Equilibrium of the Pasinetti type. On the other hand, if s_w is low enough, the corner R will lie near the horizontal axis, and the inclined section of the savings curve will be below the price-quantity curve, so that there will be no Silvery Equilibrium of the anti-Pasinetti type. It would be surprising to find that the Silvery Equilibrium of the Pasinetti type, if it exists, is necessarily associated with a rate of profit that is greater than those prevailing in Silvery Equilibria of the other type. Moreover, it is unique unless the rate of profit is singular.

Finally, it is noticed from Fig. 3(*a*) and 3(*b*) that the origin 0 is also an intersection of the price-quantity curve and the savings curve. So we are apt to conclude that it is also an equilibrium point, but a singular point like the origin must be carefully examined.

Suppose we have a growth equilibrium at $r = 0$; then $w = 1/\lambda_1$ and $w/p = 1/l_2$ from Fig. 1. These, together with $r = 0$, imply $\gamma = \beta L/\lambda_1$ and $s = bL/l_2$. As consumption γ and savings s must equal the output of the consumption good ξ_1 and the output of the capital good x_2, respectively, we obtain

$$K \geqq \frac{\alpha_1}{\lambda_1}\beta L + \frac{a_2}{l_2} bL,$$

where the strict inequality is permissible, because, as $r = 0$, there may be an excess supply of capital services. Therefore,

$$\rho = \frac{x_2}{K} \leqq \frac{b/l_2}{\dfrac{\alpha_1}{\lambda_1}\beta + \dfrac{\alpha_2}{\lambda_2} b},$$

where we assume, for the sake of simplicity, that the natural rate of growth ρ (which equals x_2/K in the state of growth equilibrium) is independent of the real-wage rate. Considering the equality, $\beta + b = 1$, and the definition of $M_{\iota,i}$, we can rewrite the above inequality as

$$a_2/M_{1,2} \leqq b/\rho$$

which states that in order for the origin to be an equilibrium point, the savings curve must be at least as steep as the price-quantity curve at the origin. This condition is fulfilled when ρ is very small. In Fig. 3(*a*) and 3(*b*) ρ is not small enough, so that the origin is not an equilibrium point.

6. Of the two methods for finding a growth equilibrium which we have discussed above, the first may be called the Oxford method because it is principally due to Harrod. The second method, on the other hand, is the one which seems to be accepted by such Cambridge economists as Joan

Robinson, N. Kaldor, P. Sraffa, R. F. Kahn, and L. Pasinetti; so we may call it the Cambridge method, although we have acknowledged that it was first rigorously formulated by the Oxford economist.[1] It remains for us to establish the equivalence of the two methods and to see what part the new theory of income distribution by Kaldor does play in the Cambridge method.

Our explanation of the Oxford method has been made on the assumption of the society's average propensity to save being constant; so we have had no Pasinetti–anti-Pasinetti trouble. In order to compare it with the Cambridge method which is closely associated with the notion of different propensities to save for capitalists and workers, let us reformulate the Oxford method for a model which has the same types of consumption and savings functions as the Cambridge school assumes. Then the workers' and the capitalists' long-run savings functions may be put in the forms, (13) and (14), and the long-run consumption-savings ratio will take on the value

$$\frac{\gamma}{ps} = \frac{c_w(W+\min(\sigma W, E))+c_c(\max(E-\sigma W, 0))}{s_w(W+\min(\sigma W, E))+s_c(\max(E-\sigma W, 0))}, \tag{15}$$

where $\sigma = s_w/(s_c-s_w)$; c_w and c_c are the workers' and the capitalists' propensities to consume, i.e., $1-s_w$ and $1-s_c$ respectively. Since (15) implies that the weight attached to the capitalists' consumption-savings ratio in the formula of the aggregate long-run consumption-savings ratio is reduced to zero when σW exceeds the total profits E, the Cambridge assumption asserting that the workers' consumption-savings ratio is greater than the capitalists' enables us to rewrite (15) as

$$\frac{\gamma}{ps} = \min\left[\frac{c_w}{s_w}, \frac{c_w(W+\sigma W)+c_c(E-\sigma W)}{s_w(W+\sigma W)+s_c(E-\sigma W)}\right]. \tag{15'}$$

Let us suppose that the consumption-good industry selects the ιth process and the capital-good industry the ith process at a given real-wage rate w. Then the formula for the warranted rate of growth is written as

$$g(w) = \frac{x}{K} = \frac{1}{\alpha_\iota \dfrac{\gamma}{s} + a_i}.$$

[1] The method suggested by Samuelson and Modigliani in their reply to Pasinetti and Mrs. Robinson is no more than a variation of the Hicksian method. See P. A. Samuelson and F. Modigliani, "Reply to Pasinetti and Robinson", *Review of Economic Studies*, Vol. XXXIII (1966), pp. 321–30.

Because of (15′), this can further be put in the form[1]

$$g(w) = \max\left[\frac{1}{\alpha_i \dfrac{c_w}{s_w} p(w) + a_i},\ s_c r(w)\right]. \tag{16}$$

On the right-hand side of (16), the first term in the brackets represents the Harrodian warranted rate of growth which is now familiar to us, whilst the second term traces out the outer envelope of the factor-price frontiers scaled down by the capitalists' propensity to save. The larger of these two gives the warranted rate of growth which we have when the Cambridge savings assumption is valid. If the warranted-growth-rate curve thus obtained intersects the natural-growth-rate curve at a point where the outer envelope of the factor-price frontiers on the reduced scale dominates the Harrodian warranted-growth-rate curve, then the Silvery Equilibrium is of the Pasinetti-type; otherwise we obtain an anti-Pasinetti growth equilibrium.

Next, the role of the Kaldorian theory of distribution in the Cambridge method is clarified by translating the saving curve into a form which is akin to Kaldors' formula. As Fig. 3(*b*) shows, the saving curve is vertical at the Pasinetti rate of interest, where the rate of growth equals the rate of interest multiplied by the capitalists' propensity to save. Taking into account the relationship that the rate of growth x/K equals the investment-income ratio divided by the capital-output ratio, we find that the Kaldor-like equation,

$$\frac{I}{Y} = s_c f, \tag{17}$$

prevails at the Pasinetti rate of interest. (17) implies the Kaldorian thesis that the share of profits, f, depends simply on the ratio of investment to output.[2]

While the rate of interest is less than the Pasinetti value, the saving curve (passing through the origin) has a constant slope that is equal to the workers' propensity to save, s_w, divided by the natural-growth-rate, ρ. Hence, s_w equals the share of profits f multiplied by ρ/r. Capitalists have no share of profits at non-Pasinetti rates of interest, so that s_w equals the society's savings ratio which in turn equals the ratio of investment to income. Thus we obtain

$$\frac{I}{Y} = \frac{\rho}{r} f, \tag{17′}$$

[1] Note that

$$\frac{1}{\alpha_i \dfrac{c_w(W+\sigma W)+c_c(E-\sigma W)}{s_w(W+\sigma W)+s_c(E-\sigma W)} p + a_i} = \frac{s_c E/p}{\alpha_i y + a_i s} = s_c \frac{E}{pK} = s_c r.$$

[2] Kaldor, loc. cit., p. 95.

which implies that, given the rate of interest, the share of profits in income is determined by the ratio of investment to output.

Thus, prior to applying the Kaldorian formula, (17) or (17′), we must determine the rate of interest and the ratio of investment to income. In the case of the Pasinetti equilibrium, the rate of interest (or the steady-state rate of return of capital) is determined by the capitalists' propensity to save at $r = s_c/\rho$, whereas in the case of an anti-Pasinetti equilibrium (as we shall see below), the rate of interest is determined by the workers' propensity to save. Next, in the state of balanced growth, the investment-income ratio is equal to the capital-output ratio multiplied by the natural rate of growth. This relationship, together with (9) and (12), gives

$$\frac{I}{Y} = \rho\frac{pK}{Y} = \frac{\rho}{r}\frac{rpK}{rpK+wL} = \frac{\rho a_i}{M_{\iota,i}+(1-M_{\iota,i})ra_i},$$

which obviously shows that the investment-income ratio is a function of the rate of interest:[1]

$$\frac{I}{Y} = F(r). \tag{18}$$

It is now seen that in the case of the Pasinetti equilibrium, we obtain exactly the same chain as Joan Robinson, N. Kaldor and other Cambridge economists assert. That is to say, the Anglo-Hungarian-Italian growth formula, $\rho = s_c r$, first determines the rate of interest, which next determines the investment-income ratio, which in turn determines the share of profits. However, it must be noted that the order of the rings of the chain is partially changed when an anti-Pasinetti equilibrium has to be established. The investment-income ratio is first equated with the workers' propensity to save; then (18) determines the rate of interest, so that we obtain the share of profits from (17′).

Finally, a short comment on the controversy between Pasinetti, Robinson, and Kaldor on the one side and Samuelson and Modigliani on the other.[2] It is recalled that the Kaldorian equation (17) (supplemented by (17′)) has been derived from the saving curve, and equation (18) from the price-quantity curve. We may, therefore, say that Kaldor's alternative theory is equivalent to Hicks' theory which regards the share of profits as being determined at the intersection of the saving curve and the price-quantity curve. The theory which Samuelson and Modigliani have developed in their reply to Pasinetti and Robinson is essentially the same as Hicks', so that a syllogism guarantees us a substantial understanding between both Cambridges.

[1] In (18), note that subscripts ι and i representing the processes selected also depend on r.

[2] *Review of Economic Studies*, Vol. XXXIII (4), 1966.

III

A NEO-CLASSICAL PASSAGE TO GROWTH EQUILIBRIUM

1. OUR task in this chapter is to investigate whether a series of the short-run equilibria starting from an arbitrarily (or historically) given capital-labour endowment will eventually approach the state of the long-run or 'silvery' (as we have called it) equilibrium. In the conventional discussion of the stability of the growth equilibrium in a two-sector economy, the relative capital-intensities of the two industries have served as a kind of litmus paper with which to test whether the Silvery Equilibrium is stable or not. Assuming that the two industries have fixed coefficients of production, Shinkai observed, for the first time, that the growth equilibrium is stable if and only if the consumption-good industry is more capital-intensive than the capital-good industry.[1] Uzawa replaced Shinkai's production functions of the Leontief type by the neo-classical ones which allow continuous substitution between labour and capital, to find that the relative capital-intensity criterion is a sufficient condition for stability but no longer a necessary condition—though Furuno later saw that the Shinkai–Uzawa finding should be subject to a proviso that the introduction of a production lag narrows the stability region and requires, for stability, that the capital intensity of the consumption-good industry should exceed that of the capital-good by an amount that corresponds to the magnitude of the lag.[2] It is to be noticed, however, that their argument is based on the assumption of steady population growth which plays a very far-reaching role in the discussion of stability. But, once we turn to a more general model of flexible population growth like ours, we find that the Silvery Equilibrium may be unstable even though the relative capital-intensity condition is satisfied. The following discussion leads to a new finding. The stability depends not only upon the capital intensities of the two industries but also upon the relative steepness of the warranted-rate-of-growth and the natural-rate-of-growth curve and the flexibility of workers' and capitalists' consumption-savings decisions.

[1] Y. Shinkai, 'On equilibrium growth of capital and labour', *International Economic Review*, Vol. I (1960), pp. 107–11.

[2] H. Uzawa, 'On a two-sector model of economic growth', *Review of Economic Studies*, Vol. XXIX (1961), pp. 40–7; Y. Furuno, 'The period of production in two-sector models of economic growth', *International Economic Review*, Vol. VI (1965), pp. 240–4.

2. Let the amount of the stock of capital and the labour force at the initial point of time be denoted by K^0 and L^0. We may take them arbitrarily or may start from the historically given endowments. It has been shown in Chapter I that K^0 and L^0 determine the short-run equilibrium prices, π^0, p^0, q^0, w^0, and activity levels, ξ_ι^0, and x_i^0. The rate of growth of the capital stock g^0 equals $\sum_i x_i^0/K^0$, and the rate of growth of the labour force ρ^0 depends on the real-wage rate, i.e. $\rho^0 = \rho(w^0)$, and g^0 is not equal to ρ^0 unless we have long-run equilibrium.

We first deal with the normal case in which a *unique* rate of growth of the capital stock g^0 is associated with w^0. The effects of increases in K and L at the rates g^0 and ρ^0 respectively can conveniently be analysed by splitting them up into (i) the effects of an increase (or a decrease) in K at the rate $g^0-\rho^0$, L being kept constant, and (ii) the effects of a proportional increase in K and L at the common rate ρ^0. The latter has already been shown to yield a proportional change in the activity levels, ξ_ι, x_i, consumption, γ, and savings, s, but to have no effect on relative prices. We, therefore, concentrate our attention on a solitary increase in the stock of capital, and show that a relative deficiency of labour thus brought about results in an increase in the real-wage rate (as would be expected).

Suppose the warranted rate of growth g^0 exceeds the natural rate ρ^0. Suppose also that prices remain constant or change in the same proportion in spite of a solitary increase in K. Since the consumption and savings functions, γ and s, are of the 'uniclass' type, so that they are homogeneous of degree zero in prices and the average propensity to consume is positive and less than one, we find that both γ and s will increase simultaneously. On the other hand, constant relative prices imply that the same processes are selected as the cheapest before and after the increase in the stock of capital. From the assumed non-singularity of the real-wage rate w^0 it follows that each industry selects a unique process at w^0. Therefore, all ξ_νs other than (say) ξ_ι and all x_js other than (say) x_i are zero before and after the increase in capital; in short-run equilibrium, activity levels ξ_ι and x_i equal consumption γ and savings s, respectively, which evidently increase when the stock of capital and hence the capitalists' income increase. We find, therefore, that a solitary increase in capital gives rise to an increase in the level of activity of each industry, so that a larger amount of labour is required for the production of goods. It is clear that this is incompatible with the constant labour force, L. Thus changes in the relative prices are inevitable.

It has been seen in the previous chapter that the attainable range of the real wages $(0, 1/\lambda_1)$ may be divided into several sub-ranges, say, $(0, w^*)$, (w^*, w^{**}), and $(w^{**}, 1/\lambda_1)$ in the case of Fig. 2(*a*). Since the real-wage rate w^0 is taken so as to yield a unique rate of growth of the capital stock, it belongs to the interior of one of the sub-ranges, say, (w^*, w^{**}). Therefore, the real-wage rate will still be in that range after a (sufficiently) small increase in the stock of capital. This means that there is no change in the processes adopted.

Let (ι, i) be the pair of processes which is chosen. Let a small increase in the stock of capital (say, $K^0 \to K^1$) give rise to changes in prices and activity levels from the values with superscript 0 to those with 1, e.g. $p^0 \to p^1$. In this comparison of the two short-run equilibria the amount of labour available is taken as remaining unchanged at L^0; the price of the consumption good is pegged on the level of unity by the normalization procedure.

We first study the case of the full employment of labour being established at the old wage rate w^0. Suppose w^0 is positive but less than the maximum value $1/\lambda_1$ that can technically be attained. For an infinitesimal increase in the stock of capital, we would have an infinitesimal increase in the rate of real wages, so that its value in the new equilibrium would still be positive and less than the maximum. The figure of the factor-price frontiers discussed in the previous chapter shows (as we have seen before) that unless the wage rate is as high as the technically attainable maximum both industries have processes that can yield positive profits; hence the short-run equilibrium prices (old and new) of the capital services are positive. The positivity of the factor prices means that the costs of production and hence the prices of the products are positive. All factors and products cannot be free; therefore, the equilibrium conditions (I.6)–(I.9) discussed in Chapter I must hold with equality. The ith and the ith processes are the only two for which we have the equilibrium conditions (I.1) and (I.2) in the form of equality. We thus have:

$$1 = q^0\alpha_\iota + w^0\lambda_\iota \quad (1), \qquad 1 = q^1\alpha_\iota + w^1\lambda_\iota, \quad (1')$$

$$p^0 = q^0 a_i + w^0 l_i \quad (2), \qquad p^1 = q^1 a_i + w^1 l_i, \quad (2')$$

$$\xi_\iota^0 = \gamma^0 = \beta(q^0 K^0 + w^0 L^0) \quad (6), \qquad \xi_\iota^1 = \gamma^1 = \beta(q^1 K^1 + w^1 L^0), \quad (6')$$

$$x_i^0 = s^0 = b(q^0 K^0 + w^0 L^0)/p^0 \quad (7), \qquad x_i^1 = s^1 = b(q^1 K^1 + w^1 L^0)/p^1, \quad (7')$$

$$K^0 = \alpha_\iota \xi_\iota^0 + a_i x_i^0 \quad (8), \qquad K^1 = \alpha_\iota \xi_\iota^1 + a_i x_i^1, \quad (8')$$

$$L^0 = \lambda_\iota \xi_\iota^0 + l_i x_i^0 \quad (9), \qquad L^0 = \lambda_\iota \xi_\iota^1 + l_i x_i^1. \quad (9')$$

Note that these two sets of equations possess the same L^0 in common since the amount of labour available is assumed to be unaltered.

Substituting for ξ_ι^0 and x_i^0 from (6) and (7) and bearing in mind (1') and (2'), we combine the equations (8) and (9) into

$$\gamma^0 + p^1 s^0 = w^1 L^0 + q^1 K^0. \quad (10)$$

It is then clear that the total expenditure in the new situation $\gamma^1 + p^1 s^1$ (which equals the new national income $q^1 K^1 + w^1 L^0$ by Walras' Law) is greater than the right-hand side of the above equation by the amount

$q^1(K^1-K^0)$. The same procedure applied to (1), (2), (8′), and (9′) leads to the parallel finding that total expenditure $\gamma^0+p^0s^0$ exceeds $\gamma^1+p^0s^1$ by $q^0(K^0-K^1)$. Hence we get

$$(q^1-q^0)(K^1-K^0) = (p^1-p^0)(s^1-s^0), \tag{11}$$

as a base for further exploration.

Besides the two equilibria, old and new, marked with superscripts 0 and 1 respectively, let us consider a third situation with superscript 2 where capital and labour are available in the same amounts as in the *old* equilibrium but prices are fixed at their *new* equilibrium values. It is a mixture of the equilibria but cannot itself be an equilibrium unless the 'old' equilibrium point is singular. In such a state, the citizens would earn an income of the amount, $w^1L^0+q^1K^0$, that is, by virtue of Walras' law, allocated exactly to consumption γ^2 and savings s^2. It is seen from (10) that the consumption-savings plan (γ^0, s^0) could be carried out in the third situation but it is not actually chosen, because (γ^0, s^0) must be different from the plan (γ^2, s^2) which would actually be carried out in that situation.[1] Thus (γ^2, s^2) is revealed to be preferable to (γ^0, s^0) at the new equilibrium prices; accordingly, when the old prices 1, p^0, q^0, w^0 prevail, the income should fall short of the amount required for carrying out plan (γ^2, s^2) because of the revealed preference axiom. We have

$$\gamma^2+p^0s^2 > \gamma^0+p^0s^0.$$

On the other hand, the right-hand side of (10) equals $\gamma^2+p^1s^2$. Subtracting the above inequality from this equality, we may derive the following inequality,

$$(p^1-p^0)(s^2-s^0) < 0;$$

in other words, if the stock of capital and the labour force remain unaltered, a rise in the price of capital goods causes savings, in terms of the capital goods, to diminish.

Finally, since the savings function is of the 'uniclass' type and s^1 and s^2 are savings planned in the two situations which differ only in the stock of capital, we have

$$s^1-s^2 = bq^1(K^1-K^0)/p^1.$$

We can now put (11) in the form

$$\left\{(1-b)+b\frac{q^1p^0-q^0p^1}{(q^1-q^0)p^1}\right\}(q^1-q^0)(K^1-K^0) = (p^1-p^0)(s^2-s^0). \tag{12}$$

[1] As the aggregate capital-labour ratio in situation 0 is different from that in situation 1, it is seen from (8), (9), (8′), and (9′) that the outputs of the two industries should be produced in different proportions in the two situations, 0 and 1. This means, together with (6), (7), (6′), and (7′), that $\gamma^0/s^0 \neq \gamma^1/s^1$; but $\gamma^1/s^1 = \gamma^2/s^2$, because (γ^1, s^1) and (γ^2, s^2) are two 'uniclass' consumption-savings plans at the same prices. (Note that (γ^0, s^0) is also a 'uniclass' plan but it is chosen at prices that are different from those at which plans (γ^1, s^1) and (γ^2, s^2) are made.)

On the left-hand side of this expression, the average propensity to save, b, is less than 1 and the fraction in the braces is, in view of the price-cost equations (1) and (2), equal to the positive number $l_i(\lambda_i p^1)$, so that the part within the braces must be positive. As the right-hand side is definitely negative, we find that an increase in the stock of capital ($K^1 > K^0$) necessarily induces a fall in the price of services ($q^1 < q^0$). Since prices are normalized, the cost of production of the consumption good is fixed at one, and hence a fall in the price of one of the factors implies a rise in the price of the other factor; hence the real-wage rate must increase (i.e. $w^1 > w^0$).

3. Next we are concerned with the case when full employment of labour is not established at w^0; labour is free, so that the wage rate w^0 is zero by the pricing rule. We can show that if an increase in the stock of capital is sufficiently small, it does not affect relative prices at all. In fact, a rise in K, which implies an increase in the national income $wL+qK$ (L and K are evaluated at w^0 and q^0), gives rise to a proportional increase in consumption γ and savings s, if the relative prices remain constant. As $w^0 = 0$, it is seen that γ and s increase at the same rate as K.

On the other hand, constant relative prices imply that there is no change in the processes selected. We find that ξ_ι and x_i which equal γ and s, respectively, also increase at the same rate as K. It is clear that the condition of full utilization of capital will be fulfilled after (as well as before) the proportional change. It is also obvious that the employment of labour will increase, so that the number of unemployed will decrease.

It is evident that a proportional change in x_i and K has no effect on the warranted rate of growth of the stock of capital; K will continue to grow at the steady rate, while the natural rate of growth of the labour force is negative when the real-wage rate is zero. The same process as above will be repeated until unemployment of labour disappears. Once full employment of labour is established, a further solitary increase in the stock of capital causes wages to increase; w ceases to be zero.

4. We have so far observed that real wages increase if the stock of capital grows at a rate higher than that of the labour force. Conversely, using exactly the same argument we obtain the result: The real wages fall when the rate of growth of the labour force exceeds that of the capital stock.

What happens when multiple rates of growth of the capital stock are associated with the given rate of real wages, that is, when w is a singular rate, say w^*, w^{**}, or $1/\lambda_1$ in Fig. 2(*a*)? Suppose $w = w^*$, and let g_* be the minimum rate of growth of the capital stock when w is fixed at w^*. Let $(1, p^*, q^*, w^*, \xi_\iota(*), x_i(*), K(*), L(*))$ be a state of short-run equilibrium which generates the warranted rate of growth $g(*)$. It is evident that $g(*)$ is as high as the minimum rate g_*; we begin with the case of $g(*)$ being larger than g_*.

Suppose the warranted rate $g(*)$ exceeds the natural rate ρ^* at w^*: $g(*) > \rho^*$. As before, changes in K and L at the rates $g(*)$ and ρ^* are examined by splitting them up into a proportional change in K and L at the common rate ρ^* and a solitary change in K at the rate $g(*)-\rho^*$. Since w^* is a real-wage rate with which multiple rates of growth of the capital stock are associated, either the consumption-good industry or the capital-good industry or both have at least two processes which they select as the cheapest among those available to them when the prices 1, p^*, q^*, w^* prevail. In the following we are concerned with the general case where μ processes are available to the consumption-good industry and m to the capital-good industry. Arrange the processes so that the first $\theta(\leqq\mu)$ and $h(\leqq m)$ processes are the short-run equilibrium processes of the consumption-good and the capital-good industries respectively; then either θ or h is greater than or equal to 2. Also arrange them in order of capital-intensity, so that

$$\alpha_1/\lambda_1 > \alpha_2/\lambda_2 > \dots > \alpha_\theta/\lambda_\theta,$$

and

$$a_1/l_1 > a_2/l_2 > \dots > a_h/l_h.$$

Let us consider the plane in which we measure capital along the vertical axis and labour along the horizontal axis. A process, as the set of capital and labour employed per unit of output, may be regarded as a point in the capital-labour plane. Let δ_1 and δ_θ be points with respective co-ordinates (α_1, λ_1) and $(\alpha_\theta, \lambda_\theta)$. (See Fig. 4.) As the price-cost equation (1) holds with prices 1, q^*, w^* for processes $l = 1, \dots, \theta$, it is seen that (i) the slope of the line segment connecting the points δ_1 and δ_θ equals the relative price w^*/q^*, and (ii) all equally profitable processes $l = 1, \dots, \theta$ lie on the segment, $\delta_1\delta_\theta$, in order of capital-intensity from one extreme point δ_1 with the highest capital-intensity to the other extreme point δ_θ with the lowest. It is the first step of Activity Analysis to recognize that any 'resultant' process (that is a simultaneous operation of the θ 'basic' processes at rates appropriate for producing one unit of the consumption good) also lies on the same segment $\delta_1\delta_\theta$. Conversely, to any point on the segment there corresponds a process, basic or resultant, which can produce one unit of the consumption good by utilizing capital and labour in the exact amounts that are specified by the point.

I hope the reader will excuse me for devoting a few pages to a piece of elementary geometry, since it is useful for examining the choice of techniques at the singular point. Let $\gamma(*)$ be the amount of the consumption good bought with income $q^*K(*)+w^*L(*)$; evidently, the demand $\gamma(*)$ is in balance with the supply $\sum_\iota \xi_\iota(*)$, as the short-run equilibrium prevails. Multiply vectors $0\delta_1$ and $0\delta_\theta$ by the scalar $\gamma(*)$, and draw a new line segment $\delta_1^*\delta_\theta^*$. It is clear that $\delta_1^*\delta_\theta^*$ is a geometrical representation of the set of all possible points $(\alpha(*), \lambda(*))$ such that

$$\alpha(*) = \alpha_1\xi_1(*)+\ldots+\alpha_\theta\xi_\theta(*), \qquad \lambda(*) = \lambda_1\xi_1(*)+\ldots+\lambda_\theta\xi_\theta(*),$$

for all non-negative $\xi(*)$s that add up to $\gamma(*)$.

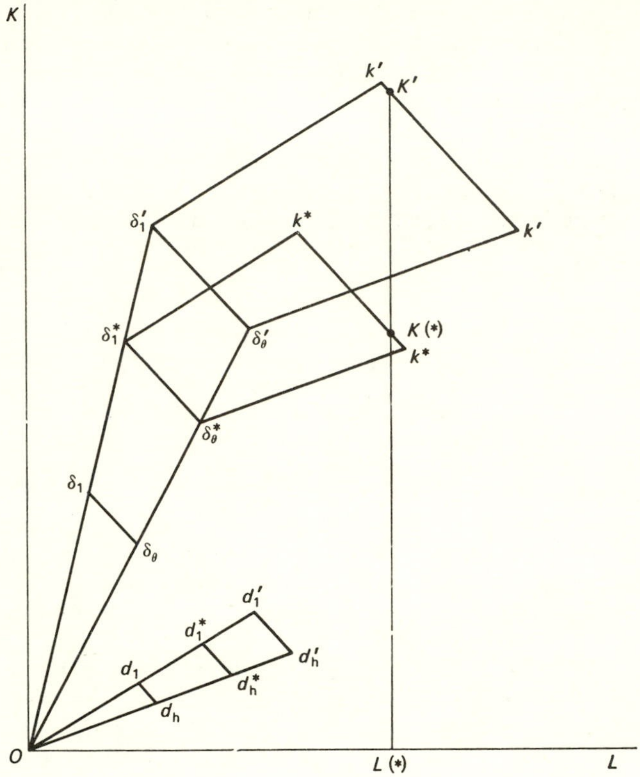

FIG. 4

Similarly we have points d_1 and d_h with coordinates (a_1, l_1) and (a_h, l_h); and the segment $d_1^*d_h^*$ is derived from d_1d_h by taking both $0d_1^*/0d_1$ and $0d_h^*/0d_h$ equal to $s(*)$. Note that all other points $(a_2, l_2), \ldots, (a_{h-1}, l_{h-1})$ are on the segment d_1d_h because they satisfy the price equation (2) with prices $\pi^*(=1), p^*, q^*, w^*$.

Let k^*k^* be the set of all points expressible as a vector sum of points on $\delta_1^*\delta_\theta^*$ and $d_1^*d_h^*$.[1] As $\delta_1^*\delta_\theta^*$ and $d_1^*d_h^*$ are parallel to each other,[2] k^*k^* is also parallel to them. It is clear that to any point on the segment

[1] Let δ be any point on $\delta_1^*\delta_\theta^*$ and d on $d_1^*d_h^*$. Let the sum of the vectors 0δ and $0d$ be $0k$; then k lies on k^*k^*.

[2] Because both the segments have the same slope $-w^*/q^*$.

k^*k^* there corresponds a set of 'admissible' levels $\xi_1(*)$, ..., $\xi_\theta(*)$, $x_1(*)$, ..., $x_h(*)$ of the cheapest processes, so that $\sum_\iota \xi_\iota(*)$ and $\sum_i x_i(*)$ are equal to $\gamma(*)$ and $s(*)$ respectively. Let $L(*)$ be the given number of workers. Let $K(*)$ be the point where k^*k^* intersects the vertical line through the point $L(*)$. At $K(*)$ we have

$$K(*) = \alpha_1\xi_1(*)+...+\alpha_\theta\xi_\theta(*)+a_1x_1(*)+...+a_hx_h(*),$$
$$L(*) = \lambda_1\xi_1(*)+...+\lambda_\theta\xi_\theta(*)+l_1x_1(*)+...+l_hx_h(*);$$

in other words, the demand for the stock of capital balances with the available amount, the labour is fully employed in operating one set of the admissible processes of both industries.

If relative prices remain unchanged, a solitary increase in the stock of capital (from $K(*)$ to K') induces a proportional increase in γ and s. Multiply vectors $0\delta_1^*$, $0\delta_\theta^*$, $0d_1^*$, $0d_h^*$ by a scalar that is equal to $\gamma'/\gamma(*) = s'/s(*)$, where γ' and s' are consumption and savings after the increase in K. Then we have the segments $\delta_1'\delta_\theta'$ and $d_1'd_h'$. We can easily verify that the new segment $k'k'$ (the set of all 'admissible' points expressible as the sum of points on $\delta_1'\delta_\theta'$ and $d_1'd_h'$) lies to the north-east of k^*k^*. If a change in K is sufficiently small, then the shift, $k^*k^* \to k'k'$, is also small, so that $k'k'$ and the vertical line through $L(*)$ have an intersection, and the following argument shows that the vertical coordinate is equal to the stock of capital after the increase.

To any point on $k'k'$ there corresponds a set of admissible activity levels ξ_ι' and x_i' ($\iota = 1, ..., \theta$; $i = 1, ..., h$). The admissibility of the activities implies the equality of the output of the consumption good $\sum_\iota \xi_\iota'$ to its demand γ' and the equality of the output of the capital good $\sum_i x_i'$ to the savings s'. In view of the price-cost equations, we get

$$q^*(\sum_1^\theta \alpha_\iota\xi_\iota' + \sum_1^h a_ix_i') + w^*(\sum_1^\theta \lambda_\iota\xi_\iota' + \sum_1^h l_ix_i') = \gamma' + p^*s'.$$

The right-hand side of this equation equals $q^*K' + w^*L(*)$ by virtue of Walras' law. Therefore, at the point where

$$\lambda_1\xi_1'+...+\lambda_\theta\xi_\theta'+l_1x_1'+...+l_hx_h' = L(*), \tag{13}$$

we have

$$\alpha_1\xi_1'+...+\alpha_\theta\xi_\theta'+a_1x_1'+...+a_hx_h' = K'. \tag{14}$$

The left-hand side of (14) gives the vertical coordinate of the intersection, while the right-hand side is obviously the amount of the stock of capital after the increase. Thus, the existence of a point fulfilling (13) and (14) is ensured if the increase in K is sufficiently small; accordingly, the relative prices will remain unchanged. A solitary increase in K with constant relative prices will result in a decrease in the growth rate of the capital stock, because the latter is given by $s/K = b(q^*K+w^*L(*))/(p^*K)$.

If the rate of growth g' after the increase in K is still larger than ρ^*, the whole process which we have discussed above is repeated. If the curve of the growth rate of the labour force intersects the vertical segment (corresponding to the singular real-wage rate w^*) of the staircase-like curve of the warranted growth rate, then the growth rate g will finally reach the level ρ^*, or otherwise it will sooner or later reach the minimum rate of growth g_* associated with w^*.

At $g = g_*$, a further solitary increase in the stock of capital necessarily affects the relative prices; the point K' coincides with the upper end of the $k'k'$ segment, and the industries select unique processes, (α_1, λ_1) and (a_1, l_1), which are the most capital-intensive among the cheapest processes $(\alpha_\iota, \lambda_\iota)$ and (a_i, l_i) ($\iota = 1, ..., \theta$; $i = 1, ..., h$). Since $g_* - \rho^*$ is still positive (that is, K is increasing at a rate greater than the rate of growth of labour), real wages will increase. The economy departs from the singular point w^*, and gets into a normal range in which the rate of growth of the capital stock uniquely corresponds to the rate of real wages.

A similar argument can be used for the converse case where the actual rate of growth $g(*)$ is less than both the maximum rate of growth g^* associated with w^* and the rate of growth of the labour force $\rho(w^*)$. The economy will climb up the vertical segment of the staircase from $g(*)$ to g^* (or to ρ^* if the $\rho(w)$ and $g(w)$ curves have an intersection at w^*).

5. We are now in a position to be able to make a definite statement about the stability of the growth equilibrium. It has been seen that if the warranted rate of growth is greater than the natural rate of growth, then the real-wage rate will tend to rise, and vice versa. On the other hand, it has been assumed that when the wage rate is low enough, the natural rate of growth is negative and, hence, falls short of the warranted rate which remains positive, while at very high rates of real wages the natural rate takes on positive values and is greater than the warranted rate as the latter drops to zero at the technically attainable maximum real-wage rate, $1/\lambda_1$. We can see clearly from Fig. 2(*a*) (in Chapter II) that if the long-run or Silvery Equilibrium is unique, any rise in the real-wage rate above the equilibrium level causes the natural rate of growth to exceed the warranted rate, and vice versa. It then follows that *any* movement away from the Silvery Equilibrium would set up forces causing the system to return to equilibrium, so that it would have *global* stability. This means that if the economy starts from any initial position, it finally approaches the equilibrium path, along which the economy grows at the rate $\rho(\bar{w})$ associated with the long-run equilibrium rate of real wages, $\bar{w}$.

When there are a number of Silvery Equilibria, a series of short-run equilibria starting from any initial point eventually approaches one of the Silvery Equilibria. (See Fig. 2(*b*).) It is seen that among the Silvery Equilibria those at the lowest and the highest real-wage rates have local stability (or stability in the small); that is to say, a *slight* movement away from them gives rise to a tendency to restore equilibrium. It is also seen that a Silvery Equilibrium w_1 is *locally* stable if and only if the slope of the natural-rate-of-growth curve at w_1 is greater than the corresponding slope of the warranted-rate-of-growth curve. Finally, Fig. 2(*b*) illustrates Samuelson's 'separation theorem' which states that consecutive Silvery Equilibria A_1, A_2, A_3, ... are alternatively stable and unstable.[1]

It should be noted that our condition for stability, which may be referred to as the local stability criterion in terms of the growth rates, has been derived on the assumption that the consumption and savings functions are of the 'uniclass' type. It is valid not only in that special case but also in more general cases, as long as the aggregate consumption-savings decisions of the community satisfy the 'weak axiom of revealed preference'. However, the condition obtained in terms of the slopes of the two growth-rate curves ceases to be either necessary or sufficient for stability if the consumption and savings decisions do not fulfil the weak axiom. It is in fact seen in the next section that if the aggregate consumption-savings decision is 'strongly contravariant' in the sense defined later, the real-wage rate diverges from the Silvery Equilibrium as time goes on, even though the slope of the natural-rate-of-growth curve is greater (algebraically) than that of the warranted-rate curve. Hence, an analysis of more general application is needed.

6. We have so far assumed that consumption and savings are 'parallel' to income. With more general consumption and savings functions which are no longer of the 'uniclass' type, the stability analysis proceeds in the following way. Suppose, for the sake of simplicity, a unique pair of processes (ι, i) is selected at a Silvery Equilibrium whose local stability is to be examined. The savings-investment equality that is established in any state of short-run equilibrium means that savings in terms of the consumption good, denoted by S, equal the output of the capital good multiplied by its price in terms of the consumption good, $x_i p$, so that $x_i = S/p$. This is combined with the supply-demand equation for the consumption good, $\gamma = \xi_\iota$, and the equation of the utilization of capital stock to yield

$$\alpha_\iota\left(\frac{\gamma}{S}p\right)+a_1=\frac{1}{g}.$$

Let us now assume that consumption γ and savings S depend on prices, p, q, w, and the workers' and the capitalists' incomes, wL and qK. We also assume that a proportional change in the income variables is accompanied by a proportional change in consumption and savings at the same rate. The assumed homogeneity of γ and S and the fact that prices p and q

[1] P. A. Samuelson, *Foundations of Economic Analysis* (Cambridge, Mass.: Harvard University Press, 1947), p. 294.

may, by virtue of the price-cost equations, be regarded as functions of the wage rate w, will lead us to the observation that the ultimate factors determining the rate of growth g (as well as the consumption-savings ratio γ/S) are the real-wage rate w and the labour-capital ratio L/K. Since the workers may be assumed to have a marginal propensity to consume that is at least as high as that of the capitalists, we may assume that the partial derivative of the consumption-savings ratio with respect to the labour-capital ratio is non-negative. This evidently means that the growth rate g is a non-increasing function of L/K.

On the other hand, it follows from the price-cost equations that p is an increasing or decreasing function of w according to whether the Shinkai–Uzawa condition, that the consumption-good industry is more capital-intensive than the capital-good industry, is satisfied or not. But an increase in the wage rate may make the consumption-savings ratio change in any direction, as γ and S are no longer proportionate; so it may offset the effect of p on g. Therefore, the rate of growth may change in either way. Thus the fact that the consumption-good industry is more (or less) capital-intensive than the capital-good industry does not necessarily imply that the rate of growth decreases (or increases) when the real wage rate increases.

Let us next classify the consumption-savings decisions into two classes according to whether they are more, or less, elastic (with respect to a change in the real wages) than the price of the capital good. We say that the aggregate consumption-savings decision is *strongly contravariant* if the total elasticity of γ/S that is obtained when we allow for responses of other prices to a given initial change in the wage rate (but with L/K remaining unchanged) and the elasticity of p with respect to w are of different signs and the former is greater in modulus than the latter; *weakly contravariant* if they have opposite signs but the former is not greater in modulus than the latter and *covariant* if they are of the same sign.[1] Then it is at once seen that in the case of a weakly contravariant or covariant consumption-savings decision, an increase (or decrease) in the wage rate (L/K fixed) gives rise to a decrease (or increase) in the rate of growth g when the chosen processes (ι, i) satisfy the Shinkai–Uzawa capital-intensity condition; while if the decision is strongly contravariant, we would have the converse relationship.

We have so far examined the correspondence between the growth rate, the labour-capital ratio and the wage rate. We obtain that correspondence under the assumption that the demand-supply equations for the consumption good, the capital good and the capital stock are fulfilled in addition to the price-cost equations. On the other hand, the demand-supply equation for labour (9), together with the similar condition (8) for the stock of capital, implies another correspondence between the

[1] In the case of the consumption and savings functions of the 'uniclass' type they are of opposite signs and equal to each other in modulus.

growth rate and the labour-capital ratio; it is seen that they are connected by the formula

$$g = \frac{\alpha_\iota L/K - \lambda_\iota}{\alpha_\iota l_i - a_i \lambda_\iota}.$$

We find that when the consumption-good (or the capital-good) industry is more capital-intensive than the other industry, an increase in the labour-capital ratio gives rise to an increase (or a decrease) in the rate of growth.

Thus the growth rate g depends, on the one hand, on w and L/K and on the other, on L/K alone; we, therefore, obtain

$$g_1(w, L/K) = g_2(L/K),$$

which gives L/K as a function of w; eliminating the parameter L/K, we obtain $g(w)$, which is called the warranted-rate-of-growth curve as before. On the basis of the relationships established above, it is found that in the case of the Shinkai–Uzawa condition being satisfied, L/K is given by a decreasing function of w if the consumption-savings decisions is weakly contravariant or covariant and conversely by an increasing function if the consumption-savings decision is strongly contravariant. As the rate of growth, g, on the right-hand side of the above equation is an increasing function of L/K, it follows that g is a decreasing function of w if the consumption-savings decision is weakly contravariant or covariant and an increasing function if it is strongly contravariant. On the other hand, when the Shinkai–Uzawa condition does not prevail, the number of possibilities is doubled. If the partial derivative of g_1 with respect to L/K is not very large in absolute value—i.e. the workers' and the capitalists' propensity to consume are not very dissimilar (or are very similar)—then the L/K curve (as a function of w) is downward sloping if the consumption-savings decision is weakly contravariant or covariant and upward sloping otherwise. This implies that the warranted rate of growth g is an increasing function of the ultimate variable w in the case of a weakly contravariant or covariant decision and a decreasing function otherwise. If, however, the workers' propensity to consume is greatly different from that of the capitalists and the effect of L/K on g_1 is greater than its effect on g_2, then the relationships are completely reversed.

Using these preliminary observations, the case where the Shinkai–Uzawa condition holds is examined as follows. Suppose the consumption-savings decision is weakly contravariant or covariant at a Silvery Equilibrium wage rate w_1. Suppose also that the warranted-rate-of-growth curve as a function of the ultimate independent variable w has, at w_1, a derivative (with respect to w) less than the slope of the natural-rate-of-growth curve. It is then evident that for w less than w_1 the warranted rate $g(w)$ is greater than the natural rate $\rho(w)$; as K increases at the rate g and L at ρ, the labour-capital ratio must diminish. This implies that w must increase, because L/K is a decreasing function of w, if the consumption-savings decision is weakly contravariant or covariant in an economy fulfilling the Shinkai–Uzawa condition. Thus w moves towards the equilibrium wage rate w_1 if it is initially set below w_1. Similarly, a rise in w above the equilibrium rate w_1 must set up forces causing w to fall. Hence the Shinkai–Uzawa condition establishes the local stability of the Silvery Equilibrium in this particular case. However, a similar argument leads to the finding that if the consumption-savings decision is strongly contravariant the Silvery Equilibrium is locally *unstable* under the same condition. We can also observe in a similar way that it may be locally *stable* even though the Shinkai–Uzawa condition does not hold; for example, it is locally stable if workers and capitalists make more or less similar consumption-savings decisions that are weakly contravariant and the slope of the natural-rate-of-growth curve is greater than that of the warranted-rate-of-growth curve. Consequently, it is seen that there is no definite relationship between the stability of the Silvery Equilibrium and the capital-intensities of the two industries.

It is interesting to note that in almost all two-sector models previously presented by many writers, as well as in the original models due to Shinkai and Uzawa, the rate of population growth is assumed to be independent of the real wage rate. It is, therefore, seen that under the Shinkai–Uzawa condition the curve $g(w)$ crosses the horizontal line ρ from north-west to south-east if the consumption-savings decision is weakly contravariant or covariant, and from south-west to north-east if it is strongly contravariant; in these cases the equilibrium has local stability. Similarly, constancy of the natural rate of growth results in eliminating all the possibilities of stability from the economy when the consumption-good industry is *less* capital-intensive than the capital-good industry. We may, therefore, conclude that it is definitely impossible for a Silvery Equilibrium to be unstable under the Shinkai–Uzawa condition and to be stable in opposite situations. Thus the Shinkai–Uzawa condition emerges as a necessary and sufficient condition for local stability of growth equilibrium.

It must, however, be emphasized that this is correct only in an economy with the population growing at a constant rate. Once a response of the labour force to changes in real wages is allowed for, this ceases to be true; as we have observed, the Shinkai–Uzawa condition is unnecessary and even insufficient for local stability. The general rule is not so simple and should be stated differently: (I) A Silvery Equilibrium at which the slope of the natural-rate-of-growth curve is greater (algebraically) than the warranted-rate-of-growth curve has local stability, irrespective of whether the capital-intensity condition is satisfied or not, if the aggregate consumption-saving decision is weakly contravariant or covariant (and workers and capitalists have very similar propensities to consume).[1] A Silvery Equilibrium at a similar intersection (as above) of the two growth-rate curves will, however, have local instability in the case of the anti-Shinkai–Uzawa case, if the aggregate consumption-savings decision is weakly contravariant or covariant and the workers' and the capitalists' propensities to consume are very dissimilar. (II) On the other hand, if the slope of the natural-rate-of-growth curve is *less* (algebraically) than that of the warranted-rate-of-growth curve and the aggregate consumption-savings decision is *strongly* contravariant at a Silvery Equilibrium, then the equilibrium is stable in the case of the Shinkai–Uzawa condition being satisfied but stable or unstable in the anti-Shinkai–Uzawa case, according to whether the workers and capitalists have similar or dissimilar propensities to consume. (III) Finally, in the case of the slope of the natural-rate-of-growth curve being greater than the slope of the warranted-rate-of-growth curve and the aggregate consumption-savings decision being strongly contravariant, the converse of (I) is valid, whilst in the case of the slope of the natural-rate-of-growth curve being less than the warranted-rate-of-growth curve and the aggregate consumption-savings decision being weakly contravariant or covariant, the converse of (II) is valid. We may thus conclude by saying that the workers' and capitalists' consumption-savings decision, the relative capital-intensities of the industries and the flexibility of the population growth are all responsible for stability.

7. The remainder of this chapter is devoted to a topic closely related to the stability problem. Using Solow's one-sector model of economic growth and giving its parameters plausible values, Ryuzo Sato has observed that the speed of convergence of the full-employment-full-capacity growth path to the Silvery Equilibrium path is very slow, that is, about one hundred years are required for the former to get within a reasonable vicinity of the latter.[2] It is, however, not difficult to construct a two-sector model which gives, again on the basis of plausible values of parameters, a much faster speed of convergence.

Let $\alpha = 4$, $\lambda = 1$, $a = 3$, and $l = 1$. Let the average propensity to consume β and the rate of population growth ρ be 94·2 and 1·6 per cent respectively; they are assumed to be constant. At Silvery Equilibrium we have

$$w = 0{\cdot}6635, \qquad p = 0{\cdot}9159, \qquad r = 0{\cdot}0919,$$

$$\frac{\xi}{K} = 0{\cdot}238, \qquad \frac{x}{K} = 0{\cdot}016, \qquad \frac{L}{K} = 0{\cdot}254,$$

[1] The proviso in parentheses is effective only in the case of the Shinkai–Uzawa condition of capital intensities being violated.

[2] R. Sato, 'Fiscal policy in a neo-classical growth model: an analysis of time required for equilibrating adjustment', *Review of Economic Studies*, Vol. XXX (1963), pp. 16–23.

which imply that $wL/Y = 0{\cdot}667$ and $pK/Y = 3{\cdot}625$, where Y represents national income. With these values of the parameters, the wage determination equation derived from the equilibrium conditions (1)–(9) may be written as[1]

$$dw/dt = 0{\cdot}5597 - 0{\cdot}6712w - 0{\cdot}2599w^2,$$

whose solution is

$$w(t) = 0{\cdot}6635 - \frac{1{\cdot}016}{0{\cdot}2599 + Ce^{1{\cdot}016t}}$$

where the constant C is determined by the initial condition.

For $C = 2$, we have $w(0) = 0{\cdot}214$ and $w(5) = 0{\cdot}660$, the corresponding values of the capital coefficient being $(pK/Y)_{t=0} = 3{\cdot}201$ and $(pK/Y)_{t=5} = 3{\cdot}622$. It is seen that it takes only five years for the difference between the current and the Silvery capital coefficient to become less than 1 per cent of the initial discrepancy. This surprisingly big difference in the speed of convergence of the one-sector and two-sector models (a century versus five years), implies that one-sector, two-sector, and such highly aggregated models are inadequate for examination of the stability of the long-run equilibrium. Hence, disaggregation of some considerable degree is inevitable.

[1] Differentiating

$$w = \frac{\alpha p - a}{\alpha l - a\lambda} \quad \text{(from the price-cost equations),}$$

$$p = \frac{1-\beta}{\beta}\frac{\xi}{x} \quad \text{(from Kahn's inter-industrial relationship),}$$

$$\frac{\xi}{K} = \frac{l - aL/K}{\alpha l - a\lambda} \quad \text{(from the resource-utilization equations),}$$

$$\frac{x}{K} = \frac{\alpha L/K - \lambda}{\alpha l - a\lambda}$$

with respect to time t and substituting, we obtain

$$\frac{dw}{dt} = \frac{\alpha}{D^2}\left(\frac{1-\beta}{\beta}\, l + p\lambda - \left(\frac{1-\beta}{\beta}\, a + p\alpha\right)\frac{lL}{x}\right),$$

where $D = \alpha l - a\lambda$. The right-hand side of this equation is quadratic with respect to w, as

$$p = \frac{a}{\alpha} + \left(1 - \frac{a}{\alpha}\right) wl, \text{ and } \frac{L}{x} = \lambda\frac{\xi}{x} + l = \lambda\frac{\beta}{1-\beta}\, p + l.$$

IV

HARRODIAN KNIFE-EDGE IN A KEYNES-TYPE 'FIXPRICE' ECONOMY

1. AMONG the assumptions underlying the foregoing analysis of stability of Growth Equilibrium, the following two have played the most important roles in deriving the conclusions: First, prices and the wage rate are perfectly flexible so that the price of any good or any factor of production will go down to zero if excess supply of it cannot be eliminated (the Rule of Free Goods). Second, unless the price of the capital service is zero, the existing stock of capital is fully utilized and investment is made according to the Acceleration Principle.[1]

It would certainly be far from the reality to suppose that all markets work according to the Rule of Free Goods. As Keynes pointed out, the Rule of Free Goods would not prevail in the labour market; there is a certain level of wages at which the supply of labour becomes perfectly elastic; and the wage rate cannot be lower than that level, even though there are a large number of workers involuntarily unemployed. Likewise, positive quasi-rents might be consistent with under-utilization of the stock of capital. For some goods, prices would be set so that they should cover costs; firms would diminish their outputs, instead of reducing prices, in case of being confronted with insufficient demand. It is seen that, as soon as we pass from the Walras-type 'flexprice' model to a 'fixprice' model,[2] either full employment of labour or full utilization of capital is not automatically established any longer. And, in the absense of full utilization of capital, it is evident that investment decisions do not obey the Acceleration Principle.

2. In order to re-interpret our match-box model from the Fixprice point of view, let us assume that the money rate of interest is determined outside the model. An entrepreneur who has a given sum of money available for expenditure can lend it to someone else at the given rate of interest or alternatively can spend it on production processes. In equilibrium it is

[1] At the outset we did not specify the form of the investment function. But it was later seen that the Rule of Profitability and the full utilization of the stock of the capital good implied the Acceleration Principle of investment decisions. Cf. section 6 of Chapter I.

[2] This flexprice-fixprice classification of economic models, which we owe to Hicks, is distinct from the conventional classification from the micro-macro viewpoint. See Hicks, op. cit., pp. 76–83.

required that neither of these two options has an advantage over the other. Because we assume that the capital good is not subject to wear and tear and that prices are rigid, the rate of return of the capital good, q/p, (or the marginal efficiency of capital, as Keynes called it) should be equated to the rate of interest. Once the rate of return of the capital good, r, is given, the real-wage rate, w, and the price of the capital good in terms of the consumption good, p, are read off from the 'factor-price frontier' figure. The Rule of Profitability states that entrepreneurs of the consumption-good industry choose processes ι such that[1]

$$\pi = 1 = \alpha_\iota rp + \lambda_\iota w, \tag{1}$$

while those of the capital-good industry choose processes i such that

$$p = a_i rp + l_i w. \tag{1'}$$

In these expressions, we adopt the same notation as before; α and λ are capital and labour coefficients in consumption-good production; a and ι are similar coefficients in capital-good production. In such 'profitable' processes ι and i may not be unique; for the sake of simplicity, however, we assume throughout this chapter that prices and the rate of return are 'non-singular' so that each industry has only one profitable process and costs of all other available processes are not covered by the prices of the respective products.

Let ξ be the output of the consumption good and x the output of the capital good. The desired (and required) amount of the capital good and the desired (required) amount of labour would be

$$K_D = \alpha_\iota \xi + a_i x, \quad \text{and} \quad L_D = \lambda_\iota \xi + l_i x, \tag{2}$$

respectively. On the other hand, the consumption and savings functions (of the Harrodian type) are written as

$$\gamma = \beta Y, \quad \text{and} \quad S = bY,$$

respectively, where β and b are positive constants adding up to unity, and Y stands for aggregate income in terms of the consumption good. The eqrations (1), (1′), and (2), together with the demand-supply equation for the consumption good and the investment-savings equation,

$$\xi = \beta Y, \quad \text{and} \quad px = bY, \tag{3}$$

yield the familiar equalities between incomes viewed from various aspects:

$$Y = \gamma + S = \xi + px = rpK_D + wL_D.$$

Let the existing stock of the capital good be denoted by K and the total number of the workers living in the society by L. The full employment

[1] As we take the consumption good as the standard commodity, we have to set its price equal to unity.

level of income is given by $rpK+wL$. It is obvious that the actual income Y will, in general circumstances, differ from the full employment income. It is, in fact, Keynes' doctrine that Y will not reach the full employment level unless there is sufficient demand for the capital good.

Since prices are rigid, no inherent forces are at work to establish full employment. For any given p, we have, from (2) and (3),

$$K_D = \left(\alpha_t \frac{\beta}{b} p + a_t\right)x, \quad \text{and} \quad L_D = \left(\lambda_t \frac{\beta}{b} p + l_t\right)x.$$

There is no reason why x should not be given such that either $K_D < K$ or $L_D < L$. Thus, in a Fixprice economy, insufficient investment would give rise to unemployment of capital or labour or both. The Saviour is Keynes' Principle of Effective Demand, but not the neo-classical principle of Competitive Pricing.

3. What form of the investment function do we assume in the following discussion? As is well known, many investment theories have been presented, among which the most powerful and familiar ones are Kaldor's Profit Principle and Hicks' and Goodwin's Nonlinear Acceleration Principle.[1] According to the former, the rate of investment I is an increasing function of the activity level or profits and a decreasing function of the existing stock of capital, with the marginal propensity to invest (with respect to an increase in the level of activity) being very small at both extremes, relative to its normal level. According to the latter, on the other hand, the rate of investment, apart from autonomous investments and investments as a result of innovations in production, is a nonlinear S-shaped function of the rate of change of income $\dot{Y}$ with a marginal acceleration coefficient, $dI/d\dot{Y}$, that is stable in the middle range of $\dot{Y}$ but passes to very small values both at very high and at very low rates of change of income.

The investment function that Harrod assumed in his *Towards* might be called an investment function of the Adaptable-Acceleration-Principle type.[2] It implies that if the desired stock of capital K_D equals the existing stock K as the result of investment at the rate x, then entrepreneurs will be left in a state of mind in which they are prepared to invest at the same rate of investment per capital, x/K, as they have done, while if K_D exceeds or falls short of K, they have to adjust upwards or downwards, and the

[1] Cf. N. Kaldor, 'A model of the trade cycle', in *Essays on Economic Stability and Growth* (London: Duckworth, 1960), pp. 177–92; R. M. Goodwin, 'The non-linear accelerator and the persistence of business cycles', *Econometrica*, Vol. XIX (1951), pp. 1–18; J. R. Hicks, *A Contribution to the Theory of the Trade Cycle* (Oxford: Clarendon, 1950). A new principle is the one of 'animal spirits' proposed by Joan Robinson (see her *Essays in the Theory of Economic Growth* (London: Macmillan, 1962).

[2] See Harrod, op. cit., pp. 82–86.

ratio x/K is increased or decreased accordingly. It is noted that the Adaptable Acceleration Principle assumes a stronger propensity to invest of entrepreneurs than that which is assumed by the conventional Flexible Acceleration Principle.[1] The Harrodian premise may be formulated as:

$$\text{sign of } \frac{d}{dt}\left(\frac{x}{K}\right) = \text{sign of } (K_D - K). \qquad (4)$$

The growth path will be examined for stability by modifying the Adaptable Acceleration Principle in the following manner. We take explicit account of the feasibility conditions:

$$K \geqq K_D, \qquad \text{and} \qquad L \geqq L_D;$$

in other words, investment is determined so that the utilization of capital and employment of labour that it requires do not exceed their availability. Then there is no possibility of K_D being greater than K; the ratio x/K will be maintained when $K_D = K$, while it will decrease when $K_D < K$.

When investment is set at a level establishing equality between the desired and the existing stock of capital, we obtain

$$\frac{x}{K} = \frac{1}{\left(\alpha_i \frac{\beta}{b} p + a_i\right)}.$$

This implies that the stock of capital increases at the 'warranted rate'. Entrepreneurs, who are satisfied with investment of the amount x, will be ready to maintain the investment ratio, x/K. Accordingly, 'progress in the current period should be equal to progress in the last preceding period' (Harrod, p. 82); the state of full utilization of capital will be perpetuated if enough labour is always available.

If the desired stock of capital K_D is less than the actual stock K, it follows from (4) that investment x increases at a *slower* rate than the stock of capital K. As K_D is proportional to x, this means that K_D increases less rapidly than K. The discrepancy between K_D and K becomes larger and larger as time goes on; the state of excess capacity is self-reproducible. Thus, a fall in K_D below K does not set up any tendency to restore the full utilization of capital, but on the contrary, a tendency for K_D to get still farther away from K. This implies the instability of the warranted growth path on the lower side.[2]

[1] It implies that there is no induced investment when the desired stock of capital equals the existing stock, whereas the accelerator works whenever there is a deficiency of capital. See, for example, R. M. Goodwin, 'Secular and cyclical aspects of the multiplier and the accelerator', *Income, Employment and Public Policy*[1] *Essays in Honor of Alvin H. Hansen* (New York: Norton, 1948), p. 120.

[2] Harrodian instability have been discussed by many writers; among those notable are, for example, S. S. Alexander, 'Mr. Harrod's dynamic model', *Economic Journal*, Vol. LX (1950); Nobuo Okishio, 'Instability of steady advance', *Economic Studies Quarterly*, Vol. V (1954), in Japanese; Dale W. Jorgenson, 'On stability in the Sense of Harrod', *Economica*, Vol. XXVII (1960).

4. When full employment of labour is not attained, the availability of labour L exceeds the demand for it L_D. The total unemployment of labour may be analysed in two parts, called Marxian and Keynesian unemployment, which are defined in terms of the quantity of labour required for the full utilization of capital in existence in the following way.

Let us divide L_D by K_D; we get

$$\frac{L_D}{K_D} = \frac{\lambda_\iota \beta p + l_i b}{\alpha_\iota \beta p + a_i b}.$$

Write L_F for L_D/K_D multiplied by K. L_F represents the amount of employment required to work the existing stock of capital at its full capacity. $L-L_D$, that is the difference between the total of labour available and the actual level of employment, gives total of unemployment; $L-L_F$ gives the 'reserve army of labour', and L_F-L_D gives unemployment due to deficiency of 'effective demand'.[1] These two kinds of unemployment are called Marxian and Keynesian unemployment, respectively.[2]

We now observe that, barring very lucky initial situations, the Fixprice economy cannot escape from violent long-term unemployment of labour. We begin with the case of the activity level of the capital-good industry x being such that it generates the demand for capital K_D that is exactly equal to the stock of capital in existence K. If the natural rate of growth ρ is greater than the warranted rate g, the labour force will expand more rapidly than the stock of capital; unemployment will increase in the form of Marxian technological unemployment. If, on the other hand, the natural rate of growth is less than the warranted rate, the stock of capital that is growing at the warranted rate will become redundant sooner or later. In fact, we have both full employment of labour and full utilization of capital at a certain point of time; at that point, the rate of growth of capital will switch from the warranted rate to the natural rate. It implies a decline in the activity level of the capital-good industry, so that the economy gets into a slump, and there will emerge unemployment of the Keynesian type. Once excess capacity appears, the rate of increase in the stock of capital will decrease by virtue of the Adaptable Acceleration Principle; hence unemployment of labour is made more serious as time goes on.

If the economy is provided, at the outset, with the stock of capital K that is greater than the stock required for production K_D, the former will, as has been seen in the previous section, increase more rapidly than the latter. This means that the deficiency of effective demand will be aggravated from one period to the next. In such circumstances, if the natural rate of

[1] Joan Robinson, *The Rate of Interest and Other Essays* (London: Macmillan, 1952), pp. 110–11.

[2] Joan Robinson, *Collected Economic Papers* (Oxford: Blackwell, 1951), p. 169.

growth exceeds the warranted rate which, in turn, exceeds the actual rate of growth of the stock of capital, then both types of unemployment, Marxian and Keynesian, will be increasingly reproduced; in the converse case, the natural rate of growth may fall short of the actual rate of accumulation; accordingly, the Marxian part of unemployment may shrink, but the Keynesian part will continue to expand.

The sole state of affairs that can be compatible with persistent full employment is the Growth Equilibrium where the natural rate of growth is equated with the warranted rate, the stock of capital is provided in an amount that is in balance with the number of workers residing in the economy, and the rate of investment is so high that the full utilization of capital is ensured. Unless all of these severe conditions are luckily fulfilled at the given rate of real wages, unemployment of labour is inevitable in a Fixprice economy.

We have thus seen that in a private-enterprise economy where entrepreneurs adjust their investment in conformity with the Harrodian law (4) it is extremely difficult to maintain full employment of labour. It is possible only in a 'mixed' economy with powerful public sectors that will supplement private investment such that private and public investment add up to the amount that is required for maintenance of full employment. In such an economy, private investment plus public investment must be exactly equal to the savings that are made by workers and capitalists out of their full-employment income. We have

$$px = bY, \qquad \text{and} \qquad L = \lambda_{\iota}\beta Y + l_i x,$$

from which we get

$$L = \left(\lambda_{\iota}\frac{\beta}{b}p + l_i\right)x. \tag{5}$$

On the left-hand side, L grows exponentially at a constant rate, ρ, i.e., $L = \bar{L}e^{\rho t}$, where $\bar{L}$ stands for the number of workers at time O. Taking account of the fact that the stock of capital increase at the rate x, we obtain from (5)

$$K(t) = \frac{\bar{L}}{\rho\Lambda}e^{\rho t} + c, \tag{6}$$

where c is a constant determined by the initial condition. Λ represents the total amount of labour directly and indirectly required to produce a unit of the capital good; that is to say,

$$\Lambda = \lambda_{\iota}\frac{\beta}{b}p + l_i.$$

On the other hand, to produce a unit of the capital good the amount of capital stock required, directly and indirectly, is

$$A = \alpha_\iota \frac{\beta}{b} p + a_i.$$

Therefore, in order to maintain the full-employment condition (5), the production of x needs the use of the stock of capital in the amount,

$$K_D(t) = Ax(t) = A \frac{\bar{L}}{\Lambda} e^{\rho t}. \tag{7}$$

As A is the reciprocal of the warranted rate of growth g, we at once find from (6) and (7) that if the natural rate of growth ρ is greater than the warranted g, $K_D(t)$ becomes greater than $K(t)$ eventually. For feasibility of production it is required that the former should not exceed the latter. Thus in an economy with the labour force growing at a rate greater than the warranted rate, full-employment growth becomes impossible at some stage in spite of wise and active spending policies of the government, because such activities of the government will necessarily result in a shortage of the stock of capital. (This would partly explain why the late Lord Keynes could not be a hero, but an enemy of the people, in the People's Republic of China.)

Terms are, however, reversed in the case of the natural rate of growth being less than the warranted rate. We find that $K_D(t)$ will not reach the existing stock $K(t)$ at some point of time and thereafter. The full-employment-growth programme guided by public sectors is feasible, but the economy will suffer from persistent excess capacity. The economy would fall into a slump as soon as public sectors stopped or checked investment. The generous Keynesian government would spoil private enterprises; after the long-continued period of full-employment growth supported by the public sectors, entrepreneurs' propensity to invest would have become degenerate, because an unused organ will atrophy.

5. We have seen that Fixprice economies where the Rule of Competitive Pricing does not work can hardly be kept in the state of full employment of labour, unless the warranted rate of growth is equated, by any chance, with the natural rate. This is true not only for pure private-enterprise economies but also for 'mixed' economies guided by public sectors. Long-term policies for full employment are, therefore, naturally concerned with measures by which the gap between the warranted and the natural rate of growth can be eliminated.

In the case of the natural rate of growth being lower than the warranted rate, as would commonly occur in Western countries, a rise in the real-wage rate (or, equivalently, a decrease in the money rate of interest) and an increase in the propensity to consume may be recommended as measures to reduce the warranted rate or to stimulate the natural rate

A rise in the real-wage rate, first of all, will probably increase the natural rate through its encouragement of immigration and births. It also affects the warranted rate by inducing a change in the price of the capital good p; if the ιth process of the consumption-good industry is more capital intensive than the ith process of the capital-good industry, then a rise of the real-wage rate will serve the purpose; that is to say, it will give rise to an increase in p, so that the warranted rate g will be diminished. If, however, the capital-good industry uses a process i that is more capital intensive than the process ι adopted by the consumption-good industry, an increase in the real-wage rate will have an adverse effect on the warranted rate. Secondly, from the definition of A as the reciprocal of the warranted rate of growth g it is obvious that an increase in the propensity to consume (i.e., an increase in β accompanied by a fall in b) will contribute to a decrease in g.

On the other hand, topsy turvy treatments for full employment should be recommended to an economy which (as do many Asiatic countries) suffers from rapid growth of the population. Besides the measures for lowering the natural rate, such as emmigration, birth control, reduction of working hours, and so on, measures for increasing the warranted rate must be taken. The reduction of the real-wage rate (if the consumption good industry is more capital intensive than the capital good industry) and the encouragement of the savings habit may be listed among effective measures to cure long-term unemployment of the Marxian type. It is obvious that these will not be received with pleasure by workers; we must conclude by saying that workers in Asiatic countries are confronted with an antinomy between full employment and austerity.

Finally, it is emphasized that the above result depends on the two basic underlying assumptions: (i) prices and the wage rate do not obey the Rule of Free Goods and are determined independently from the supply and demand for goods, and (ii) the investment function does not obey the neo-classical Acceleration Principle but satisfies the Harrodian premise (4). An economy fulfilling both of them is no more than a utopian economy where various forces working in the actual world have been eliminated. The story is no more than a parable and contrasts with the neo-classical one in various respects, but it would feature some important aspects of the real economy. Although the story has been told, we may dispense with the neo-classical assumption of no joint production which has been used. Therefore, we may say that the parable in this chapter will continue to be instructive after the Von Neumann Revolution discussed in Part II below.

V

TOWARDS MORE DISAGGREGATED MODELS

1. As WE have an enormous number of sectors in the actual world, it is of crucial importance to examine whether the main results so far confirmed in the test-tube will remain true outside it. In this chapter we return to the neo-classical model where the full employment of resources and labour is automatically attained and the Rule of Profitability and the Rule of Free Goods control behaviour of activities and prices. We shall complicate the previous two-good model so as to include many (say, n) kinds of commodities, and we will find that the neo-classical analysis of stability of long-run equilibrium will not necessarily be the same. The stability criterion may be different from model to model if the capital-good industry is divided into many sectors; though it will be shown that it is still valid in models with many consumption goods and *one* capital good. This is indeed an unhappy conclusion and means our two-sector model is inadequate to explain the actual process of capital accumulation. It may happen that in the actual world with many capital goods, the economy is getting further away from the state of long-run equilibrium, in spite of the process in our two-sector test-tube having displayed an easy passage towards a Silvery Equilibrium. Aggregation of various capital goods into one homogeneous stock of capital is a dangerous simplification; it may deform the economy in an intolerable way by forcing, for example, all instabilisers to disappear from the model altogether. An approach with many merits over the present Walrasian-type analysis will be offered in the next part; on this eve of the von Neumann Revolution in the theory of capital and growth a funeral march is played for evaluation of the neo-classical two-sector analysis.

Let us first consider a favourable case. We will show that the principles which we have been established by using the two-sector model would remain substantially unaffected even if we introduce many consumption goods. For the sake of efficiency of explanation, we take, in the following, the number of consumption goods as small as possible; we assume that each consumer is restricted to spend his income upon two sorts of goods. When expenditure is distributed between more than two goods, the argument will lose its simplicity with no addition to generality.

Let us continue to use the previous notation with the subscripts 1 and 2 indicating that the quantities or the prices at issue refer to those of the consumption good 1 and 2 respectively. For example, $\alpha_{1\iota}$ is the capital-input coefficient of the ιth process of the consumption-good industry 1, and γ_2 denotes the consumers' demand for good 2. We assume that there are μ techniques of producing good 1 and ν for good 2. Then, the short-run equilibrium is described by the following nine sets of inequalities:

$$\pi_1 \leqq q\alpha_{1\iota}+w\lambda_{1\iota} \qquad \iota = 1, ..., \mu, \tag{1.1}$$

$$\pi_2 \leqq q\alpha_{2\iota}+w\lambda_{2\iota} \qquad \iota = 1, ..., \nu, \tag{1.2}$$

$$p \leqq qa_i+wl_i \qquad i = 1, ..., m, \tag{2}$$

$$\pi_1\gamma_1 = \beta_1\left(\frac{\pi_2}{\pi_1}\right)(qK+wL), \tag{3.1}$$

$$\pi_2\gamma_2 = \beta_2\left(\frac{\pi_2}{\pi_1}\right)(qK+wL), \tag{3.2}$$

$$ps = b(qK+wL), \tag{4}$$

$$\pi_1\gamma_1+\pi_2\gamma_2+ps = qK+wL, \tag{5}$$

$$\gamma_1 \leqq \sum_\iota \xi_{1\iota}, \tag{6.1}$$

$$\gamma_2 \leqq \sum_\iota \xi_{2\iota}, \tag{6.2}$$

$$s \leqq d \leqq \sum_i x_i, \tag{7}$$

$$\sum_\iota \alpha_{1\iota}\xi_{1\iota}+\sum_\iota \alpha_{2\iota}\xi_{2\iota}+\sum_i a_i x_i \leqq K, \tag{8}$$

$$\sum_\iota \lambda_{1\iota}\xi_{1\iota}+\sum_\iota \lambda_{2\iota}\xi_{2\iota}+\sum_i l_i x_i \leqq L, \tag{9}$$

consisting of price-cost inequalities, consumption and savings functions,[1] Walras' law, and demand-supply and savings-investment inequalities. Attention should be paid to the fact that in (3.1) and (3.2) the Engel coefficients are assumed to be independent of the level of income. This assumption of unit income-elasticity evidently conflicts with the familiar Engel law, but we make it since it may be regarded as a simple first approximation to reality and since it is a necessary condition for the existence of a balanced-growth equilibrium. By the use of a powerful theorem due to Gale and Nikaido,[2] it can be shown that the system has a short-run solution for arbitrarily given positive K and L; or the same thing may alternatively be confirmed by a proof that is, in its essence, the same as that which we gave in Chapter I for the two-sector model, though the 'singular' points (i.e. the points where at least two processes

[1] Note that we are still assuming a constant propensity to save. $\beta_1(\pi_2/\pi_1)$ and $\beta_2(\pi_2/\pi_1)$ are Engel coefficients.

[2] D. Gale, 'The law of supply and demand', *Mathematica Scandinavica*, Vol. III (1955), pp. 155–69; H. Nikaido, 'On the classical multilateral exchange problem', *Metroeconomica*, Vol. VIII (1956), pp. 135–45.

of production of an industry are tied in their unit costs) are greater in number than they were before, by virtue of the multiplicity of consumption goods.[1]

The Silvery Equilibrium is defined, as before, as a state of affairs where the stock of capital K and the labour force L grow in balance, i.e., at a common rate. The existence of such a state is established in exactly the same way as in the previous two-sector model, that is to say, by the factor-price-frontier-Kahn-multiplier approach. In more detail, we can draw, on the basis of the technical coefficients of the consumption-good industry 1 and the capital-good industry, a number of factor-price frontiers which enable us to read the rate of profit and hence the price of the capital good and the price of the capital service as functions of the wage rate in terms of consumption good 1. Substituting the 'reasonable' price of the capital service thus determined into the price-cost inequalities of the consumption good 2, we get the reasonable price of good 2 (in terms of good 1). Next, in the three-sector model we have two Kahn's multipliers,[2]

$$\frac{\sum_\iota \xi_{1\iota}}{\sum_i x_i} = \frac{\beta_1\left(\dfrac{\pi_2}{\pi_1}\right)}{b}\frac{p}{\pi_1}, \qquad \frac{\sum_\iota \xi_{2\iota}}{\sum_i x_i} = \frac{\beta_2\left(\dfrac{\pi_2}{\pi_1}\right)}{b}\frac{p}{\pi_2}, \tag{10}$$

both being functions of w/π_1. As we have from (8)

$$\sum_\iota \alpha_{1\iota}\frac{\xi_{1\iota}}{\sum_i x_i} + \sum_\iota \alpha_{2\iota}\frac{\xi_{2\iota}}{\sum_i x_i} + \sum_i a_i \frac{x_i}{\sum_i x_i} = \frac{K}{\sum_i x_i},$$

the rate of growth of the stock of capital, $\sum_i x_i/K$, is seen, in view of (10), to be a continuous staircase-like function of w/π_1. The rate of growth of the labour force, on the other hand, depends on π_2/π_1 as well as w/π_1; but, as the former is adjusted to the latter, its ultimate determinant is w/π_1. We have a figure similar to Fig. 2(*a*) in Chapter II; the growth equilibrium is given by the intersection of the growth-rate curves of the capital stock and the labour force.

2. Before proceeding to the discussion of the stability of growth equilibrium, let us confirm that the consumption functions (3.1) and (3.2) are generated by utility functions of the following type. First, all consumers are 'homogeneous' in tastes in the sense that their utility functions are identical,

[1] Note that conditions (1)–(9) imply $d = s$.

[2] We assume, as before, the positivity of all technical coefficients; it is then seen t at the prices π_1, π_2, and p should be positive in the state of long-run equilibrium. This implies that (6.1), (6.2), and (7) hold with equality. We have, therefore, (10) from (3.1), (3.2), and (4).

so that we may proceed with the analysis in terms of *the* utility function, $U(\gamma_1, \gamma_2)$. Second, tastes of each consumer are 'homothetic' to the effect that a proportional change in the quantities of goods contained in two baskets to be compared with each other does not affect his choice between them. He will save a constant portion of his income and will spend the rest upon goods 1 and 2 so as to maximize his utility. It is easily seen that these specifications, together with the usual characteristics of utility functions, imply that market demands for consumers' goods are independent of the income distribution among individuals and are exactly doubled by a doubling of the aggregate income, as in (3.1) and (3.2). Moreover, it is seen that the consumption coefficients, β_1 and β_2, depend on the price ratio, π_2/π_1, alone, and Walras' law implies the following identity:

$$\beta_1\left(\frac{\pi_2}{\pi_1}\right)+\beta_2\left(\frac{\pi_2}{\pi_1}\right)+b \equiv 1. \tag{11}$$

The crucial step of proving stability is to verify that the consumers' budget (not the consumption plan but the whole plan for consumption and savings) satisfies the axiom of revealed-preference. That is to say, we must show that for any two sets of prices $(\pi_1{}^0, \pi_2{}^0, p^0)$ and $(\pi_1{}^1, \pi_2{}^1, p^1)$ the feasibility of the plan $(\gamma_1{}^1, \gamma_2{}^1, s^1)$ at $(\pi_1{}^0, \pi_2{}^0, p^0)$, i.e.

$$\pi_1{}^0\gamma_1{}^1+\pi_2{}^0\gamma_2{}^1+p^0s^1 \leqq \pi_1{}^0\gamma_1{}^0+\pi_2{}^0\gamma_2{}^0+p^0s^0, \tag{12}$$

implies the *in*feasibility of $(\gamma_1{}^0, \gamma_2{}^0, s^0)$ at $(\pi_1{}^1, \pi_1{}^1, p^1)$, i.e.

$$\pi_1{}^1\gamma_1{}^1+\pi_2{}^1\gamma_2{}^1+p^1s^1 < \pi_1{}^1\gamma_1{}^0+\pi_2{}^1\gamma_2{}^0+p^1s^0. \tag{13}$$

As a general rule, it is of course true that the specification of the consumption and savings functions in the forms, (3.1), (3.2), and (4), does not necessarily imply the revealed-preference axiom for the whole plan (γ_1, γ_2, s). But if we further assume that β_2 is a non-increasing function of π_2/π_1, i.e.[1]

$$\frac{\partial\beta_2}{\partial(\pi_2/\pi_1)} \leqq 0, \quad \text{or} \quad \left\{\beta_2\left(\frac{\pi_2{}^1}{\pi_1{}^1}\right)-\beta_2\left(\frac{\pi_2{}^0}{\pi_1{}^0}\right)\right\}\left(\frac{\pi_2{}^0}{\pi_2{}^1}-\frac{\pi_1{}^0}{\pi_1{}^1}\right) \geqq 0, \tag{14}$$

the axiom holds as is shown in the following way.

Bearing in mind (3.1), (3.2), and (4), inequalities (12) and (13) can be written as

$$\left[\pi_1{}^0\frac{\beta_1{}^1}{\pi_1{}^1}+\pi_2{}^0\frac{\beta_2{}^1}{\pi_2{}^1}+p^0\frac{b}{p^1}\right](q^1K+w^1L)$$
$$\leqq \left[\pi_1{}^0\frac{\beta_1{}^0}{\pi_1{}^0}+\pi_2{}^0\frac{\beta_2{}^0}{\pi_2{}^0}+p^0\frac{b}{p^0}\right](q^0K+w^0L), \tag{12'}$$

[1] This is a slight generalization of the assumption of the constant consumption coefficient and implies that the price elasticity is not less than 1.

and

$$\left[\pi_1{}^1\frac{\beta_1{}^1}{\pi_1{}^1}+\pi_2{}^1\frac{\beta_2{}^1}{\pi_2{}^1}+p^1\frac{b}{p^1}\right](q^1K+w^1L)$$
$$<\left[\pi_1{}^1\frac{\beta_1{}^0}{\pi_1{}^0}+\pi_2{}^1\frac{\beta_2{}^0}{\pi_2{}^0}+p^1\frac{b}{p^0}\right](q^0K+w^0L), \qquad (13')$$

where $\beta_i{}^0 = \beta_i(\pi_2{}^0/\pi_1{}^0)$; $\beta_i{}^1 = \beta_i(\pi_2{}^1/\pi_1{}^1)$. There are two cases to be discussed: The easier one is the case where relative prices remain unchanged in both situations, and the other case is where some (small) changes in prices occur. With prices of the consumption goods and the capital good being unchanged, it is clear that (12′) holds if and only if the real income in situation 1 is not greater than that in situation 0. This weak inequality between the incomes in the two situations is, however, a strict one since $(\gamma_1{}^0, \gamma_2{}^0, s^0) \neq (\gamma_1{}^1, \gamma_2{}^1, s^1)$—a basic assumption in the revealed-preference discussion though we have not made an explicit statement of it in the above. In fact, if the incomes were equal to each other, the plans in the two situations would be identical—a contradiction. Now (13′) directly follows from the strict inequality thus established.

In the case of relative prices in situation 1 differing from those in situation 0, it is seen that the product of the parts in the square brackets on the left-hand side of (12′) and right-hand side of (13′) is greater than $(\beta_1{}^0+\beta_2{}^0+b)^2$, the product of the parts in the square brackets on the right-hand side of (12′) and left-hand side of (13′). This is so because (i) the inequality,

$$\left(\pi_1{}^0\frac{\beta_1{}^1}{\pi_1{}^1}+\pi_2{}^0\frac{\beta_2{}^1}{\pi_2{}^1}+p^0\frac{b}{p^1}\right)\left(\pi_1{}^1\frac{\beta_1{}^0}{\pi_1{}^0}+\pi_2{}^1\frac{\beta_2{}^0}{\pi_2{}^0}+p^1\frac{b}{p^0}\right)$$
$$>(\beta_1{}^0+\beta_2{}^0+b)^2+\left(\beta_1{}^0\frac{\pi_1{}^1}{\pi_1{}^0}+\beta_2{}^0\frac{\pi_2{}^1}{\pi_2{}^0}+b\frac{p^1}{p^0}\right)(\beta_2{}^1-\beta_1{}^0)\left(\frac{\pi_2{}^0}{\pi_2{}^1}-\frac{\pi_1{}^0}{\pi_1{}^1}\right), \qquad (15)$$

is true in all circumstances so long as there is at least one price that is changed, and (ii) the last part on the right-hand side of (15) is non-negative because of (14).[1] Hence inequality (12′) does imply (13′);[2] the

[1] (15) holds with strict inequality since we have at least one relative price, say $p^1/\pi_1{}^1$, such that $p^1/\pi_1{}^1 \neq p^0/\pi_1{}^0$, so that

$\frac{p^1}{p^0}\frac{\pi_1{}^0}{\pi_1{}^1}+\frac{p^0}{p^1}\frac{\pi_1{}^1}{\pi_1{}^0} > 2$. In verifying (15), use the relationship,

$$(\beta_2{}^1-\beta_2{}^0)\left(\frac{\pi_2{}^0}{\pi_2{}^1}-\frac{\pi_1{}^0}{\pi_1{}^1}\right) = (\beta_1{}^1-\beta_1{}^0)\frac{\pi_1{}^0}{\pi_1{}^1}+(\beta_2{}^1-\beta_2{}^0)\frac{\pi_2{}^0}{\pi_2{}^1},$$

which follows from (11).

[2] Dividing (15) by (12′), we get (13′).

whole consumption-savings plan, therefore, satisfies the revealed-preference axiom.

It is not difficult to confirm that the other part of the stability proof of the neo-classical model in Chapter III holds *mutatis mutandis* in a system with two (or many) consumption goods. We have an equation similar to (III.12); as the right-hand side of that equation is definitely negative (because of the axiom of revealed preference), we get the Neo-classical Dynamic Rule: An increase in the stock of capital per man reduces the price of capital services and hence raises the real-wage rate. If the warranted rate of growth is initially set to be greater than the natural rate, the real wage will continue to increase until the two rates of growth are finally equated with each other. The path towards the Silvery Equilibrium is exactly the same as that which we had in the two-sector model. There is nothing to gain in complicating the system by considering many consumption goods; there is no loss in the explanatory capacity of the model by aggregating them into a single representative consumption good, such as Wheat.

3. If the capital good is disaggregated, a completely different result is obtained. Savings should now be distributed among various new capital goods, such that the total value of investments equals savings at any moment. It is assumed, as before, that prices are so flexible that each capital good is fully utilized unless it is a free good. When prices are set such that each industry will choose one and only one process available to it, we have, in an economy with one consumption and two capital goods,

$$K_1 = \alpha_1\xi + a_{11}x_1 + a_{12}x_2,$$

$$K_2 = \alpha_2\xi + a_{21}x_1 + a_{22}x_2, \tag{16}$$

where K_i is the stock of capital good i, α_i and a_{ij} the volume of capital good i used in the production of one unit of the consumption good and capital good j, respectively, ξ the output of the consumption good, and x_i the output of capital good i.

As we are assuming that capital goods do not suffer wear and tear, capital good i is regarded as increasing at the rate x_i, so that $x_i = dK_i/dt$. It is clear that in any short-run equilibrium, investment I is the sum over i of the products of x_i and p_i. Since the output of the consumption good ξ must equal *ex ante* consumption i.e. $\gamma = \beta(\sum_i q_iK_i + wL)$, equations (16) may be solved with respect to the x_is, so that the x_is are expressed in terms of K_1, K_2, and $\sum_i q_iK_i + wL$. Taking into account the fact that the prices, q_1, q_2, p_1, p_2, take on definite value depending on the real-wage rate w, we find that investment I is a function of w, K_1, K_2, and L. By the same argument, savings depend on the same variables. The savings-investment equality may, therefore, be put in the form

$$S(w, K_1, K_2, L) = I(w, K_1, K_2, L). \tag{17}$$

Equations (16) and (17) are combined with the growth rate function, $\dot{L}/L = \rho(w)$, of the labour force to give a complete dynamic path of capital accumulation. With arbitrarily given K_1, K_2, and L, the real-wage rate is determined so as to establish equation (17);[1] the demand for the consumption good is then determined, and equations (16) are solved with respect to the x_is, the amounts of capital goods produced, in terms of K_1, K_2, and L. The capital stocks, K_1 and K_2, increase at the rates, x_1/K_1 and x_2/K_2, respectively, while the labour force grows at the (known) natural rate, $\rho(w)$; so that we have the capital stocks and labour force at the next point of time, with which exactly the same process of accumulation is repeated.

Let us now show, by presenting a numerical example, that in an economy with heterogeneous capital goods the path of accumulation, $(K_1(t), K_2(t), L(t))$, so far discussed does not necessarily approach the equilibrium-growth path (or the Silvery Equilibrium path) along which all the capital stocks and the labour force grow steadily at a common fixed rate. We assume that industries choose at Silvery Equilibrium the processes with the following input coefficients:

	Consumption-good industry	Capital-good industry 1	Capital-good industry 2
Capital-good 1	1·52	4	2
Capital-good 2	1·52	2	4
Labour	1·74	1	1

We also assume that the labour force grows at the rate of 3 per cent when the real-wage rate is fixed at 0·4, and that citizens save 10 per cent of their income. It is then seen that the Silvery Equilibrium is established at prices, $(\pi, p_1, p_2, q_1, q_2) = (1, 1, 1, 0{\cdot}1, 0{\cdot}1)$, and with capital stocks per man, $(K_1/L, K_2/L) = (1, 1)$.

Let us now suppose strong price-stabilizing forces prevail, so that the real-wage rate is kept within a very close neighbourhood of the Silvery Equilibrium. The consumption function γ may then safely be approximated by

$$\gamma = 0{\cdot}9(0{\cdot}1K_1 + 0{\cdot}1K_2 + 0{\cdot}4L).$$

[1] It is interesting to compare this mechanism of wage determination with Kaldor's theory of income distribution among workers and capitalists.

This, together with the above values of the coefficients, enables us to put (16) in the form,

$$
\begin{aligned}
0{\cdot}8633K_1 - 0{\cdot}1367K_2 &= 0{\cdot}5467L + 4x_1 + 2x_2, \\
-0{\cdot}1367K_1 + 0{\cdot}8633K_2 &= 0{\cdot}5467L + 2x_1 + 4x_2.
\end{aligned} \tag{16'}
$$

Taking into consideration that the labour force expands at the natural rate of 3 per cent, we can easily solve differential equations (16′); by the use of a desk calculator we get three characteristic numbers, 0·03, 0·12, and 0·50; hence the solutions are

$$
\begin{aligned}
K_1(t) &= C_1e^{0.03t} + C_{11}e^{0.12t} + C_{12}e^{0.50t}, \\
K_2(t) &= C_2e^{0.03t} + C_{21}e^{0.12t} + C_{22}e^{0.50t}, \\
L &= C_3e^{0.03t},
\end{aligned} \tag{18}
$$

where the *C*s are constants determined by the initial conditions. As the natural rate is the smallest among the characteristic numbers, we find from (18) that with a lapse of time the capital stocks per worker, K_1/L and K_2/L, will diverge further and further from their Silvery Equilibrium values.

This is indeed a remarkable conclusion. In our previous model with many consumption goods and one capital good (as well as in the original two-sector model) the stability of the real-wage rate implied the stability of every other variable. But, as soon as heterogeneous capital goods are introduced and the equality between supply and demand has to be established in each capital market, we can no longer observe definite relationships between the wage stability and the stability of other variables. Activity variables may not be stable even if the price-wage system is stable; and the converse may also happen. The phenomena of 'mixed stability-instability' which have never been observed in two-sector models may appear in many-sector models, depending, *inter alia*, on the relative magnitudes of various capital-input coefficients. It is thus seen that systems containing heterogeneous capital goods can no longer be aggregated; only detailed multi-sector models can give the correct answer to the stability problem.

4. In the rest of this chapter we shall try to liberate ourselves from a number of other unrealistic assumptions. The first assumption to be abandoned is the classical one that firms can be classified into industries producing *distinct* outputs: consumption goods and capital goods. Instead we assume (as Leontief and many other contemporary economists do) that each good may serve as a production requirement of all the various industries in the economy. There is no clear line of demarcation between consumption and capital goods: A good is a consumption good if it is bought by a consumer, and a capital good if it is used as a factor of production. The lifetime of a capital good is usually longer than the production period of goods, so that it can be used in production more than once. Current production requirements (fuel, material, etc.) which cease to exist once they are used up in production may, however, be treated as special capital goods with the length of life equal to the production period.

In our previous two-sector model it is assumed that factors of production (labour and the capital service) are instantaneously transformed into a product (the consumption good or the capital good). It is clear that this instantaneous or 'synchronized' process of production is a limiting case of the so-called 'point-input-point-output' process that transforms factors entering production simultaneously at some point of time into a product after a certain length of time; while the latter is also a special case of a more general process with continuous inputs and continuous outputs. In the following we make, for the sake of simplicity, two assumptions: (i) all the processes are of the point-input-point-output type; (ii) each of them has the same period of production which is taken as one unit of time. We also assume that to each of the n industries there are available a number of manufacturing processes producing homogeneous outputs. Let the s_jth process of industry j consume b_{is_j} units of capital good i and l_{s_j} units of labour to produce one unit of good j. Industry j can choose from among m_j processes, so that the subscript s_j runs from 1_j to m_j for a given j.

We next abandon another unrealistic assumption to the effect that all capital goods do not suffer wear and tear. Let τ_{is_j} be the *average* life of good i when it is used for further production by the s_jth process. A unit of capital good i produced at the beginning of period $t-v$ and used from $t-v$ to t by that process is regarded and treated as equivalent to $\left(1-\frac{1}{\tau_{is_j}}\right)^v$ units of brand-new capital good i produced at the beginning of period t. Thus our procedure presumes that a capital good loses a constant percentage (depending on its use) of the existing quantity as a result of damage from normal use, but the remaining quantity has the same quality as a new unit of that good.

Let $p_i(t)$ be the price of good i in period t. It is clear that the total value of capital stocks used per unit level of the s_jth process is

$$b_{1s_j}p_1(t)+b_{2s_j}p_2(t)+\cdots+b_{ns_j}p_n(t),$$

the depreciation accruing from which amounts to

$$\frac{b_{1s_j}}{\tau_{1s_j}}p_1(t)+\frac{b_{2s_j}}{\tau_{2s_j}}p_2(t)+\cdots+\frac{b_{ns_j}}{\tau_{ns_j}}p_n(t);$$

the rate of depreciation is, therefore, seen to be a weighted average of $1/\tau_{1s_j}$, $1/\tau_{2s_j}$, ..., $1/\tau_{ns_j}$. It is noted that the rate of depreciation thus defined is much greater than the usual figure, because our formula includes the current inputs (fuel, material, and so on), i.e., the inputs of those goods whose τ_{is_j}s are unity.

As production takes time, industries are required to decide when they should pay workers, at the beginning or in the middle or at the end of the production period. In the following we assume that wages are paid in advance at the beginning of the period; then an entrepreneur who intends to produce good j by the use of the s_jth process must prepare, per unit of the output, wage funds of the amount $l_{s_j}w(t)$, where $w(t)$ is the money-wage rate in period t. The total value of capital is the sum of the value of fixed capital and the value of working capital including wage funds.

At the beginning of the next period (that is, when the production process is completed), the entrepreneur will have one unit of output j and an outfit of capital equipment of

$$\left\{b_{1s_j}\left(1-\frac{1}{\tau_{1s_j}}\right), \ldots, b_{ns_j}\left(1-\frac{1}{\tau_{ns_j}}\right)\right\}$$

after deducting the portions worn in the process of production. They are evaluated at the prices in period $t+1$, and the rate of profit of the s_jth process $r_{s_j}(t)$ is obtained by dividing the excess of output over total costs (i.e. current costs *plus* depreciation of fixed capital goods *plus* capital losses due to price changes) by the total amount of capital; that is to say, we have

$$r_{s_j}(t) = \frac{p_j(t+1)+\sum_i b_{is_j}\left(1-\frac{1}{\tau_{is_j}}\right)p_i(t+1)-\sum_i b_{is_j}p_i(t)-l_{s_j}w(t)}{\sum_i b_{is_j}p_i(t)+l_{s_j}w(t)}.$$

Let $r_j(t)$ be the maximum of $r_{1_j}(t), r_{2_j}(t), \ldots, r_{m_j}(t)$. By definition, we have

$$p_j(t+1) \leqq \{1+r_j(t)\}\{\sum_i b_{is_j}p_i(t)+l_{s_j}w(t)\}-\sum_i b_{is_j}\left(1-\frac{1}{\tau_{is_j}}\right)p_i(t+1)$$

$$i, j = 1, \ldots, n;\ s_j = 1_j, \ldots, m_j.$$

The entrepreneur will choose, from among m_j possible processes, those which give the maximum rate of profit; therefore, he will adopt only those processes which fulfil the above relationship with equality (the Rule of Profitability).

In a competitive situation, entrepreneurs switch from the production of a good with a low rate of profit to another with a higher rate; so that different profit rates are equalized throughout the economy to a uniform rate; that is

$$r(t) = r_j(t) \qquad \text{for all} \quad j = 1, \ldots, n.$$

Hence the above inequalities may be put in the form

$$p_j(t+1) \leqq \sum_i b_{is_j}\left(1-\frac{1}{\tau_{is_j}}\right)\{p_i(t)-p_i(t+1)\}+\sum_i \frac{b_{is_j}}{\tau_{is_j}}p_i(t)$$
$$+r(t)\{\sum_i b_{is_j}p_i(t)+l_{s_j}w(t)\}+l_{s_j}w(t),$$
$$s_j = 1_j, \ldots, m_j. \qquad (19)$$

after rearranging the terms. In an economy where the entire profits are paid to the owners of capital as interest, $r(t)$ equals the rate of interest. Then on the right-hand side of (19), the first term stands for capital losses due to price changes, the second for the value of the current inputs (including the depreciation of fixed capital goods), the third for the interest charge on fixed and working capital, and the last for wage costs. It is noticed that our former price inequalities (1.1), (1.2), and (2) in the three sector model are extended to inequalities (19), when the production period is not null and capital goods suffer wear and tear. By denoting

$$a_{is_j} = b_{is_j}/\tau_{is_j},$$

(19) may be put in the matrix form

$$P_m(t+1) \leqq \{P(t)-P(t+1)\}(B-A)+P(t)A$$
$$+r(t)\{P(t)B+w(t)L\}+w(t)L, \qquad (20)$$

where

$$P(t) = \{p_1(t), p_2(t) \ldots p_n(t)\}$$

and $P_m(t)$ is an m-dimensional vector whose components can be partitioned into n groups such that the first m_1 are all $p_1(t)$s, the next m_2 all $p_2(t)$s, and so on; A, B, and L are

$$A = \begin{pmatrix} a_{11_1} \ldots a_{1m_1} & a_{11_2} \ldots a_{1m_2} \ldots a_{11_n} \ldots a_{1m_n} \\ \cdot\ \cdot\ \cdot\ \cdot\ \cdot\ \cdot & \cdot\ \cdot\ \cdot\ \cdot\ \cdot\ \cdot\ \cdot\ \cdot\ \cdot\ \cdot\ \cdot \\ a_{n1_1} \ldots a_{nm_1} & a_{n1_2} \ldots a_{nm_2} \ldots a_{n1_n} \ldots a_{nm_n} \end{pmatrix},$$

$$B = \begin{pmatrix} b_{11_1} \ldots b_{1m_1} & b_{11_2} \ldots b_{1m_2} \ldots b_{11_n} \ldots b_{1m_n} \\ \cdot\ \cdot\ \cdot\ \cdot\ \cdot\ \cdot & \cdot\ \cdot\ \cdot\ \cdot\ \cdot\ \cdot\ \cdot\ \cdot\ \cdot\ \cdot\ \cdot \\ b_{n1_1} \ldots b_{nm_1} & b_{n1_2} \ldots b_{nm_2} \ldots b_{n1_n} \ldots b_{nm_n} \end{pmatrix},$$

$$L = (l_{1_1} \ldots l_{m_1} \quad l_{1_2} \ldots l_{m_2} \ldots l_{1_n} \ldots l_{m_n}),$$

which are referred to as the matrix of current-input coefficients, the matrix of capital-input coefficients, and the vector of labour-input coefficients, respectively.

We now pass on to the output-determination side of the system. Let

$x_{s_j}(t)$ be the level of the s_jth activity of industry j during period t; it is clear that $x_{s_j}(t)$ is non-negative for those s_j for which (20) holds with equality, while it is zero otherwise. The total stock of good i, $Q_i(t+1)$, made available at the beginning of period $t+1$, is the stock of good i existing at the end of period t *plus* the output of good i available at the beginning of period $t+1$; we can at once see

$$Q_i(t+1) = \sum_j \sum_{s_j} (b_{is_j} - a_{is_j}) x_{s_j}(t) + \sum_{s_i} x_{s_i}(t), \qquad i = 1, \ldots, n.$$

If we assume that each good is perfectly transferable from one industry to another, and denote the consumption of good i in period t by $c_i(t)$, we have inequalities[1]

$$Q_i(t+1) \geqq \sum_j \sum_{s_j} b_{is_j} x_{s_j}(t+1) + c_i(t+1), \qquad i = 1, \ldots, n,$$

which imply that no more goods can be used for production during any period than are available after deducting the amounts devoted to consumption, at the beginning of the period. Eliminating $Q_i(t+1)$ from the above two sets of conditions, we have the following inequalities that are put in matrix form,

$$X(t) \geqq AX_m(t) + B\{X_m(t+1) - X_m(t)\} + C(t+1), \tag{21}$$

where $X_m(t)$ is the m-dimensional column vector of activity levels

$$X_m(t) = \{x_{1_1}(t), \ldots, x_{m_1}(t), x_{1_2}(t), \ldots, x_{m_2}(t), \ldots, x_{1_n}(t), \ldots, x_{m_n}(t)\};$$

$X(t)$ is the n-dimensional column vector whose first component is the sum of the first m_1 components of $X_m(t)$, the second the sum of the next m_2 components, and so on. $C(t)$ is the n-dimensional (column) consumption vector consisting of elements, $C_i(t)$, $i = 1, \ldots, n$. It is easily seen that inequalities (21) correspond to (6.1), (6.2), and (8) of the three-sector model.

Finally, it is obvious that the labour constraint (9) may now be written as

$$\rho_{t-1}\rho_{t-2} \ldots \rho_0 N \geqq \sum_j \sum_s l_{s_j} x_{s_j}(t), \tag{22}$$

where $\rho_t - 1$ is the rate of growth of the labour force in period t, and N the number of workers available at the beginning of period 0; we may assume, as before, that ρ_t depends on the real-wage rate in period t.

[1] We assume (like Hicks, in *Value and Capital*) that consumers can only buy goods at the beginning of each period, say, on his 'Monday'. Goods are delivered until the beginning of the next period when new contracts can be made.

5. The multi-sectoral model described by inequalities (20)–(22) was examined in Chapter 4 of my previous book.[1] But it seems that some further remarks are helpful before we proceed to examine how the model works through time. First of all, it should be noticed that in multi-sectoral models (unlike the two-sector model but like the model with many capital goods discussed above) a definite conclusion about the stability of the long-run equilibrium does not follow from specifying that the consumption and the savings functions satisfy the axiom of revealed preference. In order to be able to say something definite about the paths of economic activities through time, it is necessary to specify not only the households' consumption and saving decisions but also entrepreneurs' investment decisions; the latter is completely independent of the former in an economy in which there are more than two kinds of capital goods. It is true that the total amount of investment is set by the savings decisions of the households; but it is always possible for entrepreneurs to allocate it among various capital goods in any proportions;[2] the axiom of revealed preference obviously has no connection with the principles of allocating investment. In the multisectoral analysis, therefore, we would not gain by assuming the axiom: We would instead benefit by neglecting capitalists' consumption as well as workers' savings. This procedure which is popular especially among Cambridge economists results in an over or underestimation of the rate of growth according to whether the capitalists' consumption is greater or less than the workers' savings; but, as will be seen below, it can establish a simple relationship between the long-run equilibrium rate of interest and the rate of balanced growth.

Secondly, we assume that workers are identical in their tastes for consumption goods and can offer only one unit of homogeneous labour. As workers spend their income upon various commodities without making any savings, the budget equation takes the form,

$$\sum_i p_i(t)c_i(p_i(t), \ldots, p_n(t), w(t)) = w(t), \tag{23}$$

where $c_i(p_i, \ldots, p_n, w)$ is the consumption of goods i per worker; c_is are, according to the classical theory of consumer's behaviour, homogeneous of degree zero in prices and the wage rate, so that they remain invariant with respect to any type of normalization. It is evident that the total consumption of good i is given by the formula

$$c_i(t) = c_i(p_1(t), \ldots, p_n(t), w(t))\{\sum_j \sum_{s_j} l_{s_j} x_{s_j}(t)\}, \tag{24}$$

as the number of workers employed is given by $\sum_j \sum_{s_j} l_{s_j} x_{s_j}(t)$.

[1] *Equilibrium, Stability and Growth: A Multi-sectoral Analysis* (Oxford: Clarendon Press), 1964.

[2] In the previous model with two kinds of capital goods total investment is distributed between them according to the multi-sectoral Acceleration Principle.

In a state of price equilibrium which is defined as a state where prices and the wage rate remain unchanged over time, we may take labour as the *numéraire* and fix the wage rate at unity. We call prices measured in terms of labour, wage-prices. We have, as in the previous two-sector model, two important rules of competition: One is the Rule of Profitability (or the principle of profit-rate maximization) which implies that entrepreneurs do not use those processes fulfilling (20) with strict inequality; while the other is the Rule of Free Goods or the rule of charging zero prices for those goods which are over-produced, i.e. those goods fulfilling (21) with strict inequality. Being armed with these rules, we obtain, in a state of 'tranquility', where the activity levels grow at a common rate g {i.e., $X_m(t+1) = (1+g)X_m(t)$} at stationary prices (i.e., $P(t+1) = P(t) = P$), the aggregative price-cost equation,

$$P_m X_m(t) = PAX_m(t) + rPBX_m(t) + (1+r)LX_m(t), \tag{25}$$

by post-multiplying (20) by $X_m(t)$, and the aggregative supply-demand equation,

$$PX(t) = PAX_m(t) + gPBX_m(t) + PC(t+1), \tag{26}$$

by premultiplying (21) by P. It is noted that $w(t)$ is unity by normalization, and P stands for the vector of wage-prices. It is also noted that a state of 'tranquility' exists only when r is set at an appropriate value not exceeding the technically attainable maximum.[1] In view of (23) and (24) as well as the fact that prices are constant over time, we find that $PC(t+1) = (1+g)LX_m(t)$. Moreover, we have $P_m X_m(t) = PX(t)$ by definition. Hence (25) and (26) imply $r = g$; that is, with the Cambridge type (or the J. von Neumann–Joan Robinson type) of savings function, the 'tranquil' rate of growth is equal to the (preassigned) rate of interest.

Let $[0, \bar{r})$ be the (semi-open) range of r within which a set of positive (or non-negative) stationary wage-prices is associated with a given value of r. When r increases in that range, wage prices also increase, so that the real-wage rate decreases correspondingly; in particular, when r approaches the upper bound $\bar{r}$, wage prices tend to infinity, with the result that the real-wage rate falls to zero. On the other hand, when r approaches the lower bound zero, wage-prices become very small and the real-wage rate, therefore, becomes large. We assume that the technology is 'sustainable', i.e., that the real-wage rate corresponding to zero rate of profit is at least as high as the subsistence level which enables workers to buy the necessities of life. Then, on the assumption that the rate of growth of the labour force is a function of the real-wage rate such that it is negative if the real-wage rate is less than the subsistence level and positive if it is

[1] Ibid., p. 96.

greater than that level, we find that there is an intersection of the curve showing the growth rate of the labour force as a function of the rate of profit[1] with the curve (the 45° line) showing the tranquil rate of balanced growth of outputs as a function of the rate of profit. These two curves are our old friends; the natural-rate-of-growth and the warranted-rate-of-growth curve, respectively. The intersection gives an equilibrium rate of profits. The long-run equilibrium thus established with the Cambridge savings function (excluding capitalists' consumption and workers' savings) is referred to as the Golden Equilibrium which is, as will be shown later, superior to the Silvery Equilibrium. It will in fact be shown that the former gives an optimum, in comparison with which the latter is no more than a 'second-best' state.

6. The working of the model is now examined on the basis of a number of assumptions. First, the money-wage rate $w(t)$ is taken to be unchanged over time. Second, the interest rate is fixed at the 'golden' rate, $\bar{r}$. Third, the growth rate of the labour force is considered to take on a positive value, independently of any of the variables in the system. These assumptions are too stringent to generate dynamic movements of prices and activity levels that could simulate their real behaviour in the actual world. But it would still be of interest to find that, under these assumptions, dual stability-instability of prices and outputs (a curiosum due to Jorgenson) almost inevitably presents itself.[2]

We begin with prices historically given in period 0, a stationary money-wage rate, $\bar{w}$, and the rate of interest set at the golden rate, $\bar{r}$. Substituting these values in the price-cost inequalities (20) for $t = 0$ we obtain the prices in period 1.[3] The consumption coefficients in period 1 are, therefore, determined, so that we may find the output levels in period 1 by solving inequalities (21) and (22), as stocks of goods at the beginning of period 1 (or equivalently activity levels in period 0) and the labour force available at the same point of time may be regarded as given for period 1. We thus have two inter-temporal relationships giving $P(t+1)$ and $X(t+1)$ as a function of $P(t)$ and $X(t)$, respectively.

Before proceeding further with the work of establishing the dual stability-instability theorem, let us compare the above procedure of determining prices and activity levels with the one in the previous two-sector model. In that model it was assumed that there is no production lag and no depreciation; the price-subsystem may then be described in terms of the

[1] The natural rate of growth can be reduced to a function of the rate of profits, because the real-wage rate is a decreasing function of the profit rate.

[2] D. W. Jorgenson, 'A dual stability theorem', *Econometrica*, Vol. XXVIII (1960), pp. 892–99.

[3] Note that throughout the following, $w(t)$ and $r(t)$ in (20) are fixed at $\bar{w}$ and $\bar{r}$, respectively.

static, simultaneous inequalities[1]

$$p_j(t) \leqq r(t)\sum_i b_{is_j}p_i(t)+l_{s_j} \qquad s_j = l_j, ..., m_j; j = 1, 2, \tag{27}$$

while the output-subsystem is reduced to a system containing a dynamic (or differential) relationship. We have[2]

$$\sum_{s_1} x_{s_1}(t) \geqq c_1(t) \tag{28}$$

for consumption good 1, and

$$Q_2(t) \geqq \sum_{s_1} b_{2s_1}x_{s_1}(t)+\sum_{s_2} b_{2s_2}x_{s_2}(t) \tag{29}$$

$$dQ_2/dt = \sum_{s_2} x_{s_2}(t) \tag{30}$$

for capital good 2. If the rate of profit $r(t)$ is given, (27) can determine prices at time t which, in turn, determines the capital coefficients chosen. Therefore, with the capital stock $Q_2(t)$ inherited from the past, the activity levels at t can be fixed but they must still fulfill inequalities (28) and (29); and the capital stock in the immediate future is given by the differential equation (30). This process of determining prices and outputs is comparable with that of the multi-sectoral system (20) and (21) with production lags and depreciation, although prices are simultaneously determined in our two-sector model, and not in a successive way as in the multi-sector model.

Apart from the presence or absence of time lags, an essential difference between our two-sector model and the multi-sector model lies in the fact that the former is furnished with a relationship between the real-wage rate on the one hand, and the growth rates of the stock of capital and labour force on the other; that is, the rate of real wages will increase (or decrease) when the rate of growth of the capital stock is greater (or less)

[1] In (20) the one period lag is to be replaced by zero, so that the first term on the right-hand side vanishes; furthermore, the absence of the production lag implies that no interest is charged on the working capital; hence the term $r(t)w(t)L$ disappears from the right-hand side. We also have $a_{is_j} = 0$ or $\tau_{is_j} = \infty$ by the assumption that the capital good does not suffer wear and tear.

[2] All $a_{is_j} = 0$ as before. In view of the fact that there is no production lag, we have

$$Q_1(t) = \sum_{s_1} x_{s_1}(t) \qquad \text{and} \qquad Q_1(t) \geqq c_1(t)$$

for the consumption good 1, because $b_{is_1} = 0$. For the capital good 2 it is clear that (29) and (30) follow from the two inequalities preceding (21); one of them, if it is put in the form

$$Q_2(t+1)-\sum_j \sum_{s_j} b_{2s_j}x_{s_j}(t) = \sum_{s_2} x_{s_2}(t)$$

means that the capital stock increases at a time-rate equal to the rate of production of the capital good; so that it may be written as (30) in the differential form.

than that of the labour force. This inter-temporal law which follows from the axiom of revealed preference may be applied to determine the rate of profit in the immediate future, because it is a decreasing function of the real-wage rate as is seen from Fig. 1 in Chapter II (the factor-price frontiers). And it has been shown in Chapter III that the stability of the long-run equilibrium and hence the convergence of the rate of profit to the long-run rate are ensured by that law. In the multi-sector model, however, we have no basis for applying that axiom; we have, therefore, no law which enables us to tell how the rate of profit will change. As a result of this incompleteness of the model we must be content with conditional paths of prices and outputs that are derived on the assumption that the rate of profit is fixed at the golden level.

It should be emphasized that, even if the convergence of the rate of profit to its golden value is ensured in some way or other, the multiplicity of capital goods may cause instability. Suppose there is a mechanism which causes the profit rate to tend strongly towards the golden value $\bar{r}$ and keeps it there. Suppose also that the principle of the profit maximization prevails as well as the rule of competitive pricing; then the activity level $x_{s_j}(t)$ is set at zero in period t for any process fulfilling (20) with strict inequality; and each good fulfilling (21) with strict inequality is marketed at zero price in period $t+1$. Accordingly, we have

$$P_m(t+1)X_m(t) = P(t+1)AX_m(t)+(1+\bar{r})P(t)BX_m(t) \\ -P(t+1)BX_m(t)+(1+\bar{r})\bar{w}LX_m(t), \quad (31)$$

and

$$P(t+1)X(t) = P(t+1)AX_m(t)+P(t+1)BX_m(t+1) \\ -P(t+1)BX_m(t)+P(t+1)C(t+1), \quad (32)$$

from (20) and (21) respectively. By definition, the left-hand side of (31) is identical with that of (32). As the money-wage rate is fixed at $\bar{w}$, the Cambridge assumption that the total amount of consumption equals wages may be written as

$$P(t+1)C(t+1) = \bar{w}LX_m(t+1). \quad (33)$$

Hence we obtain

$$P(t+1)BX_m(t+1)+\bar{w}LX_m(t+1) = (1+\bar{r})\{P(t)BX_m(t)+\bar{w}LX_m(t)\}, \quad (34)$$

an equation from which we can observe the 'dual stability-instability character' of the Golden Equilibrium.

Let us now suppose that full employment of labour is sustained, so that $LX_m(t)$ is always equal to the supply of labour which grows at the golden rate $\bar{r}$. We thus have

$$LX_m(t+1) = (1+\bar{r})LX_m(t), \quad (35)$$

and from (34), we find that

$$P(t+1)BX_m(t+1) = (1+\bar{r})P(t)BX_m(t)$$

holds for all t. It follows, therefore, that the capital per man $P(t)BX_m(t)/\bar{w}LX_m(t)$ remains constant over time and hence its initial deviation from the golden value of capital per man is preserved forever. This shows that the Golden Path of outputs cannot be stable if the golden prices are stable.

On the other hand, it is clear that when the path of outputs eventually approaches the Golden Path, we also have equation (35). When $X_m(t+1)$ approaches the Golden State which grows at the balanced rate $\bar{r}$, we obtain

$$P(t+1)B\bar{X}_m = P(t)B\bar{X}_m,$$

where $\bar{X}_m$ is a vector describing the relative intensities of operating the available processes along the golden output path. We are again led to the same conclusion that once capital per man deviates from its golden value, then the deviation will be preserved forever; it follows, therefore, that the stability of the golden output path implies that the golden prices cannot be stable.

Thus the stability of the output side is incompatible with stability on the price side. We must, however, give warning not to put too much confidence in this conclusion that has only been established on a number of restrictive assumptions. Among them, the following three seem to be most responsible for it. First, stability-instability has been discussed in a partial system where the wage rate is kept constant through time and the rate of profit is fixed at the golden level. Second, it has been assumed (i) that entrepreneurs choose activities so as to maximize the rate of profit, and (ii) that the rule of competitive pricing always prevails in the market. As a choice of processes is not possible unless the prices $P(t+1)$ and $P(t)$ are given, (i) means that the activity levels in period t, $X_m(t)$, depend on $P(t+1)$ as well as $P(t)$; and as the excess demands for goods in period $t+1$ are defined for given $X_m(t)$ and $X_m(t+1)$, (ii) means that $P(t+1)$ depends on $X_m(t)$ and $X_m(t+1)$. Thus, $X_m(t)$ depends on $P(t+1)$, which in turn depends on $X_m(t+1)$. The dependence of $X_m(t)$ upon $X_m(t+1)$ is recurrent, so that $X_m(t)$ cannot be determined exactly and correctly unless entrepreneurs are able to foresee the remote future perfectly. When entrepreneurs' expectations are imperfect and more or less subject to uncertainty, rules (i) and (ii) will not be workable; hence we do not have equations (31) and (32) on which the dual stability-instability of the Golden Equilibrium is based.

Finally, the Cambridge savings function we have so far assumed is also very unrealistic. In the actual world, capitalists do consume and workers do save; in fact, the value of consumption is greater than total wages in many economies. Therefore, we do not have (33) which plays a crucial part in deriving the 'conclusion'.[1] Thus the dual stability-instability theorem is no more than an abstract law that can be valid only for partial or conditional movements generated in the laboratory; it must be modified in order to have any application to the actual world.

[1] In the previous model consisting of one consumption and *two* capital sectors, it is assumed that the saving function is not Cantabrigian but of the uniclass type. It can be seen that in that economy the stability of prices does not necessarily imply instability of the capital (or output) structure; it is possible that the Golden Equilibrium is stable with respect to both prices and outputs.

PART II

THE VON NEUMANN REVOLUTION

VI

ECONOMIC IMPLICATIONS OF THE 'REVOLUTION'

1. THE neo-classical model so far examined in full detail assumes, among other things, (a) that firms can be classified into two or several industries, each producing a single output, (b) that capital goods do not suffer wear and tear, or they depreciate by evaporation, (c) that the stock of capital goods can be transferred freely from one firm to another, and (d) that the neo-classical price mechanism does work so as to automatically establish the full employment of capital stocks and the labour force. All these assumptions are unrealistic; they crucially affect the model's capacity to analyse the capital structure of the economy.

According to the neo-classical evaporation treatment of depreciation, capital goods that were produced several years ago and have been subject to wear and tear are considered to be physically equivalent to some smaller amounts of new capital goods of the same kind. This is a useful assumption simplifying the matter, but it does over-simplify the age structure of the available endowments and cannot very well deal with the mortality of the capital goods. It is even self-contradictory, because if an entrepreneur has a certain amount of a capital good that is in its final stage of wear and tear, he will have no capital equipment at the beginning of the next year; while if he has a certain amount, however small, of a new capital good, he may use it for production throughout its whole lifetime. As this extreme case shows, it is generally impossible to find *quantitative* equivalents, in terms of a new capital good, of capital goods damaged in various degrees from past use. Only by treating capital goods at different stages of wear and tear as *qualitatively* different goods, can we adequately deal with the age structure of capital stock.

Von Neumann suggested that used capital goods appearing simultaneously with products at the end of the production period could be treated as by-products of the manufacturing process. A process that uses capital equipment is regarded as a process that converts a bundle of 'inputs' into a bundle of 'outputs'; inputs are defined to include capital goods left over from the preceding period and outputs are defined to include qualitatively different capital goods left over at the end of the current period.[1] As long as we use some capital goods which may be

[1] Cf. J. von Neumann, 'A model of general economic equilibrium', *Review of Economic Studies*, Vol. XIII (1945–6), pp. 1–9.

used for a number of periods, there must appear at least two goods in the list of 'outputs': ordinary products and 'deformed' capital goods; the process of production should, therefore, inevitably be 'multi-productive', even if it produces no by-product in the ordinary sense.

This treatment of capital goods, on the one hand, requires us to throw away the first assumption of no joint products and to confront the 'joint production' problem, but, on the other, enables us to discard the third assumption of perfect transferability of capital equipment, an unwelcome parasite in the previous 'no joint production' model. In addition to being more productive, a new capital good is generally more transferable than a used one. A new machine will be sold to any factory that demands it, while a machine that has already been set up in a factory will not usually be transferred to another factory, even if the factory that owns the machine is overequipped and some other factory is underequipped. This inequality in the transferability of capital goods can readily be incorporated in the growth model, by permitting joint production in the sense von Neumann suggested and treating capital goods produced at different dates and installed in different factories as different goods. We can rule out the transference of used fixed capital goods between factories by specifying technology such that production processes which use those capital goods fixed in factory *A* are unavailable to all other factories except *A*. It is true that even in our new model each good is still perfectly transferable among those sectors to which it is useful; but the transferability of a machine installed in sector *A* is limited within *A* since it is useless to other sectors. Machines placed in different sectors are different goods and have different spheres of transference. They may have different prices even though they are the same kind in the ordinary sense. In particular, they become free goods in those sectors (or factories) which are overequipped with them but have positive imputed prices in other sectors where they are utilized at full capacity.

Another task assigned to the theory of capital is to find out when a capital good ceases to be used and is replaced by new one. In growth theory this problem is especially important, because otherwise we could not estimate correctly the amount of replacement investment and we would obtain a more or less distorted figure of the rate of growth. It is evident that the economic lifetime of a fixed capital good cannot exceed its natural or physical lifetime (a technological constant). But the former is a variable that depends on economic circumstances and may be less than the latter, as a capital good would be discarded if all processes utilizing it turned out to be unprofitable at a certain point in its physical lifetime. The traditional Dynamic Input–Output Analysis (based on the Generalized Leontief Model) as well as the neo-classical theories of economic growth assumes, however, that the rates of depreciation of various capital goods are given coefficients in the list of parameters of the system, to the effect that the average lifetime of each capital good is a constant determined independently of its profitableness. The von Neumann device of regarding capital goods at different ages as different goods grants us the privilege of determining, endogenously, their economic lifetime simultaneously with other economic unknowns; in fact, capital goods will die economically and become free goods when they become unprofitable. Thus von Neumann's theory of capital accumulation, though it may be considered as an extension of the Dynamic Input–Output Analysis from the formal or mathematical point of view, has entirely different implications. He brought about a revolution—bloodless but still violent—in the theory of capital and growth.

2. It is obvious that the length of time that it takes for the initial inputs to be transformed into the final products is different from process to process. We can, however, 'standardize' processes so that each of them is of unit time duration; those of longer duration may be considered as being composed of a number of 'standardized' processes of unit duration, if we are prepared to enlarge our list of goods so as to include fictitious intermediate products. Suppose the augmented list consists of n goods and there are, after the standardization, a finite number m of production processes available to the economy. As some or all of the processes may produce several kinds of goods, it is possible, though improbable, that the number of processes available is less than the number of goods produced.

Let a_{ij} be the quantity of good j technically required per unit intensity of process i, l_i the number of workers employed per unit intensity of process i, and b_{ij} the quantity of good j produced per unit intensity of process i. Each process converts a bundle of n commodities and labour into a different bundle of n commodities, and the transformation can be symbolized in the following way:

$$(a_{i1}, a_{i2}, ..., a_{in}, l_i) \rightarrow (b_{i1}, b_{i2}, ..., b_{in}).$$

Our treatment of capital goods necessitates the introduction of h kinds of goods for a capital good k with a life of $h+1$ periods; good k is the brand-new capital good k, good $k+1$ the one-year-old capital good k, and so on until the h-year old capital good k. By our convention, the process i using the brand-new capital good k 'produces' the one-year-old capital good k; so that $b_{i,k+1}$ must be positive if a_{ik} is positive. We have

$$(a_{i1}, a_{i2}, ..., a_{ik}, ..., a_{in}, l_i) \rightarrow (b_{i1}, b_{i2}, ..., b_{i,k+1}, ..., b_{in}),$$

where a_{ij} other than a_{ik} and b_{ij} other than $b_{i,k+1}$ may be zero. Since we may use, instead of the new capital good 'k', one of the old capital goods

'$k+1$', '$k+2$', ..., '$k+h$', we have, as well, the following h similar processes labelled $i+1$, ..., $i+h$, respectively:

$$(a_{i+1,1}, a_{i+1,2}, \ldots, a_{i+1,k+1}, \ldots, a_{i+1,n}, l_{i+1})$$
$$\rightarrow (b_{i+1,1}, b_{i+1,2}, \ldots, b_{i+1,k+2}, \ldots, b_{i+1,n}),$$
$$\cdots\cdots\cdots\cdots\cdots\cdots$$
$$(a_{i+h,1}, a_{i+h,2}, \ldots, a_{i+h,k+h}, \ldots, a_{i+h,n}, l_{i+h})$$
$$\rightarrow (b_{i+h,1}, b_{i+h,2}, \ldots, b_{i+h,n}),$$

where $a_{i+1,k+1}$, $b_{i+1,k+2}$, ..., $a_{i+h,k+h}$ are positive.

A similar symbolization would facilitate the reader's comprehension of our procedure of standardizing the periods of production. A process i, which takes $h+1$ periods to transform the initial inputs a_{i1}, ..., a_{in}, l_i into the final outputs b_{i1}^*, ..., b_{in}^* can be converted into $h+1$ standardized processes, i, $i+1$, ..., $i+h$, of unit time duration, by using h fictitious intermediate products, 1, ..., h. From the initial inputs we obtain at the end of the first period b_{i1} units (say) of the first intermediate product; the capital goods which participate in that production also appear as outputs, b_{ij}, $b_{ij'}$, etc. In the second round of the pluri-period production process, some of these capital goods may be released from work, while others continue to be utilized and are transformed, at the end of the second period, into different capital goods. This process denoted by $i+1$ transforms the first intermediate product of amount, $a_{i+1,1} = b_{i1}$, into the second intermediate product of amount, $b_{i+1,2}$. We proceed in this way until the hth intermediate product, $a_{i+h,h} = b_{i+h-1,h}$, is transformed into the final products. Since the first h goods in the list of commodities are intermediate products, so that a_{i1}, ..., a_{ih} of the initial inputs and b_{i1}^*, ..., b_{ih}^* of the final outputs evidently vanish, we find that an ($h+1$)-period production process $(0, \ldots, 0, a_{i,h+1}, \ldots, a_{in}, l_i) \rightarrow (0, \ldots, 0, b_{i,h+1}^*, \ldots, b_{in}^*)$ is equivalent to the following $h+1$ 'standardized' processes:

$$(0, 0, \ldots, 0, a_{i,h+1}, \ldots, a_{in}, l_i) \rightarrow (b_{i1}, 0, 0, \ldots, 0, b_{i,h+1}, \ldots, b_{in})$$
$$(a_{i+1,1}, 0, \ldots, 0, a_{i+1,h+1}, \ldots, a_{i+1,n}, 0) \rightarrow (0, b_{i+1,2}, 0, \ldots, b_{i+1,h+1}, \ldots, b_{i+1,n}),$$
$$\cdots\cdots\cdots\cdots\cdots\cdots$$
$$(0, 0, \ldots, a_{i+h,h}, a_{i+h,h+1}, \ldots, a_{i+h,n}, 0) \rightarrow (0, 0, 0, \ldots, 0, b_{i+h,h+1}, \ldots, b_{i+h,n}),$$

where $b_{i+h,j} = b_{ij}^*$ ($j = h+1, \ldots, n$).

Including all the fictitious goods and processes thus introduced, let us define matrices A and B and a column vector L as:[1]

$$A = \begin{pmatrix} a_{11} & a_{12} & \dots & a_{1n} \\ a_{21} & a_{22} & \dots & a_{2n} \\ \dots & \dots & \dots & \dots \\ a_{m1} & a_{m2} & \dots & a_{mn} \end{pmatrix},$$

$$B = \begin{pmatrix} b_{11} & b_{12} & \dots & b_{1n} \\ b_{21} & b_{22} & \dots & b_{2n} \\ \dots & \dots & \dots & \dots \\ b_{m1} & b_{m2} & \dots & b_{mn} \end{pmatrix},$$

$$L = \{l_1, l_2, \dots, l_m\};$$

and call them the input-coefficient matrix, the output-coefficient matrix and the labour-input-coefficient vector respectively. The ith row of A obviously gives the inputs of various goods per unit intensity of process i, and the ith row of B the outputs of that process, while the jth column of A gives the quantities of good j required by various processes, and the jth column of B the amounts of good j produced. The current state of technology is described by the matrix $\{A, B, L\}$ referred to as the 'catalogue of activities' (by myself) or the 'book of blue prints' (by Samuelson).[2]

If constant returns to scale prevail, inputs and outputs per unit intensity of each process remain unchanged with respect to changes in the intensities at which processes operate; all coefficients a_{ij}, b_{ij}, and l_i, therefore, are constant by this assumption. All of them are naturally non-negative; it is conventional to sharpen the non-negativity of a_{ij} to the following semi-positivity:

(Ia) for each process $i = 1, \dots, m$ there is at least one good j for which $a_{ij} > 0$.

Similarly, we may assume that

(Ib) for each good $j = 1, \dots, n$ there is at least one process i with $b_{ij} > 0$.

The former implies that each process uses at least one input, while the latter that there is no good which cannot be produced. Both assumptions are plausible, but we do not assume (Ia) throughout this and the next

[1] Note that a process is defined as a row vector, while it is defined in Chapter V as a column vector. We denote column vectors by braces { } and row vectors by square brackets [ ].

[2] Morishima, loc. cit., p. 95; P. A. Samuelson, 'Parable and realism in capital theory: the surrogate production function', *Review of Economic Studies*, Vol. XXIX (1962), p. 194.

chapter, since (Ib), if it is combined with (Ic) below, is powerful enough so that there is nothing to gain by making (Ia).

Since the 'catalogue of activities' includes the fictitious processes introduced for standardizing the periods of production, the strict positivity of the labour-input coefficients in vector L ought not to be assumed. It is possible and likely that a pluri-period production process employs labour in some particular (but not all) periods only; so that it is decomposed into elementary processes with $l_i = 0$ as well as those with $l_i > 0$. Vector L is now assumed to be merely semi-positive, and on it is imposed the assumption of indispensability of labour (Ic) which is introduced later.

Suppose processes 1, ..., m operate at intensities $x_1, ..., x_m$, respectively; then goods, $j = 1, ..., n$, are consumed in the amounts

$$I_j = a_{1j}x_1 + a_{2j}x_2 + \cdots + a_{mj}x_m \qquad j = 1, ..., n,$$

and are produced in the amounts

$$O_j = b_{1j}x_1 + b_{2j}x_2 + \cdots + b_{mj}x_m \qquad j = 1, ..., n.$$

If outputs O_j are as large as α times I_j (where α is a positive number), then we can, in the next period, repeat the same production activity at more (if $\alpha > 1$) or less (if $\alpha < 1$) intensive degrees, $\alpha x_1, ..., \alpha x_m$, because all goods consumed in the present period are again available in different quantities (possibly, in the same quantities) at the beginning of the next period. We say that activities $x_1, ..., x_m$ are *repeatable* or commodities are *reproducible*, if such a positive α exists. We assume that

(Ic) for all repeatable $x = (x_1, ..., x_m)$, $\Sigma l_i x_i > 0$.

This evidently means that labour is indispensable for the reproduction of commodities.

3. From the considerations in the previous section, it is clear that the growth model, if it is not to be a model in an empty dream, must be multisectoral and must also be capable of dealing successfully with joint production. A model fulfilling these requirements was first proposed by von Neumann. He assumed the following: (a) there are constant returns to scale in the production of all goods; (b) the supply of labour can be expanded indefinitely; (c) the wage rate is fixed at a level at which workers can only purchase the minimum amounts of goods biologically required for subsistence; (d) the whole of the capitalists' income is automatically invested in new capital goods. It is evident that the model ignores capitalists' consumption as well as the role of the supply of labour in determining the real wage rate: Workers are like farm animals, and capitalists are simply self-service stands for capital.

Let us now follow von Neumann and assume that 'consumption of goods takes place only through the processes of production which include necessities of life consumed by workers and employees'.[1] Let e_j be the minimum of good j needed to persuade a man to work; then $l_i e_j$ is the quantity of good j required for supporting the lives of the people employed per unit intensity of process i. We may define the 'augmented input coefficient', c_{ij}, as the sum of the material and the labour-feeding input coefficients, a_{ij} and $l_i e_j$.

It is assumed that wages are fixed at the subsistence level, so that we have

$$w = \sum_j e_j P_j,$$

where w denotes the wage rate and P_j the price of good j. For an assigned interest factor β,[2] the total cost (including interest on working and fixed capital) of process i operating at unit intensity amounts to

$$\beta(\sum_j a_{ij} P_j + w l_i), \qquad \text{or more simply,} \qquad \beta \sum_j c_{ij} P_j.$$

This amount is compared with the total 'receipts' from that process, $\sum_j b_{ij} P_j$, to calculate the profitableness of the process. With given prices and rate of interest, some processes are likely to be more profitable than others. In equilibrium, however, there can be no process which yields a return greater than the prevailing interest rate; for under perfect competition positive supernormal profits would attract competitors to use the same process, so that prices of factors would rise. Thus in the state of equilibrium, we have for all $i = 1, ..., m$

$$\sum_j b_{ij} P_j \leqq \beta \sum_j c_{ij} P_j.$$

Moreover, if process i earns negative profits after payment of interest, it will not be used; namely, if the strict inequality '$<$' applies in the above inequality for i, the intensity of operation of process i, denoted by q_i, is set at zero (the Rule of Profitability).

Next, since each process is of unit time duration, $\sum_i b_{ij} q_i$ gives the quantity of good j produced at the end of the period concerned, while $\sum_i c_{ij} q_i$ gives the quantity of good j used up in production (including workers' consumption) at the beginning of the same period. Von Neumann concentrated his attention on the state of balanced growth, where processes operate at intensities growing (or decaying) at a common, constant geometric rate; the inputs in any period are proportional to the inputs in the preceding period. As the inputs in the next period, i.e. the inputs

[1] J. von Neumann, loc. cit., p. 2.
[2] The interest factor is defined as 1 + the rate of interest.

in the current period multiplied by the common expansion factor α (= 1+the rate of growth), should be provided from the current outputs, we have for all goods $j = 1, \ldots, n$

$$\sum_i b_{ij}q_i \geqq \alpha \sum_i c_{ij}q_i.$$

This is so simply because it is impossible to use more of a good in the production processes than is available. In equilibrium those goods that are overproduced will be free goods, and zero prices are charged for them; that is to say, if the strict inequality '>' applies in the above inequality for j, the price of good j, P_j, is set at zero (the Rule of Free Good).

Von Neumann's problem was to establish the existence of a state of Growth Equilibrium fulfilling the Rule of Profitability and the Rule of Free Goods. It is important to observe that the Rule of Profitability governs the choice of production processes, but does not apply to consumers' behaviour, while the Rule of Free Goods applies in the goods markets but not in the labour market. As soon as the intensities of the processes are determined, the demand for labour is determined, the supply of labour, by hypothesis, adjusts itself quickly and smoothly to the demand, and consumption of goods is directly proportional to the volume of employment. In the von Neumann drama goods and processes (or industries) are actors, but labour and consumption (or families) wear, like *kurokos* in *Kabuki*, black clothes and appear on the stage, not as actors but as prompters.

An alternative but invalid interpretation of the model is popular even among such distinguished economists as Georgescu-Roegen and DOSSO. It has often been stated that von Neumann's formal theory could be applied to a closed economy by including labour in the list of goods, say, as the nth good and treating 'consumption of consumers' goods as a labour-producing process'.[1] It is of course true that such an interpretation is possible; but it would be an unsatisfactory interpretation. We would in fact depart from reality if we regarded our homes, however humble, as 'pigsties' where 'hogs and piggies' are fed and bred according to the Rule of Profitability. It seems that there is no rationale for requiring that 'rate of profits' be equalized throughout all industries and families. Moreover, it would contradict von Neumann's explicit statement that he assumed that 'the natural factors of production, including labour, can be expanded in unlimited quantities'.[2] The reproduction of the labour force was not his

[1] See, for example, N. Georgescu-Roegen, 'The aggregate linear production function and its applications to von Neumann's economic model', *Activity Analysis of Production and Allocation*, ed. T. C. Koopmans (New York: Wiley, 1951), p. 107; R. Dorfman, P. A. Samuelson and R. M. Solow, *Linear Programming and Economic Analysis* (New York: McGraw-Hill, 1958), p. 382.

[2] J. von Neumann, loc. cit.

concern; labour was regarded as an exogenous factor which could be imported from outside the model as it was needed.

4. Let us now turn from technology to consumer's choice. In reducing the worker-consumer to a farm animal and the capitalist-saver to a self-service stand for capital, the original von Neumann model could simulate the earlier stage of the development of capitalist and communist countries. It could also describe a slave-economy whose object is mere enlargement of production. Since, on the one hand, the real-wage rate is fixed at the subsistence level (so that workers can only buy the minimum amounts of goods biologically required for existence) and on the other, the whole of the capitalists' income is accumulated for investment, there is no room in the model for consumer choice.

Consumer choice was first introduced into the model in one of my previous papers[1] by relaxing the von Neumann assumption, so that workers still consume their entire income, but capitalists spend a portion of their income on consumption goods. In this part of the book, however, I am concerned with the more general and realistic case where workers, like capitalists, save a constant proportion of their income and consume the rest so that their demand for each good depends on relative prices and their income. Despite the additional assumption that all workers have identical tastes as we assumed for the capitalists, our savings function is sufficiently general so that it covers the case discussed by Mrs. Robinson, Kaldor, and Pasinetti as well as the 'uniclass-type' savings function.

When a worker saves a part of his income, he owns, directly or through loans to entrepreneurs, a part of the total stock of capital and will receive a share of the total profits according to his ownership. Thus any worker in the system is not a pure worker by a 'capitalist-worker'; he is a double-faced person who may be disintegrated into a pure worker and a pure capitalist. In the following, however, we suppose (like Pasinetti) that the proportion saved out of the workers' profit income is equal to the proportion saved out of their wage income, which may possibly (and probably) be different from the savings ratio s_c of the pure capitalists. Workers' savings S_w may then be written as

$$S_w = s_w(W+E_w),$$

where W denotes the total amount of wages, E_w the total amount of profits accruing to them, and s_w the workers' savings ratio. On the assumption that all workers have identical tastes, they can be aggregated into one giant, the Worker, whose utility function is assumed, besides fulfilling the law of diminishing marginal rates of substitution between goods in all directions, to be *quasi-homogeneous* or *homothetic* with respect to the

[1] See Morishima, op. cit., pp. 131–53.

Worker's demand for goods, $e_1, \ldots, e_n$,[1] as well as fulfilling the traditional law of diminishing marginal rates of substitution between all goods. The assumption of quasi-homogeneity is rather unconventional and implies that a proportional change in the quantities of goods does not give rise to any change in the preference ordering. It is a restrictive assumption, for it means the Engel-elasticities of all goods (i.e., the elasticities of demand with respect to income) are unity. However, once we allow for the Worker's savings, the proportionality between his consumption and his income is a necessary condition for a balanced growth of the economy.[2]

The Worker consumes only a constant proportion of his income; his budget constraint is

$$\sum_j P_j e_j = c_w(W+E_w),$$

where c_w $(= 1-s_w)$ is his propensity to consume. (c_w is a positive constant not exceeding unity.) Maximizing his utility with respect to the quantities of goods demanded, subject to his budget constraint, we obtain the familiar conditions that the marginal rates of substitution between goods should equal the ratios of their prices. These, together with the budget constraint, imply that the Worker's demand for each good depends on all prices and his income. It is well-known that all the quantities demanded are homogeneous functions of degree zero in their arguments, so that they remain unaffected when prices and the income are multiplied or divided by any positive number.

Furthermore, it follows from the quasi-homogeneity that the income-elasticity of e_j is unity. This is seen by inquiring what change in the quantities demanded would be necessary to meet the budget constraint and the marginal-rate conditions after an increase, say a doubling, of income, all prices remaining unchanged. It is obvious that the doubling of the income enables the Worker to double the quantities of goods and, by virtue of the quasi-homogeneity of the utility function, the order of preferences is not disturbed by doubling the quantities bought. Thus an increase in the Worker's income results in an increase of $e_1, \ldots, e_n$ in the same proportion, that is to say, the Engel-elasticities all equal unity.

The above considerations lead to the presentation of the demand functions in the form

$$e_j = g_j(y_1, \ldots, y_n)\frac{W+E_w}{\sum_j P_j} \qquad j = 1, \ldots, n,$$

[1] A function is said to be *quasi-homogeneous* if $u(x) \geqq u(x')$ implies $u(qx) \geqq u(qx')$ for all sets of variables $x = (x_1, \ldots, x_n)$ and $x' = (x_1', \ldots, x_n')$ and all scalars $q \geqq 0$.

[2] On the other hand, if the Worker does not save, we can dispense with the assumption of unitary Engel-elasticities of the Worker's demands for goods. In such a case, we may substitute a weaker assumption for the assumption in the text, but the argument of Chapter VII concerning the existence of a balanced growth equilibrium would not be essentially different.

where y_h is the normalized price of good h, i.e., the price P_h divided by $\sum_j P_j$. As these must fulfil the budget constraint, we have the identity,

(IIa) $\sum_j g_j(y_1, ..., y_n)y_j = c_w$ for all non-negative, non-zero sets of prices, $y_1, ..., y_n$.

The capitalists may also be aggregated into one giant, because they are assumed to have similar tastes. It is assumed that their tastes are well described by a utility function that follows the conventional law of diminishing marginal rates of substitution. We make for the Capitalist, as we did for the Worker, the assumption of quasi-homogeneity of his utility function, which implies that the Engel-elasticity of his consumption is unity. We can, therefore, write

$$d_j = f_j(y_1, ..., y_n)\frac{E_c}{\sum_j P_j} \qquad j = 1, ..., n,$$

where d_j is the Capitalist's demand for good j and E_c profits accruing to the Capitalist; the identity

(IIb) $\sum_j f_j(y_1, ..., y_n)y_j = c_c$ for all non-negative, non-zero sets of prices, $y_1, ..., y_n$,

must follow from the budget constraint

$$\sum_j d_j P_j = c_c E_c,$$

where c_c stands for the (constant) average propensity to consume of the Capitalist.

In my *Equilibrium, Stability, and Growth*, it was assumed that when capitalists' income is non-positive, their consumption is zero and when it is positive, it is proportional to their income. Here, however, we assume for the sake of simplicity that the Capitalist always consumes a constant proportion of his income even if it is negative. It is of course true that no one can consume a negative amount of a good. But we dare to make this assumption in order to simplify the resulting formulas. It is harmless, because the non-linearity caused by switching the Capitalist's pattern of consumption at the zero income level has already been well treated in my earlier book.[1] Furthermore, at the state of Silvery Equilibrium which is our main concern in this chapter and the following, the income of the Capitalist is shown to be positive.[2]

[1] Ibid., pp. 139–45.

[2] As to the Worker, a similar non-linearity would occur at the subsistence level of his income. But we need not bother about that, because the income of the Worker at the state of Silvery Equilibrium will be shown to be in excess of the amount required to buy the necessities of life.

Remarks on two points are now in order. First it is true that no general relationship exists between the normalized wages, $W/(\sum_j P_j)$, and the real wages. However, let $\sigma_1, ..., \sigma_n$ be positive numbers such that for consumption goods they are those quantities which enable the Worker to maintain a given standard of living, and for non-consumption goods they are taken as very small; then the Laspeyre index-number of prices of consumption goods is well approximated by

$$P(\sigma) = \frac{P_1\sigma_1 + \cdots + P_n\sigma_n}{P_1{}^0\sigma_1 + \cdots + P_n{}^0\sigma_n},$$

where $P_j{}^0$ is the price of good j in the base year. (The effect of including non-consumption goods in the formula is not far-reaching, because their σs may be arbitrarily small.) We may, therefore, measure the real wages by $W/P(\sigma)$. Let us now transform the standard of measuring the quantities of goods so that $\sigma_j = 1$ for all j; then the index-number and the real wages will respectively be written as

$$\frac{\sum_j P_j}{\sum_j P_j{}^0} \qquad \text{and} \qquad W \Bigg/ \left(\frac{\sum_j P_j}{\sum_j P_j{}^0}\right)$$

in terms of the new units. As $\sum_j P_j{}^0$ is constant, we may leave it out. We may thus refer to $W/(\sum_j P_j)$ as the 'real wages' (as we shall in fact do throughout the following), provided that quantities of goods are measured in terms of appropriate standards.

The second remark is about (IIa, b) which may be called the Walrasian identity. We have so far implicitly assumed that every good can be consumed by anybody. However, pure capital goods such as blast furnaces, bulldozers and electronic computers never enter into the list of goods one consumes in normal situations; it would, therefore, be realistic to assume that the Worker's and the Capitalist's demands for these goods are identically zero; so that

$$g_j(y_1, y_2, ..., y_n) = 0 \qquad \text{and} \qquad f_j(y_1, y_2, ..., y_n) = 0$$

for pure capital goods. If all the prices of consumption goods approach zero, then the left-hand side of (IIa) tends to zero unless the Worker's demand for some consumption goods becomes infinitely large. This is a contradiction, so that the Walrasian identity (IIa) requires

$$g_j(y_1, y_2, ..., y_n) = +\infty \qquad \text{for some good } j$$

at the points where prices of all consumption goods are zero; similarly for the Capitalist.

So long as we proceed this way, we will be much disturbed by the infinity problem even though we can finally attain our aim of establishing the existence of a state of equilibrium growth. Therefore, it would be wise to adopt another mathematically easier approach unless it implies very implausible economic assumptions. We assume:

(IIc) all Engel-coefficients $g_j(y_1, y_2, ..., y_n)$ and $f_j(y_1, y_2, ..., y_n)$ $(j = 1, ..., n)$ are non-negative, finite, and continuous for every non-negative set of normalized prices $(y_1, y_2, ..., y_n)$.

From this it follows that when all prices of the consumption goods (in the ordinary sense) are zero, the Worker and the Capitalist will spend all their incomes on some capital goods. It seems absurd and very unrealistic at first sight. But no one can refute that in Paradise the Capitalist will use a blast furnace to heat his dog's house, while the Worker's children will do their homework with the aid of electronic computers(!).

5. We are now in a position to set out the conditions for equilibrium growth. In the state of equilibrium, the rate of returns of various processes will, first of all, not exceed the current rate of interest, otherwise one could borrow money and purchase these capital goods with the highest rate of return and earn the difference between the returns and the interest rate paid for borrowing money. Thus the rate of interest should not fall short of the maximum rate of return; we have the following inequality:

$$\text{return of any process} \equiv \text{receipts} - \text{cost of that process}$$
$$\leqq \text{interest payments},$$

or

$$\text{total cost (including interest on working and fixed capital)}$$
$$\text{of any process} \geqq \text{total receipts from that process.}$$

The rule of choice of techniques, on the other hand, requires that those processes whose rates or return are not as high as the rate of interest should not be put into operation; it thus rules out discrepancies among rates of return of the *active* manufacturing processes chosen by the Capitalist. We thus find that throughout the processes in operation there prevails a uniform rate of return that is as high as the ruling rate of interest; and in the complete list of processes available to the economy there is no process that could realize returns at a rate higher than the uniform rate (the Rule of Profitability).

Let $r(t)$ be the rate of interest in period t, $P_j(t)$ the price of good j in period t,[1] and $w(t)$ the money-wage-rate in period t. We define $\beta(t)$ as

[1] As capital goods are non-transferable once they have been installed in a factory, there are no markets for second-hand capital goods. Similarly, we have no markets for the (fictitious) intermediate goods. The prices of those goods are not market prices, of course, but imputed or shadow prices calculated from the cost equations.

$1+r(t)$ and call it the interest factor. As the period of production is assumed to be one unit of time, the returns of process i operating at unit intensity are

$$\sum_j b_{ij}P_j(t+1)-\sum_j a_{ij}P_j(t)-l_i w(t),$$

which cannot exceed, in equilibrium, the interest payments

$$r(t)\{\sum_j a_{ij}P_j(t)+l_i w(t)\};$$

hence, bearing in mind the definition of $\beta(t)$, we have[1]

$$\sum_j b_{ij}P_j(t+1) \leqq \beta(t)\{\sum_j a_{ij}P_j(t)+l_i w(t)\} \qquad i = 1, ..., m. \tag{1}$$

In matrix terms these inequalities may equivalently and more concisely be written as

$$BP(t+1) \leqq \beta(t)\{AP(t)+Lw(t)\},$$

where $P(t)$ is an n-dimensional column vector $\{P_1(t), ..., P_n(t)\}$.

Next let $q_i(t)$ be the intensity at which process i operates in period t. As an unprofitable process i is not used, the intensity of that process i which fulfills (1) with strict inequality should be zero. It is obvious that for the other processes, $q_i(t)$s are non-negative. Thus,

$$q_i(t) \geqq 0, \text{ and if (1) holds with '<', } q_i(t) = 0;$$

or equivalently, by multiplying inequalities in (1) by $q_i(t)$ and adding them up we have

$$\sum_i\sum_j b_{ij}P_j(t+1)q_i(t) = \beta(t)[\sum_i\sum_j a_{ij}P_j(t)q_i(t)+\{\sum_i l_i q_i(t)\}w(t)], \tag{2}$$

which we can put, in matrix terms, in the simpler form:

$$q(t)BP(t+1) = \beta(t)\{q(t)AP(t)+q(t)Lw(t)\},$$

where $q(t)$ is an m-dimensional row vector $[q_1(t), ..., q_m(t)]$.

Let us now turn from prices to 'demand-supply' (or 'input-output')

[1] These inequalities are based on the assumption that wages are paid in advance at the beginning of each period; so that the total cost includes not only the interest charge on fixed capital but also the interest charge on wages (i.e. the interest charges on 'variable capital' in the Marxian terminology). On the other hand, if we assume that wages are paid at the end of period t after workers have done their work in that period, we have, instead of (1),

$$\sum_j b_{ij}P_j(t+1) \leqq \beta(t)\{\sum_j a_{ij}P_j(t)\}+l_i w(t) \qquad i = 1, . . ., m.$$

Two models which I have called the Marx-von Neumann and the Walras-von Neumann models in my former book are derived from the respective assumptions. (See ibid., pp. 136–53.) In this chapter we are concerned only with the Marx-von Neumann model.

relations. It is evident that no more goods can be consumed in any period than are available in that period. The amounts of goods that are available and 'supplied' in period t are 'outputs' produced in the previous period $t-1$; while the 'demand' consists of the 'inputs' in the production process and the personal consumption of the Worker and the Capitalist. It is noted that storage processes are recognized as 'productive' processes in our list of techniques, so that the 'supply' includes bequests from the past and the 'demand' stores for the future. We have:

supply of any good $\geqq$ industrial demand+personal demand for that good.

If there is an excess supply of some good, its price will decrease until an equilibrium is obtained between the supply and demand for that good. Those goods for which the demand is still less than the supply, even if their prices have fallen to zero, will be discarded as 'free goods' or 'junk'. In equilibrium, only those goods for which the equality between supply and demand is established may have positive prices. At equilibrium prices, therefore, the aggregate supply of all goods should equal the aggregate (industrial and personal) demand for all goods.

In the notation we are using, the output of good j available in period t, the input of good j used in the production process in period t, and the Capitalist's and the Worker's consumption of good j in period t are respectively denoted by

$$\sum_i b_{ij}q_i(t-1), \qquad \sum_i a_{ij}q_i(t), \qquad d_j(t), \qquad e_j(t).$$

We may thus put the above inequality between supply and demand in the following form:

$$\sum_i b_{ij}q_i(t-1) \geqq \sum_i a_{ij}q_i(t)+d_j(t)+e_j(t) \qquad j=1,\ldots,n, \tag{3}$$

or

$$q(t-1)B \geqq q(t)A+d(t)+e(t),$$

where $d(t)$ and $e(t)$ are n-dimensional row vectors representing $[d_1(t), \ldots, d_n(t)]$ and $[e_1(t), \ldots, e_n(t)]$, respectively. From the rule of pricing (or the Rule of Free Goods) discussed above, we have the following neo-classical switching:

$$P_j(t) = 0, \text{ if (3) holds with '>', and } P_j(t) \geqq 0 \text{ otherwise.}$$

It ensures that at equilibrium prices $P_1(t), \ldots, P_n(t)$ there is equality between the aggregate demand and the aggregate supply:

$$\sum_i\sum_j b_{ij}q_i(t-1)P_j(t) = \sum_i\sum_j a_{ij}q_i(t)P_j(t)+\sum_j d_j(t)P_j(t)+\sum_j e_j(t)P_j(t), \tag{4}$$

which may more conveniently be put in the matrix form,

$$q(t-1)BP(t) = q(t)AP(t)+d(t)P(t)+e(t)P(t).$$

It is evident that there can be no outputs, no inputs, no wages and no profits without productive activities; the conditions (3) and (4) are thus met when $q_i(t-1) = q_i(t) = 0$ for all $i = 1, ..., m$. Similarly, the conditions (1) and (2) are trivially met when all prices and the wage rates are zero. But such obviously meaningless states should be avoided. In order to assure that a state of equilibrium fulfilling the conditions (1)–(4) is economically meaningful, we make the additional condition that the total value of all goods produced must be positive. This condition in the form,

$$\sum_i \sum_j b_{ij} q_i(t-1) P_j(t) > 0, \quad \text{or} \quad q(t-1)BP(t) > 0, \tag{5}$$

was first imposed by Kemeny, Morgenstern, and Thompson but it is not used in the original von Neumann model.[1]

The final condition describes the equilibrium in the labour market. In the original von Neumann model it is assumed that the supply of labour can be expanded indefinitely at the subsistence level of real wages, so that the problem of deficiency of labour, one of the most serious obstacles to rapid growth, is completely ignored. In fact, it is a defect of von Neumann's theory of growth that no attention is paid to Harrod's observation that the natural rate of growth sets a limit to the average value of the actual rate of growth over a long period.

Let ρ_t be the growth factor (1 + the rate of growth) of the labour force in period t, and N the number of workers in period 0; then the supply of labour in period t will be $\rho_{t-1} \ldots \rho_1 \rho_0 N$. Since the demand for labour in period t is $\sum_i l_i q_i(t)$, the demand–supply equilibrium is described by

$$\sum_i l_i q_i(t) = \rho_{t-1} \ldots \rho_1 \rho_0 N.$$

It would be more realistic to assume that the 'natural rate of growth' $\rho - 1$ depends on the real-wage rate rather than to assume it is constant. But it will help the reader's comprehension to begin with examining the simpler case. When ρ is constant, we have

$$\sum_i l_i q_i(t) = \rho^t N, \qquad \text{or} \qquad q(t)L = \rho^t N. \tag{6}$$

After attaining proficiency in this simple case, we shall consider, in Part IV, the more general and realistic case of flexible population growth. The discussion there will (particularly, in Chapter XIV) proceed on the same assumption as that in Part I above; that is, ρ is negative, zero, or positive according to whether the real-wage rate is less than, equal to, or greater than the subsistence level. Throughout Parts II and III, we assume that ρ is a constant and greater than 1.

[1] See J. G. Kemeny, O. Morgenstern, and G. L. Thompson, 'A generalization of the von Neumann model of an expanding economy', *Econometrica*, Vol. XXIV (1956), pp. 117–18. They first introduced assumption (Ia) and (Ib) to ensure (5) in the original von Neumann model.

6. Let us now pass on to the determination of prices and activity levels in the model described above. We have two possible approaches: the Competitive Equilibrium Approach of the Hicks-Malinvaud type and the Balanced Growth Approach of the Cassel-von Neumann type.[1] According to the Temporary Equilibrium Approach, which is a special case of the Competitive Equilibrium Approach over a longer period,[2] we concentrate attention on some particular period, and classify the variables concerned into expected, current, and lagged endogenous variables. As we have observed before, consumptions $d_j(t)$ and $e_j(t)$ depend on the Capitalist's income $E_c(t)$ and the Worker's income $W(t)+E_w(t)$ as well as on prices $P_j(t)$. As we are assuming that the period of production is one unit of time, the profits from activities in period t are only realized in period $t+1$; the profits at the Capitalist's and the Worker's disposal at the beginning of period t accrue from the activities in the past period $t-1$, which are taken as given in period t. On the other hand, the Worker's wage income $W(t)$ in period t depends on activities in the current period. It is, therefore, seen that the system (1)–(6) includes the $2m+3n+4$ variables, $q_i(t-1)$, $q_i(t)$, $P_j(t-1)$, $P_j(t)$, $P_j(t+1)$,$w(t-1)$, $w(t)$, $\beta(t-1)$, and $\beta(t)$ $(i = 1, ..., m; j = 1, ..., n)$; among them $q_i(t-1)$, $P_j(t-1)$, $w(t-1)$, and $\beta(t-1)$ $(i = 1, ..., m; j = 1, ..., n)$ are lagged endogenous variables; $q_i(t)$, $P_j(t)$, $w(t)$, and $\beta(t)$ are current endogenous variables; $P_j(t+1)$ are expected variables. The Temporary Equilibrium Approach starts with historically given values of lagged endogenous variables for the first year of the recursive process. With the supplementary functions of expected prices, we may solve the system (1)–(6) for the first year with respect to the current variables, $q_i(1)$, $P_j(1)$, $w(1)$, $\beta(1)$, of that year, we then have the values of the lagged endogenous variables for the second year, so that we can solve the system for the second year with respect to the current endogenous variables of that year; and so on. (Note that values of all the parameters of the system are supplied exogenously: all coefficients a_{ij}, b_{ij}, l_i, are given technologically, N historically, and ρ biologically.)

On the other hand, according to the Balanced Growth Approach which will be adopted in the next chapter as well as the rest of this chapter, we do not investigate the working of the economy in terms of a series of temporary (or short-run) equilibria, but instead we focus attention on a state of long-run equilibrium where all sectors of the economy are in harmony with each other, and hence the economy changes only in scale but not in composition. It is useless as a theory of short-run fluctuations, but may effectively describe the long-run growth; it will be especially

[1] G. Cassel, *Theory of Social Economy* (New York: Harcourt, Brace and Co., 1932), 708pp.

[2] The Competitive Equilibrium Approach will be discussed later in full detail, but we are content, in this chapter, with the following rough sketch of the Temporary Equilibrium Approach.

powerful as a normative theory which provides programmes for the long-run optimal growth (i.e., the so-called Turnpike Theorems and others).

This approach does not start with given initial values of the lagged endogenous variables. Indeed, it imposes $m+2n+3$ additional conditions on prices, the wage rate, the interest rate, intensities of activities, and the distribution of profits between the Capitalist and the Worker. The growth equilibrium which this approach sets up is a state of balanced growth, where prices, the wage rate and the interest rate remain stationary over time, and the intensities of production grow at a constant geometric rate. We thus have

$$\alpha q_i(t-1) = q_i(t), \qquad P_j(t-1) = P_j(t) = P_j(t+1),$$
$$w(t-1) = w(t), \qquad \beta(t-1) = \beta(t),$$
$$(i = 1, ..., m; j = 1, ..., n) \text{ for all } t,$$

where α is $1+$the rate of balanced growth.

The remaining condition on the distribution of profits was introduced by Pasinetti. Since the total profits are distributed among individuals in proportion to their ownership of capital and the distribution remains unchanged over time in the state of growth equilibrium, the rate of growth of the amount of capital that each individual owns (i.e., the amount of one's savings divided by the amount of one's capital) must be the same if there is long-run balanced growth. Hence it is found that, for the Capitalist and the Worker, profits should be proportional to their savings:

$$\frac{E_w}{s_w(W+E_w)} = \frac{E_c}{s_c E_c}. \tag{7}$$

This Pasinetti condition for a stationary distribution[1] implies

$$E_w = \frac{s_w}{s_c - s_w} W; \tag{8}$$

hence

$$E_c = E - \frac{s_w}{s_c - s_w} W, \tag{9}$$

where E is the total profits. We can write

$$d_j(t)+e_j(t) = f_j E(t) + \left(\frac{s_c}{s_c - s_w} g_j - \frac{s_w}{s_c - s_w} f_j\right) W(t). \tag{10}$$

In the state of balanced growth we may delete letters $t-1$, t, etc.

[1] Luigi L. Pasinetti, 'Rate of profit and income distribution in relation to the rate of economic growth', *Review of Economic Studies*, Vol. XXIX (1962), p. 273. In deriving (8), we assume that $1 \geqq s_c > s_w \geqq 0$.

denoting dates. Normalizing prices and activity levels by dividing (1) and (2) by $\sum_j P_j(t)$ and $\sum_i q_i(t)$, we obtain

$$\sum_j b_{ij} y_j \leqq \beta\left(\sum_j a_{ij} y_j + l_i \Omega\right) \qquad i = 1, \ldots, m, \tag{1'}$$

$$\sum_i \sum_j b_{ij} x_i y_j = \beta\left\{\sum_i \sum_j a_{ij} x_i y_j + \left(\sum_i l_i x_i\right)\Omega\right\}, \tag{2'}$$

where x_i is the normalized intensity, y_j the normalized price, and Ω the real-wage rate; they are quotients of q_i divided by the sum of the qs, P_j by the sum of the Ps, and w by the sum of the Ps, respectively. Similarly, divide (3), (4), and (5) by $\sum_i q_i(t-1)$ and $\sum_j P_j(t)$. In the state of balanced growth they can then be written as follows:[1]

$$\sum_i b_{ij} x_i \geqq \alpha \sum_i a_{ij} x_i + (\beta - 1)\left\{\sum_i \sum_k a_{ik} x_i y_k + \left(\sum_i l_i x_i\right)\Omega\right\} f_j(y)$$
$$+ \alpha \left\{\frac{s_c}{s_c - s_w} g_j(y) - \frac{s_w}{s_c - s_w} f_j(y)\right\}\left(\sum_i l_i x_i\right)\Omega \qquad j = 1, \ldots, n, \tag{3'}$$

$$\sum_i \sum_j b_{ij} x_i y_j = \alpha \sum_i \sum_j a_{ij} x_i y_j + (\beta - 1)\left\{\sum_i \sum_j a_{ij} x_i y_j + \left(\sum_i l_i x_i\right)\Omega\right\} c_c$$
$$+ \alpha\left(\sum_i l_i x_i\right)\Omega, \tag{4'}$$

$$\sum_i \sum_j b_{ij} x_i y_j > 0. \tag{5'}$$

Finally (6) is equivalent to the following two equations:

$$\alpha = \rho, \tag{6'}$$

and

$$\left(\sum_i l_i x_i\right)\xi = N,$$

where ξ (a scalar) represents the absolute level of the intensities in period 0. Once the x_is are determined, ξ is trivially obtained. In the following,

[1] By definition, $E(t) = \text{Receipts}\{\sum_i \sum_j b_{ij} q_i(t-1) P_j(t)\}$ *minus* $\text{Cost}\{\sum_i \sum_j a_{ij} q_i(t-1) P_j(t-1) + \sum_i l_i q_i(t-1) w(t-1)\}$. Hence, from (2)

$$E(t) = (\beta(t-1) - 1)\ \{\sum_i \sum_j a_{ij} q_i(t-1) P_j(t-1) + \sum_i l_i q_i(t-1) w(t-1)\}. \tag{11}$$

As labour is fully employed in the state of growth equilibrium, we have

$$W(t) = w(t)\ \sum_i l_i q_i(t). \tag{12}$$

In deriving (3′), (4′), and (5′), we use these relationships, in addition to the identities $\sum f_j(y) y_j = c_c$ and $\sum_j g_j(y) y_j = c_w$ that follow from (IIa) and (IIb).

therefore, our attention is focused on the inequalities (1′)–(6′), which may more simply be written in matrix form as:[1]

$$By \leqq \beta(Ay+\Omega L), \tag{1′}$$

$$xBy = \beta x(Ay+\Omega L), \tag{2′}$$

$$xB \geqq \alpha\left[xA+x\Omega L\left\{\frac{s_c}{s_c-s_w}g(y)-\frac{s_w}{s_c-s_w}f(y)\right\}\right] + (\beta-1)(xAy+x\Omega L)f(y), \tag{3′}$$

$$xBy = (\alpha+(\beta-1)c_c)(xAy+x\Omega L), \tag{4′}$$

$$xBy > 0, \tag{5′}$$

$$\alpha = \rho. \tag{6′}$$

A state of affairs fulfilling these inequalities is referred to as a Silvery Equilibrium which would be obtained in an economy where the Worker's propensity to save is less than the Capitalist's. It reduces to the Golden Equilibrium when no worker is allowed to save and no capitalist is allowed to consume. The Golden Equilibrium in which the Golden Rule holds would be akin to the original von Neumann equilibrium, though the former (unlike the latter) is generated in models which allow for workers' choice of consumption goods. In the following, we only assume that the Capitalist's propensity to save s_c is greater than that of the Worker, s_w.

It is evident that if the labour force grows at a very high rate, it is impossible to provide all workers in the economy with opportunities to work; unemployment of labour is inevitable, so that condition (6′) for full employment cannot be satisfied. We thus notice that in order to establish the existence of a solution (x_1, ..., x_m, y_1, ..., y_n, α, β, Ω) to (1′)–(6′), we need not only the conditions (Ib, c) on technology, and the conditions (IIa,b,c) on Engel-coefficients, but also some condition (say, (III) below) that prevents the rate of growth of the labour force from getting too large.

As I showed in my previous book, and as many authors have also observed, there is a relationship between the rate of interest $(\beta-1)$ and the rate of growth $(\rho-1)$.[2] It was originally derived on the assumption of no saving by the workers, but Pasinetti later found that the result is independent of the assumption.[3] In fact, since $s_c = 1-c_c$, it is seen that in a state fulfilling (1′)–(6′) (if it exists), we must have

$$\rho-1 = (\beta-1)s_c; \tag{13}$$

[1] It is seen from (2′) that the net national product $xBy-xAy$ equals the profits $(\beta-1)x(Ay+\Omega L)$ *plus* the wages $x\Omega L$; while (4′) states that the net national product equals investment $(\alpha-1)xAy$ *plus* the Capitalist's and the Worker's consumption. These together imply the familiar 'saving-investment' equation. As in the two-sector prototype, investment is automatically equal to savings at the full-employment level, when the Rule of Profitability and the Rule of Competitive Pricing both prevail.

[2] See Morishima, loc. cit., p. 145.

[3] Pasinetti, loc. cit., pp. 270–2.

in other words, the equilibrium rate of interest is determined independently of the Worker's propensity to save and is equal to the natural rate of growth divided by the Capitalist's propensity to save. This follows since we have

$$\rho+(\beta-1)c_c = \beta;$$

from (2′), (4′), and (6′). As both ρ and s_c are exogenously given constants, the rate of interest at the state of balanced growth is uniquely determined as the ratio $(\rho-1)/s_c$. It is of course independent of the intensities, prices, and wages.

Let us now derive the restriction on the growth rate of the labour force. In the state of balanced growth, the aggregate demand for good j (for consumption purposes) by the Capitalist and the Worker would be

$$h_j = \frac{\rho-1}{s_c}\{\sum_i\sum_k a_{ik}x_i y_k+(\sum_i l_i x_i)\Omega\}f_j(y)$$
$$+\rho\left\{\frac{s_c}{s_c-s_w}g_j(y)-\frac{s_w}{s_c-s_w}f_j(y)\right\}(\Sigma l_i x_i)\Omega \qquad i = 1, ..., n,$$

where h_j is the sum of $d_j(t)$ and $e_j(t)$ divided by $\sum_i q_i(t-1)$ and $\sum_j P_j(t)$. This equation follows from (10)–(13) ((11) and (12) are found in the footnote on p. 107). Together with (IIa,b) and $\rho > 1$, we get

$$\sum_j h_j y_j \geqq \frac{(\rho-1)c_c}{s_c}(\sum_j\sum_i a_{ij}x_i y_j).$$

Consequently, one of the h_js must be at least as large as the corresponding f$(\rho-1)c_c/s_c\}(\Sigma a_{ij}x_i)$. In the state of balanced growth, therefore, the total demand for some good j (including the demand for production purposes $\rho\sum_i a_{ij}x_i$) is at least as large as

$$(\rho+(\rho-1)c_c/s_c)(\sum_i a_{ij}x_i).$$

Hence, if we had for all non-negative $x_1, ..., x_m$

$$\sum_i b_{ij}x_i < \{(\rho-c_c)/s_c\}(\sum_i a_{ij}x_i) \qquad j = 1, ..., n,$$

then it would obviously be impossible for the economy to grow in balance at the natural rate ρ even if the wage rate were reduced to zero. From this consideration, we assume that

(III) the natural rate of growth is so low that there is a non-negative set $(x_1, x_2, ..., x_m)$ which fulfils inequalities,

$$\sum_i b_{ij}x_i > \{(\rho-s_c)/c_c\}(\sum_i a_{ij}x_i), \qquad j = 1, ..., n.$$

7. We have so far tacitly assumed that inequalities (1′)–(6′) have a solution $(x, y, \alpha, \beta, \Omega)$ that is *non-negative* in the sense that not only is every component of x and y (as well as α, β, and Ω) non-negative but also both the Capitalist's and the Worker's shares of the total profits are non-negative. It is true that the share of the Worker E_w is positive because W is positive in the Silvery Equilibrium state (see (8) above). However, the Capitalist's share E_c may be negative, because no ceiling has been set on E_w to prevent it exceeding total profits E.

It is obvious that a mathematical solution to (1′)–(6′) is economically meaningless unless each member of the society receives a non-negative amount of profits in the state of affairs corresponding to that solution. In order for the equilibrium conditions (1′)–(6′) to give a genuinely meaningful solution, the Worker's and the Capitalist's share E_w and E_c must, therefore, explicitly be subject to the constraints that E_w should not exceed E and that E_c should not be negative. These conditions are put in the following forms:

$$E_w = \min\left(\frac{s_w}{s_c - s_w} W, E\right), \tag{8'}$$

$$E_c = \max\left(E - \frac{s_w}{s_c - s_w} W, 0\right), \tag{9'}$$

where $\min(a, b)$ means the smaller of a and b and $\max(a, b)$ the larger of them. They imply that whenever $\frac{s_w}{s_c - s_w} W$ is less than E, the worker receives that amount and the Capitalist the remainder as the Pasinetti condition (7) requires (hence (8) and (9) hold true), but when $\frac{s_w}{s_c - s_w} W$ reaches E or exceeds it, the entire profits fall into the Worker's hands so that the Capitalist receives nothing.

Replacing (8) and (9) by (8′) and (9′), we have

$$d_j(t) + e_j(t) = f_j \max\left\{E(t) - \frac{s_w}{s_c - s_w} W(t), 0\right\} + g_j\left[W(t) + \min\left\{\frac{s_w}{s_c - s_w} W(t), E(t)\right\}\right] \tag{10'}$$

instead of (10). We then find, in view of (11) and (12), that the demand-supply conditions (3′) and (4′) can be written in the state of balanced growth as:

$$\sum_i b_{ij} x_i \geqq \alpha \sum_i a_{ij} x_i + f_j(y) \max\left\{\pi - \frac{s_w}{s_c - s_w} \alpha\left(\sum_i l_i x_i\right)\Omega, 0\right\} + g_j(y)\left[\alpha\left(\sum_i l_i x_i\right)\Omega + \min\left\{\frac{s_w}{s_c - s_w} \alpha\left(\sum_i l_i x_i\right)\Omega, \pi\right\}\right], \tag{3''}$$

$$\sum_i\sum_j b_{ij}x_iy_j = \alpha\sum_i\sum_j a_{ij}x_iy_j + c_c \max\left\{\pi - \frac{s_w}{s_c - s_w}\,\alpha(\sum_i l_ix_i)\Omega,\ 0\right\}$$
$$+c_w\left[\alpha(\sum_i l_ix_i)\Omega + \min\left\{\frac{s_w}{s_c-s_w}\,\alpha(\sum_i l_ix_i)\Omega,\ \pi\right\}\right], \qquad (4'')$$

where

$$\pi = (\beta-1)\{\sum_i\sum_j a_{ij}x_iy_j + (\sum_i l_ix_i)\Omega\}.$$

It is seen that if the Pasinetti assumption

$$\pi > \frac{s_w}{s_c - s_w}\,\alpha(\sum_i l_ix_i)\Omega \qquad (14)$$

is fulfilled, (3″) and (4″) are reduced to (3′) and (4′); we would then obtain a 'Pasinetti' Silvery Equilibrium. On the other hand, when condition (14) does not hold, (3″) and (4″) are reduced to

$$\sum_i b_{ij}x_i \geqq \alpha\sum_i a_{ij}x_i + (\beta-1)\{\sum_i\sum_k a_{ik}x_iy_k + (\sum_i l_ix_i)\Omega\}g_j(y)$$
$$+\alpha(\sum_i l_ix_i)\Omega g_j(y), \qquad (3''')$$

$$\sum_i\sum_j b_{ij}x_iy_j = \alpha\sum_i\sum_j a_{ij}x_iy_j + (\beta-1)\{\sum_i\sum_k a_{ik}x_iy_k + (\sum_i l_ix_i)\Omega\}c_w$$
$$+\alpha(\sum_i l_ix_i)\Omega c_w. \qquad (4''')$$

These, together with the other conditions for equilibrium, (1′), (2′), (5′), and (6′), would give an 'anti-Pasinetti' Silvery Equilibrium, where we have (from (2′), (4‴), and (6′))

$$\frac{\rho-1}{s_w} = \frac{\pi + \alpha(\sum_i l_ix_i)\Omega}{\sum_i\sum_j a_{ij}x_iy_j + (\sum_i l_ix_i)\Omega}. \qquad (15)$$

In this expression, π is the (normalized) total profits accruing from the activities in period $t-1$ (say) and $\alpha(\Sigma l_ix_i)\Omega$ stands for the (normalized) wages in period t. The denominator on the right-hand side represents the total stock of capital in period $t-1$ including both fixed and working capital. Note that there is a time lag between the receipt of profits and the payment of wages because we have assumed that the production of goods is not instantaneous. If it were instantaneous, or if wages were paid at the end of each period after the Worker had done his work as in the so-called Walras–von Neumann model,[1] we would have 1 in place of α in the numerator on the right-hand side of (15). Accordingly, the numerator would give the net product from the activities in period $t-1$,

[1] Morishima, loc. cit., pp. 148–53.

and (15) would be reduced to the Samuelson-Modigliani formula for anti-Pasinetti equilibrium:[1]

$$(\rho-1)/s_w = \text{the average product of capital.}$$

Thus (15) may be regarded as an extension of their formula to the case with production lags.

In any case, we have either Pasinetti or anti-Pasinetti equilibrium. All the parameters of the model participate in determining which equilibrium prevails in the model as the long-run solution. When a Pasinetti equilibrium is obtained, the profit rate is equal to the natural rate of growth divided by the Capitalist's propensity to save, and the other parameters which include the Worker's propensity to save have no part in the formula determining the profit rate. On the other hand, in the case of anti-Pasinetti equilibrium, the average product of capital (in the 'extended' sense) is, irrespective of the input-output coefficients and the Capitalist's propensity to save, always equal to the natural rate of growth divided by the Worker's propensity to save. Since the definition of π and (6′) enable us to rewrite (15) as

$$\beta-1 = \frac{\rho-1}{s_w} - \rho\frac{1}{1+(\sum_i\sum_j a_{ij}x_i y_j)/(\sum_i l_i x_i \Omega)},$$

we find that when an anti-Pasinetti equilibrium prevails, the rate of profit is simultaneously determined with $(\Sigma\Sigma a_{ij}x_i y_j)/(\Sigma l_i x_i \Omega)$, Marx's 'organic composition of capital'.[2]

8. Prior to giving a proof of the existence of a balanced growth solution, we devote the final part of this chapter to reviewing the 'no joint production' model (or the Generalized Leontief Model) of the previous chapter as a special case of the Generalized von Neumann Model. In the 'no joint production' economy, it is assumed that industry j can choose between m_j different manufacturing processes for good j; b_{is_j} denotes the quantity of good i used per unit of output j by the s_jth process, and l_{s_j} the labour-input coefficient of that process. Let δ_{is_j} be the rate of depreciation of good i when used by the s_jth process, it is the reciprocal of the average length of life of factor i used by that process. In the model of the previous chapter, quantity adjustments are made for old capital goods, but they are not treated as goods which are *qualitatively* different from the corresponding brand-new capital goods. The amount of good i left over by process s_j for the following period would then be $c_{is_j} = (1-\delta_{is_j})b_{is_j}$ per unit of output j; according to the von Neumann convention, c_{1s_j}, ...,

[1] See P. A. Samuelson and F. Modigliani, 'The Pasinetti paradox in neoclassical and more general models', *Review of Economic Studies*, Vol. XXXIII (1966), p. 278.
[2] Cf. ibid., p. 27–9.

c_{ns_j} are regarded as outputs. The input- and output-coefficient matrices are then

$$A' = \begin{pmatrix} b_{11_1} \dots b_{1m_1} & b_{11_2} \dots b_{1m_2} \dots b_{11_n} \dots b_{1m_n} \\ b_{21_1} \dots b_{2m_1} & b_{21_2} \dots b_{2m_2} \dots b_{21_n} \dots b_{2m_n} \\ \dots & \dots \\ b_{n1_1} \dots b_{nm_1} & b_{n1_2} \dots b_{nm_2} \dots b_{n1_n} \dots b_{nm_n} \end{pmatrix},$$

$$B' = \begin{pmatrix} 1+c_{11_1} \dots 1+c_{1m_1} & c_{11_2} \dots c_{1m_2} & \dots & c_{11_n} \dots c_{1m_n} \\ c_{21_1} \dots c_{2m_1} & 1+c_{21_2} \dots 1+c_{2m_2} & \dots & c_{21_n} \dots c_{2m_n} \\ \dots & \dots & \dots & \dots \\ c_{n1_1} \dots c_{nm_1} & c_{n1_2} \dots c_{nm_2} & \dots & 1+c_{n1_n} \dots 1+c_{nm_n} \end{pmatrix},$$

$$L' = [l_{1_1} \dots l_{m_1} \quad l_{1_2} \dots l_{m_2} \dots l_{1_n} \dots l_{m_n}].^1$$

The matrix notation we are using here is different from that in the previous chapter: the present A is the previous B, and the present B is $E+B-A$ in the previous symbols, where

$$E' = \begin{pmatrix} 1 \dots 1 & 0 \dots 0 \dots 0 \dots 0 \\ 0 \dots 0 & 1 \dots 1 \dots 0 \dots 0 \\ \dots & \dots \\ 0 \dots 0 & 0 \dots 0 \dots 1 \dots 1 \end{pmatrix},$$

whose ith row has, first, $(m_1+m_2+\dots+m_{i-1})$ zeros, and then m_i ones followed by $(m_{i+1}+\dots+m_n)$ zeros.

With this notation the two fundamental inequalities of the previous chapter (V.20) and (V.21) can now be written in the following forms:

$$BP(t+1) \leqq \{1+r(t)\}\{AP(t)+w(t)L\},$$
$$q(t)B \geqq q(t+1)A+c(t+1),$$

where $r(t)$ is the rate of interest in period t, $P(t)$ the (column) vector of prices in period t, $q(t)$ the activity vector in period t, $c(t)$ the consumption vector in period t. The above price-inequality is a mere translation of (V.20) into the present language. We can derive the above quantity-inequality from (V.21), because $X(t)+BX_m(t)-AX_m(t)$ (in the notation of Chapter V) represents the outputs including capital goods left over from the previous period, i.e., $q(t)B$ in the present symbols, and $BX_m(t+1)$ in Chapter V is no more than $q(t+1)A$ in the present notation. The price- and quantity-inequalities thus obtained are nothing more than the two fundamental inequalities (1) and (3) of the von Neumann model; the great simplicity and unreality of the 'no joint production' model follows from the special output matrix used.

[1] Prime applied to matrices denote, as usual, their transpose.

It is true that (i) if there were no by-products in the ordinary sense and (ii) if old capital goods damaged from past use could quantitatively be transformed into equivalent brand-new capital goods, the von Neumann method of analysis would be reduced to the dynamic input-output analysis discussed in the preceding chapter;[1] but assumption (i) and (ii) prevent us from approaching the problem of age composition of capital equipment and other related problems. Once they are taken into consideration (as they should be in the theory of long-run economic growth), old capital goods must be treated as qualitatively different goods. We must part from our old friends, Walras and Leontief; von Neumann is our new horse.

[1] In spite of the fact that many economists including McKenzie and Solow are interested in it, the generalized Leontief model discussed in this section has the following unsatisfactory properties: (i) perfect malleability and (ii) perfect transferability of capital goods. A less objectionable model which is free from these unrealities but which still belongs to the Leontief family has been presented by Morishima and Murata; it lies between the 'generalized Leontief model' and the 'generalized von Neumann model', and should, however, be superseded by the latter since it assumes some kind of malleability for capital goods. Cf. L. W. McKenzie, 'Turnpike theorems for a generalized Leontief model', *Econometrica*, Vol. XXXI (1963), pp. 165–80; R. M. Solow, 'Competitive valuation in a dynamic input-output system', *Econometrica*, Vol. XXVII (1959), pp. 30–53; M. Morishima and Y. Murata, 'An input-output system involving non-transferable goods', *Econometrica*, Vol. XXXV (1968).

VII

EQUILIBRIUM GROWTH (I) CASSEL–VON NEUMANN RAY

1. IN THE previous chapter, the state of balanced growth of all outputs with continued full employment of labour was described in terms of six sets of inequalities (VI.1′)–(VI.6′).[1] Such a state of affairs has been called a Silvery Equilibrium which is reduced to the familiar Golden Equilibrium in the particular case where no worker saves and no capitalist consumes at all. Existence of a Silvery Equilibrium thus defined has been established in my former book by the argument which proceeds in the following way. For any arbitrarily chosen real-wage rate Ω, we find the prices and interest rate which would induce a perfectly competitive economy to grow in balance at a steady rate. This rate of growth which was called the 'warranted rate of growth' by Sir Roy Harrod as well may be different from the 'natural rate of growth' $\rho-1$, so that the condition of continued full employment may not be fulfilled. The real-wage rate, therefore, would have to be adjusted so as to give a Silvery Equilibrium. Thus my previous argument consisted of two parts yielding the following conclusions: (i) given any real-wage rate there is a warranted rate of growth at which all outputs can grow in balance, and (ii) there is a real-wage rate making the warranted rate equal the given natural rate of growth. I was successful in giving a complete proof to the first proposition (i), while the second proposition (ii) could only be asserted with a proviso ruling out some perverse cases.[2]

In this chapter we establish the existence of a balanced growth at the natural rate in one step but not two. It will be shown that perverse cases are impossible if we make assumptions (Ia, b), (IIa, b, c), and (III) in Chapter VI. Our new argument uses game-theory as before, although I received hints from H. Haga and M. Otsuki's proof which uses linear programming.[3] It is indeed not surprising that the method of linear

[1] Strictly speaking, (VI.3″) and (VI.4″) should replace (VI.3′) and (VI.4′) if the possibility of 'anti-Pasinetti' Silvery Equilibrium is allowed for. But in the present chapter, we accept, for the sake of simplicity, the Pasinetti assumption and get through without being bothered with the switching operations min (a, b) and max (a, b) in (VI.3″) and (VI.4″). As far as the analytical aspect of the problem is concerned, we would not lose much by doing so; we have in fact, dealt well with troubles caused by a similar switching operation (see my *Equilibrium, Stability and Growth*, pp. 139–45).

[2] See ibid., pp. 151–3.

[3] H. Haga and M. Otsuki, 'On a generalized von Neumann model', *International Economic Review*, Vol. VI (1965), pp. 115–23.

programming can be applied effectively to a problem whose solution is warranted by a game-theory argument, and vice versa.

Let us consider the following preliminary production-pricing game. It does not give the balanced growth solution, unless by chance it is an equilibrium game. It will nevertheless be a useful tool when we grope for the equilibrium state. Just as Walras imagined a process of *tâtonnement* to examine a number of arbitrary sets of prices for the possibility of equilibrium prices, we play a number of shadow games of production and pricing to find the full-dress equilibrium game.

The game is described in terms of the 'net outputs' and the 'augmented labour-inputs'. Consider a situation where there is an *arbitrary* wage-price system (Ω, y), although the economy is in a state of balanced growth (i.e., the activity levels are growing at the natural rate $\rho-1$). When process i is operating at unit intensity, outputs $(b_{i1}, b_{i2}, ..., b_{in})$ of the n goods will be produced in period $t+1$ from the material inputs $(a_{i1}, a_{i2}, ..., a_{in})$ and the labour input (l_i) which enter the process in period t. Workers consume various goods in the proportions described by the vector of Engel-coefficients $g(y)$, so that the labour input l_i implies $\Omega l_i g_1(y)$, $\Omega l_i g_2(y)$, ..., $\Omega l_i g_n(y)$ amounts of goods are consumed.

At the end of period t, profits of the amount

$$\sum_k b_{ik} y_k - \sum_k a_{ik} y_k - \Omega l_i \qquad (i = 1, ..., m),$$

are earned; note that they include not only normal profits but also supernormal profits because (Ω, y) may not be an equilibrium wage-price system. Let $\beta-1$ be the normal profit rate; it follows from the Pasinetti equation discussed in the previous chapter that $\beta-1$ is equal to the natural rate of growth $\rho-1$ divided by the Capitalist's propensity to save s_c. Obviously, the normal profits are

$$\pi_i = (\beta-1)(\sum_k a_{ik} y_k + \Omega l_i) \qquad (i = 1, ..., m).$$

The difference between the actual and the normal profits is called the supernormal profits. In the preliminary production-pricing game it is assumed that only the normal part of profits is shared among individuals in proportion to ownership of capital, the whole of the supernormal part being retained by the firm. This is of course different from the original assumption which asserted that the total profits are distributed among individuals. We need not bother ourselves about this deviation, because in the state of equilibrium we are searching for there can be no supernormal profits, so that the two assumptions yield the same result.

The normal profits π_i are distributed between the Capitalist and the Worker in the way discussed in the last chapter. When process i is operated at unit intensity in period t, it will be operated at intensity ρ in period

$t+1$ since the economy is assumed to grow at the rate $\rho-1$ per period. In period $t+1$, the Worker will get, as well as wages of the amount $\Omega\rho l_i$, a part π_{wi} of the normal profits π_i, the rest π_{ci} being received by the Capitalist; the distribution should obey the Pasinetti formula

$$\frac{\pi_{wi}}{s_w(\Omega\rho l_i+\pi_{wi})}=\frac{\pi_{ci}}{s_c\pi_{ci}}.$$

As $\pi_{wi}+\pi_{ci}=(\beta-1)(\sum_k a_{ik}y_k+\Omega l_i)$, we get

$$\pi_{wi}=\frac{s_w}{s_c-s_w}\,\Omega\rho l_i,$$

$$\pi_{ci}=(\beta-1)\sum_k a_{ik}y_i+\left(\beta-1-\frac{\rho s_w}{s_c-s_w}\right)\Omega l_i.$$

The worker spends π_{wi} to buy various goods in amounts which are proportional to the Engel-coefficients $g(y)$:

$$\frac{s_w}{s_c-s_w}\,\Omega\rho l_i g_1(y),\;\dots,\;\frac{s_w}{s_c-s_w}\,\Omega\rho l_i g_n(y).$$

On the other hand, the Capitalist's consumption is distributed among n goods in proportion to the Engel-coefficients $f_1(y), \dots, f_n(y)$, so that he consumes good j (say) in the amount

$$\left\{(\beta-1)\sum_k a_{ik}y_k+\left(\beta-1-\frac{\rho s_w}{s_c-s_w}\right)\Omega l_i\right\}f_j(y),$$

which can be split up further into the following $n+1$ components:

$$(\beta-1)a_{i1}y_1f_j(y),\;(\beta-1)a_{i2}y_2f_j(y),\;\dots,$$
$$(\beta-1)a_{in}y_nf_j(y),\;\left(\beta-1-\frac{\rho s_w}{s_c-s_w}\right)\Omega l_i f_j(y).$$

The first n of them increase proportionally with the value of the material inputs, and the last with the wage payments. Thus the use of various inputs has multiplier effects on the demand for goods through the Worker's and the Capitalist's consumption, so long as the Worker saves a part of his income and the Capitalist spends a portion of the profits he receives on consumption.

The multiplier effects have a one period lag, so that they have to be discounted if they are synchronized with the original inputs. In the state of balanced growth where the intensity of any process in period t is ρ

times as large as that in period $t-1$, it is evident that it must be discounted at the rate ρ. If the multiplier effects are induced, the labour input (l_i) entering process i causes $\Omega n_{i1}(y), \ldots, \Omega n_{in}(y)$ amounts of goods to be used, where

$$\Omega n_{ij}(y) \equiv \Omega l_i g_j(y) + \frac{s_w}{s_c - s_w}\,\Omega l_i g_j(y) + \left(\frac{\beta-1}{\rho} - \frac{s_w}{s_c - s_w}\right)\Omega l_i f_j(y)$$

$$(j = 1, \ldots, n).$$

These may be called the 'augmented labour inputs' (in terms of goods). They are defined as the sum of the Worker's consumption from his wage income (the first term on the right-hand side of the above formula) and the Worker's and the Capitalist's consumption induced by profits on the labour input (the second and the third term). The last two terms stand for the multiplier effects which are discounted at the rate ρ. In matrix notation we may write

$$N(y) \equiv \left(\frac{s_c}{s_c - s_w}\right) Lg(y) + \left(\frac{\beta-1}{\rho} - \frac{s_w}{s_c - s_w}\right) Lf(y),$$

where $N(y)$ is an m by n matrix whose typical element is $n_{ij}(y)$.

On the other hand, the material inputs cause

$$a_{ij} + \frac{\beta-1}{\rho}(a_{ik} y_k) f_j(y)$$

amounts of goods ($j = 1, \ldots, n$, respectively) to be used up. The 'augmented material inputs' thus defined consist of the original material inputs and the multiplier effects discounted by ρ. Subtracting the augmented material inputs from the outputs available in period t which are, in the state of balanced growth, $\frac{1}{\rho} b_{i1}, \frac{1}{\rho} b_{i2}, \ldots, \frac{1}{\rho} b_{in}$, and not $b_{i1}, \ldots, b_{in}$, we get the 'net outputs'; they are typically written in the form,

$$m_{ij}(y) \equiv \frac{1}{\rho} b_{ij} - a_{ij} - \frac{\beta-1}{\rho}\Big(\sum_k a_{ik} y_k\Big) f_j(y),$$

or they can be put in the matrix form:

$$M(y) \equiv \frac{1}{\rho} B - A - \frac{\beta-1}{\rho} Ayf(y).$$

The generalized von Neumann model (of the Pasinetti type) discussed in Chapter VI is repeated (in matrix form) as follows:

$$By \leqq \beta(Ay+\Omega L), \tag{1}$$

$$xBy = \beta x(Ay+\Omega L), \tag{2}$$

$$xB \geqq \alpha\left\{xA+x\Omega L\left(\frac{s_c}{s_c-s_w}g(y)-\frac{s_w}{s_c-s_w}f(y)\right)\right\}$$
$$+(\beta-1)(xAy+x\Omega L)f(y), \tag{3}$$

$$xBy = (\alpha+(\beta-1)c_c)(xAy+x\Omega L), \tag{4}$$

$$xBy > 0, \tag{5}$$

$$\alpha = \rho. \tag{6}$$

(1) represents the price-cost inequalities, and (3) the demand-supply inequality. (2) and (4) follow from the Rule of Profitability and the Rule of Free Goods, respectively. (5) is evidently required for a meaningful solution. (6) is the Harrodian condition for persistence of the growth equilibrium.

The Pasinetti equality (VI.13) between the interest rate and the equilibrium growth rate divided by the Capitalist's propensity to save, and the Harrod equality between the equilibrium growth rate and the natural growth rate, both hold in the state of balanced growth we are discussing. These two equalities together with Assumption (IIa, b) mean we can rewrite (1) and (3), in our new terminology of 'net outputs' and 'augmented labour-inputs' as follows:

$$\sum_j m_{ij}(y)y_j \leqq \Omega\sum_j n_{ij}(y)y_j, \qquad i = 1, ..., m, \tag{1'}$$

$$\sum_i m_{ij}(y)x_i \geqq \Omega\sum_i n_{ij}(y)x_i, \qquad j = 1, ..., n, \tag{3'}$$

or equivalently,

$$M(y)y \leqq \Omega N(y)y, \tag{1'}$$

$$xM(y) \geqq \Omega xN(y). \tag{3'}$$

Inequalities (1′) imply that the value of net outputs of any process cannot exceed the value of the augmented labour-inputs; in other words, in equilibrium there can be no process which can pay workers a higher rate than the prevailing wage rate. Inequalities (3′) assure the feasibility of growth; hence the total augmented labour-input of any good does not exceed the total available net output of that good.

These inequalities can be examined from the game-theoretic point of view. Let y^* be an arbitrary set of normalized prices whose elements are non-negative with unit sum. Consider the following set of inequalities:

$$\sum_j m_{ij}(y^*)y_j \leqq \Omega \sum_j n_{ij}(y^*)y_j, \tag{1*}$$

$$\sum_i m_{ij}(y^*)x_i \geqq \Omega \sum_i n_{ij}(y^*)x_i, \tag{3*}$$

or

$$M(y^*)y \leqq \Omega N(y^*)y, \tag{1*}$$

$$xM(y^*) \geqq \Omega xN(y^*). \tag{3*}$$

The matrices M and N now assume constant values, and we can interpret (1*) and (3*) as a game between two persons: the Entrepreneur and the Market.

Given prices, the net output and the augmented labour-input coefficients, $m_{ij}(y^*)$ and $n_{ij}(y^*)$, are determined. For a while, suppose they are independent of the activities of the Market, in spite of the fact that prices are fixed in the market and the coefficients respond to the prices. The game is defined as follows. There are m pure strategies available to the Entrepreneur from among which he chooses one or a mixture. Similarly, the Market has n pure strategies; they and their mixtures give the set of all strategies open to 'him', from which he chooses a strategy. It is a rule of the game that if the Entrepreneur chooses his ith pure strategy and the Market his jth pure strategy, the latter pays to the former an amount of money equal to

$$m_{ij}(y^*) - \Omega n_{ij}(y^*).$$

An overall picture of the amount paid under each pair of strategies is given by

$$M(y^*) - \Omega N(y^*),$$

which is, therefore, called the pay-off matrix, or the pay-off table.

When the Entrepreneur employs a mixed strategy $x = (x_1, ..., x_m)$ and the Market $y = (y_1, ..., y_n)$, the amount paid by the Market to the Entrepreneur is

$$v = \sum_{i=1}^{m} \sum_{j=1}^{n} \{m_{ij}(y^*) - \Omega n_{ij}(y^*)\} x_i y_j.$$

Thus the Entrepreneur will naturally seek to maximize his expected income v which is the excess of the value of the net outputs over the value of the augmented labour-inputs, while the Market will protect himself by choosing y so as to minimize his expected loss v. It is obvious that if the wage rate Ω is set too low, the game favours the Entrepreneur, i.e. he wins the game, however skilfully the Market plays; and vice versa. If the wage rate is set so that the game is fair, neither player can expect positive (or negative) gains; hence conditions (1*) and (3*) are fulfilled when both players choose optimum strategies. Thus the state which satisfies (1*) and (3*) may be regarded as an optimum state of the game at the fair wage rate.

2. The existence and uniqueness of the fair wage rate are rigorously established in the following way. As the natural rate of growth is positive (i.e., $\rho > 1$) and $c_c + s_c = 1$ by definition, it is at once seen that $(\rho - c_c)/s_c$ is greater than ρ. Bearing in mind assumption (III) in Chapter VI, we find *a fortiori* that there is a non-negative set of intensities $(x_1, x_2, ..., x_m)$ such that

$$\sum_i \left(\frac{1}{\rho} b_{ij} - a_{ij}\right) x_i > 0 \qquad j = 1, ..., n.$$

As these activities $x_1, ..., x_m$ are repeatable in the sence defined in the previous chapter, it follows from (Ic) in the same chapter that $\sum_i l_i x_i$ is positive. Then the strict inequality

$$\sum_i \{m_{ij}(y^*) - \Omega n_{ij}(y^*)\} x_i > 0$$

holds for negative and very large (in modulus) Ω, unless $g_j(y^*) = f_j(y^*) = 0$. It is evident that, for js for which $g_j(y^*) = f_j(y^*) = 0$, we have similar inequalities for any Ω, because when $g_j(y^*)$ and $f_j(y^*)$ vanish, $m_{ij}(y^*)$ reduces to $\frac{1}{\rho} b_{ij} - a_{ij}$ and $n_{ij}(y^*)$ to zero. The above inequality thus holds for all $j = 1, ..., n$ when Ω is negative and very large in modulus.

Next, the catalogue contains processes with $l_i = 0$. Let I be the set of all such processes. The processes belonging to I can be grouped into a number of subsets, $I_1, I_2, ..., I_u$, in the following way. Set x_i^0 positive for all i in I and zero for all other i. Clearly, $\sum_i l_i x_i^0 = 0$, that is to say, something is produced without labour. By virtue of assumption (Ic) the activities, $x_1^0, ..., x_m^0$, cannot be repeated; that is to say, there is at least one good j such that

$$0 = \sum_i b_{ij} x_i^0 < \sum_i a_{ij} x_i^0,$$

the set of such goods being denoted by J_1. All is which belong to I and have $a_{ij} > 0$ for some j in J_1 form the subset I_1.

Now replace x_i^0 for each i in I_1 by zero. It is clear that we still have $\sum_i l_i x_i^0 = 0$; therefore, the activity vector x^0 after the replacement is not repeatable. In exactly the same way as we defined J_1 and I_1, a set of goods J_2 and a set of processes I_2 are defined, in terms of the new activities $x_1^0, ..., x_m^0$, as a set of all goods which are required for production but not produced by the activities $x_1^0, ..., x_m^0$, and a set of all processes which use some non-reproducible goods (i.e. some goods j in J_2), respectively. Proceeding likewise, we get the sets, $I_1, I_2, ..., I_u$, and $J_1, J_2, ..., J_u$. Finally, those goods which are not classified in $J_1, ..., J_u$ form the remainder J_{u+1}.

It is now clear that we obtain inequalities

$$\sum_j b_{ij} y_j < \rho \sum_j a_{ij} y_j$$

for the processes in I_r by setting prices of goods grouped in J_r sufficiently high in comparison with prices of goods in $J_{r+1}, ..., J_u, J_{u+1}$; r can run from 1 to u. We have a strictly positive price set $y = (y_1, ..., y_n)$ such that the above inequality holds for each process in I. As $l_i = 0$ for i in I, this means, in view of the definitions of $m_{ij}(y^*)$ and $n_{ij}(y^*)$, that we have the inequality

$$\sum_j m_{ij}(y^*) y_j < \Omega \sum_j n_{ij}(y^*) y_j, \qquad \text{for all } i \text{ in } I.$$

On the other hand, for i with $l_i > 0$ we have $\sum_j n_{ij}(y^*) y_j > 0$ because all $y_1, ..., y_n$ are taken to be positive, the Engel coefficients $g_j(y^*)$ and $f_j(y^*)$ $(j = 1, ..., n)$ are non-negative and at least one of them is positive; therefore, when Ω is large enough, each $\Omega \sum_j n_{ij}(y^*) y_j$ exceeds the corresponding $\sum_j m_{ij}(y^*) y_j$. We can thus choose $\tilde{y} = (\tilde{y}_1, ..., \tilde{y}_n)$ so that

$$\sum_j \{m_{ij}(y^*) - \Omega n_{ij}(y^*)\} \tilde{y}_j < 0 \qquad \text{for all} \qquad i = 1, ..., m,$$

if Ω is positive and very large.

In this way, we have found that for very large (in modulus) negative Ω the Entrepreneur can always (irrespective of the play of the Market) expect a positive gain by choosing an appropriate strategy, say, $\tilde{x} = (\tilde{x}_1, ..., \tilde{x}_m)$, while for very large positive Ω the Market's choice of prices $\tilde{y} = (\tilde{y}_1, ..., \tilde{y}_n)$ yields a negative gain irrespective of the Entrepreneur's choice of activities. The value of the game (the expected pay-off) is in favour of the Entrepreneur or the Market, according to whether the parameter Ω is very small (negative) or very large. Since the value of the game is a continuous function of Ω, there must be a fair wage rate Ω at which both players can expect no gain.

Let us next establish that the fair wage rate is unique. Suppose the contrary, namely, that there exist two different fair wage rates, Ω^0 and Ω^1. Let x^0 and y^0 be the optimum strategies for the Entrepreneur and the Market associated with the wage rate Ω^0, and x^1 and y^1 those associated with Ω^1. From the assumption that all workers have identical tastes in consumption, it follows that if the augmented labour-input coefficient $n_{ij}(y^*)$ of some process i is positive with respect to some good j, then it is positive, with respect to the same good, for all processes i with $l_i > 0$. Goods can then be grouped (after rearranging them) into two classes, $j = 1, ..., h$ and $j = h+1, ..., n$, such that for i with $l_i > 0$

$$n_{ij}(y^*) > 0 \qquad \text{if} \quad j = 1, ..., h,$$

and

$$n_{ij}(y^*) = 0 \qquad \text{if} \quad j = h+1, ..., n.$$

It is clear that h is independent of i and such a pattern of the matrix of the augmented labour-input coefficients implies the uniqueness of the fair wage rate.

Suppose Ω^0 is greater than Ω^1; we would then have, for i with $l_i > 0$,

$$\sum_{j=1}^{n} m_{ij}(y^*)y_j{}^1 \leqq \Omega^1 \sum_{j=1}^{n} n_{ij}(y^*)y_j{}^1 < \Omega^0 \sum_{j=1}^{n} n_{ij}(y^*)y_j{}^1$$

unless $y_1{}^1 = y_2{}^1 = \cdots = y_h{}^1 = 0$. The strict inequalities holding between the extreme right-hand and the extreme left-hand sides imply that $x_i{}^0 = 0$ for all i with $l_i > 0$; hence $\sum_i l_i x_i{}^0 = 0$. The activities $x_1{}^0, ..., x_m{}^0$ are not repeatable, so that

$$0 = \sum_i b_{ij}x_i{}^0 < \rho \sum_i a_{ij}x_i{}^0 \qquad \text{for some } j.$$

Therefore,

$$\sum_i \{m_{ij}(y^*) - \Omega^0 n_{ij}(y^*)\} x_i{}^0 < 0 \qquad \text{for some } j.$$

It is then seen that the Market (who minimizes the pay-off) could have a negative expected gain. This result clearly contradicts the fairness of Ω^0. Hence we must have $y_j{}^1 = 0$ for $j = 1, ..., h$.

We now have

$$\sum_j m_{ij}(y^*)y_j{}^1 \leqq \Omega^1 \sum_j n_{ij}(y^*)y_j{}^1 = 0 \qquad \text{for all } i;$$

so that

$$\sum_{i=1}^{m} \sum_{j=h+1}^{n} m_{ij}(y^*)x_i y_j{}^1 \leqq 0$$

for any non-negative x_is. On the other hand, the fact that $n_{ij}(y^*) = 0$ for $j = h+1, ..., n$ means that not only $g_j(y^*) = 0$ but also $f_j(y^*) = 0$ for those j; accordingly,

$$m_{ij}(y^*) = \frac{1}{\rho} b_{ij} - a_{ij} \qquad i = 1, ..., m; j = h+1, ..., n.$$

As we have seen before, assumption (III) implies that there are non-negative x_is such that

$$\sum_i b_{ij} x_i > \rho \sum_i a_{ij} x_i \qquad j = 1, \ldots, n.$$

Hence,

$$\sum_{i=1}^{m} \sum_{j=h+1}^{n} \left(\frac{1}{\rho} b_{ij} - a_{ij} \right) x_i y_j^1 = \sum_{i=1}^{m} \sum_{j=h+1}^{n} m_{ij}(y^*) x_i y_j^1 > 0,$$

a contradiction. This establishes the uniqueness of the fair wage rate: $\Omega^0 = \Omega^1$.

The final part of this section is devoted to proving rigorously that an optimum solution of the *fair* preliminary game between the Entrepreneur and the Market is also a 'balanced growth' solution to inequalities (1*) and (3*), and vice versa. First, let (x^0, y^0, Ω^0) be a set of game-theory solutions. Since Ω^0 is fair, the value of the game vanishes, i.e.,

$$\sum_i \sum_j \{m_{ij}(y^*) - \Omega^0 n_{ij}(y^*)\} x_i^0 y_j^0 = 0.$$

Since x^0 and y^0 are optimum strategies, the pay-off is maximized with respect to x at x^0 and minimized with respect to y at y^0. Therefore, (1*) and (3*) should be fulfilled at (x^0, y^0, Ω^0); otherwise, the value of the game would be positive or negative.

Next, let (x^0, y^0, Ω^0) be a solution to (1*) and (3*). Suppose that the wage rate Ω^0 is unfair, so that the value of the game is not zero; we would have

$$\hat{v} = \max_x \min_y \sum_i \sum_j \{m_{ij}(y^*) - \Omega^0 n_{ij}(y^*)\} x_i y_j \neq 0,$$

where x and y are probability vectors, i.e. their elements are non-negative and add up to one. First, assume $\hat{v} > 0$. Then there is an $x^1 = (x_1^1, \ldots, x_m^1)$ such that

$$\sum_i \{m_{ij}(y^*) - \Omega^0 n_{ij}(y^*)\} x_i^1 > 0 \qquad j = 1, \ldots, n.$$

These strict inequalities yield

$$\sum_i \sum_j \{m_{ij}(y^*) - \Omega^0 n_{ij}(y^*)\} x_1^1 y_j > 0$$

for any vector y whose elements are non-negative and not all zero;[1] on the other hand, if there is a y fulfilling (1*), then the above bilinear form takes on a non-positive value at that y, because x^1 is non-negative. Thus we have a contradiction, which means that there is no y satisfying (1*). Similarly, if $\hat{v} < 0$, (3*) is not satisfied. Hence the wage rate Ω^0 fulfilling both (1*) and (3*) is fair.

[1] Such a vector is referred to as a non-negative, non-zero vector.

Finally, inequalities (1*) and (3*) imply

$$\sum_i \sum_j \{m_{ij}(y^*) - \Omega^0 n_{ij}(y^*)\} x_i{}^0 y_j \geqq \sum_i \sum_j \{m_{ij}(y^*) - \Omega n_{ij}(y^*)\} x_i{}^0 y_j{}^0$$
$$\geqq \sum_i \sum_j \{m_{ij}(y^*) - \Omega^0 n_{ij}(y^*)\} x_i y_j{}^0.$$

It is seen that the pay-off is minimized at y^0 when the Entrepreneur chooses the strategy x^0, while it is maximized at x^0 when the Market chooses y^0. This means that y^0 is an optimum strategy for the Market, and x^0 that for the Entrepreneur. The equivalence between the balanced growth solution and the game-theoretic optimum solution is thus secured. (Note, however, that the solution is not necessarily unique, each preliminary game may have several (or infinitely many) solutions.)

3. In the Walrasian process of tâtonnement, consumers and producers respond to prices cried in the market, and the custodian of the market (or a stroker of clappers) changes prices until he finally finds equilibrium prices which equate the demand and supply of each good in the market. Likewise, our preliminary games give correspondences between prices and other variables; that is to say, to any preassigned set of prices y^*, there corresponds a fair wage rate Ω, a set $T(y^*)$ of optimum strategies for the Market and a set $U(y^*)$ of optimum strategies for the Entrepreneur. We are now in a position to find an equilibrium game such that the preassigned price set itself is an optimum strategy for the Market; in other words, we are groping for a point $\bar{y}$ such that $\bar{y} \in T(\bar{y})$.

We call such a point a fixed point (or an equilibrium point) of the correspondence, $y \to Y(y)$, to which we will apply Kakutani's fixed-point theorem,[1] since our correspondence satisfies the requirements of that theorem:

Let S be a non-empty, bounded, closed, convex subset in a Euclidean space. If a multi-valued correspondence $z \to R(z)$ from S into S is upper semicontinuous and $R(z)$ is non-empty and convex for all $z \in S$, then there is a point $\bar{z}$ in S such that $\bar{z} \in R(\bar{z})$.[2]

In our application, we take S as

$$\{y \mid y_j \geqq 0, \sum_j y_j = 1\},$$

i.e. the set of all n-dimensional non-negative vectors with unit sums. It is of course a non-empty, bounded, closed, convex subset in a Euclidean

[1] S. Kakutani, 'A generalization of Brouwer's fixed point theorem', *Duke Mathematical Journal*, Vol. VIII (1941), pp. 457–59. Kakutani's theorem is a generalization of Brouwer's fixed-point theorem and is further generalized by Eilenberg and Montgomery, whose theorem is also used later.

[2] For the definitions of convexity and upper semicontinuity, see footnotes 1 and 2, p. 13.

space, so that it satisfies the requirements of the theorem. For $z \to R(z)$ we take $y \to T(y)$, of course. To any preassigned y^* we have $T(y^*)$, a non-empty set of all n-dimensional non-negative vectors y (with unit sums) which realize (1*) at the fair wage rate Ω corresponding to y^*. By construction, $y^* \to T(y^*)$ is a multi-valued (possibly a single-valued) correspondence from S into S ($T(y^*)$ is a subset of S).

The remaining requirements are the upper semicontinuity of the correspondence $y^* \to T(y^*)$ and the convexity of $T(y^*)$, the former is verified as follows. Let y^{*k} and y^k be any sequences of points in S that converge to y^* and y respectively. Corresponding to each y^{*k}, we have the fair wage rate Ω^k and the 'optimum price' set $T(y^{*k})$. Suppose $y^k \in T(y^{*k})$ for all k; then

$$\sum_j m_{ij}(y^{*k})y_j^k \leqq \Omega^k \sum_j n_{ij}(y^{*k})y_j^k \qquad (i = 1, \ldots, m) \qquad (1^k)$$

for every k. The fairness of Ω^k implies that with each Ω^k there is associated a non-negative intensity vector x^k (with unit sum) such that

$$\sum_i m_{ij}(y^{*k})x_i^k \geqq \Omega^k \sum_i n_{ij}(y^{*k})x_i^k \qquad (j = 1, \ldots, n). \qquad (3^k)$$

This is so because, if for any non-negative x^k with unit sum there were a j not satisfying inequality (3^k), then the minimizing player (the Market) could always choose y^k to make the expected pay-off negative; clearly, this contradicts the fairness of Ω^k. We have shown that Ω^k is finite for every k and we can easily show that it does not tend to infinity when k does. Let Ω and x be the limit points of $\{\Omega^k\}$ and $\{x^k\}$ respectively, when k tends to infinity. It is obvious that (1^k) and (3^k) which hold for every k must also hold in the limit. As we have from (IIc) in Chapter VI

$$m_{ij}(y^*) = \lim_{k \to \infty} m_{ij}(y^{*k}), \qquad \text{and} \qquad n_{ij}(y^*) = \lim_{k \to \infty} n_{ij}(y^{*k}),$$

we get

$$\sum_j m_{ij}(y^*)y_j \leqq \Omega \sum_j n_{ij}(y^*)y_j \qquad (i = 1, \ldots, m), \qquad (1^*)$$

$$\sum_i m_{ij}(y^*)x_i \geqq \Omega \sum_i n_{ij}(y^*)x_i \qquad (j = 1, \ldots, n). \qquad (3^*)$$

These show the fairness of the limiting wage rate Ω. Thus the limit y of y^k satisfies (1*) at the fair wage rate; hence $y \in T(y^*)$, or $\lim_{k \to \infty} y^k \in \lim_{k \to \infty} T(y^{*k})$. The upper semicontinuity of the correspondence $y^* \to T(y^*)$ is thus established.

Next suppose there are two price-systems y^0 and y^1 that belong to $T(y^*)$. Since the fair wage rate with which they are associated is unique, y^0 and

y^1 satisfy (1*) at the same fair wage rate Ω^0. Consequently, for all μ such that $0 \leqq \mu \leqq 1$, we have

$$\sum_j m_{ij}(y^*)y_j(\mu) \leqq \Omega^0 \sum_j n_{ij}(y^*)y_j(\mu) \qquad i = 1, ..., m,$$

where $y_j(\mu) = (1-\mu)y_j{}^0 + \mu y_j{}^1$. These m inequalities for y, together with the n inequalities (3*) which hold for Ω^0 and x^0, imply that all convex combinations of y^0 and y^1 (i.e. $y(\mu)$ for all μ in [0, 1]) belong to the optimum strategy set $T(y^*)$. Hence it is a convex set.

We now find that the existence of a point such that $\bar{y} \in T(\bar{y})$ is insured by the Kakutani theorem, so that

$$\sum_i m_{ij}(\bar{y})\bar{y}_j \leqq \bar{\Omega} \sum_i n_{ij}(\bar{y})\bar{y}_j \qquad i = 1, ..., m,$$

where $\bar{\Omega}$ is the fair wage rate associated with $\bar{y}$. The fairness of $\bar{\Omega}$ implies the existence of a non-negative, non-zero intensity vector $\bar{x}$ such that

$$\sum_i m_{ij}(\bar{y})\bar{x}_i \geqq \bar{\Omega} \sum_i n_{ij}(\bar{y})\bar{x}_i \qquad j = 1, ..., n.$$

It is noticed here that the uniqueness of the fair wage rate played a very important role in the above argument. As we have seen, uniqueness follows when we make a restrictive assumption such as the assumption of workers having identical tastes, but it does not follow under more general assumptions. In fact, the fair wage rate is not unique if workers operating different processes, say sailors and mine workers, have different Engel-coefficients. It is, however, to be noticed that even in such general cases the above argument does hold *mutatis mutandis*, so long as the net output coefficients m_{ij} and the augmented labour-input coefficients n_{ij} continue to be independent of the real wage rate Ω. It is seen that alterations in the assumptions subject to the qualification mentioned above do not affect the convexity of the optimum strategy set $T(y^*)$ and the correspondence, $y^* \rightarrow T(y^*)$, remains upper semicontinuous; so that we can apply the Kakutani theorem to those cases also, and obtain a fixed point $(\bar{\Omega}, \bar{y}, \bar{x})$.[1]

4. We have thus shown that inequalities (1′) and (3′) (and hence (1) and (3)) are fulfilled at the fixed point $(\bar{\Omega}, \bar{x}, \bar{y})$. Once they are established, it is easy to see that all other equilibrium conditions are also satisfied at that point. As $\bar{x}$ is non-negative, we have from (1′)

$$\sum_i \sum_j m_{ij}(\bar{y})\bar{x}_i\bar{y}_j \leqq \bar{\Omega} \sum_i \sum_j n_{ij}(\bar{y})\bar{x}_i\bar{y}_j.$$

[1] A further generalization can be made so that m_{ij} and n_{ij} may depend on Ω also. We cannot, however, apply the Kakutani theorem to this case; instead we must use the Eilenberg–Montgomery fixed point theorem (as we will do in Chapter XIV below).

Similarly, we have from (3′) and the non-negativity of $\bar{y}$

$$\sum_i \sum_j m_{ij}(\bar{y})\bar{x}_i\bar{y}_j \geqq \bar{\Omega} \sum_i \sum_j n_{ij}(\bar{y})\bar{x}_i\bar{y}_j.$$

It is evident that these expressions can hold simultaneously only with equality; hence

$$\sum_i \sum_j m_{ij}(\bar{y})\bar{x}_i\bar{y}_j = \bar{\Omega} \sum_i \sum_j n_{ij}(\bar{y})\bar{x}_i\bar{y}_j. \qquad (2')$$

Remembering the relations between the equilibrium rate of interest $\beta - 1$, the warranted rate of growth $\alpha - 1$ and the natural rate of growth $\rho - 1$, we can easily convert equation (2′) in terms of the net outputs and the augmented labour-inputs into the alternative forms (2) and (4) originally stated in terms of outputs, material inputs, and labour inputs.

We have seen that in equilibrium the rate of growth equals the rate of interest times the Capitalist's propensity to save. Accordingly, we have $\beta = (\rho - c_c)/s_c$. From assumption (III) we find that there is an activity vector x such that $x(B - \beta A) > 0$. Hence, $x(B - \beta A)\bar{y} = \rho x M(\bar{y})\bar{y} > 0$;[1] in words, the Entrepreneur can choose processes to produce net outputs whose total value (evaluated at the equilibrium prices) is positive. On the other hand, it is clear from (1′) that he cannot choose processes which make the total value of the augmented labour inputs less than the value of net outputs. Hence the wage payments are positive at x; therefore the equilibrium real-wage rate $\bar{\Omega}$ is positive.

On the other hand, (3) implies that the 'balanced growth' activities $\bar{x}_1, \ldots, \bar{x}_m$ are 'repeatable'; it follows, therefore, from assumption (Ic) that $\sum_i l_i\bar{x}_i$ is positive. In the state of equilibrium growth the total value of inputs (as it includes the wages $\bar{\Omega} \sum_i l_i\bar{x}_i$) is positive; thus it follows from (2) that the value of the equilibrium outputs is also positive. Hence (5) is fulfilled at $(\bar{\Omega}, \bar{x}, \bar{y})$. We have thus succeeded in finding a Silvery Equilibrium solution to the model.

5. On the basis of the inequalities, (1′) and (3′), of the 'game' between the Market and the Entrepreneur that describe the mechanism of competitive pricing and the technological feasibility of the balanced growth of outputs respectively, it has so far been shown that the equilibrium real-wage rate is fair. We will now examine the fairness of the equilibrium price-wage system and choice of techniques from a somewhat different angle.

We continue to assume that the Capitalist spends a constant proportion of the *normal* profits for consumption and the remainder of the normal profits for expanding production; but the part of actual profits which

[1] The equality follows immediately from the definition of $M(y)$, the budgetary identity of the Entrepreneur, $f(y)y = c_c$, and the equilibrium interest-population-growth-rate relationship, $\beta - 1 = (\rho - 1)/s_c$.

exceeds the normal profits has no effect on the Capitalist's consumption and investment. Consider, as before, a state where the economy is growing at the natural rate of growth $\rho-1$, and fix the interest rate at the level appropriate to it. We then have $\alpha = \rho$ and $\beta-1 = (\rho-1)/s_c$. For any price-set y^* the net output coefficients $m_{ij}(y^*)$ and the augmented labour-input coefficients $n_{ij}(y^*)$ are determined in the same way as we explained before. It is clear that those rates of real wages which satisfy the input-output inequalities

$$\sum_i m_{ij}(y^*)x_i \geqq \Omega \sum_i n_{ij}(y^*)x_i \qquad j = 1, ..., n \qquad (3'')$$

are technically possible; if one of them is not fulfilled, then there is a good whose output falls short of its input. The *greatest technically possible real-wage rate* $\Omega_T(y^*)$ is defined as the maximum of those Ω with which are associated a set of activity levels $(x_1, x_2, ..., x_m)$ fulfilling (3″). As can be easily verified, this definition implies that $\Omega_T(y^*)$ is the fair real-wage rate[1] determined by the game between the Entrepreneur and the Market with the pay-off coefficients $m_{ij}(y^*) - \Omega n_{ij}(y^*)$.

In defining the greatest real-wage rate comparison is made between various states of balanced growth at the natural rate. If we did not make such restrictions, the workers could be paid at a wage rate higher than $\Omega_T(y^*)$. A state of balanced growth at a lower rate of growth would obviously result in a higher wage rate. If unbalanced growth were allowed for, there might be no finite maximum of the real-wage rate.

On the other hand, the *warranted real-wage rate* is defined as follows. Suppose a price-set $y^* = (y_1^*, y_2^*, ..., y_n^*)$ prevails in the market. If the real-wage rate is fixed so low that the value of augmented labour-inputs (evaluated at $y_1^*, ..., y_n^*$) of some production process is less than the value of net outputs of that process, the Capitalist can earn profits at a rate greater than the normal. The Workers can force the Capitalist to accept an increase in the wage rate by resorting to various devices such as strikes. With $y_1^*, ..., y_n^*$, therefore, should be associated a real-wage rate such that

$$\sum_j m_{ij}(y^*)y_j^* \leqq \Omega \sum_j n_{ij}(y^*)y_j^* \qquad i = 1, ..., m; \qquad (1'')$$

and the *smallest* non-negative Ω fulfilling (1″) is called the warranted rate of real-wages (denoted by $\Omega_W(y^*)$).[2] It is clear that if the wage rate is pushed up to a level greater than Ω_W, inequalities (1″) must hold with strict inequality for all processes with positive labour-input coefficients; so that capitalists will find that no process with $l_i > 0$ can yield profits at the normal rate. There is, therefore, no process (with $l_i > 0$) in action,

[1] Or the largest fair wage rate, if we have several fair wage rates.

[2] If $\sum_j m_{ij}(y^*)y_j^* \leqq 0$ for all i, then $\Omega_W(y^*)$ is taken as zero.

and no worker is employed. Thus the 'warranted' rate of real wages is the only rate which will make both the Capitalist and the Worker accept the current price system.

We can now summarize what we are trying to find. We shall find that the Silvery Equilibrium is established if and only if a warranted price system prevails with a real-wage rate which is a maximum among all technically possible rates. It is very easy to get this result if we can confirm that for any given prices $y_1^*, \ldots, y_n^*$, the technically possible maximum rate $\Omega_T(y^*)$ cannot exceed the warranted rate of real wages $\Omega_W(y^*)$.

The Lemma is prove at once in the following way. We obtain from (1″) and (3″)

$$\Omega_T(y^*)\sum_i\sum_j n_{ij}(y^*)x_i y_j^* \leqq \sum_i\sum_j m_{ij}(y^*)x_i y_j^* \leqq \Omega_W(y^*)\sum_i\sum_j n_{ij}(y^*)x_i y_j^*,$$

because x and y^* are non-negative vectors with unit sums. In view of the definition of $n_{ij}(y^*)$ and assumption (IIa, b) in Chapter VI we have

$$\sum_i n_{ij}(y^*)x_i y_j^* = \left\{1+\frac{1}{\rho}(\beta-1)c_c\right\}\sum_i l_i x_i,$$

which is strictly positive by virtue of (Ic)[1] and the fact that $\beta > 1$. Hence, the above inequality leads to the following important relationship:

$$\Omega_W(y^*) \geqq \Omega_T(y^*) \qquad \text{for any } y^* = (y_1^*, \ldots, y_n^*). \tag{7}$$

It is now easy to show that (7) holds with equality at any Silvery Equilibrium. This is intuitively obvious, for if at some prices $y_1^*, \ldots, y_n^*$, the greatest technically possible real-wage rate is less than the warranted rate, then any wage rate which is technically permissible will not be accepted by workers. Equilibrium will not be established so long as $y_1^*, \ldots, y_n^*$ prevail; prices will, therefore, change until the wage-price system finally settles down at an equilibrium structure $(\bar{\Omega}, \bar{y})$ such that

$$\bar{\Omega} = \Omega_W(\bar{y}) = \Omega_T(\bar{y}). \tag{8}$$

More rigorously speaking, we have $\bar{\Omega} \geqq \Omega_W(\bar{y})$ from (1′) and $\bar{\Omega} \leqq \Omega_T(\bar{y})$ from (3′). These relationships yield (8) since we have (7). Conversely, it trivially follows from the definitions of Ω_W and Ω_T that the conditions (1′) and (3′) for a Silvery Equilibrium are satisfied at the point $(\Omega, \bar{y})$ fulfilling (8).[2]

We now find an important efficiency property of the Silvery Equilibrium

[1] Assumption (Ic) is applied to the activities $x_1, \ldots, x_m$ satisfying (3″) since they are repeatable.

[2] A similar equation was found by Gale to be established between the growth and the interest factor in the original von Neumann model. See D. Gale, 'The closed linear model of production', *Linear Inequalities and Related Systems*, ed. H. W. Kuhn and A. W. Tucker (Princeton: Princeton University Press, 1956), pp. 285–330.

Growth. Expressions (7) and (8) imply that, so long as the economy is restricted to grow in balance at the natural rate of growth and the Worker and the Capitalist save constant fractions of their incomes, the Silvery Equilibrium is the only viable state of affairs in which the competition among workers and capitalists can be consistent with the available technology. In any Silvery State the real-wage rate is determined and equal to the greatest technically permissible wage rate with which there can be associated normal long-run supply prices $\bar{y}_1, ..., \bar{y}_n$. In all other states, the wage rate determined by competition is too high to meet the condition of technology unless the economy grows at a rate less than the natural rate, or outputs of various goods grow at different rates.

6. We conclude this chapter by showing that if the aggregate consumption-demand functions fulfil the weak axiom of revealed preference, one and only one equilibrium wage-price system $(\bar{\Omega}, \bar{y})$ corresponds to the silvery equilibrium output path $\bar{x}$. It is evident that the axiom is equivalent, as far as an individual is concerned, to the law of the diminishing marginal rates of substitution, but for the consumers as a whole, it is a stringent condition. If, however, the Capitalist and the Worker are assumed to have the same utility function, so that there is only one type of consumer in the economy, the axiom necessarily follows from the law of the diminishing marginal rates of substitution imposed on the utility function of the Consumer.

Let π and ω be the Capitalist's and the Worker's income respectively. The aggregate consumption-demand for good j, h_j, is defined as follows:

$$h_j(y, \omega, \pi) = \pi f_j(y) + \omega g_j(y).$$

Assume now that two different sets $(\bar{y}, \bar{\omega}, \bar{\pi})$ and (y', ω', π') are associated with the same silvery structure $\bar{x}$. The weak axiom states:

$$\text{If } \sum_j \bar{h}_j y_j' \leqq \sum_j h_j' y_j', \text{ then } \sum_j \bar{h}_j \bar{y}_j < \sum_j h_j' \bar{y}_j,$$

where $\bar{h}_j = h_j(\bar{y}, \bar{\omega}, \bar{\pi})$ and $h_j' = h_j(y', \omega', \pi')$.

The argument continues in exactly the same way as that in Chapter I where we found a similar result. Suppose the first inequality of the axiom holds, then the second inequality follows from the hypothesis. On the other hand, if the first inequality does not hold, then $\sum_j \bar{h}_j y_j' > \sum_j h_j' y_j'$, which reduces to the second inequality, by changing (y', ω', π') into $(\bar{y}, \bar{\omega}, \bar{\pi})$ and vice versa. Hence, in any case we have the second inequality. As h_j' is the equilibrium consumption-demand for good j associated with $\bar{x}$, it follows from (3) that for all j

$$\sum b_{ij}\bar{x}_i - \rho \sum_i a_{ij}\bar{x}_i \geqq h_j'.$$

Therefore, taking into account the second inequality of the axiom just established, we have

$$\sum_i \sum_j b_{ij}\bar{x}_i \bar{y}_j - \rho \sum_i \sum_j a_{ij}\bar{x}_i \bar{y}_j \geqq \sum_j h_j' \bar{y}_j > \sum_j \bar{h}_j \bar{y}_j.$$

On the other hand, (4) states that the extreme left-hand side equals the extreme right-hand side, since $\bar{h}_1, \ldots, \bar{h}_n$ are equilibrium consumption demands, a contradiction. Thus there corresponds a unique set $(\bar{y}, \bar{\omega}, \bar{\pi})$ of prices, wages, and profits to a given silvery activity structure $\bar{x}$; from this it at once follows that the equilibrium wage rate $\bar{\Omega}$ is also uniquely determined.

VIII

EQUILIBRIUM GROWTH (II) HICKS–MALINVAUD TRAJECTORIES

1. In spite of the elegance of the theory of balanced growth, it must be recognized that neither a competitive equilibrium over time nor a succession of temporary equilibria through time generates a monotonic expansion in the economy, unless it is endowed with the stocks of goods and the labour force exactly in the balanced growth proportions. When the historically given initial point is off the balanced growth path, a path produced by the competitive mechanism would regularly or irregularly wind through the economic field. The rhythm is not monotonic; nevertheless, it is still equilibrated as no dissonance is heard throughout the whole process of development.

Such paths, along which the competitive or 'neo-classical' (as we may call it) system develops from the given historical point, are classified according to the numbers of periods involved. If an equilibrium over T periods is established in an economy whose residents can correctly foresee events in those periods, then that equilibrium is said to be of order T. It is evident that this classification is an extension of the Marshallian tripartite division into the temporary, the short period and the long period equilibrium. The Temporary Equilibrium that rules within any single period is an equilibrium of order 1, while at the other extreme there is the Perfect Equilibrium over Time (or the equilibrium of infinite order) that will occur when prices in any period in the future (as well as tastes, resources and technology in the future) are correctly predicted. As was observed by Malinvaud and others and will in the next chapter be reconfirmed, in the present von Neumann-like model a 'Pareto optimality' of order T is realized along a competitive equilibrium path of the same order.[1] The economy can, therefore, work for ever in an optimum way with perfect efficiency if it travels along the path of competitive equilibrium of infinite order. It would supply a useful standard of reference in the theory of growth and could be compared with the Silvery Equilibrium path (a balanced growth path) discussed in the previous chapter—the other standard of reference. The comparison is the subject matter of one of the later chapters; we devote the present and the next chapter to

[1] See, for example, E. Malinvaud, 'Capital accumulation and efficient allocation of resources', *Econometrica*, Vol. XXI (1953), pp. 233–68.

establishing, respectively, the existence and optimality of the Competitive Equilibrium paths of various orders.

We take the temporary equilibrium first and will then turn to the more general case of equilibrium of order T and finally to the perfect equilibrium over time that is approached as the limit as T tends to infinity. It is clear that the model of competitive equilibrium is, in many respects, similar to the model of balanced growth. There are, however, two relationships which the former should take into explicit account, whereas the latter has no room for them.

The balanced growth analysis, which concentrates attention upon a steady state of proportional growth at constant prices, implicitly assumes that people's expectations of future prices are 'static', that is to say, prices are expected to remain unchanged for ever. In competitive equilibrium analysis, on the other hand, this restrictive assumption is replaced by the more general one that the price of a good j expected to prevail in a specific period t in the future depends on current prices of various goods and labour in addition to t. We then have the relation

$$P_j(t) = \psi_{jt}(P_1(0), ..., P_n(0), w(0))$$

for each good available in the future, and we call it the expectation function. In the Temporary Equilibrium Analysis which we first take up, entrepreneurs' prospects are confined to one period; the relevant expectation functions are only those for $t = 1$. Accordingly, we will eliminate, for the sake of simplicity, the second subscript, $t = 1$, applied to ψ, and write

$$P_j(1) = \psi_j(P_1(0), ..., P_n(0), w(0)),$$

or more simply, write ψ_j for $P_j(1)$.

Techniques of production are now evaluated at current prices and expected prices. Processes will be selected so as to maximize the expected profits, i.e. expected value of output *minus* current costs including interest charges. So long as profits are positive, the prices of the factors of production will be bidded up, and we obtain, in the state of equilibrium, the familiar inequalities

$$\sum_j b_{ij}\psi_j \leqq \beta(\sum_j a_{ij}P_j + l_i w), \qquad i = 1, ..., m,$$

or

$$\sum_j b_{ij}\psi_j z \leqq \sum_j a_{ij}P_j + l_i w, \qquad i = 1, ..., m, \tag{1}$$

where z is the reciprocal of β ($\beta = 1+$the rate of interest). The former is an obvious variant of (VI. 1) and the latter is a restatement of the former. For the sake of simplicity, the script 0 denoting the fact that the relevant variables belong to the current period is completely deleted from these inequalities.

The other relationship to be spotlighted is the equalization of aggregate investment to aggregate savings which was eliminated from the balanced growth analysis as a redundant equation following from the rest of the inequalities of the model. Investment is the increment in the value of the stocks of goods during the current period. The stocks of good j available at the end and the beginning of the current period 0 are

$$b_j = \sum_i b_{ij} q_i$$

and

$$b_{j,-1} = \sum_i b_{ij} q_{i,-1},$$

respectively, where q_i and $q_{i,-1}$ are the levels of activity of the ith process in the current and the previous period, respectively. $b_1, ..., b_n$ are evaluated at prices $\psi_1, ..., \psi_n$, which are expected to prevail in period 1, and are then discounted by the factor β. $b_{1,-1}, ..., b_{n,-1}$ would similarly be evaluated if they were kept intact until the end of the period. The increment $\sum_j (b_j - b_{j,-1})\psi_j z$ thus obtained, together with the appreciation of the stocks, $b_{1,-1}, ..., b_{n,-1}$, due to price changes during the current period, gives the investment; that is to say,

$$\text{investment} = \sum_j (b_j - b_{j,-1})\psi_j z + \sum_j b_{j,-1}(\psi_j z - \psi_{j,-1} z_{-1}),$$

where $\psi_{j,-1}$ is the price of good j that was expected in the previous period to prevail in the current period, and z_{-1} is the reciprocal of 1 *plus* the rate of interest in the previous period. In view of the definitions of b_j and $b_{j,-1}$ above, we have in matrix notation

$$\text{investment} = qB\psi z - q_{-1}B\psi_{-1}z_{-1}, \tag{2}$$

where q is the m-dimensional row vector with elements q_i, while ψ is the n-dimensional column vector with elements ψ_j; similarly for q_{-1} and ψ_{-1}.

On the other hand, aggregate savings are the difference between income and consumption. The aggregate income consists of wages and profits. The total wages which the labour force N expects to earn in period 0 will amount to wN in the state of full employment, while the profits accruing in period 0 to the capitalists from their activities in the previous period amount to

$$q_{-1}BP - q_{-1}AP_{-1} - q_{-1}Lw_{-1}.$$

Subtracting the workers' and the capitalists' consumption from their income, we have

$$\text{savings} = wN + q_{-1}(BP - AP_{-1} - Lw_{-1}) - (e+d)P, \tag{3}$$

where e and d stand, respectively, for the workers' and the capitalists' consumption vectors (row vectors) in the current period.

For there to be a temporary equilibrium in period 0 the total demand (industrial and personal demands) for each good must not exceed its supply and a similar relationship must hold for labour. These $n+1$ conditions for goods and labour are put in vector notation as follows:

$$q_{-1}B \geqq qA+e+d, \tag{4}$$

$$N \geqq qL. \tag{5}$$

The final relationship necessary to complete the model is the Keynesian savings-investment inequality which requires that investment should be at least as high as savings, because otherwise the economy would be drawn into the quicksand of a depression; hence,

$$\text{investment} \geqq \text{savings}. \tag{6}$$

It is to be remembered that among the (in-)equalities (1)–(6) making up the system of temporary equilibrium equations (2), (3), and (6) did not appear in the balanced growth model in Chapters VI and VII. (6) was dispensed with as it holds with equality once the other inequalities hold in the Silvery Equilibrium state. To observe this fact and to facilitate the proof of the existence of a temporary equilibrium, we shall begin by transforming the system into an equivalent form in terms of 'profits' and 'excess demands'.

Let us define the profits from process i as the excess of the discounted expected value of outputs of process i over the value of goods and labour used in production. When i operates at unit intensity, profits are given as

$$E_i = \sum_j b_{ij}\psi_j z - \sum_j a_{ij}P_j - l_i w. \tag{7}$$

The excess demand for good j is defined as the excess of the demand for good j over its supply; and similarly for labour. We have

$$F_j = \sum_i q_i a_{ij} + e_j + d_j - \sum_i q_{i,-1} b_{ij}, \tag{8}$$

$$G = \sum_i q_i l_i - N. \tag{9}$$

Finally, a formal definition of excess savings as

$$H = \text{savings–investment} \tag{10}$$

will be useful in the following argument.

From the definitions of investment and savings (2) and (3), and the assumption that the economy at any past moment was in temporary equilibrium (i.e., the total expected value of outputs (discounted) equalled the total value of inputs in the previous period,[1]) we obtain the following

[1] That is,

$$q_{-1}B\psi_{-1}z_{-1} = q_{-1}AP_{-1} + q_{-1}Lw_{-1}.$$

identity that may be referred to as 'Walras' law':

$$\sum_i q_i E_i + \sum_j F_j P_j + Gw + H \equiv 0. \tag{11}$$

H must be zero (i.e. investment must equal savings) in Silvery Equilibrium, because the Rule of Profitability and the Rule of Free Goods obtains, which apply to that state imply the following three equations:

$$\text{(i) } \sum_i q_i E_i = 0, \qquad \text{(ii) } \sum_j F_j P_j = 0, \qquad \text{(iii) } Gw = 0.$$

Equation (i) holds because unprofitable processes are not used (the Rule of Profitability), while (ii) and (iii) hold because goods and labour are free when they are excessively supplied (the Rule of Free Goods).

2. In the Balanced Growth Approach we are able to shut out the equality between investment and savings behind the screen, when the two neo-classical rules regarding profitability and pricing are brought before the foot-lights. On the other hand, in the Temporary Equilibrium Approach we derive the latter from the former by assuming there is inequality (6) between savings and investment. As E_i, F_j, and G are all non-positive in temporary equilibrium and activity levels q_i, prices P_j, and the wage rate w are non-negative, we have

$$\text{(i}'\text{) } \sum_i q_i E_i \leqq 0, \qquad \text{(ii}'\text{) } \sum_j F_j P_j \leqq 0, \qquad \text{(iii}'\text{) } Gw \leqq 0.$$

Together with these, the identity (11) requires that H be non-negative. However, from (6) we find the 'excess supply of savings' H ought to be non-positive. Therefore, H vanishes in temporary equilibrium. Once savings equal investment, it immediately follows from Walras' law that excess profits and excess demands for goods and labour cancel out. This last fact implies that (i′), (ii′), and (iii′) must hold with equality; that is to say, unprofitable processes are not used, and goods and labour in excess supply are free—the neo-classical rules.[1]

Before we proceed to the rigorous proof of the existence of a temporary equilibrium, let us count inequalities and unknown variables included in the system. First of all, we have subsystem (1) consisting of m inequalities, subsystem (4) consisting of n inequalities, equations (2) and (3), and inequalities (5) and (6). We also have identity (11).

Next, unknowns are m activity levels q_i, n prices P_j, the wage rate w, the discount factor z, investment, and savings. The other variables to be

[1] Note that this demonstration of equivalence of the savings-investment equality to the neo-classical rules will not be valid when the full employment of labour cannot be automatically established. In case of an equilibrium attended by possible unemployment the equality of investment to savings does not imply neo-classical flexibility of the wage rate. It is well-known that Keynes could have developed the theory of unemployment as soon as he denied the rule for labour.

found in the system are expected prices ψ_j, lagged expected prices $\psi_{j,-1}$, the lagged discount factor z_{-1}, lagged activity levels $q_{i,-1}$, lagged prices $P_{j,-1}$, the lagged wage rate w_{-1}, workers' and capitalists' consumption demands e_j and d_j, and the available labour force N. When we confine ourselves to the determination of temporary equilibrium and not the dynamic workings of the system, expected prices are treated as variables depending on current prices and the current wage rate, and all lagged variables as parameters or historically given constants. The supply of labour is assumed, in this part of the book, to be an exogenous variable, although we may (as we will in fact do in Part IV) treat it as a factor determined within the system by introducing a 'production' function for the labour force. Finally, it is noticed that consumption demands are not independent variables but depend upon current prices and the workers' and the capitalists' income; the profits from activities in the previous period are distributed among workers and capitalists in proportion to their ownership of the capital accumulated from their past savings, so that they commence the 'game' with inherited handicaps.

The number of independent variables, $m+n+4$, thus obtained equals the number of (in-)equalities. Since identity (11) holds for these variables, our temporary equilibrium model, like Walras' system of equations, has one degree of freedom. For the perfect determination of temporary equilibrium values of the unknowns, one more condition needs to be added. We complete the model by using the following two-step approach: we first treat one of the unknowns as if it is given and determine the temporary equilibrium values of the remaining unknowns; we shall then append one equation to fix the value of the unknown left for a later examination.

It is to be remembered that we are now confronted with a problem very similar to that which the classical economists have met when they fix the absolute level of prices. In models like ours in which lagged price variables appear, prices must be viewed from two points of views, intratemporal and intertemporal. A price must, on the one hand, be examined in relationship to other contemporary prices, and, on the other, in relationship to prices at a different point of time. To distinguish these two aspects from each other, we convert our price variables into new variables defined as[1]

$$p_j = P_j/\sum_k P_k, \qquad v = w/\sum_k P_k$$

and

$$p_{j,-1} = P_{j,-1}/\sum_k P_{k,-1}, \qquad v_{-1} = w_{-1}/\sum_k P_{k,-1}.$$

[1] The symbol v representing the real-wage rate should not be confused with the v in the last chapter that was used for designating the value of the game.

Evidently, $p_1, \ldots, p_n$ describe the intratemporal relation between current prices, while τ defined as

$$\tau = \sum_k P_{k,-1} / \sum_k P_k$$

gives the intertemporal relationship.

Let us, for the sake of simplicity, assume throughout the rest of this chapter that the expectation functions are homogeneous of degree one, i.e., when all current prices and the current wage rate change proportionately, entrepreneurs' expected prices are induced to change in the same proportion. We can then regard the 'normalized expected prices', $\psi_j / \sum_k P_k$, as functions of normalized current prices and wage rate; we write

$$\psi_j / \sum_k P_k = \phi_j(p_1, \ldots, p_n, v) \qquad j = 1, \ldots, n.$$

It is now easily verified that the discounted profits, the excess demands and the excess savings can be put in the following normalized forms:

$$E_i = \sum_j b_{ij}\phi_j z - \sum_j a_{ij} p_j - l_i v, \tag{7'}$$

$$F_j = \sum_i q_i a_{ij} + e_j + d_j - \sum_i q_{i,-1} b_{ij}, \tag{8'}$$

$$G = \sum_i q_i l_i - N, \tag{9'}$$

$$H = \{Nv + \sum_i \sum_j q_{i,-1} b_{ij} p_j - \sum_i q_{i,-1}(\sum_j a_{ij} p_{j,-1} + l_i v_{-1})\tau \tag{10'}$$
$$- \sum_j (e_j + d_j) p_j\} - \{\sum_i \sum_j q_i b_{ij} \phi_j z - \sum_i \sum_j q_{i,-1} b_{ij} \phi_{j,-1} z_{-1} \tau\}.$$

It is noted that the same symbols, E_i, F_j, etc., as those having so far represented the *non-normalized* discounted profits, etc. are now used to signify the *normalized* ones, since no confusion is expected. It is also noted that consumption demands, e_j and d_j, that appear in the expressions of F_j and H depend not only on normalized prices but also on normalized wages Nv, normalized lagged profits,

$$\sum_i \sum_j q_{i,-1} b_{ij} p_j - \sum_i q_{i,-1}(\sum_j a_{ij} p_{j,-1} + l_i v_{-1})\tau,$$

and their distribution among individuals. Finally, the Walras' law can be put in the normalized form,

$$\sum_i q_i E_i + \sum_j F_j p_j + Gv + H = 0. \tag{11'}$$

3. We are now ready to steam out of the harbour. Let us embark on a long logical journey to search for an equilibrium—a still uncharted 'fixed point'. In finding an economic state such that

$$E_i \leqq 0, \quad F_j \leqq 0, \quad G \leqq 0, \quad H \leqq 0, \quad \text{for all } i \text{ and } j, \tag{12}$$

we treat all q_i, p_j, v, and z as unknowns to be determined, while the lagged values of them, as well as the initial distribution of the labour force and profits among households, are given as historical data. The determination of the intertemporal price ratio τ is a subject in section 5 below; but, as far as this section is concerned, it is regarded as if it had already been given somewhere in a more extensive system.

From the history of economic analysis we know that pseudo- (or quasi-) economic processes, which are not intended to give a precise description of the actual movement in the market but can still simulate it more or less, have often been devised with the purpose of groping towards a solution of the equations (inequalities) for equilibrium. The 'tâtonnement' in the Walrasian economics, the 'abstract economy' by Arrow and Debreu, and the 'game' in the previous chapter are such examples.[1] Similarly, in the following we imagine, for the same purpose, a pseudo-economy consisting of m entrepreneurs each managing a production process and a custodian of the market whose task is to find prices of goods and services in the market.

It is true that prices in the actual world are sensitive to excess supply as well as to excess demand. It is also true that it is unlikely that some prices have exactly the same sensitivities on either side of an equilibrium; in fact, as Keynes emphasized, the money-wage rate will not fall when there is an excess supply of labour, although it rises when there is an excess demand. In the following argument we shall assume that responses of the entrepreneurs and the custodian are entirely asymmetric. We define

$$E_i^* = \max\,(E,0),\ F_j^* = \max\,(F,0),\ G = \max\,(G,0),\ H = \max(H,0),$$

where max (a, b) means the larger of the numbers, a and b, in the parentheses. As the entrepreneurs and the custodian do not react to negative E_i, F_j, G, and H at all, their responses can be described in terms of the modulated functions, E_i^*, F_j^*, G^*, and H^*.

In more detail we assume that the custodian raises the *non-normalized* price P_j when excess demand for good j, F_j, is positive, whereas he does not change P_j at all when F_j is negative. Thus the custodian manipulates P_j in response to F_j^*. This means that the *normalized* price p_j defined as $P_j/\sum_k P_k$ would respond not only to F_j^* (in a positive way) but also to

[1] Cf. K. J. Arrow and G. Debreu, 'Existence of an equilibrium for a competitive economy', *Econometrica*, Vol. XXII (1954), pp. 265–90.

other F_k^*s ($k \neq j$) (in a negative way). From among those fulfilling the requirements we may choose a response function of the form:

$$\pi_j = \frac{1}{1+\sum_k F_k^*}(p_j+F_j^*), \qquad j = 1, ..., n,$$

where π_j stands for the normalized price of good j after the response. It is easily seen from the formula that π_j is greater than p_j if F_j^* is positive, but less than it if some of the other F_k^*s are positive.[1] (Note that even though F_j^* appears in the denominator too, an increase in F_j^* gives rise to an increase in π_j since p_j is less than unity.)

Next, when the real-wage rate is set at a very high level, at $\bar{\bar{v}}$ say, there would be, regardless of prices of goods, at least one good for which the workers' demand becomes so great that it exceeds the initial availability of that good; hence it is evident that $\bar{\bar{v}}$ cannot be an equilibrium rate. Thus the real-wage rate, if it is to be an equilibrium rate, is required, first of all, to be less than $\bar{\bar{v}}$. On the other hand, it is obvious from its definition that the real-wage rate increases when the money-wage rate rises, while it diminishes when prices of goods rise. The money-wage rate and the non-normalized prices are, in turn, assumed to respond to the modulated excess demand functions G^* and F_j^*s, respectively. A class of response functions fulfilling all these requirements includes the formula,

$$\nu = \frac{\bar{\bar{v}}}{\bar{\bar{v}}+\sum_k F_k^*+G^*}(v+G^*),$$

stating that the responses mentioned above shift the real-wage rate from v to ν.

Thirdly, the rate of interest is assumed to adjust so as to equate savings and investment. The rate of interest will decrease (hence z, i.e. the reciprocal of 1+the rate of interest, will increase) when savings exceed investment, whereas no effect on the interest rate is noticed in the opposite situation because of the (assumed) absence of the symmetry of the response. Moreover, it is assumed that the custodian is 'conservative' or 'moderate' in altering the rate of interest in the sense that he will reduce it less, when he is confronted with excess demands for goods so that he raises their non-normalized prices, than in other situations. (This means that the custodian tends to raise the interest rate when non-normalized prices of goods rise and there are no excess savings.) Thus H^* is a positive factor

[1] It would be interesting to see that our response equation, though it is not put in a differential form, is equivalent to the so-called Brown-von Neumann differential equation, $dp_j/dt = F_j^*(p) - \{\sum_k F_k^*(p)\}p_j$, which was devised for solving 'games'. See H. Nikaido, 'Stability of equilibrium by the Brown–von Neumann differential equation', *Econometrica*, Vol. XXVII (1959), pp. 654–71.

and the F_j^*s are negative factors in the adjustment of z. We may take them as if they were affecting z according to the following formula,

$$\zeta = \frac{\bar{\bar{z}}}{\bar{\bar{z}}+\sum_k F_k^*+H^*}(z+H^*),$$

where ζ is the value of z after the response, and $\bar{\bar{z}}$ is a large enough number to bring about that inequality

$$\bar{\bar{z}}\sum_j b_{ij}\phi_j > \sum_j a_{ij}p_j+l_i v$$

is satisfied for at least one process i, no matter how the prices and the real-wage rate are fixed. In the following we assume that the b_{ij}s are big enough and expectations are good enough for $\bar{\bar{z}}$ to be less than one. ζ does not exceed $\bar{\bar{z}}$ as long as z does not.

Let us now turn from the custodian's to the entrepreneurs' responses. Each process i uses some inputs, i.e., goods produced in the preceding period or labour or probably both. $\bar{\bar{q}}_i$ is defined as a number which is greater than the smallest among $\sum_k b_{k1}q_{k,-1}/a_{i1}$, ..., $\sum_k b_{kn}q_{k,-1}/a_{in}$ and N/l_i. When the denominators vanish, they are regarded as plus infinity. As at least one of a_{i1}, ..., a_{in} and l_i does not vanish, $\bar{\bar{q}}_i$ is well defined. It is then seen that some of the inequalities

$$\bar{\bar{q}}_i a_{ij} > \sum_k b_{kj}q_{k,-1}, \qquad \bar{\bar{q}}_i l_i > N, \qquad j = 1, ..., n$$

are valid; so that operation of process i at intensity $\bar{\bar{q}}_i$ is not feasible. It is now assumed that entrepreneurs are sensitive to discounted profits. Process i would tend to be operated more intensively, whenever positive profits are expected from that process. On the same assumptions of 'asymmetric' and 'moderate' reactions that we have made for the custodian, we may think of entrepreneurs behaving according to the formula,

$$\theta_i = \frac{\bar{\bar{q}}_i}{\bar{\bar{q}}_i+\sum_k F_k^*+E_i^*}(q_i+E_i^*) \qquad i = 1, ..., m.$$

The 'respondent' θ_i does not exceed the barrier $\bar{\bar{q}}_i$ unless the 'petitioner' q_i does. It is noted that F_k^*s appear in the denominator of the response function because entrepreneurs are assumed to be moderate with respect to increases in non-normalized prices. This moderation of entrepreneurs may be justified since, if they are conscious of inflation, they will lower the intensity of production when non-normalized prices rise. Any way, it is an assumption which makes our work easier.

4. Let us consider a set R of all possible economic states (q, p, v, z) such that

$$\text{(i) } \bar{\bar{q}}_i \geqq q_i \geqq 0, \qquad \text{(ii) } p_j \geqq 0, \quad \sum_j p_j = 1,$$

$$\text{(iii) } \bar{\bar{v}} \geqq v \geqq 0, \qquad \text{(iv) } \bar{\bar{z}} \geqq z \geqq 0.$$

The above $m+n+2$ response functions convert a state (q, p, v, z) in R into another state $(\theta, \pi, \nu, \zeta)$. The functions are constructed in such a way that the four properties in terms of which R is defined are preserved by the conversion; that is to say, if (q, p, v, z) belongs to R, then the respondent $(\theta, \pi, \nu, \zeta)$ is also an element of R. We thus have a transformation of R into itself. Furthermore, since the denominators of the response functions do not vanish anywhere, the continuity of the transformation follows from the continuity of the modulated profit and excess demand functions, E_i^*, F_j^*, etc. All the requirements for applying the Brouwer fixed-point theorem are realized;[1] so that there exists a fixed point $(\bar{q}, \bar{p}, \bar{v}, \bar{z})$ that is not changed by the transformation. $(\bar{q}, \bar{p}, \bar{v}, \bar{z})$ is transformed onto itself; that is, $(\bar{q}, \bar{p}, \bar{v}, \bar{z}) = (\bar{\theta}, \bar{\pi}, \bar{\nu}, \bar{\zeta})$. Hence we have

$$\begin{aligned}
\bar{q}_i &= \frac{\bar{\bar{q}}_i}{\bar{\bar{q}}_i + \sum_k \bar{F}_k^* + \bar{E}_i^*}(\bar{q}_i + \bar{E}_i^*), \qquad i = 1, \ldots, m, \\
\bar{p}_j &= \frac{1}{1 + \sum_k \bar{F}_k^*}(\bar{p}_j + \bar{F}_j^*), \qquad j = 1, \ldots, n, \\
\bar{v} &= \frac{\bar{\bar{v}}}{\bar{\bar{v}} + \sum_k \bar{F}_k^* + \bar{G}^*}(\bar{v} + \bar{G}^*), \\
\bar{z} &= \frac{\bar{\bar{z}}}{\bar{\bar{z}} + \sum_k \bar{G}_k^* + \bar{H}^*}(\bar{z} + \bar{H}^*),
\end{aligned} \tag{13}$$

where the single bar over any symbol signifies its evaluation at the fixed point.

It is important to observe that all E_i^*, F_j^*, G^*, and H^* vanish at any fixed point, because if some of them were positive, then the point could not be an equilibrium point. In order to prove that a temporary equilibrium is established at a fixed point, we assume the contrary. Suppose that one of the excess demands F_j $(j = 1, \ldots, n)$ is positive at the fixed point;

[1] Brouwer's theorem asserts that if R is a non-empty, compact, convex set in a (multi-dimensional) Euclidean space and F is a continuous function from R into R, then F has a fixed point, $x = F(x)$, in R.

then we have $\sum_k F_k^* > 0$ in (13). The first equation of (13) can, accordingly, be put in the form

$$\bar{q}_i = \frac{\bar{q}_i \bar{E}_i^*}{\sum_k \bar{F}_k^* + \bar{E}_i^*}.$$

It is then evident that $\bar{q}_i$ is zero if $\bar{E}_i^*$ is zero, and positive otherwise. This means that $\bar{q}_i \bar{E}_i$ is zero if $\bar{E}_i \leqq 0$, and positive if $\bar{E}_i > 0$. In exactly the same way, each $\bar{F}_j \bar{p}_j$ ($j = 1, \ldots, n$) and $\bar{G}\bar{v}$ are non-negative in all circumstances, and in particular they are positive if the corresponding $\bar{F}_j$ or $\bar{G}$ is positive. As one of $\bar{F}_j$s is positive by hypothesis, these non-negativities imply the following strict positivity:

$$\sum_i \bar{q}_i \bar{E}_i + \sum_j \bar{F}_j \bar{p}_j + \bar{G}\bar{v} > 0,$$

which, together with Walras' law (11′), implies that $\bar{H} < 0$ which further implies $\bar{z} = 0$ from the last equation of (13).

On the other hand, the definition of excess savings (10′) leads to

$$\text{(normalized) savings} + \sum_i \sum_j q_{i,-1} b_{ij} \phi_{j,-1} z_{-1} \pi < 0$$

when $\bar{H} < 0$ and $\bar{z} = 0$. Hence savings must be negative at the fixed point. As it is assumed that the workers' and the capitalists' marginal propensity to consume can never exceed unity, we have negative savings only when income from the ownership of capital is negative. We also assume, on the other hand, that capitalists with negative incomes would not consume any goods at all. The above inequality is therefore reduced to

$$\text{Capitalists' income} + \text{Workers' income} - \text{Workers' consumption}$$
$$+ \sum_i \sum_j q_{i,-1} b_{ij} \phi_{j,-1} z_{-1} \tau < 0.$$

It is evident that the total profits are distributed among capitalists and workers in proportion to their ownership of capital; so the capitalists receive a fraction of the total profits, or a fraction of the difference between the total value of outputs and the total value of inputs. The total value of inputs equals the *discounted* expected value of outputs, $\sum_i \sum_j q_{i,-1} b_{ij} \phi_{j,-1} z_{-1} \tau$, in the last period, as was assumed earlier in the footnote on p. 136. Taking these into account, we find that the above inequality can be written as

$$\text{a fraction of total output} + \text{a fraction of total input}$$
$$+ \text{Workers' income} - \text{Workers' consumption} < 0. \tag{14}$$

Hence the workers must consume more than their income which is impossible when their marginal propensity is always less than (or equal to) unity. Hence $\bar{F}_j$ should not be positive for any j.

As soon as we have $\sum_k \bar{F}_k^* = 0$, we obtain from (13)

$$\begin{aligned} &\text{(a)}\ \bar{q}_i = \bar{\bar{q}}_i && \text{if } \bar{E}_i^* > 0, \\ &\text{(b)}\ \bar{v} = \bar{\bar{v}} && \text{if } \bar{G}^* > 0, \\ &\text{(c)}\ \bar{z} = \bar{\bar{z}} && \text{if } \bar{H}^* > 0. \end{aligned}$$

These properties imply the equilibrium conditions, $\bar{E}_i \leqq 0$, $\bar{G} \leqq 0$, and $\bar{H} \leqq 0$. Let us now recall that $\bar{\bar{v}}$ is taken very large so that, at $\bar{\bar{v}}$, excess demand for at least one good is positive. We then find that in order for excess demand for each good to be non-positive as is required by $\sum_k \bar{F}_k^* = 0$, $\bar{v}$ must be less than the upper bound $\bar{\bar{v}}$. Hence, it follows from (b) that the excess demand for labour should not be positive. Next non-positive excess demands for goods and labour imply that, for all i, $\bar{q}_i$ is less than $\bar{\bar{q}}_i$; because $\bar{\bar{q}}_i$s are defined such that if $\bar{q}_i = \bar{\bar{q}}_i$ for some i, then excess demand for some good or excess demand for labour is positive; a contradiction. Hence, it follows from (a) that no process can yield positive profits. Finally, $\bar{\bar{z}}$ is defined such that some process gains positive profits at $\bar{\bar{z}}$. Clearly, the non-positivity of profits just established contradicts the equality $\bar{z} = \bar{\bar{z}}$; in view of property (c), we obtain the final equilibrium condition that savings must not exceed investment.

5. We have verified our conjecture that any fixed point $(\bar{q}, \bar{p}, \bar{v}, \bar{z})$ gives an equilibrium. Before we also saw that at any equilibrium point the rule of competitive pricing and the rule of general equality of the rates of profit must prevail and savings must equal investment (i.e. $\bar{H} = 0$). Furthermore, the equilibrium price vector $\bar{p}$ is non-negative and non-zero, as it is normalized so that the sum of its elements is unity. The remaining properties we will now establish are the non-singularity of $\bar{z}$ (that prevents the equilibrium rate of interest from getting infinite) and the non-triviality of the intensity vector (implying that some production activities take place in any temporary equilibrium).

Let us first prove the non-singularity of $\bar{z}$. For this purpose we introduce the assumption that all goods are available at the beginning of the period, i.e.,

$$\sum_i q_{i,-1} b_{ij} > 0 \qquad \text{for all } j = 1, \ldots, n.$$

At first sight this might be considered very restrictive; in fact, it is a stringent and unrealistic assumption if it is an addition to the more popular assumption that the list of goods remains unchanged through time. However, this last assumption is not of great importance to the Temporary Equilibrium Approach, although it is fundamental to the Balanced Growth Approach. Alternatively we may assume that the catalogue of goods may (and will) change from period to period. In each period, only those goods which are available at the beginning of that period can be traded, so that the catalogue for the present period (say) need not contain the goods which are no longer used in the economy (rickshaws in Japan, mammoth meat, etc.) as well as the goods which have never been available but are expected to be in the future (*gan-kerollin*—a miraculously efficacious medicine for cancer, estates on the moon, etc.).[1]

Equipped with this assumption, we can now easily show that $\bar{z}$ cannot be zero. If $\bar{z}$ vanished, we could obtain from $\bar{H} = 0$, an equation which is similar to (14) except for having '=' in place of '<'. The total value of outputs available at the beginning of the period is the sum $\sum_i q_{i,-1}b_{ij}$ multiplied by p_j ($j = 1, ..., n$), which is positive by the assumption just made. We then find that the workers' income is less than their consumption—a contradiction to the fact that the workers' propensity to consume cannot exceed unity. Because of the assumption $\bar{\bar{z}} < 1$, we now obtain $0 < \bar{z} < 1$, which implies that the rate of interest is positive and finite.

Finally, let us consider the non-triviality of the equilibrium activities. Suppose the contrary, namely, that $\bar{q}_i$s are zero for all $i = 1, ..., n$. Then there is no industrial demand for goods, and no demand for labour. All workers will be unemployed, so that they have no income to spend on consumption. On the other hand, we find from (2) that investment is negative when all $\bar{q}_i$s vanish, and, therefore, savings must be so too. Endowed with the assumed properties of the savings function, negative savings imply negative income for the capitalists, which, in turn, implies that there is no capitalists' consumption of goods. We now find no demand for goods at all. Hence every good is free, that is to say, every price is zero. This clearly contradicts the fact that the sum of $\bar{p}_j$s is one. Therefore, the null hypothesis that $\bar{q}_i$s are zero for all i is rejected, and the non-triviality of the activities is established.

6. We have so far treated the intertemporal price ratio $\tau(= \sum_k P_{k,-1}/\sum_k P_k)$ as a parameter or a variable constant. To any given positive value of it there corresponds a temporary equilibrium. A change in τ will give rise to a shift of the equilibrium point. We shall be left with many 'equilibria' unless the value of τ is specified. The second step of the existence proof is to select among such equilibria a true one at which prices are equilibrated not only in relation to other contemporary variables (activity levels and others) but also in their intertemporal aspect, i.e., in relation to the level of prices in the past period. Thus, instead of the *ex ante* equilibrium conditions

[1] Corresponding to this qualification for goods to be put on the list of the goods, we eliminate from the catalogue of processes for a period those processes which use some goods unavailable in that period.

examined in the last section, an *ex post* condition now appears before the footlights.

Considering the definition of excess savings H given in (10′), we find that the *ex ante* equilibrium condition, savings = investment, can be put in the form,

$$\sum_j b_{j,-1}\phi_{j,-1}\bar{z}_{-1}\,\tau + \text{savings in period } 0 = \sum_j b_j\phi_j\bar{z},$$

where $b_{j,-1} = \sum_i \bar{q}_{i,-1}b_{ij}$ and $b_j = \sum_i \bar{q}_i b_{ij}$. The stocks of goods which will be available at the end of period 0 are expected, at the beginning of that period, to have a capitalized (or discounted) value,[1] $\sum_j b_j\phi_j\bar{z}$, while the corresponding value in period -1 is $\sum_j b_{j,-1}\phi_{j,-1}\bar{z}_{-1}$ that appears on the left-hand side of the above equation. The above *ex ante* condition for equilibrium is also required to hold in period -1, because we conceive the economic system as one which is always in temporary equilibrium. We have

$$\sum_j b_{j,-2}\phi_{j,-2}\bar{z}_{-2}\,\tau_{-1} + \text{savings in the last period} = \sum_j b_{j,-1}\phi_{j,-1}\bar{z}_{-1}. \tag{15}$$

This savings-investment condition must hold in the *ex post* sense as well. The stocks of goods are retrospectively evaluated at their actual prices $\bar{p}_j$ but not, of course, at the expected prices ϕ_j. The *ex post* equation between savings and investment is then written as

$$\sum_j b_{j,-2}\bar{p}_{j,-1}\bar{z}_{-2} + \text{savings in the last period} = \sum_j b_{j,-1}\bar{p}_j\bar{z}_{-1}/\tau. \tag{16}$$

The *ex ante* and *ex post* valuations of the stocks of goods are consistent if the expectations of prices are correct in the macroscopic sense; we then see that in periods -1 and -2 the *ex ante* total value of the stocks evaluated at their expected prices is equal to the *ex post* total value at the actual prices. It is obviously true that a sufficient condition for the macroscopic correctness is that the expectations of prices are correct microscopically, i.e., the price of every and each good is realized just as it was previously expected to turn out. But, even though this condition is not met, it is still

[1] This value was referred to in the previous section as the discounted expected value of 'outputs'. Since we follow von Neumann in treating used capital goods appearing simultaneously with products at the end of the period as by-products of that production process, the total value of 'outputs' and the total value of stocks are identical with each other.

possible that the expectations may macroscopically be correct; so that we have

$$\Sigma\, b_{j,-1}\phi_{j,-1} = \Sigma\, b_{j,-1}\bar{p}_j/\tau \tag{17}$$

and a similar equation for period -2. These two equations together ensure (15) and (16) simultaneously. In fact, the terms of (15) are equal to the corresponding terms of (16). It is from equation (17) that we can determine the remaining unknown τ.

As $q_{i,-1}$s were fixed in the previous period, $b_{j,-1}$s are regarded as given in the current period. They are all positive, because those goods which do not exist currently are excluded from the present list of goods. The equilibrium values of $\bar{p}_j$s depend on the parameter τ, are non-negative and add up to unity. Hence the (normalized) *ex post* value of the stocks, $\Sigma\, b_{j,-1}\bar{p}_j$, has a lower bound as well as an upper bound.

Taking into account the boundedness and the dependence on τ of the *ex post* value of the stocks, we find that the right-hand side of (17) becomes indefinitely large when τ tends to zero, and becomes very small when it tends to infinity. The left-hand side of (17), on the other hand, is a constant determined in the previous period. Accordingly, we have a τ (or τs) at which the savings-investment equality does hold *ex post* as well as *ex ante*.

7. We have so far assumed that the producers' expectations of prices are correct macroscopically but may not be microscopically. For some goods, the prices which have to be realized in the next period may differ from those which were previously expected to prevail in that period. Such errors in expectations evidently mean that plans laid down for the future are not right and must be more or less revised before execution. A producer's plan for the present period is made as a part of his entire plan which extends to his time-horizon; his plan for the present period and his plan for the future form an inseparable whole. If the latter should later be revised because of imperfect expectations, it may happen that the former will not fully suit or even conflicts with the revised version. We have already carried out the plans for the present period. Thus, when we have imperfect foresight, we cannot protect ourselves from malinvestment and the consequent waste of resources; the equilibrium established in any given period will not be perfect but merely temporary.

We may conceive of entrepreneurs who can precisely foresee the prices to be established in the coming $T-1$ periods, but whose expectations of the prices in the Tth future period may be correct only in the macroscopic sense. In an economy guided by such informed entrepreneurs, no divergence between expected and realized prices would be observed throughout the first $T-1$ future periods; realized prices will first depart from their expected prices in the Tth period. From the realistic point of view the usefulness of such an imaginary economy would be doubtful. However, it is clear that the general idea includes at the one extreme where $T = 1$, the temporary equilibrium or the pure 'Spot Economy' and at the other where $T = \infty$, a system where all entrepreneurs have 'perfect foresight' or the pure 'Futures Economy'. As was stated at the beginning of this chapter and will later be confirmed, the idea of equilibrium of order T based on the assumption of entrepreneurs' expectations of order T is very important in both the analytical and normative senses. It is so because it plays a role of a bridge connecting Hicks' *Value and Capital* path with Malinvaud's full equilibrium path. Along the former, competitive pricing does work through time and *temporary* Pareto optimality is ensured at each moment of time under the realistic assumption of imperfect foresight, while along the latter not only a temporary Pareto optimum is established in every period but also a full Pareto optimum is realized over time, owing to the ideal condition of perfect foresight.

Let $P_j(t)$, $w(t)$, and $\beta(t)$ denote the price of good j, the wage rate, and the interest factor (i.e. 1+the interest rate), respectively, which are all expected to prevail in period t; define $z(t)$ as the reciprocal of $\beta(t)$ as before. Since entrepreneurial expectations are correct so far as the coming $T-1$ periods are concerned, $P_j(t)$ $w(t)$, and $z(t)$ $(t = 1, 2, ..., T-1)$ will turn out in due course to be actual prices, actual wage rates and actual discount factors that are determined in the market by the rules of competitive pricing. They must first of all satisfy inequalities,

$$\sum_j b_{ij}P_j(t+1)z(t) \leqq \sum_j a_{ij}P_j(t)+l_i w(t), \qquad t = 0, 1, ..., T-2$$

which state that in periods $t = 0, 1, ..., T-2$, the discounted values of outputs of production processes $i = 1, ..., m$ cannot exceed their costs. Secondly, the quantities of goods demanded at these prices, wages and interest rates must not exceed the quantities offered; so that for each $j = 1, ..., n$, we have

$$\sum_i q_i(t-1)b_{ij} \geqq \sum_i q_i(t)a_{ij}+e_j(t)+d_j(t) \qquad t = 0, 1, ..., T-1.$$

We have similar conditions for labour,

$$N(t) \geqq \sum_i q_i(t)l_i \qquad t = 0, 1, ..., T-1,$$

that is to say, no more labour can be employed in any period than is available.

Thirdly, prices must satisfy the savings-investment inequalities. As usual, aggregate savings in period t are defined as an excess of income in period t (wages received in t *plus* profits accruing in t to the owners of capital from the activities in $t-1$) over consumption in period t. Aggregate investment in period t, on the other hand, is the increment in the value of the stocks of goods during period t, that is to say, the difference between the value of the stocks of goods at the end of period t and the corresponding value at the beginning. The stocks of goods available at the end of period t are expected to have the market values, $P_1(t+1)$, ..., $P_n(t+1)$ in the next period $t+1$ when they will be used for consumption and production, so that they are evaluated at discounted expected prices, $P_1(t+1)z(t)$, ..., $P_n(t+1)z(t)$; whereas the stocks of goods available at the beginning of period t are evaluated at their *cost* prices.[1] Such procedures enable us to put the investment in period t in the form

$$\sum_i \sum_j q_i(t) b_{ij} P_j(t+1) z(t) - \sum_i q_i(t-1)\{\sum_j a_{ij} P_j(t-1) + l_i w(t-1)\}.$$

As a result of the assumption of correct foresight of order T prices expected to prevail in period $t = 0, 1, ..., T-1$ are correct prices that will actually be established, but $P_1(T)$, ..., $P_n(T)$ appearing in the evaluation of the end value of the stocks of goods of period $T-1$ are merely expected prices $\psi(T)$ that are possibly different from those which will be realized in period T. In equilibrium, we have inequalities,

$$\text{investment in period } t \geqq \text{savings in period } t, \quad t = 0, 1, ..., T-1.$$

Finally, the Rule of Profitability which states that processes can at most yield zero profits after payment of interest, must hold for the final period $T-1$. We have m inequalities,

$$\sum_j b_{ij} \psi_j(T) z(T-1) \leqq \sum_j a_{ij} P_j(T-1) + l_i w(T-1), \quad i = 1, ..., m,$$

where $\psi_j(T)$ stands for the price of good j expected to rule in the market in period T. It is remembered that $\psi_j(T)$ is not an independent variable but is related to current prices and the wage rate by a subjective expectation function.

8. Let us now discount and normalize prices and wage rates. The discount factor over multiple periods is defined as

$$Z(t) = z(t-1)z(t-2) ..., z(0),$$

the present value of a variable in period t being given by multiplying it by $Z(t)$. We use the following notation:

$$p_j(0) = P_j(0)/P, \qquad p_j(t) = P_j(t)Z(t)/P,$$
$$v(0) = w(0)/P, \qquad v(t) = w(t)Z(t)/P,$$

[1] This evaluation of the initial stocks is somewhat different from the one we adopted in the Temporary Equilibrium Analysis above; the goods available at the beginning of period t were therein valued at the discounted market prices expected in the preceding period $t-1$ to prevail in period t. It is true that from the *ex ante* point of view these two evaluations are not equivalent, but as soon as an equilibrium is established in period $t-1$, they become identical. See the footnote on p. 136.

where the normalization factor is defined as

$$P = \sum_{k=1}^{n} P_k(0) + \sum_{t=1}^{T-1} \sum_{k=1}^{n} P_k(t)Z(t).$$

Excess demand for good j in period t, $F_j(t)$, is a function of activity levels, $q_i(t)$, normalized discounted prices, $p_j(t)$, normalized discounted wage rate, $v(t)$, and normalized discounted profits in period t accruing from the activities in period $t-1$; while excess demand for labour in period t, $G(t)$, depends only upon activities in period t. Profits from each process, as well as investment and savings, are discounted and normalized. $E_i(t)$ represents the normalized, discounted profits gained when process i is operated in period t at unit intensity, and $H(t)$ stands for the normalized, discounted excess savings over investment in period t.[1]

The equilibrium conditions over T periods are written in terms of these 'excess functions'; we have

$$\text{(i) } E_i(t) \leqq 0, \qquad \text{(ii) } F_j(t) \leqq 0, \tag{18}$$

$$\text{(iii) } G(t) \leqq 0, \qquad \text{(iv) } H(t) \leqq 0.$$

They must hold for all $t = 0, 1, ..., T-1$; they are $T(m+n+2)$ in number. In addition to these we have an equality requiring that all $p_j(t)$s add up to unity (by normalization). Moreover, we have Walras' law,

$$\sum_i q_i(t)E_i(t) + \sum_j F_j(t)p_j(t) + G(t)v(t) + H(t) = 0,$$

being identically true for each $t = 0, 1, ..., T-1$. This system, consisting of $T(m+n+2)+1$ conditions with T identities, contains as unknowns Tm activity levels $q_i(t)$, Tn prices $p_j(t)$, T wage rates $v(t)$ and T interest rates $z(t)$. The number of unknowns exceeds the number of conditions less identities by $T-1$; the system can be solved if $T-1$ unknowns, say, $z(1)$, ..., $z(T-1)$, are fixed in some way or other. Alternatively, we must have $T-1$ additional conditions in order that all unknowns in the system should be completely determined.

Malinvaud has presented a number of such conditions.[2] For example, if it is supposed that there is a commodity j^0 that can be stored without any cost, its price ('non-normalized' in the sense of the present chapter but 'normalized' in the sense of Malinvaud) will be kept constant, so that $z(t)$ may be computed by

$$z(t) = \frac{p_{j^0}(t+1)}{p_{j^0}(t)} \qquad t = 1, ..., T-1.$$

[1] The definitions of $E_i(t)$, $F_j(t)$, $G(t)$, and $H(t)$ are similar to those of E_i, F_j, G, and H given by (7′)–(10′) above.

[2] Malinvaud, loc. cit., pp. 257–8.

In the following we are instead concerned with a path along which the rate of profits remains unchanged. We have $T-1$ equations:

$$z(0) = z(1) = \dots = z(T-1),$$

so that $Z(T)$ is given as the Tth power of $z(0)$.

The following pseudo-economic adjustment functions are devised for searching for a fixed point:

$$\theta_i(t) = \frac{\bar{\bar{q}}_i}{\bar{\bar{q}}_i+\sum_k \sum_t F_k^*(t)+E_i^*(t)} \{q_i(t)+E_i^*(t)\},$$

$$\pi_j(t) = \frac{1}{1+\sum_k \sum_t F_k^*(t)} \{p_j(t)+F_j^*(t)\},$$

$$v(t) = \frac{\bar{\bar{v}}(t)}{\bar{\bar{v}}(t)+\sum_k \sum_i F_k^*(t)+G^*(t)} \{v(t)+G^*(t)\},$$

$$\zeta = \frac{\bar{\bar{z}}}{\bar{\bar{z}}+\sum_k \sum_t F_k^*(t)+\sum_t H^*(t)} \{z+\sum_t H^*(t)\},$$

where $E_i^*(t)$ represents the modulated profit function of process i, $F_j^*(t)$ and $G^*(t)$ the modulated excess demand functions for good j and labour, and $H^*(t)$ the modulated excess savings function. $\bar{\bar{q}}_i$ is taken to be greater than the technically feasible, maximum activity level of process i in period t, and $\bar{\bar{v}}(t)$ is greater than the technological barrier to the real-wage rate in period t. They will be defined exactly in section 9. $\bar{\bar{z}}$ is taken to be so large that at $\bar{\bar{z}}$ the strict inequality

$$\bar{\bar{z}}^T\{\sum_j b_{ij}\phi_j(T)\} > \sum_j a_{ij}p_j(T-1)+l_i v(T-1),$$

where $\phi_j(T) = \psi_j(T)/P$, is necessarily satisfied for at least one process i, no matter how the prices and the real-wage rates are fixed.

The proof developed in sections 3–6 above to establish a temporary equilibrium can be applied *mutatis mutandis* to the present pseudo-economic process. We find a fixed point by applying Brouwer's theorem; we see that all the conditions (18) are fulfilled at any fixed point, so that the point is identified with the equilibrium over time which is obtained, under the hypothesis of perfect foresight, when a positive value is assigned to $\tau = \sum_k P_k(-1)/P$. Finally, the imposition that the savings-investment equation holds *ex post* as well as *ex ante* determines the value of τ (the intertemporal price ratio) which has so far been treated as a parameter.

It remains to establish the non-triviality of the equilibrium of order T. The equilibrium rate of profits (or the interest rate) must be *finite*; the equilibrium set of prices in any period must be non-negative and *non-vanishing*. The first italicized property is equivalent to $z \neq 0$ and the second to $\sum_{j=1}^{n} p_j(t) \neq 0$ for all $t = 0, 1, \ldots, T-1$ at the fixed point. Throughout the rest of this section, which is devoted to verifying these properties, we write the values of the variables at the fixed point simply as $p_j(t)$, etc. without the bar that has been used in the previous sections to distinguish the equilibrium values from non-equilibrium values.

Suppose $z = 0$.[1] If we designate $\phi_j(T)$ as the normalized price (not discounted) of good j expected to prevail in period T, we may write the normalized, discounted investment in period $T-1$ as

$$z^T \sum_i \sum_j q_i(T-1) b_{ij} \phi_j(T) - z \sum_i q_i(T-2)\{\sum_j a_{ij} p_j(T-2) + l_i v(T-2)\};$$

when z vanishes, the two terms vanish. Then one of the equilibrium conditions is reduced to

$$H(T-1) = S(T-1) \leqq 0, \tag{19}$$

where $S(T-1)$ is the normalized discounted savings in period $T-1$. (19) implies that the total profits received at the beginning of period $T-1$ should be non-positive, that is to say,

$$\sum_i \sum_j q_i(T-2) b_{ij} p_j(T-1) - z \sum_i q_i(T-2)\{\sum_j a_{ij} p_j(T-2) + l_i v(T-2)\} \leqq 0, \tag{20}$$

because otherwise capitalists, as well as workers, would save a portion of their income. As capitalists' consumption is now zero, their savings equal their income, which is added to workers' savings to make the total savings $S(T-1)$. On the other hand, it follows from $z = 0$ that the second term of (20) vanishes, so that we have

$$\sum_i \sum_j q_i(T-2) b_{ij} p_j(T-1) = 0. \tag{21}$$

We now find that capitalists and workers receive no profits (either positive or negative) at the beginning of period $T-1$; consequently, (19) can be written as:

$$\text{wages} - \text{workers' consumption} \leqq 0. \tag{22}$$

By assumption the workers' propensity to consume is less than one; therefore the workers' consumption cannot be as great as wages unless both are zero. Accordingly (22) implies that wages (and hence the wage rate) must be zero in period $T-1$; we thus obtain $v(T-1) = 0$.

[1] In the application of Brouwer's theorem an argument similar to the following has to be made in order to show that the supposition of one of $F_j^*(t)$s being positive at the fixed point leads to a contradiction.

Similarly, from (21) we have, for $t = T-2$, inequalities similar to (19)–(22), from which we can get $v(T-2) = 0$. Repeating the same reasoning we finally obtain

$$\sum_i \sum_j q_i(-1)b_{ij}p_j(0) = 0 \qquad \text{and} \qquad v(0) = 0. \tag{23}$$

Since the catalogue for the present period O contains only those goods which are available from the activities in the last period, we have

$$\sum_i q_i(-1)b_{ij} > 0 \qquad \text{for all } j,$$

so that (23) implies $p_j(0) = 0$ for all j. Thus the cost of production of each good in period 0 is zero; it then follows from the cost-price inequalities that all prices must vanish in period 1. We now again find that each good can be produced without any cost in period 1. We may proceed in this way until we at last get $p_j(t) = 0$ for all $j = 1, ..., n$ and $t = 0, 1, ..., T-1$. This clearly contradicts the fact that prices are normalized such that they sum to unity. Hence z should be positive.[1]

A similar argument enables us to find that for any t some $p_j(t)$s are not zero. Suppose the contrary, namely, that all prices are zero in a certain period t_0. It is then evident that we have $\sum_i \sum_j q_i(t_0-1)b_{ij}p_j(t_0) = 0$, which yields

$$\sum_i \sum_j q_i(t_0-2)b_{ij}p_j(t_0-1) = 0 \qquad \text{and} \qquad v(t_0-1) = 0 \tag{24}$$

in the same way as we obtained similar equations in the above argument. Equations (24) in turn result in equations of the same sort for t_0-2; and so on until we finally obtain (23) for $t = 0$. As all goods are available at the beginning of period 0, all $p_j(0)$s must vanish. This, together with the fact that the wage rate remains null up to t_0-1, implies that prices of all goods are zero until period t_0.

It is easy to see that the wage rate in period t_0 would be zero when all prices are zero in that period. If the wage rate were positive although commodity prices are zero, then there should be a great amount of demand for some goods which would be enough to exhaust their availability; this would contradict the hypothesis that all $p_j(t_0)$s vanish in period t_0. Once all $p_j(t_0)$ and $v(t_0)$ are zero, then all $p_j(t_0+1)$s are zero by the cost-price argument, which in turn implies $v(t_0+1) = 0$; and so forth. Thus we find that if all $p_j(t)$s are zero for some t, then they are so for all t. It is evident that this 'permanent' nullity of prices violates the normalization requirement. Hence, for any t some $p_j(t)$s are not zero. We have thus established the non-triviality of the equilibrium of order T.

[1] It is further seen that the interest rate is positive (z is less than 1), when expectations of prices are such that $\bar{\bar{z}}$ may be taken as small as unity.

9. Being escorted by Malinvaud, we can now safely cross the bridge to the opposite shore.[1] The central problem there is to establish the existence of an equilibrium of *infinite* order under the hypothesis that entrepreneurs can perfectly foresee all affairs in the eternal future; that is to say, we discuss whether a limiting path is obtained or not, as the horizon T recedes to an unlimited extent.

Let us now pay explicit attention to an assumption which has implicitly been used in proving the existence of a fixed point of order T in the previous section. Namely, it is now assumed that every process must consume a positive amount of at least one good or labour as an input. Then each process i cannot be operated, in period 0, at an intensity greater than the upper bound $\bar{\bar{q}}_i(0)$ of the activity level of process i. $\bar{\bar{q}}_i(0)$ is defined as

$$\bar{\bar{q}}_i(0) > \min\left\{\frac{\sum_i q_i(-1)b_{i1}}{a_{i1}}, \dots, \frac{\sum_i q_i(-1)b_{in}}{a_{in}}, \frac{N(0)}{l_i}\right\}$$

where the quotient on the right-hand side is regarded as infinity for j (or labour) when $a_{ij} = 0$ (or $l_i = 0$). It follows from the assumption just stated that each $\bar{\bar{q}}_i(0)$ is finite; and because

$$\sum_i q_i(-1)b_{ij} \geqq \sum_i q_i(0)a_{ij}, \qquad j = 1, \dots, n,$$

$$N(0) \geqq \sum_i q_i(0)l_i,$$

for feasible activities $q_1(0), \dots, q_m(0)$, it is evident that feasible activities are subject to inequalities, $q_i(0) \leqq \bar{\bar{q}}_i(0)$, $i = 1, \dots, m$. Similarly, define $\bar{\bar{q}}_i(1)$ as

$$\bar{\bar{q}}_i(1) > \min\left\{\frac{\sum_i \bar{\bar{q}}_i(0)b_{i1}}{a_{i1}}, \dots, \frac{\sum_i \bar{\bar{q}}_i(0)b_{in}}{a_{in}}, \frac{N(1)}{l_i}\right\}.$$

Then operation of process i at the intensity $q_i(1)$ is not feasible in period 1 if $q_i(1) > \bar{\bar{q}}_i(1)$. Proceeding this way, we get an infinite sequence of the bounding activity levels, $\bar{\bar{q}}(0), \bar{\bar{q}}(1), \dots, \bar{\bar{q}}(t), \dots,$ where $(\bar{\bar{q}}t)$ represents an m-dimensional vector with elements, $\bar{\bar{q}}_1(t), \dots, \bar{\bar{q}}_m(t)$.

The argument has so far proceeded in terms of the normalized, discounted prices and the discounted, real-wage rate; and the base of the normalization has been taken such that the sum of the discounted prices through T periods becomes unity, while the discounted real-wage rate has been defined in terms of such prices. In the following, however, we

[1] See E. Malinvaud, loc. cit. See also his 'Corrigendum', *Econometrica*, Vol. XXX (1962), pp. 570–3.

normalize prices and the wage rate *period-wise* by dividing $P_j(t_0)Z(t_0)$ and $w(t_0)Z(t_0)$ in a particular period t_0 not by the total sum, $\sum_k^n \sum_{t=0}^{T-1} P_k(t)Z(t)$, but by the period-wise sub-total, $\sum_k^n P_k(t_0)Z(t_0)$.[1] We write the new normalized prices and the new real-wage rate as

$$\pi_j(t) = P_j(t)Z(t)/\sum_k P_k(t)Z(t),$$

$$v(t) = w(t)Z(t)/\sum_k P_k(t)Z(t), \qquad t = 0, 1, \ldots \textit{ ad inf.},$$

since no confusion is expected between these π_j and v and the tâtonnement prices π_j and the tâtonnement wage rate v which have appeared in the proof of the existence of an equilibrium of order T.

As we have seen before, workers' demand for any good j in any period t, $e_j(t)$, is a homogeneous function of degree zero with respect to prices and wages in the same period. The homogeneity permits the normalization; we may write

$$e_j(t) = e_j(\pi_1(t), \ldots, \pi_n(t), v(t)\sum_i q_i(t)l_i) \qquad j = 1, \ldots, n.$$

When the employment, $\sum_i q_i(t)l_i$, of labour does not reach the supply, $N(t)$, the wage rate will be set at zero by the rule of competitive pricing. On the other hand, when full employment of labour is established, the wages will be positive; an increase in the real-wage rate $v(t)$ will give rise to an increase in the workers' demand for at least one good. For a sufficiently high wage rate, there will be, regardless of prices $\pi_1(t), \ldots, \pi_n(t)$, a good j whose $e_j(t)$ becomes greater than the barrier, $\sum_i \bar{\bar{q}}_i(t-1)b_{ij}$, so that such a wage rate is impossible. This means that in each period t there is a barrier that prevents the equilibrium real-wage rate in that period from becoming greater than a certain fixed amount $\bar{\bar{v}}(t)$.[2]

It is obvious that the previous price-cost inequalities in terms of the non-normalized prices, $P_j(t)$, $P_j(t+1)$ and the non-normalized wage rate $w(t)$ can be transformed into the following inequalities in terms of the new normalized variables $\pi_j(t)$, $\pi_j(t+1)$ and $v(t)$:

$$\{\sum_j b_{ij}\pi_j(t+1)\}\tau(t) \leq \sum_j a_{ij}\pi_j(t)+l_i v(t) \qquad i = 1, \ldots, m, \tag{25}$$

where

$$\tau(t) = \sum_k P_k(t+1)Z(t+1)/\sum_k P_k(t)Z(t),$$

[1] Such normalization is meaningful, because in equilibrium $\sum_k P_k(t) > 0$ for all t, i.e. the equilibrium prices are non-null period-wise.

[2] $\bar{\bar{v}}(t)$ that has appeared in the pseudo-economic process for finding the fixed point in section 8 above is similarly defined in terms of the 'over-all' normalization.

and $v(t)$ cannot exceed $\bar{v}(t)$. Since $\pi(t)$ and $\pi(t+1)$ are non-negative and have been normalized and every good can be produced by some processes, we find that the part in the braces on the left-hand side of (25) is necessarily positive for some j. Hence, it follows from (25) that $\tau(t)$ is bounded from above; that is to say, there are fixed, positive numbers, $\bar{\bar{\tau}}(t)$, $t = 0, 1, \ldots$, *ad infinitum*, such that

$$\sum_k P_k(t+1)Z(t+1) \leqq \bar{\bar{\tau}}(t) \sum_k P_k(t)Z(t).^1 \tag{26}$$

Finally, z, the reciprocal of one plus the rate of interest, must be bounded in order to establish the existence of an equilibrium path of infinite order. We have seen that z is positive and that it has an upper bound at $\bar{\bar{z}}$. More specifically, in the footnote on p. 154, it has been seen that $\bar{\bar{z}}$ will not be greater than one when optimistic expectations prevail.

Without making any explicit reference to the order of an equilibrium, we have so far written activities, prices, wage rate and discount factor in period t simply as $q_i(t)$, $\pi_j(t)$, $v(t)$, and z, respectively. From now on, we designate them as $q_i^{(T)}(t)$, etc., where t may take any integral number from zero up to $T-1$, and T stands for the order of the equilibrium path.

Let t_0 be any specific value of t. It has been seen that all $q_i^{(T)}(t_0)$s are bounded, i.e., $0 \leqq q_i^{(T)}(t_0) \leqq \bar{q}_i(t_0)$ for all $T = t_0+1, t_0+2, \ldots$, *ad infinitum*. Then by the Bolzano–Weierstrass theorem asserting that a bounded set containing infinitely many points has an accumulation point, the sequence $\{q_i^{(T)}(t_0)\}$, $T = t_0+1, t_0+2, \ldots$ has a limit, $q_i^*(t_0)$. Similarly, for any t, $\pi_j^{(T)}(t)$, $v^{(T)}(t)$, and $z^{(T)}$ are bounded, from which it follows that they have limits, $\pi_j^*(t)$, $v^*(t)$, and z^*, respectively. The path, $q_i^*(t)$, $\pi_j^*(t)$, $v^*(t)$, z^*, $t = 0, 1, \ldots$, gives an equilibrium of infinite order which would prevail when entrepreneurs are able to foresee the future perfectly. By multiplying the normalized prices $\pi_j^*(t)$ by their corresponding level factor, $\sum_k P_k(t)Z(t)$, we obtain the absolute discounted prices, $P_j^*(t)Z^*(t)$. The level factors are bounded because of (26), and therefore absolute prices are finite in any period.

[1] Our $\bar{\bar{\pi}}(t)$ corresponds to Malinvaud's α_t in his 'Corrigendum', p. 571.

IX

EQUILIBRIUM GROWTH. (III) NORMATIVE PROPERTIES

1. WE HAVE so far discussed three kinds of equilibrium growth paths, the Cassel–von Neumann path of balanced growth, the Lindahl–Hicks sequence of temporary equilibria and the Hicks–Malinvaud perfect equilibrium over time, which we will now examine for efficiency and optimality. Each of them will in succession be compared with any other feasible path to see in what sense the former is superior. The subject is important for its own sake; from the results obtained we may decide our attitude towards the conventional but yet unsolved choice between competition or planning. It is also important as a prelude to the Turnpike problem, one of central and most attractive up-to-date topics of growth economics, which we shall discuss in a number of the following chapters.

Let us begin by giving the necessary definitions. First, the efficiency of a growth path is defined in terms of 'net' or 'consumable' outputs. Following our previous notation, we write $q_i(t-1)$ for the intensity of process i operating in period $t-1$. The total output of good j available at the beginning of period t is then written as $\sum_{i=1}^{m} b_{ij}q_i(t-1)$, and the total amount of the same good used by various manufacturing processes for further production as $\sum_{i=1}^{m} a_{ij}q_i(t)$. It is evident that the remainder of the total output, after subtracting the total input, might be devoted to consumption by workers and capitalists; we call

$$h_j(t) = \sum_{i=1}^{m} b_{ij}q_i(t-1) - \sum_{i=1}^{m} a_{ij}q_i(t)$$

the 'net' or 'consumable' output of good j in period t. For the last period T, $h_j(T)$ is defined as

$$h_j(T) = \sum_{i=1}^{m} b_{ij}q_i(T-1),$$

which is the amount of good j bequeathed to the future generations after T.

In the following we say that a path of order T with a net output stream, $H^* = \{h_1^*(t), ..., h_n^*(t);\ t = 0, 1, ..., T\}$, is *weakly efficient* (of order T) if there is no other feasible path yielding a different sequence of net outputs $H = \{h_1(1), ..., h_n(t);\ t = 0, 1, ..., T\}$, such that there is more of some commodity and no less of any other commodity to consume in H than in H^*. This definition of efficiency in kind may be strengthened to the following efficiency in value: we say that a path with H^* is *strongly efficient* (of order T) if no possible path can provide us with net outputs H, whose total value, evaluated at some positive prices $\{p_1(t), ..., p_n(t)\}$, $t = 0, 1, ..., T$, is greater than the corresponding value of H^*. Weak efficiency rules out the existence of a net output stream H fulfilling

$$h_j(t) \geqq h_j^*(t) \qquad j = 1, ..., n;\ t = 0, 1, ..., T$$

with at least one strict inequality, whereas strong efficiency means that inequality

$$\sum_{t=0}^{T} \sum_{j=1}^{n} h_j(t)p_j(t) > \sum_{t=0}^{T} \sum_{j=1}^{n} h_j^*(t)p_j(t)$$

should not hold for any feasible path of order T. Evidently, the strong definition implies the weak one, but not vice versa.

The classical criteria for Pareto optimality in production and consumption make sense on the basis of a set of fundamental assumptions. It is first assumed that there is no Veblen–Duesenberry effect. Unlike Japanese girls following the latest styles in Western countries but like Indian ladies always wearing saris anywhere in the world, people in our economy have independent tastes for goods, so that no one's act of consumption affects any other person's preferences of goods unless some prices are induced to change. Second, in the previous discussions of equilibrium growth, balanced or unbalanced, we regarded capitalists' and workers' demands for consumption goods as depending on prices and their incomes and we assumed that their demand functions remained unchanged through time. This last assumption implies that no autonomous shift takes place in the utility functions from which the demand functions are derived. In the following we formulate the problem of Pareto-optimal development on the assumption of stationary tastes, and unless otherwise stated each individual's propensity to consume is assumed to be a constant exogenously determined. In the third place the assumed independence of the utility functions implies that a social optimum may be obtained in conflict with social equity. In many cases, however, one will feel that an increase in capitalists' consumption of goods with no increase in workers' consumption would not lead to a better social distribution of goods. It is really true that those who are sensitive to fairness of rationing more than the absolute amounts distributed would not regard an 'optimum' in the sense exactly defined below as a best state, nor even as an allowable state of affairs. But throughout this chapter, interpersonal and intertemporal comparisons of utilities are completely ruled out; we proceed on the assumption that there is no divergence between social and private satisfaction.

A Pareto optimum of the economy is now defined as follows. Along a feasible growth path, say, of order T, we have a stream of net outputs which can be distributed among workers and capitalists in various ways. A possible distribution is said to be a Pareto optimum (of order T) if there is no other feasible path of order T, such that every individual enjoys his consumption on the second path at least as much as that on the first, with some individuals really preferring their consumption on the second to the corresponding one on the first, *and* those who come after period T are bequeathed as much of every good on the second path as on the first. It follows directly from the definitions of the weak efficiency and the Pareto optimality that the former is a necessary condition for the latter, because if a feasible path associated with a Pareto optimum distribution were not weakly efficient, then there would be another feasible path that could provide us with the net output of at least one good in a larger amount than on the first path without entailing a reduction in the net output of any other good; so that every individual would prefer the second path to the first. This clearly contradicts the supposed Pareto optimality of the first path.

In view of DOSSO's finding that efficiency of order T implies efficiency of any lower order $t \leqq T$ but a sequence of efficient paths of order t_1, t_2, ... does not necessarily make the resulting path of order $T = t_1+t_2+...$ efficient,[1] and in taking the necessity of efficiency for optimality into account, we get a similar proposition concerning optimality: a state is a Pareto optimum of any order $t \leqq T$ if it is a Pareto optimum of order T, but the contrary is not true, so that a t-period Pareto optimum may not be so over $2t$, $3t$, ... periods.

2. The concept of competitive equilibrium of order T is so general that it includes the Lindahl–Hicks temporary equilibrium as a special case when $T = 1$ and the Malinvaud full equilibrium over time as another special case when T is infinite.[2] We shall see, in this section, that the efficiency and Pareto optimality of each of these two extremes result from an argument that holds for a general T.

Let us write equilibrium prices and wage rates, all *discounted and normalized*, of order T as

$$p^*(0), p^*(1), ..., p^*(T-1), p^*(T),$$

$$v^*(0), v^*(1), ..., v^*(T-1),$$

[1] See R. Dorfman, P. A. Samuelson, and R. Solow, loc. cit., pp. 310–12.

[2] Cf. E. Lindahl, *Studies in the Theory of Money and Capital* (London: George Allen and Unwin Ltd., 1939); J. R. Hicks, *Value and Capital* (Oxford: Clarendon, 1939); E. Malinvaud, 'Capital accumulation and efficient allocation of resources', *Econometrica*, Vol. XXI (1953).

respectively, and non-normalized equilibrium intensities of order T as

$$q^*(0), q^*(1), \ldots, q^*(T-1).$$

$p^*(t)$ with subscript j denotes the price of a particular good j in period t and $q^*(t)$ with i denotes the intensity of a particular process i in period t. Prices, $p_1^*(T), \ldots, p_n^*(T)$, at the end of the path are merely expected prices which are determined by subjective expectation functions. We have for all i

$$\sum_j b_{ij}p_j^*(t+1) \leqq \sum_j a_{ij}p_j^*(t)+l_iv^*(t) \tag{1}$$

$$i = 1, \ldots, m;\ t = 0, 1, \ldots, T-1,$$

because in equilibrium the discounted values of outputs of production processes must not exceed their costs. Since unprofitable processes are not adopted in the state of equilibrium, the intensities $q_i^*(t)$ in association with strict inequalities (1) are zero; multiplying (1) by $q_i^*(t)$ and summing over i and t we have, from the definition of $h_j(t)$ above, an equation,

$$\sum_{t=0}^{T}\sum_{j=1}^{n} h_j^*(t)p_j^*(t) = \sum_{t=0}^{T-1}\{\sum_{i=1}^{m} l_iq_i^*(t)\}v^*(t)-\sum_{j=1}^{n}\sum_{i=1}^{m} b_{ij}\bar{q}_ip_j^*(0), \tag{2}$$

where $\bar{q}_i$s are the intensities in period -1 which are historically given.

In a similar way, for any feasible path of order T, $\{q(0), q(1), \ldots, q(T-1)\}$, starting from the historical initial point $\bar{q}$ we obtain an *in*equality,

$$\sum_{t=0}^{T}\sum_{j=1}^{n} h_j(t)p_j^*(t) \leqq \sum_{t=0}^{T-1}\{\sum_{i=1}^{m} l_iq_i(t)\}v^*(t)-\sum_{j=1}^{n}\sum_{i=1}^{m} b_{ij}\bar{q}_ip_j^*(0). \tag{3}$$

For a feasible path we require that the part in the braces on the right-hand side of (3) must not exceed the available labour $N(t)$ in period t. The Rule of Free Goods operates in the state of equilibrium, so that the wage rate $v^*(t)$ is set at zero if the equilibrium demand for labour, $\sum_{i=1}^{m} l_iq_i^*(t)$, is less than $N(t)$. We then find that the first term on the right-hand side of (2) equals $\sum_{t=0}^{T-1} N(t)v^*(t)$; hence it is greater than or equal to the corresponding term of (3). We therefore obtain

$$\sum_{t=0}^{T}\sum_{j=1}^{n} h_j(t)p_j^*(t) \leqq \sum_{t=0}^{T}\sum_{j=1}^{n} h_j^*(t)p_j^*(t),$$

which means that the competitive equilibrium of order T is strongly efficient. From this general result it follows that short-run efficiency is ensured on the Lindahl–Hicks path. We again note that perpetual short-run efficiency does not necessarily imply efficiency of longer-run so that the two paths, the Lindahl–Hicks path of perpetual temporary equilibrium and the Hicks–Malinvaud path of perfect equilibrium, may diverge from each other.

3. Let us now establish the Pareto optimality of competitive equilibrium. We begin by recalling the assumptions so far made about the consumer's preference. In addition to the conventional assumptions, we have assumed that there are only two different types of consumers, capitalists and workers, their tastes being identical within each group; i.e., the utility functions do not differ from capitalist to capitalist, and from worker to worker. Moreover, we have assumed that the marginal rates of substitution between goods are not affected if the quantities of all goods purchased by an individual are increased by the same proportion. These assumptions, however, have no relevance to the optimality proof, although for the sake of simplicity we continue to regard the economy as if it consisted of only two persons, the Capitalist and the Worker.

Pareto optimality can be discussed in two alternative ways: first we can assume that each consumer has a utility function which describes his preferences among possible consumption programmes extending over T periods; second we can assume the absence of intertemporal complementarity and regard a person at a certain date and the same person at another date as different persons. We take the second option; this means that we have T Capitalists and T Workers in the following discussion of Pareto optimality of order T, since contemporary uniformity has been assumed for capitalists as well as for workers.

Let us compare the competitive equilibrium of order T (marked with an asterisk) with a feasible path producing net outputs $\{h(0), h(1), ..., h(T)\}$ such that for net outputs at the end of the final period we have

$$h_j(T) \geqq h_j^*(T) \qquad j = 1, ..., n. \tag{4}$$

In each period t consumable outputs $h(t)$ are shared between the Capitalist and the Worker; the distribution is feasible if the Capitalist's share of good j (denoted by $h_j'(t)$) together with the Worker's one (denoted by $h_j''(t)$) does not exceed the available quantity $h_j(t)$. Let the Capitalist and the Worker consume $d_j^*(t)$ and $e_j^*(t)$ amounts of good j, respectively, when the equilibrium wage-price system prevails in period t. Since the equilibrium distribution is of course feasible, the sum of $d_j^*(t)$ and $e_j^*(t)$ cannot exceed the equilibrium net output $h_j^*(t)$ produced in the same period. If the Capitalist preferred $h'(t)$ to $d^*(t)$ at the equilibrium prices and wages, we would have the inequality,

$$\sum_{j=1}^{n} h_j'(t)p_j^*(t) \geqq \sum_{j=1}^{n} d_j^*(t)p_j^*(t), \qquad t = 0, 1, ..., T-1. \tag{5}$$

Otherwise the Capitalist would be worse off in the second state where he buys $h'(t)$ than in the original state of the competitive equilibrium, because the fact that he buys the commodity bundle $d^*(t)$ although he could buy $h'(t)$ if he chose, reveals that $h'(t)$ is not preferred to $d^*(t)$, a contradiction to the hypothesis that $h'(t)$ is preferred to $d^*(t)$. In the same way, an inequality similar to (5) holds between $h''(t)$ and $e^*(t)$, provided that the Worker is not worse off when he consumes the commodity bundle $h''(t)$ rather than $e^*(t)$.

To show that the competitive equilibrium is a Pareto optimum, we now suppose the contrary. Then it is possible to raise the satisfaction of the Worker (or the Capitalist) at some date t, without lowering the satisfaction of the other people (including the Workers at the other dates). That is to say, there is a possible path fulfilling (4) and enabling the Capitalist and the Worker in any period t to consume goods in the amounts $h'(t)$ and $h''(t)$ such that both $h'(t)$ and $h''(t)$ are at least as desirable as $d^*(t)$ and $e^*(t)$, respectively, and one of them, say $h''(t_0)$ in a certain period t_0, is definitely preferred to $e^*(t_0)$. We have inequalities (5) for the Capitalist and similar inequalities for the Worker, at least one of which, say the one for t_0, must hold with strict inequality; hence we have

$$\sum_{t=0}^{T-1} \sum_{j=1}^{n} \{h_j'(t)+h_j''(t)\}p_j^*(t) > \sum_{t=0}^{T-1} \sum_{j=1}^{n} \{d_j^*(t)+e_j^*(t)\}p_j^*(t). \qquad (6)$$

As each equilibrium price $p_j^*(t)$ is competitively determined, it is set at zero under the Rule of Free Goods when in period t the total consumption of good j, $d_j^*(t)+e_j^*(t)$, is less than the supply of the net output $h_j^*(t)$. It then follows that the right-hand side of (6) equals $\sum_{t=0}^{T-1} \sum_{j=1}^{n} h_j^*(t)p_j^*(t)$. This together with (4) and the fact that the left-hand side of (6) cannot exceed $\sum_{t=0}^{T-1} \sum_{j=1}^{n} h_j(t)p_j^*(t)$, leads to

$$\sum_{t=0}^{T} \sum_{j=1}^{n} h_j(t)p_j^*(t) > \sum_{t=0}^{T} \sum_{j=1}^{n} h_j^*(t)p_j^*(t).$$

Clearly, the existence of such a feasible path contradicts the efficiency of order T established for the equilibrium path; we, therefore, find that the competitive equilibrium yields a Pareto optimum.

4. The relationship is now examined from the opposite direction. We shall see that a Pareto optimum of order T is a competitive equilibrium of the same order if by some chance or other the historically given, initial distribution of wealth among workers and capitalists is the exact distribution which generates that Pareto optimum *and* if entrepreneurs can precisely foresee prices over T periods in the future. The first condition is necessary because our economy is under private ownership, so that a Pareto optimum requiring an alteration in the given distribution of wealth could not occur, under the competitive mechanism, in an economy where each consumer maximizes his satisfaction subject to his wealth constraint; the second condition is needed in an economy with production lags because changing views of entrepreneurs about the future are capable of affecting the present situation.

Let us begin by confirming a lemma of a purely mathematical nature which is pivotal in establishing the desired relationship. It is called Farkas' theorem and states:[1] *If a linear inequality*

$$R_1\zeta_1+R_2\zeta_2+\ldots+R_n\zeta_n \leqq 0$$

holds for all $\zeta_1, \ldots, \zeta_n$ *fulfilling m linear inequalities,*

$$R_{i1}\zeta_1+R_{i2}\zeta_2+\ldots+R_{in}\zeta_n \leqq 0 \qquad i = 1, \ldots, m,$$

then there is a set of non-negative multipliers $\eta_1, \ldots, \eta_m$, *such that*

$$\eta_1 R_{1j}+\eta_2 R_{2j}+\ldots+\eta_m R_{mj} = R_j \qquad j = 1, \ldots, n.$$

To get such a set, we consider the quadratic,

$$V = \frac{1}{2}\sum_{j=1}^{n} (\eta_1 R_{1j}+\eta_2 R_{2j}+\ldots+\eta_m R_{mj}-R_j)^2,$$

which is minimized, with respect to the ηs, subject to the condition that none of the ηs can be negative. It is evident that there exists a minimum point, $\eta_1^0, \ldots, \eta_m^0$, at which

$$\frac{\partial V}{\partial \eta_i} = 0 \qquad \text{if} \quad \eta_i > 0, \tag{7}$$

and

$$\frac{\partial V}{\partial \eta_i} \geqq 0 \qquad \text{if} \quad \eta_i = 0 \tag{8}$$

The latter condition is weaker than the usual, necessary condition for a minimum that is familiar in differential calculas and implies that a smaller value of V would be obtained if we could diminish η_i; but none of such variations is admissible because η_i has already reached its lowest value.

The values of ηs at which V takes on a minimum give the values of the multipliers we are seeking. From the quadratic form V, we have

$$\frac{\partial V}{\partial \eta_i} = -\sum_{j=1}^{n} R_{ij}\zeta_j^0 \geqq 0 \qquad i = 1, \ldots, m,$$

where

$$-\zeta_j^0 = \eta_1^0 R_{1j}+\eta_2^0 R_{2j}+\ldots+\eta_m^0 R_{mj}-R_j, \qquad j = 1, \ldots, n. \tag{9}$$

Taking (7) and (8) into account, we have $\sum_{i=1}^{m}\sum_{j=1}^{n} \eta_i^0 R_{ij}\zeta_j^0 = 0$; hence we get from (9)

$$\sum_{j=1}^{n} (\zeta_j^0)^2 = \sum_{j=1}^{n} R_j\zeta_j^0.$$

1 Cf. R. Dorfman, P. A. Samuelson, and R. Solow, ibid., p. 191 and pp. 502–6.

It is obvious that the left-hand side is non-negative, while it follows from the premise of the Farkas theorem that the right-hand side is non-positive. We must, therefore, have $\zeta_j^0 = 0$, for all $j = 1, ..., n$, so that (9) now gives the desired result.

5. As the necessary scaffolding has been set up, we may now proceed to the main issue. Let $u_c = U^c(h_1'(t), ..., h_n'(t))$ denote the Capitalist's utility function which gives the degree of the Capitalist's satisfaction in period t as a function of his consumption in the same period. Similarly, we write $u_w = U^w(h_1''(t), ..., h_n''(t))$ for the Worker's utility function. Also, let $u_c^0(t)$ and $u_w^0(t)$ be the degree of satisfaction which the Capitalist and the Worker enjoy in period t in a particular state of Pareto optimum. It follows from the definition of optimality of that kind that any $u_c^0(t)$ or $u_w^0(t)$, $t = 0, 1, ..., T-1$, say $u_w^0(0)$, takes on a maximum value subject to

$$U^c(h_1'(t), ..., h_n'(t)) \geqq u_c^0(t), \tag{10}$$

$$U^w(h_1''(t), ..., h_n''(t)) \geqq u_w^0(t), \tag{11}$$

$$\sum_{i=1}^{m} b_{ij}q_i(t-1) - \sum_{i=1}^{m} a_{ij}q_i(t) - h_j'(t) - h_j''(t) \geqq 0, \quad j = 1, ..., n, \tag{12}$$

$$\sum_{i=1}^{m} b_{ij}q_i(T-1) \geqq h_j^0(T), \qquad = 1, ..., n, \tag{13}$$

$$N_t \geqq \sum_{i=1}^{m} l_i q_i(t), \tag{14}$$

where (11) must hold for $t = 1, ..., T-1$, while all the other constraints must hold for $t = 0, 1, ..., T-1$. (10) and (11) are required because Capitalists in periods $t = 0, 1, ..., T-1$ and Workers in periods $t = 1, ..., T-1$ should not be made worse off. (13) implies that $h_j^0(T)$ amounts of good j should be bequeathed to future generations living beyond the horizon T. Finally, (12) and (14) are necessary for the optimum state to be feasible.

It is evident that in the state of Pareto optimum all variables take on non-negative values; they are not all zero but some of them may be zero. Let a small change in a variable, say $h_j'(t)$, from its optimum value, $h_j'^0(t)$, be denoted by $\delta h_j'(t)$. With regard to those variables which vanish at the optimal point, variations are restricted to non-negative values; that is to say,

$$\left.\begin{aligned} \delta h_j'(t) &\geqq 0 \quad \text{if} \quad h_j'^0(t) = 0, \\ \delta h_j''(t) &\geqq 0 \quad \text{if} \quad h_j''^0(t) = 0, \\ \delta q_i(t) &\geqq 0 \quad \text{if} \quad q_i^0(t) = 0. \end{aligned}\right\} \tag{15}$$

On the other hand, since the restrictions (10)–(14) are applied after the variation as well as in the optimum state, the same restrictions must apply for infinitesimal variations if the original restrictions are 'binding' at the optimal point. More specifically, variations must satisfy the following five sets of conditions, if the *if*-clauses added to the conditions are valid at the point of Pareto optimum we are dealing with:

$$\left.\begin{aligned}
&\sum_{j=1}^{n} \frac{\partial U^c}{\delta h_j'(t)}\,\delta h_j'(t) \geqq 0, && \text{if (10) holds with equality;}\\
&\sum_{j=1}^{n} \frac{\partial U^w}{\partial h_j''(t)}\,\delta h_j''(t) \geqq 0, && \text{if (11) holds with equality;}\\
&\sum_{j=1}^{m} b_{ij}\delta q_i(t-1)-\sum_{i=1}^{m} a_{ij}\delta q_i(t)-\delta h_j'(t)-\delta h_j''(t) \geqq 0, &&\\
& && \text{if (12) holds with equality;}\\
&\sum_{i=1}^{m} b_{ij}\delta q_i(T-1) \geqq 0, && \text{if (13) holds with equality;}\\
&0 \geqq \sum_{i=1}^{m} l_i\delta q_i(t), && \text{if (14) holds with equality;}
\end{aligned}\right\} \quad (16)$$

where $\delta q_i(-1) = 0$ because the activities in the past, $q_i(-1)$, are historically given and cannot be altered. The first two *if*-clauses are always valid at a Pareto optimum, so that the corresponding inequalities are standing members of (16).

As $u_w^0(0)$ is a maximum subject to (10)–(14), we also have the inequality,

$$\sum_{j=1}^{n} \frac{\partial U^w}{\partial h_j''(0)}\,\delta h_j''(0) \leqq 0.$$

This, together with (15) and (16), gives a set of inequalities, to which Farkas' theorem is applied. (In fact, the senses of the inequalities in (15) and (16) can be reversed, if necessary, by multiplying by -1 so that they satisfy the hypothesis of the theorem.) Hence it is seen that in association with inequalities listed in (15) and (16), there exist non-negative numbers, which are denoted by $\lambda_j'(t)$, $\lambda_j''(t)$, $\mu_i(t)$, $\nu'(t)$, $\nu''(t)$, $p_j(t)$, $p_j(T)$, $v(t)$, respectively, such that

$$p_j(t)-\frac{\partial U^c}{\partial h_j'(t)}\,\nu'(t)-\lambda_j'(t) = 0, \tag{17}$$

$$p_j(t)-\frac{\partial U^w}{\partial h_j''(t)}\,\nu''(t)-\lambda_j''(t) = 0, \tag{18}$$

$$\sum_{j=1}^{n} a_{ij}p_j(t)+l_i v(t)-\sum_{j=1}^{n} b_{ij}p_j(t+1)-\mu_i(t) = 0, \tag{19}$$

where $\nu''(0)$ is defined as 1; $i = 1, ..., m$; $j = 1, ..., n$; and $t = 0, 1, ..., T-1$.

If $h_j'(t)$ is positive and the restriction on $\delta h_j'(t)$ is absent from (15), then we have $\lambda_j'(t) = 0$ in (17); hence

$$\frac{\partial U^c}{\partial h_j'(t)} v'(t) = p_j(t).$$

On the other hand, in the case where $h_j'(t) = 0$, the above equality is replaced by $\leqq$ since $\lambda_j'(t)$ is non-negative. Similar findings emerge from (18) and (19). Thus

$$\frac{\partial U^c}{\partial h_j'(t)} v'(t) \begin{cases} = p_j(t) & \text{if} \quad h_j'^0(t) > 0, \\ \leqq p_j(t) & \text{if} \quad h_j'^0(t) = 0, \end{cases} \tag{17'}$$

$$\frac{\partial U^w}{\partial h_j''(t)} v''(t) \begin{cases} = p_j(t) & \text{if} \quad h_j''^0(t) > 0, \\ \leqq p_j(t) & \text{if} \quad h_j''^0(t) = 0, \end{cases} \tag{18'}$$

$$\sum_{j=1}^{n} b_{ij} p_j(t+1) \begin{cases} = \sum_{j=1}^{n} a_{ij} p_j(t) + l_i v(t) & \text{if} \quad q_i^0(t) > 0, \\ \leqq \sum_{j=1}^{n} a_{ij} p_j(t) + l_i v(t) & \text{if} \quad q_i^0(t) = 0. \end{cases} \tag{19'}$$

Moreover, if (12) is an inequality for some particular t_0, the corresponding inequality of variations disappears from (16), and $p_j(t_0)$ is regarded as zero; similarly for (13) and (14).

We have thus derived the conditions usually referred to as the Kuhn–Tucker optimality conditions.[1] They are no more than the mathematical conditions for a point to be the optimum of a nonlinear programming problem. Sound economic implications, however, are at once derived from them as soon as we interpret the Farkas (or Lagrange) multipliers, $p_j(t)$s and $v(t)$s, as discounted prices and discounted wage rates. The first two sets of inequalities of the Kuhn–Tucker conditions imply that relative to each Pareto optimum there exists a system of wage rates and prices such that prices are, roughly speaking, 'proportional' to the Capitalist's and the Worker's marginal utilities of goods. The third set implies that a state cannot be a Pareto optimum so long as unprofitable processes are used. Finally, it is seen that the Rule of Free Goods prevails: if there is an excess supply of good j (i.e. (12) or (13) holds with strict inequality), its price is set at zero. The same rule is applied to labour, so that the wage rate will be zero in those periods when workers are not fully employed.

[1] H. W. Kuhn and A. W. Tucker, 'Nonlinear programming', in J. Neyman (ed.), *Proceedings of the Second Berkeley Symposium on Mathematical Statistics and Probability*, (Berkeley, Calif.: University of California Press, 1951).

6. It is clear that the Kuhn–Tucker conditions thus interpreted constitute a part of the conditions for competitive equilibrium, but, in order for a given Pareto optimum to be a full competitive equilibrium, several additional conditions need to be satisfied. First, every household has a budget constraint to be met in each period. Let $E_c(t)$ and $E_w(t)$ stand for profits (discounted) which the Capitalist and the Worker, respectively, receive at the beginning of period t. They accrue from the activities in period $t-1$ but are as yet indeterminate, because they depend, among other things, on the rate of interest in $t-1$, and although conditions (17′)–(19′) determine the discounted prices and wage rates that are associated with the given point of Pareto optimum, they leave the discount ratios (and hence the rates of interest) indeterminate. Let $W(t)$ be the discounted wages which the Worker is paid in period t. With the given average propensities, c_c and c_w, the Capitalist's and the Worker's consumption in period t must satisfy

$$\sum_j^n h_j'^0(t)p_j(t) = c_c E_c(t)$$
$$(20)$$
$$\sum^n h_j''^0(t)p_j(t) = c_w\{W(t)+E_w(t)\}$$

respectively.

Since $t = 0, 1, ..., T-1$, we have T sets of budget equations. In each of them, members of the left-hand sides and $W(t)$ are given once the point of Pareto optimum is given, while $E_c(t)$ and $E_w(t)$ depend on the rate of profits (or the interest rate) and the ownership of capital in the previous period. (Profits are distributed among the Capitalist and the Worker in proportion to the amounts of capital they own.) We have the recursive relationship that the capital one owns at the beginning of period t is the sum of the capital one owned at the beginning of $t-1$ and one's savings in period $t-1$. We have the saving functions of the type that one's savings in period t are proportional to the income one receives in period t and, therefore, depend on one's wages in period t and one's capital at the beginning of period $t-1$ as well as the profit rate in period $t-1$; and wages are given at the point of Pareto optimum. Consequently, we find that the ultimate variables which determine the right-hand sides of (20) are the stream of the profit (or interest) rates and the *initial* distribution of capital between the Capitalist and the Worker. Thus the $2T$ conditions (20) contain only T variables $r(t)$, $t = -1, 0, ..., T-2$, and one parameter.[1] This means that

[1] We might at first sight regard $r(-1)$ as a parameter of the problem, because it looks from the notation as if it were a variable in the past period -1. It must, however, be remembered that $r(-1)$ does not stand for the *ex ante* (or equilibrium) rate of interest determined in period -1 but is the *ex post* rate of profits calculated in period 0; hence it is treated as a current variable.

every Pareto optimum does not necessarily satisfy all the budget conditions. It is, however, always possible to find a number of Pareto optima (or possibly a unique Pareto optimum) that are consistent with the budget constraints, because we can adjust the values of T parameters of the optimality problem, say those of $u_c^0(t)$, $t = 0, 1, ..., T-1$, of (10) such that generated Pareto optimal consumption quantities fulfil the $2T$ budget constraints for some profit rate. Obviously such values of $u_c^0(t)$s are relative to the initial distribution of wealth between the Capitalist and the Worker. If the historically given distribution does not bear such a relationship to the prescribed $u_c^0(t)$ and $u_w^0(t)$, then it is evident that the generated Pareto optimum cannot be a competitive equilibrium.

Second, the prices of goods $p(T)$ in the final period T are calculated according to the optimization rules (17′)–(19′). They may generally differ from those values of the prices which entrepreneurs expect to prevail in period T. The equalization of them is a part of the conditions for competitive equilibrium, but no account is taken of it in the Pareto optimization procedure. In order to secure the equalization it must be assumed that the amounts of goods, $h_i^0(T), ..., h_n^0(T)$, which will be bequeathed at the horizon T to the future generations are given such that the optimization calculations result in the same final prices $p(T)$ as those expected by entrepreneurs. Such particular specification of the bequests $h^0(T)$ is a necessary condition for coincidence of Pareto optimum and competitive equilibrium.

7. We have so far seen that every competitive equilibrium is a Pareto optimum and conversely every Pareto optimum (if it is consistent with budget conditions and expectations of prices) is a competitive equilibrium.[1] We have also seen that the Silvery Equilibrium growth or the (generalized) von Neumann growth is a particular equilibrium over time that is obtained when the initial state is somewhere on the von Neumann path. Accordingly, the von Neumann growth is superior to other feasible paths which start from the same initial position as the von Neumann path; more precisely, it is a strongly efficient path, along which the consumable outputs are distributed among capitalists and workers in a Pareto optimum way.

It must be emphasized that we have obtained this superiority of the von Neumann growth on the assumption that the economy was in the state of

[1] Recent literature concerning this classical proposition includes: K. J. Arrow, 'An extension of the basic theorems of classical welfare economics', in J. Neyman (ed.), *Proceedings of the Second Berkeley Symposium on Mathematical Statistics and Probability* (Berkeley, Calif.: University of California Press, 1951), pp. 507–32; G. Debreu, 'Valuation equilibrium and Pareto optimum', *Proceedings of the National Academy of Sciences*, Vol. XL (1954), pp. 588–92; also his *Theory of Value* (New York: John Wiley, 1959); R. Dorfman, P. A. Samuelson, and R. Solow, loc. cit., pp. 408–15.

Silvery Equilibrium at the beginning of the journey. It is evident that this is an extremely unrealistic assumption which can only be satisfied by chance. In general, an economy is not so luckily situated; there will be some goods whose initial stocks are relatively superfluous or deficient. In comparison with a path starting with such historically given stocks of goods the von Neumann growth path will not necessarily be revealed as an optimum path.

It must also be emphasized that we have obtained the Silvery Growth Equilibrium on the assumption that the propensity to save is given to each member of the economy. It is evident that the solution is relative to these parameters. If individuals had different propensities to save, the economy would be directed to grow along a different path of balanced growth. In fact there are a number of balanced growth states, each could be turned into a Silvery Equilibrium growth state if capitalists and workers saved at the appropriate rates. A problem which naturally presents itself is: how much of its income should a nation save to obtain the best one among all the possibilities of balanced growth? This is clearly a limited Ramsey problem—'limited' in the sense that a restriction is made on the 'menu' so that it consists of balanced growth states only, all other feasible states having been ruled out from the field of selection for some reason or other. The solution to it (which is called the Golden Equilibrium) would generally differ from the solution to the general Ramsey problem of choosing the best from among all feasible growth paths.[1] However, if sufficient time is allowed, any solution to the latter problem is seen to approach the Golden Equilibrium (in the case where the subjective time-preference factor does not exceed the growth factor) or some specific Silvery Equilibrium (in all other cases),[2] remaining within a sufficiently small neighbourhood of the Golden or the Silvery Equilibrium over the greater part of the course (the Consumption Turnpike Theorem). Leaving this convergence problem to later chapters, we venture in this section to work further on the assumption that choice is restricted within the family of balanced growth paths. The study will result in the famous Golden Rule of Accumulation due to E. S. Phelps and others;[3] it provides a foundation for Turnpike Theorems and justifies the classical saving programme of the Marx–von Neumann–Joan Robinson type which lays down that aggregate savings equal the total amount of profits.

Let us consider two states which grow in balance at the given natural

[1] F. P. Ramsey, 'A mathematical theory of saving', *Economic Journal*, Vol. XXXVIII (1928), pp. 543–59.

[2] More accurately, it is that Silvery Equilibrium which is obtained as the balanced Ramsey-optimum path (referred to later) when the subjective time-preference factor is greater than the growth factor.

[3] See, for example, E. S. Phelps, 'The golden rule of accumulation', *American Economic Review*, Vol. LI (1961), pp. 638–43, as well as his *Golden Rules of Economic Growth* (New York: Norton, 1966), pp. 189.

rate, $\rho-1$, with initial intensities $(\bar{q}_1, \bar{q}_2, ..., \bar{q}_m)$ and $(\bar{\bar{q}}_1, \bar{\bar{q}}_2, ..., \bar{\bar{q}}_m)$, respectively. The intensities of processes in period t are $\rho^t\bar{q}_1, \rho^t\bar{q}_2, ..., \rho^t\bar{q}_m$ in the first state and $\rho^t\bar{\bar{q}}_1, \rho^t\bar{\bar{q}}_2, ..., \rho^t\bar{\bar{q}}_m$ in the second. From them result in period $t+1$ consumable outputs $\rho^t\bar{h}_1, \rho^t\bar{h}_2, ..., \rho^t\bar{h}_n$, and $\rho^t\bar{\bar{h}}_1, \rho^t\bar{\bar{h}}_2, ..., \rho^t\bar{\bar{h}}_n$ respectively, which are distributed between the Capitalist and the Worker. We have the normalized equations,

$$\sum b_{ij}\bar{q}_i = \rho \sum_i a_{ij}\bar{q}_i + \bar{h}_j, \qquad i = 1, ..., n$$

and

$$\sum b_{ij}\bar{\bar{q}}_i = \rho \sum_i a_{ij}\bar{\bar{q}}_i + \bar{\bar{h}}_j, \qquad j = 1, ..., n.$$

Let $\bar{u}_c(t)$ and $\bar{u}_w(t)$ denote the utilities which the Capitalist and the Worker realize in the first state from their consumption of goods in period t; similar utilities in the second state are referred to as $\bar{\bar{u}}_c(t)$ and $\bar{\bar{u}}_w(t)$.

The criteria of Pareto optimality enable us to sort out Pareto optima from other non-optimal points; but they are ineffective in ordering points belonging to the set of Pareto optima. In fact, for two different Pareto optimal states, I and II, there must be at least two strict inequalities having opposite senses; for example, we must have, for some t and t', inequalities

$$\bar{u}_c(t) > \bar{\bar{u}}_c(t) \qquad \text{and} \qquad \bar{u}_i(t') < \bar{\bar{u}}_i(t'),$$

where $i = c$ or w. In words, if a person, say the Capitalist in period t, prefers his choice in the state I to that in II, then there must be another person, the Capitalist in period t' or the Worker, who prefers his choice in II to that in I. This is obvious because otherwise state II would not be a Pareto optimum. It is evident that in such a situation we cannot put these states in any particular socially preferred order unless a further criterion of social choice is introduced so that utilities of various persons at various points of time can interpersonally and intertemporally be compared with each other.

The problem of finding that balanced growth path which workers and capitalists prefer to the other balanced growth paths is now investigated under the following special assumptions. We assume that the utility functions $U^c(h')$ and $U^w(h'')$ are quasi-homogeneous and similar. The definition of the quasi-homogeneity has already been given; it means that a proportional change in the consumption quantities of goods does not at all disturb the marginal rate of substitution of goods for one another. We say that $U^c(h')$ and $U^w(h'')$ are similar if $h' = h''$ implies the equality of the marginal rates of substitution between the Capitalist and the Worker. Since we are only concerned with states of balanced growth, these properties are sufficient to allow us to consolidate the Capitalist and the Worker into a single person.

First, in the state of balanced growth, there is no change in prices and the wage rate, but the Capitalist's and the Worker's income grow at the natural rate. It then follows, under the assumption of $U^c(h')$ being quasi-homogeneous, that an increase in the Capitalist's income gives rise to a proportional increase in his consumption quantities, $h_1', ..., h_n'$, so that his Engel-coefficients remain unchanged; and the same constancy is observed with regard to the Worker. Second, the similarity of the utility functions implies that the Engel-coefficients of the Capitalist and the Worker are identical. Therefore, along any balanced growth path, the Capitalist's Engel-coefficients take on the same constant values as the Worker's.

For each period t we may consider an *instantaneous* Pareto optimization problem to maximize, say, the Worker's degree of satisfaction in period t,

$$U^w(h_1''(t), ..., h_n''(t)),$$

subject to the constraints in the same period:

$$\begin{aligned} U^c(h_1'(t), ..., h_n'(t)) &\geqq u_c(t), \\ h_j'(t)+h_j''(t) &\leqq h_j(t), \\ \sum_i b_{ij}q_i(t-1)-\sum_i a_{ij}q_i(t) &= h_j(t), \\ \sum_i l_i q_i(t) &\leqq \rho^t \bar{N}, \end{aligned}$$

where $j = 1, ..., n$; $u_c(t)$, and $\bar{N}$ are regarded as given. It is noted that in this problem the usual restriction that $q_1(t-1), ..., q_m(t-1)$ are historically given is removed and, instead, $q(t-1)$ and $q(t)$ are required to fulfil the proportionality conditions,

$$q_i(t) = \rho q_i(t-1) \qquad i = 1, ..., m. \tag{21}$$

Because of the quasi-homogeneity of the utility functions, the solutions to the above problem can be written as

$$\begin{aligned} q_i(t) &= \rho^t \bar{q}_i, & h_j(t) &= \rho^t \bar{h}_j, \\ h_j'(t) &= \rho^t \theta \bar{h}_j, & h_j''(t) &= \rho^t (1-\theta)\bar{h}_j, \end{aligned} \tag{22}$$

where $i = 1, ..., m$ and $j = 1, ..., n$; 'barred' symbols are independent of time t, and θ is the distribution factor depending upon the prescribed value of $u_c(t)$. Under the condition that U^c and U^w are 'similar', it can be verified that this Pareto optimality is equivalent to the following problem: to maximize, instead of $U^w(h'(t))$, the aggregate utility function

$$U(h_1(t), ..., h_n(t)) \tag{23}$$

subject to

$$\sum_i b_{ij}q_i(t-1)-\sum_i a_{ij}q_i(t) = h_j(t) \tag{24}$$

$$\sum_i l_i q_i(t) \leqq \rho^t \bar{N}, \tag{25}$$

$j = 1, ..., n$, and then to distribute aggregate consumable outputs $h(t)$ between the Capitalist and the Worker such that

$$U^c(\theta h_1(t), ..., \theta h_n(t)) = u_c(t) \qquad \text{and} \qquad h_j''(t) = (1-\theta)h_j(t),$$

where U is a function 'similar' to U^c and U^w; $u_c(t)$ is the prescribed degree of satisfaction of the Capitalist; and the qs are regarded as satisfying the proportionality conditions (21).[1] It is thus found that when individual utility functions are quasi-homogeneous and similar, any Pareto optimum to be established under the condition of balanced growth is reduced to a solution of a single-person optimization problem which disregards the distribution of aggregate consumable outputs among the members and simply maximizes the aggregate utility function (23) subject to the technical conditions (24). An argument identical with that developed in section 3 above gives the Kuhn–Tucker conditions for this new optimum which demand that the following inequalities hold at the balanced growth state $h(t) = \rho^t \bar{h}$ and $q(t) = \rho^t \bar{q}$:

$$\nu(t)\,\frac{\partial U}{\partial h_j}\begin{cases} = p_j & \text{if} \quad \bar{h}_j > 0, \\ \leqq p_j & \text{if} \quad \bar{h}_j = 0, \end{cases} \tag{26}$$

$$\sum_j b_{ij} p_j \begin{cases} = \rho \sum a_{ij} p_j + \rho l_i v & \text{if} \quad \bar{q}_i > 0, \\ \leqq \rho \sum_j a_{ij} p_j + \rho l_i v & \text{if} \quad \bar{q}_i = 0, \end{cases} \tag{27}$$

where the ps are normalized such that $\sum_j p_j = 1$, and the marginal utilities $\partial U/\partial h$ are functions of $\rho^t h$. It is noted that $p_1, ..., p_n$, and v and $\nu(t)$ are the Farkas multipliers, among which, because of the quasi-homogeneity of U, $\nu(t)$ is dependent on t, but the ps and v are not.

The multipliers ps and v are interpreted as implicit (or shadow) prices and wage rate which will prevail along the optimal balanced growth path. If labour is a free good, i.e., if (25) holds with strict inequality, then v will be set at zero. Considering this fact and the proportionality of the activities, $q(t) = \rho^t \bar{q}$, we get from (24), (25), and (27) the equation

$$\sum_j p_j h_j(t) = \rho^t \bar{N} v \qquad \text{for all } t, \tag{28}$$

which implies the Golden Rule of Accumulation holds: when the Capitalist's and the Worker's propensity to save are such that the sales value of consumable outputs equals the total wages bill, the corresponding balanced growth path is 'optimal', i.e., it produces a consumption stream which is uniformly preferred to the consumption stream associated with any other balanced growth path.

[1] In fact, the Kuhn–Tucker conditions for both problems are identical.

Optimum consumable outputs thus determined are distributed between the Capitalist and the Worker in the following manner. The postulated Pareto optimality requires that they are distributed between them in the proportion of θ to $1-\theta$, where θ is a constant determined in response to the prescribed value of u_c. In general, θ may take on any number between 0 and 1. But, if the Golden State should be a state of long-run equilibrium (either of the Pasinetti type or of the anti-Pasinetti type), the distribution factor θ must, as will be seen below, be fixed at zero; or, in other words, the Capitalist must devote his whole income for accumulation purposes. This means that only a particular Pareto optimum which corresponds to the degree of satisfaction of the Capitalist set at $u_c = U^c(0)$ can be a Golden Equilibrium which is perpetually maintained.

We reach this important finding in the following way. Since consumption plus savings equals the total product which in turn equals wages plus profits, (28) implies

$$\text{savings} = s_c E_c + s_w(W+E_w) = E_c + E_w = \text{profits},$$

where profits E_c accrue to the Capitalist and E_w to the Worker. In the Pasinetti long-run equilibrium, profits are distributed between the Capitalist and the Worker in proportion to their savings; we have

$$\frac{E_c}{s_c E_c} = \frac{E_w}{s_w(W+E_w)} \quad \text{or} \quad s_w(W+E_w) = s_c E_w. \tag{29}$$

Hence,

$$s_c(E_c+E_w) = E_c+E_w,$$

from which we find that the Golden Rule requires the Capitalist's propensity to save to be unity; hence θ is zero.

The second equation of (29) can now be put in the form

$$s_w W = c_w E_w. \tag{30}$$

This states that in the state of Golden Equilibrium the consumption from the Worker's profit income must just compensate the savings from his wage income. It is evident that it holds in any society where the Worker saves all his profit income and consumes all his wage income. It is also evident that when no profits accrue to the Worker, it is reduced to the classical condition that the Worker should not save at all.

On the other hand, in the Golden Equilibrium of the anti-Pasinetti type with E_c zero, we have no savings and no consumption by the Capitalist. Hence, $\theta = 0$ again. The Golden Equilibrium will be established when the Worker saves according to rule (30).

Finally, it is recollected that we have so far considered the problem of choosing the best one from among all possible balanced growth paths and we obtained the Golden Rule of Accumulation. It is clear that the

Silvery Equilibrium will be superseded by the Golden Equilibrium if we can freely choose the initial stocks of goods but the choice has to be made from among the balanced growth paths. There is, however, no reason why we should stick to balanced or proportional growth. All feasible paths that start with *given* initial stocks of goods are compared with each other; and on the basis of some dynamic utility function, one of them will be chosen as the best. In Chapter XIII below, this path is given the name of the Ramsey optimum path. It is evident that it is relative to the given initial point and need not be a balanced growth path.

To each possible initial point there corresponds a Ramsey optimum path. Among all such paths we can find one that is a balanced growth path. In Chapter XIII we show that this balanced Ramsey-optimum path is relative to the parameters of the assumed dynamic utility function, especially to the 'time-preference factor'. Also, along that path a Silvery Equilibrium is established with an equilibrium rate of profits that equals the assumed value of the subjective time-preference factor. This observation is referred to as the Silvery Rule of Accumulation. Applying it to the Silvery Equilibrium established in a purely private-enterprise economy, we may think of it, even though it was not chosen with any particular welfare consideration in mind, as if the society choose it as a Ramsey optimum on the basis of a 'shadow' dynamic utility function which discounts the future generations at an appropriate rate.

We now conclude this chapter by noting that the two Rules of Accumulation characterize the corresponding equilibria differently: the Golden Equilibrium is the optimum path chosen from among all possible paths of balanced growth, while the Silvery Equilibrium is the balanced path among all possible paths which are Ramsey optimum, provided that the time-preference factor of the Ramsey optimization is taken such that it equals the profits factor (i.e., 1 + the rate of profits) prevailing at the Silvery Equilibrium.

PART III

AFTER THE REVOLUTION

X

MAXIMIZATION OF BEQUESTS: THE FIRST TURNPIKE THEOREM

1. HAVING found the conditions for the Golden Equilibrium we naturally turn to examine the economy for stability. Does a Hicks–Malinvaud competitive equilibrium trajectory starting from the historically given initial point approach nearer and nearer to the state of Golden Equilibrium when the order of the path gets larger? This problem, which amounts to asking whether an economy obeying the principle of competition can attain a Golden Age, will be discussed repeatedly in this chapter and the following. The convergence of this sort will be compared with another kind of convergence recently dealt with by many writers under the common heading of Turnpike Theorems, particular applications of which may occur in more or less planned economies but not in purely competitive economies.

In this chapter, we confine ourselves to the simple case of 'L-shaped' indifference curves. We assume that (i) the Capitalist's propensity to save is unity and the Worker's is zero not only in Golden Equilibrium but also in all other circumstances, and (ii) the Worker has a family of parallel indifference curves to the effect that, unless a commodity is a 'limiting' factor, an increase in the supply of it (the supply of other commodities remaining constant) does not leave the Worker better off than before. It then follows that although the Worker is permitted to choose between alternative bundles of commodities which are equal in value, Engel-coefficients derived from such indifference curves do not respond to price changes at all; they are taken as constant, as in the original von Neumann model which does not allow for consumers' choice. Our model is probably applicable to communist economies in the early stage of their development. It is evident that there is no bourgeoisie in such economies; and when they are put under the dictatorship of Stalinists, all surpluses of production are automatically reinvested, all consumption goods are rationed and workers cannot choose goods according to their own tastes but are only fed at some subsistence level.

Apart from T inequalities stating that in each period t, $t = 0, 1, ..., T-1$, investment must be at least as large as savings, the Hicks–Malinvaud path of order T is characterized (as was shown in Chapter VIII) by the following four sets of inequalities:

$$\sum b_{ij}q_i(t-1) \geqq \sum_i c_{ij}q_i(t), \tag{1}$$

$$N(t) \geqq \sum_i l_i q_i(t), \tag{2}$$

$$\sum_j b_{ij} P_j(t+1) z(t) \leqq \sum_j a_{ij} P_j(t) + l_i w(t), \tag{3}$$

$$P_j(T) = \psi_{jT}(P_1(0), \ldots, P_n(0), w(0)), \tag{4}$$

where $i = 1, \ldots, m$; $j = 1, \ldots, n$; $t = 0, 1, \ldots, T-1$. (1) and (2) are the supply-demand inequalities for good j and labour, respectively; (3) is the price-cost inequality for process i; (4) is the price-expectation function. Symbols other than c_{ij} are familiar. b_{ij} represents an output coefficient of process i; l_i the labour-input coefficient of process i; $N(t)$ the number of workers in period t; $q_i(t)$ the intensity of process i in period t; $P_j(t)$ the price of good j in period t; $w(t)$ the wage rate in period t; and $P_j(T)$ the expected price of good j in period T. The symbol c_{ij} has the same meaning as it had when it was used in the original von Neumann model; that is to say, it denotes the sum of the quantity, a_{ij}, of good j technologically required per unit level of operation of process i and the quantity of good j consumed by the workers employed per unit level of operation of process i—an 'augmented' input coefficient. Each Engel-coefficient, though it depends on the real-wage rate, is assumed to be independent of all prices, so that the quantities consumed by workers are independent of prices. The analysis, however, has to be confined to the case where the real-wage rate is fixed at some, say subsistence, level in order for each c_{ij} to be regarded completely as a constant.

Let us now assume, throughout this chapter, that the stream of labour supply $N(t), t = 0, 1, \ldots,$ *ad infinitum*, is given such that it causes a constant real-wage rate to prevail. We have the Worker's budget equation

$$w(t) = \sum_j e_j P_j(t), \tag{5}$$

where e_j stands for the consumption of good j per worker. It is again noted that all e_js, as well as the real-wage rate $w(t)/\sum_j P_j(t)$, are taken as constant throughout this chapter. In view of the definition of c_{ij}, we then put (3) in the form

$$\sum_j b_{ij} p_j(t+1) \leqq \sum_j c_{ij} p_j(t) \qquad i = 1, \ldots, m, \tag{3'}$$

in terms of discounted prices $p_j(t) = P_j(t)Z(t)$.[1]

As we have decided to assume that $w(0)$ is a constant, we may eliminate it from the arguments of the expectation functions (4). They may be written as

$$p_j(T) = \phi_{jT}(p_1(0), \ldots, p_n(0))Z(T), \qquad j = 1, \ldots, n. \tag{4'}$$

[1] The discount factor $z(t)$ is defined as the reciprocal of 1+the rate of interest in period t. The long-term discount factor $Z(t)$ is the product of t short-term factors, $z(0), z(1), \ldots, z(t-1)$.

With these modifications the original inequalities (1)–(4) characterizing the Hicks–Malinvaud path are equivalent to the system of inequalities (1), (3′), and (4′) (where the first two hold for $t = 0, 1, \ldots, T-1$) provided the supply of labour is adjusted so as to keep the real-wage rate unchanged.

Instead of directly investigating whether the path thus particularized will converge to the Golden Equilibrium, we take the following indirect method. We imagine long-run efficient paths starting with historically given initial endowments and aiming at a stock structure specified by the planning authorities. Such paths are called DOSSO paths, because Dorfman, Samuelson, and Solow were the first to show that *any* of the paths will run near the Golden Equilibrium path (nicknamed 'Turnpike' by DOSSO) for most of the programming period, when it is sufficiently long (the Turnpike Theorem).[1] The efficiency of a DOSSO path implies that it is a path obtained by maximizing a scalar u subject to

$$\sum_i b_{ij} q_i(t-1) \geqq \sum_i c_{ij} q_i(t), \qquad t = 0, 1, \ldots, T-1, \tag{6}$$

$$\sum_i b_{ij} q_i(T-1) \geqq b_j^* u, \tag{7}$$

where $j = 1, \ldots, n$; $b_1^*, \ldots, b_n^*$ are the desired proportions of the stocks of goods at a prescribed point of time T. Those goods which are superfluous at that time will be discarded so that the desired proportions are left; the remaining stocks will be bequeathed to the coming generation in exactly those proportions. The scalar, u, may be taken as an index of attainment of the aim, in terms of which all feasible paths are evaluated. It is easy to see that the Kuhn–Tucker conditions for this optimization problem are formulated in terms of the Farkas multipliers $p(t)$ as

$$\sum_j b_{ij} p_j(t+1) \begin{cases} = \sum_j c_{ij} p_j(t), & \text{if } q_i^0(t) > 0 \\ \leqq \sum_j c_{ij} p_j(t), & \text{if } q_i^0(t) = 0, \end{cases} \tag{8}$$

$$\sum_j b_j^* p_j(T) \begin{cases} = 1, & \text{if } \quad u^0 > 0, \\ \geqq 1, & \text{if } \quad u^0 = 0, \end{cases} \tag{9}$$

at the maximum point $\{q^0(0), \ldots, q^0(T-1), u^0\}$. The DOSSO path characterized by inequalities (6)–(9)[2] can now readily be compared with the Hicks–Malinvaud path. First, (6) is identical with (1); in other words, both paths are chosen from among the same set of feasible paths. Second, (8) is identical with (3′). In other words, both paths choose processes according to the Rule of Profitability; processes are evaluated at market

[1] See Dorfman, Samuelson, and Solow, op cit., Chapter 12.

[2] Note that (9) is no more than a formula for the normalization of prices when optimization is 'meaningful' in the sense that there is a feasible path with $u > 0$.

prices in the case of the Hicks–Malinvaud path and at (officially fixed) efficiency prices in the case of the DOSSO. These prices are set according to the rule of competitive pricing. Finally, both paths are different from each other in the final states reached. The DOSSO path is so selected that it will, in period T, arrive at a point on the 'terminal ray' specified by the authorities, as is required by (7), while the Hicks–Malinvaud path is guided by entrepreneurs' expectations (4′). However, this difference is irrelevant for the first half of the stability proof for the Hicks–Malinvaud equilibrium trajectory; besides, its convergence to the Golden Equilibrium will follow as a corollary to the Turnpike Theorem. For the efficiency of argument, let us now turn the steering-wheel in the direction of the Turnpike Theorem and drive on as far as we can, with the intention that we will finally come back to the problem of the Hicks–Malinvaud competitive equilibrium path in order to establish its stability. This is indeed the way of Turnpike theorists.

2. In this section and the following we are concerned with a simple Turnpike Theorem established on a number of von Neumann assumptions mentioned in the previous section. They are: (1) the real-wage rate is held constant, which means that as soon as the demand for labour is found to increase at a rate greater than the natural rate of population growth, the supply of labour is expanded by immigration, to whatever extent is necessary; (2) the Worker only consumes and the Capitalist only saves; (3) the Worker buys consumption goods in the same fixed amounts in any circumstances as he does in the state of Golden Equilibrium. These assumptions are of course restrictive; but some of them are necessary for convergence, while others are unnecessary. Those which are found to be unnecessary will be removed in more far-reaching discussions in later chapters. Also, we shall later discuss the significance of the other assumptions to the Turnpike Theorem.

Once provided with these assumptions, we may put our basic inequalities for balanced growth equilibrium into the following original von Neumann forms:

$$\sum_j b_{ij} y_j \leqq \beta \sum_j c_{ij} y_j, \qquad i = 1, \ldots, m, \tag{10}$$

$$\sum_i \sum_j b_{ij} x_i y_j = \beta \sum_i \sum_j c_{ij} x_i y_j, \tag{11}$$

$$\sum_i b_{ij} x_i \geqq \alpha \sum_i c_{ij} x_i, \qquad j = 1, \ldots, n, \tag{12}$$

$$\sum_i \sum_j b_{ij} x_i y_j = \alpha \sum_i \sum_j c_{ij} x_i y_j, \tag{13}$$

$$\sum_i \sum_j b_{ij} x_i y_j > 0, \tag{14}$$

where $x_1, ..., x_m$ are normalized intensities, and $y_1, ..., y_n$ are normalized prices. The existence of non-negative solutions $(\bar{x}, \bar{y}, \bar{\alpha}, \bar{\beta})$ to the system (10)–(14) has been established by Kemeny, Morgenstern, and Thompson under the following two assumptions:[1]

(a) for each process $i = 1, ..., m$ there is at least one good j for which $c_{ij} > 0$;
(b) for each good $j = 1, ..., n$ there is at least one process i for which $b_{ij} > 0$.

(b) has already been used in the proof of the existence of a balance growth solution to the generalized von Neumann model in Chapter VII. The other assumption (a), though it has not been utilized there, is also plausible enough, because there would be no process i whose a_{ij}, $j = 1, ..., n$, and l_i are all zero and some goods are required to feed labour; we at once find that as it is impossible for any process to produce some goods without consuming either a material input or a labour-feeding input, every process must have at least one positive augmented input coefficient, c_{ij}.

There may be a number of balanced growth states satisfying inequalities (10)–(14), among which those solutions with the largest $\bar{\alpha}$ give the Golden Equilibrium path or the Turnpike. We assume that the wage rate is given so that the largest $\bar{\alpha}$ equals the natural growth factor, ρ, of the labour force. We also assume throughout the rest of this chapter that:

(i) the Turnpike intensity vector $\bar{x}$ is unique,
(ii) the Turnpike price vector $\bar{y}$ is strictly positive.

The former implies the system is to some extent indecomposable, while the latter rules out the possibility of free goods, so that $\bar{x}$ fulfils each inequality of (12) with equality. They are of course rather restrictive assumptions. Tremendous mathematical efforts to remove them will, however, only lead to a generalization that is not very important from the economic view-point; it seems to me that in our present case the marginal revenue will not compensate for the marginal cost.

Let us now consider feasible paths of length T which start with given stocks of goods, $b(0) = \{b_1(0), ..., b_n(0)\}$, inherited from the past (where $b_j(0) = \sum_i b_{ij}q_i(-1)$ in the other expression) and aim to have the terminal composition of stocks, $b^* = (b_1{}^*, ..., b_n{}^*)$, specified by the planning authorities. No restriction is made on the initial stock vector $b(0)$ except that:

(iii) $b(0)$ is given such that the economy can move from $b(0)$ to a point on the Turnpike in a finite number of periods, say T_0.

[1] See J. G. Kemeny, O. Morgenstern, and G. L. Thompson, loc. cit., pp. 116–19.

The only restriction that is made on the final composition b^* is that:

(iv) b^* is given such that the economy can move in a finite number of periods, T_1, from a point on the Turnpike to a state with the stock composition b^*.

We may normalize b^* so that

$$\bar{y}_1 b_1^* + \ldots + \bar{y}_n b_n^* = 1.$$

Let $b_j(t)$ denote the stock of good j available at the beginning of period t, i.e.,

$$b_j(t) = \sum_i b_{ij} q_i(t-1).$$

All the feasible paths are evaluated in terms of the final composition b^*. A DOSSO path that maximizes the index of attainment, u, or the minimum of the ratios $b_1(T)/b_1^*, \ldots, b_n(T)/b_n^*$, will be chosen out of the set of all feasible paths of order T. We can state the Turnpike Theorem as follows:[1]

If the programming period T is sufficiently long, then any DOSSO path starting from b(0) *will remain most of that period within a very small neighbourhood of the Turnpike* (*or of the Golden Equilibrium*).

The theorem has been discussed for various models; but most of them, if they are examined as economic models, are not so satisfactory as our present model. For example, Radner assumes that only one process is profitable when the Turnpike prices $\bar{y}$ and the Turnpike interest rate $\bar{\beta}$ prevail; while McKenzie's model, though it is more general than my previous 'no joint production' model, belongs to the family of neo-classical Dynamic Input-Output models which we have rejected in Chapter VI above.[2] In the present model which is very similar to Hicks' in *Capital and Growth* we will offer a proof that may be regarded as a mathematical brother of his 'economic' reasoning.[3]

3. The previous studies have, however, succeeded in finding a *jyoseki*[4] for attacking the Turnpike problem; the proofs various writers have presented are fundamentally the same in spite of their *prima facie* differences. Following Hicks, all available processes are classified into two groups: the 'top' and the 'non-top' processes. All 'profitable' processes, i.e. all those which satisfy the profitability condition (10) with equality at the

[1] See, for example, Dorfman, Samuelson, and Solow, op. cit., Chapter 12 and Morishima, op. cit., Chapter 6. The simple device of fixing the terminal composition can be replaced by a more general evaluation function discussed by Radner. Cf. R. Radner, 'Paths of economic growth that are optimal with regard only to final states: a Turnpike Theorem', *Review of Economic Studies*, Vol. XXVIII (1961), pp. 98–104.

[2] L. W. McKenzie, 'Turnpike Theorems for a generalized Leontief model', *Econometrica*, Vol. XXXI (1963), pp. 165–80.

[3] J. R. Hicks, *Capital and Growth* (1966), pp. 227–37 and pp. 322–31.

[4] A formula in the game of *go*.

Turnpike prices and interest rate, are arranged in the 'top' class, while all others are put in the 'non-top' class. Non-top processes are unprofitable when the Turnpike prices and interest rate prevail, so that they enter into the equilibrium vector $\bar{x}$ with zero intensity. We define a 'top' state as a state of affairs where all the non-top processes are not used; then the Golden Equilibrium state is a particular 'top' state, where top processes are used with balanced growth intensities, $\bar{x}_1, \bar{x}_2, \ldots, \bar{x}_m$. Following Hicks again, we shall sometimes refer to it as the 'top-balanced' state.[1]

Our proof also follows the *jyoseki*. It will be shown that when the programming period T becomes very long, any DOSSO path will approach some sequence of states, which in turn converges to the Turnpike. For this purpose we introduce a sequence of stock indices $\{K(t)\}$ in which the stocks of various goods at the beginning of each period t are weighted by their Turnpike prices $\bar{y}$; we define

$$K(t) = \sum_j \bar{y}_j b_j(t).$$

Summing the products of $\bar{y}_j$ and each of the feasibility inequalities (6) and summing the products of $q_i(t)$ and each of the price–cost inequalities (10), we get a very important inequality which sets an upper bound to the rate of growth of the stock index:

$$\bar{\beta} K(t) \geqq K(t+1) \qquad \text{or} \qquad K(t+1)/K(t) \leqq \bar{\beta} = \bar{\alpha}.^2$$

It clearly asserts that it is impossible for the stock index to grow at a rate greater than the Turnpike rate of growth. We find that if and only if top processes only are used in period t with full employment of all stocks of goods, the stock index can increase at the 'top' rate, i.e., we have $K(t+1)/K(t) = \bar{\alpha}$.

It follows from assumptions (iii) and (iv) that among feasible paths there are paths with the following properties. First, they start from given $b(0)$ and reach a point on the Turnpike at the beginning of period T_0. Second, once on the Turnpike they continue along it until the beginning of period $T - T_1$ and reach the aimed stock composition b^* at the beginning of period T. Take one of such paths, and call it the 'bottom' path, because any DOSSO path must, by definition, be at least as high as that path at the beginning of period T. Let the rate of growth of the index K in period t be η_t along the bottom path and θ_t along a DOSSO path; the former gives $K(T)$ as

$$\bar{K}(T) = K(0)(1+\eta_0)(1+\eta_1) \ldots (1+\eta_{T-1}),$$

while the latter gives it as

$$K(T) = K(0)(1+\theta_0)(1+\theta_1) \ldots (1+\theta_{T-1}).$$

[1] The set of all top states is called the von Neumann facet by McKenzie.

[2] Note that the famous von Neumann equality between $\bar{\alpha}$ and $\bar{\beta}$ directly follows from equations (11) and (13).

Since the bottom path is a path that realizes the composition b^* at the beginning of period T, the ratios $\bar{b}_1(T)/b_1^*, \ldots, \bar{b}_n(T)/b_n^*$, are equal to each other (where $\bar{b}_j(T)$ is the 'bottom' stock of good j at the beginning of period T). It follows from the efficiency of a DOSSO path that it must have an index of attainment of the aim, u, which is at least as high as the common ratio $\bar{b}_j(T)/b_j^*$. Hence, from the definition of u, we have $b_j(T) \geqq \bar{b}_j(T)$ for all j. Thus efficiency in the sense of DOSSO requires $K(T) \geqq \bar{K}(T)$.

Let us rearrange the sequence of the growth rates $\{\theta_t\}$ $(t = 0, 1, \ldots, T-1)$ in a monotonic increasing way. Let θ_{t_i} denote the ith smallest rate of growth, and let θ_{t_N} be less than the Turnpike rate of growth by δ. Then

$$1+\theta_{t_i} \leqq \bar{\alpha}-\delta \qquad i = 1, \ldots, N,$$
$$\bar{\alpha} \geqq 1+\theta_{t_j} \geqq \bar{\alpha}-\delta \qquad j = N+1, \ldots, T;$$

hence we find that the DOSSO stock index $K(T)$ cannot exceed the 'ceiling' values, $K(0)(\bar{\alpha}-\delta)^N\bar{\alpha}^{T-N}$.

On the other hand, because the bottom path is so constructed that the index K increases at the Turnpike rate from period T_0 to $T-T_1-1$, we may write $\bar{K}(T)$ as $J\bar{\alpha}^{T-T_0-T_1}$, where J represents the accumulation of K in the introduction and the finale, or more exactly,

$$J = K(0)(1+\eta_1) \ldots (1+\eta_{T_0-1})(1+\eta_{T-T_1}) \ldots (1+\eta_{T-1}).$$

We now get, from the comparison of the ceiling value of K with the bottom value,

$$\frac{J}{K(0)}\,\bar{\alpha}^{-(T_0+T_1)} \leqq \left(\frac{\bar{\alpha}-\delta}{\bar{\alpha}}\right)^N, \tag{15}$$

where $\dfrac{J}{K(0)}\,\bar{\alpha}^{-(T_0+T_1)}$ is a constant independent of the length of the DOSSO path. This inequality gives the maximum difference δ which the Nth smallest rate of growth θ_{t_N} can take from the Turnpike rate; and for all $i > N$, $1+\theta_{t_i}$ should be between $\bar{\alpha}$ and $\bar{\alpha}-\delta$. It follows from (15) that δ tends to zero as N tends to infinity.

Now let ε be a small positive number. Define N as the integer which is nearest to $\varepsilon\sqrt{T}$, and δ as the discrepancy between θ_{t_N} and the Turnpike growth rate. When T tends to infinity, N will also tend to infinity (so that δ becomes negligible), but the ratio of N to T becomes smaller and smaller and finally approaches zero. Thus, not only does the number of periods, in which the rate of growth of K (along a DOSSO path) is approximately equal to the Turnpike rate, increase indefinitely but also its ratio to the total number of periods approaches unity, because $(T-N)/T \doteqdot (T-\varepsilon\sqrt{(T)})/T$. Accordingly, if the programming period T is sufficiently long, we may take a very long period, throughout which the difference between the Turnpike and the DOSSO growth rate is negligible.

The following two important properties are obtained for the behaviour of the DOSSO path during the 'long period'. First, all the available stocks of goods are required to be almost fully utilized in the long period. For if the stock of a good exceeded the input and consumption of that good by a significant amount in a certain period belonging to the long period, then the remainder (which is valuable by the assumption that there is no free good in the economy) would be thrown away; hence the index K could not grow at the maximum rate in that period. This means that δ is significantly positive, so that (15) would be reduced to a contradiction. Second, the use of the non-top processes must be negligible throughout the long period. For if they were not and the non-top processes appeared in the input-output inequalities (6) with significant weights, the growth rate of K would also be significantly less than the Turnpike rate. Hence, throughout the long period, both excess supply of stocks and utilization of non-top processes can safely be neglected. Thus the behaviour of a DOSSO path can well be approximated, throughout the long period, by solutions to the set of difference equations

$$\sum_i{}^* b_{ij} q_i(t-1) = \sum_i{}^* c_{ij} q_i(t) \qquad j = 1, ..., n \tag{16}$$

where $\sum_i{}^*$ denotes the summation over the 'top' range. For the convenience of exposition processes are rearranged, in the rest of this chapter, such that the first m^* processes are the top processes and others are non-top; consequently, the summation $\sum^*$ includes the m^* terms from $i = 1$ to $i = m^*$.

4. We now turn to the second part of the proof to show the convergence of DOSSO paths to the Turnpike. But the argument does not proceed straight forwardly; we must begin by establishing a lemma (with a somewhat long proof, I am afraid) whereby we can reduce (16) to a set of ordinary difference equations. We shall show that the number of the Golden Equilibrium processes (i.e. the top processes with *positive* $\bar{x}_i$) is at most as large as the number of goods n,[1] and that the number of the top processes m^* is equal to the number of the Golden Equilibrium processes if the technology is suitably 'canonized' and an appropriate Turnpike price set $(\bar{y}_1, \bar{y}_2, ..., \bar{y}_n)$ is chosen.

A kind of net output coefficient may be defined as

$$v_{ij} = b_{ij} - \bar{\beta} c_{ij} \qquad j = 1, ..., n,$$

in terms of which production processes may be redefined as

$$v_i = (v_{i1}, v_{i2}, ..., v_{in}).$$

[1] This has been observed by Gale. See his excellent article, 'Closed model of production', in H. W. Kuhn and A. W. Tucker (ed.), *Linear Inequalities and Related Systems*, p. 295.

There are available m such processes in the economy, among which we have, for all top processes $i = 1, ..., m^*$,

$$v_{i1}\bar{y}_1+v_{i2}\bar{y}_2+...+v_{in}\bar{y}_n = 0$$

by definition. Hence it is seen that the vectors v_i, $i = 1, ..., m^*$, lie in a linear subspace of dimension at most $n-1$. As $\bar{\alpha} = \bar{\beta}$ and no goods can be free by assumption (ii), we have

$$\sum_i {}^*v_{ij}\bar{x}_i = 0$$

along the Turnpike; it follows that the origin of that subspace corresponds to the Golden Equilibrium point, $\bar{x}$.

Let us classify the top processes into the Golden Equilibrium and other top processes. Let m' ($\leqq m^*$) be the number of Golden Equilibrium processes; we arrange them so that they are the first m' processes labelled by numerals 1, 2, ..., m'. Clearly the origin is a positive linear combination of them. We obtain a convex polyhedron with at most m' vertices spanned by the vectors $v_1, ..., v_{m'}$, having the origin in its interior.[1] (See Fig. 5(a)–(c) with $n = 3$). It is clear that if the number of vertices r of that polyhedron is less than m', then $m'-r$ processes (for example, v_5 and v_6 in Fig. 5(a)) can be expressed as non-negative linear combinations of the other Golden Equilibrium processes; there are *at least two* sets of processes, each giving the origin as a positive linear combination of its component processes. This is a contradiction to the uniqueness of the Turnpike intensity vector. Hence our polyhedron must have m' vertices. The figure obtained by eliminating v_5 and v_6 from Fig. 5(a) illustrates that if m' is greater than n, there are more than two positive linear combinations of the Turnpike processes giving the Golden Equilibrium state as the origin. We again have a contradiction of the same type. Hence m' cannot exceed n.

Let us now consider a 'top' polyhedron spanned not only by the Golden Equilibrium processes but also by all other top processes. If the number of vertices r^* of that polyhedron is less than the number of the top processes m^*, then each of the remaining m^*-r^* top processes (not lying on the vertices) can be expressed as a non-negative linear combination of the vertices. Such 'dependent' processes are eliminated from the list of the 'basic' processes of production; so that we may assume $m^*= r^*$ by making a canonization.

Suppose now $m^* > m'$; suppose also $m' = n$, implying that the origin lines inside the polyhedron spanned by the Golden Equilibrium processes

[1] If the origin lies on a face (or on an intersection of several faces) of the polyhedron, some vertices (v_1, v_4, v_5 in Fig. 5(d)) have zero weights in the equilibrium positive linear combination; this contradicts the definition of the Golden Equilibrium process as a top process with positive $\bar{x}_i$.

(as illustrated by Fig. 5(b)). Then the 'top' polyhedron with m^* vertices would be of the type illustrated by Fig. 5(e). Hence as we have already seen, the Turnpike intensity vector $\bar{x}$ cannot be unique, a contradiction. We find, therefore, that if $m' = n$, then m^* cannot be greater than m'; thus $m^* = n$.

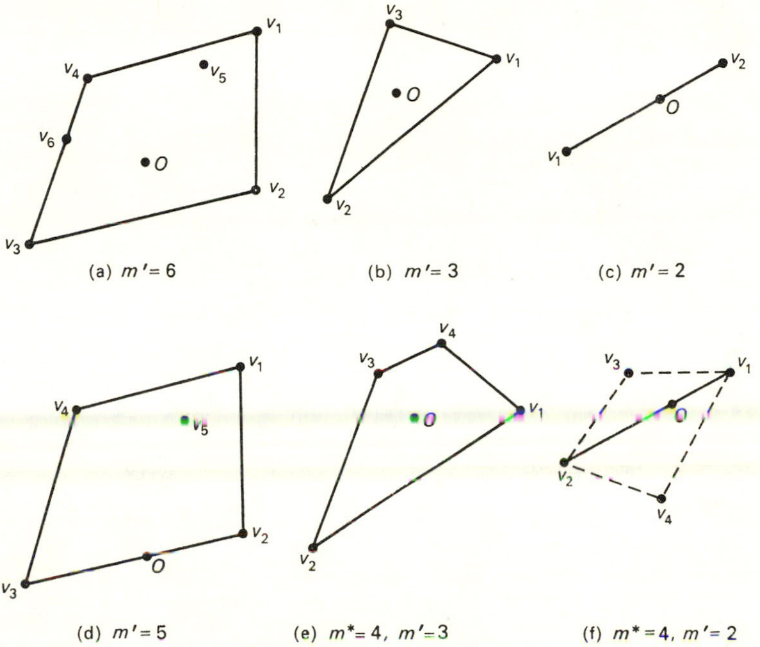

FIG. 5

Next we consider the case with $m' < n$. Let R_n be the $(n-1)$-dimensional subspace in which all top processes lie, and Π the polyhedron spanned by all the Golden Equilibrium processes. As $m' < n$, there is an $(n-2)$-dimensional hyperplane which contains all Golden Equilibrium processes in one halfspace[1] produced by that hyperplane and all other top processes are in the other halfspace. Otherwise, if there were top processes on both sides of Π, the equilibrium intensity vector $\bar{x}$ could not be unique (see Fig. 5(f), where v_1 and v_2 are the Golden Equilibrium processes and v_3 and v_4 are other top processes). Also all non-top processes are located in an n-dimensional half-space produced by the hyperplane R_n, because

$$v_{i1}\bar{y}_1 + \ldots + v_{in}\bar{y}_n < 0$$

1 The part of the space which lies on one side of the dividing hyperplane.

for all non-top processes. We find, therefore, that a *slight* rotation of the hyperplane R_n about Π results in having all non-Golden Equilibrium processes (top or non-top) in only one of the *open* half-spaces[1] produced by the new R_n. Such a rotation implies changes in prices; as prices are originally chosen positive, they are still positive after the slight rotation. At the new equilibrium prices there are no top processes other than the Golden Equilibrium processes, that is, $m^* = m' < n$. This completes the proof of our lemma.

5· Let us now assume, throughout this section, that the technology has been 'canonized' and 'appropriate' positive equilibrium prices have been chosen; we can then group equations (16) into two classes:

$$\sum_i{}^* b_{ij} q_i(t-1) = \sum_i{}^* c_{ij} q_i(t), \qquad j = 1, ..., m^* \tag{17}$$

and

$$\sum_i{}^* b_{ik} q_i(t-1) = \sum_i{}^* c_{ik} q_i(t), \qquad k = m^*+1, ..., n, \tag{18}$$

where (17) gives a usual system of simultaneous difference equations in m^* unknown functions $q_1(t), ..., q_{m^*}(t)$, and (18) is empty, when $m^* = n$.

Equations (17) are solved by the usual method; that is, all possible particular solutions (hence the general solutions as linear combinations of them) are obtained by finding latent roots of the characteristic equation:

$$\begin{vmatrix} b_{11}-\lambda c_{11} & b_{21}-\lambda c_{21} & \dots & b_{m^*1}-\lambda c_{m^*1} \\ b_{12}-\lambda c_{12} & b_{22}-\lambda c_{22} & \dots & b_{m^*2}-\lambda c_{m^*2} \\ \dots & \dots & \dots & \dots \\ b_{1m^*}-\lambda c_{1m^*} & b_{2m^*}-\lambda c_{2m^*} & \dots & b_{m^*m^*}-\lambda c_{m^*m^*} \end{vmatrix} = 0, \tag{19}$$

or

$$|B^*-\lambda C^*| = 0,$$

where B^* stands for the $m^* \times m^*$ matrix (b_{ij}) and C^* for the $m^* \times m^*$ matrix (c_{ij}). If the rank of C^* is m^*, then (19) gives m^* roots; but no *a priori* information is given about the rank of C^*. We only know that (19) gives *at most* m^* roots. Let $\bar{m}(\leqq m^*)$ be the total number of the latent roots, and denote them by $\lambda_1, ..., \lambda_{\bar{m}}$. It is shown that the general solution to (17) can be written as

$$q_i(t) = \sum_k^{\bar{m}} v_k q_{ik} \lambda_k{}^t, \qquad i = 1, ..., m^*, \tag{20}$$

1 A half-space not including the dividing hyperplane.

where $Q_k = (q_{1k}, q_{2k}, ..., q_{m^*k})$ is the characteristic solution associated with λ_k and $v_1, ..., v_{\bar{m}}$ depend on the initial conditions.[1]

Notice that when $\bar{m} < m^*$, the initial values of $q_1(t), q_2(t), ..., q_{m^*}(t)$ cannot arbitrarily be given; we must start from a point in the non-negative part of the convex polyhedral cone spanned by $\bar{m}$ vectors $Q_1, Q_2, ..., Q_{\bar{m}}$. Notice also that further restrictions are imposed on the initial position in order for the solution (20) to (17) to satisfy $n-m^*$ equations (18) too. In fact, if

$$\sum_i{}^* b_{ij} q_{ik} \neq \lambda_k \sum_i{}^* c_{ij} q_{ik} \tag{21}$$

for some $j = m^*+1, ..., n$, then the v_k corresponding to the particular solution $q_{ik}\lambda_k{}^t$ must be zero. However, there is a particular solution which satisfies all of equations (17) and (18) for any value of t, that is, the Turnpike solution. It can be verified, as would be expected, that $\bar{\alpha}$ is a latent root of (19) and that $\bar{x}_1, \bar{x}_2, ..., \bar{x}_{m^*}$ are not only the characteristic solutions associated with $\bar{\alpha}$ but also fulfil

$$\sum_i{}^* b_{ij} \bar{x}_i = \alpha \sum_i{}^* c_{ij} \bar{x}_i \qquad j = m^*+1, ..., n.$$

For other particular solutions with $|\lambda_k| = \bar{\alpha}$, we now assume that:

(v) (a) When $m^* = n$, there is no negative or complex root of (19) that has absolute value $\bar{\alpha}$. (b) When $m^* < n$, (19) is allowed to have negative or complex roots of modulus $\bar{\alpha}$, but for each of such roots (21) must hold for some $j = m^*+1, ..., n$.

This is the conventional 'joker' ruling out exceptions discussed later. It amounts to assuming that all particular solutions corresponding to those λ_k with modulus $\bar{\alpha}$ do not enter the general solution.

If there is a latent root λ_k such that $|\lambda_k| > \bar{\alpha}$, it is seen that the initial point has to be situated in a more restricted zone in order for (17) and (18) to hold for a long period. Suppose λ_k is a positive number greater than $\bar{\alpha}$. Then some of $q_{1k}, q_{2k}, ..., q_{m^*k}$ must be negative; because otherwise there would be a balanced growth solution at a rate, λ_k, greater than $\bar{\alpha}$. This contradicts the fact that the Turnpike is a path of balanced growth at the maximum rate. If, say, q_{1k} is negative, then $q_1(t)$ will become negative sooner or later, because $q_{1k}\lambda_k{}^t$ will dominate other terms of $q_1(t)$ when t is large. In order that $q_1(t)$ can remain non-negative throughout a very

[1] For the sake of simplicity, we assume, throughout the rest of this chapter, that all the latent roots are distinct.

Owing to Samuelson's *Foundations of Economic Analysis*, a system of linear difference (or differential) equations, say (17), is now familiar to economic students when its λ-matrix, $B^*-\lambda C^*$, has a non-singular leading coefficient matrix C^*, whereas the case with C^* singular is still left unfamiliar to many of them. About that case, however, one may consult, for example, R. A. Frazer, W. J. Duncan, and A. R. Collar, *Elementary Matrices*, (Cambridge: University Press, 1955) pp. 156–63. See p. 163 particularly.

long period, the importance of the particular solution $q_{ik}\lambda_k^t$ in the general solution (20) must be negligible; that is, ν_k is restricted to be a very small number. Similar observations are made for negative and complex roots which are greater than $\bar{\alpha}$ in modulus.

6. We are now at the stage of *yosse*.[1] We have seen that if the programming period T is sufficiently long, any optimum path has a long stretch throughout which (17) and (18) are approximately fulfilled. This implies that at the beginning of that stretch the optimum path has already arrived in the restricted zone just discussed above. Some ν_k must be zero, and the ν_ks corresponding to those λ_ks which are greater than $\bar{\alpha}$ in modulus must be zero or negligible. Every particular solution entering the general solution with a ν_k of some 'macroscopic' magnitude has a characteristic value λ_k which is less than $\bar{\alpha}$ in modulus, unless it is the Turnpike solution. It is now clear that as time goes on, the Turnpike solution will become dominant in the general solution. This means that the DOSSO path remains within a very small neighbouring cone of the Turnpike for most of the programming period.[2]

However, the Turnpike Theorem is not an exception to the rule that every rule has its exception. There is no reason (economic or mathematical) why the 'joker' (v) should be in our hand. If it is not, there may be, as will be seen below, a path which is viable over an infinitely long period but does not converge to the Golden Equilibrium path, eternally oscillating around it with a 'relatively' constant amplitude.[3]

Suppose the characteristic equation has altogether m_1 roots of absolute value $\bar{\alpha}$. If m_1 is even, they are

$$\bar{\alpha},\ -\bar{\alpha}, \text{ and } \bar{\alpha}\Lambda(\pm\theta_k) \qquad k = 1, 2, ..., (m_1-2)/2,$$

where

$$\Lambda(\theta_k) = \cos\theta_k + \sqrt{(-1)}\sin\theta_k.$$

If it is odd, the negative root $-\bar{\alpha}$ is eliminated from the list. It is evident that the negative root can be regarded as a special complex root having

[1] The final part of a game of *go*.

[2] It has been seen that the percentage of the exceptional periods, in which the DOSSO growth rate is significantly less than the Turnpike growth rate, is negligible when the programming period T is very long. But we have not seen what parts of the DOSSO path the exceptional periods belong to. With no further reasoning, it is conceivable that they may be scattered over the whole path. It is, however, a part of the Turnpike *jyoseki* to show that they are, in fact, located only in the beginning and final parts of the path (Nikaido). I do not go into this highly sophisticated problem here and would like to leave it to mathematicians. See H. Nikaido, 'Persistence of continual growth near the von Neumann ray: a strong version of the Radner Turnpike Theorem', *Econometrica*, Vol. XXXII (1964), pp. 151–62.

[3] An amplitude that increases at the same rate as the Turnpike growth rate.

$\theta_k = \pi$; therefore, we shall only be concerned with a representative complex root $\bar{\alpha}\Lambda(\theta_1)$.

We begin by examining the simple case where $2\pi/\theta_1$ is an integer σ_1. Suppose the contrary of (v), i.e., that the characteristic solutions, $\zeta_i+\sqrt{(-1)}\eta_i$, $i = 1, ..., m^*$, that are associated with the root $\bar{\alpha}\Lambda(\theta_1)$[1] satisfy

$$\sum_i{}^* b_{ij}\{\zeta_i+\sqrt{(-1)}\eta_i\} = \bar{\alpha}\Lambda(\theta_1)\sum_i{}^* c_{ij}\{\zeta_i+\sqrt{(-1)}\eta_i\} \tag{22}$$

for *all* $j = 1, ..., n$. It can then be easily verified that conjugate relationships

$$\sum_i{}^* b_{ij}\{\zeta_i-\sqrt{(-1)}\eta_i\} = \bar{\alpha}\Lambda(-\theta_1)\sum_i{}^* c_{ij}\{\zeta_i-\sqrt{(-1)}\eta_i\} \tag{23}$$

also hold for $j = 1, ..., n$.

Let τ be any positive integer. Multiply (22) and (23) by $\Lambda(\tau\theta_1)$ and $\Lambda(-\tau\theta_1)$, respectively, and sum the corresponding equations; we get

$$\sum_i{}^* b_{ij}x_i(\tau) = \bar{\alpha}\sum_i{}^* c_{ij}x_i(\tau+1), \qquad j = 1, ..., n,$$

where

$$x_i(\tau) = \zeta_i\cos(\tau\theta_1)-\eta_i\sin(\tau\theta_1), \qquad i = 1, ..., m^*. \tag{24}$$

Since

$$\sum_i{}^* b_{ij}\bar{x}_i = \bar{\alpha}\sum_i{}^* c_{ij}\bar{x}_i$$

for all j, we get

$$\sum_i{}^* b_{ij}\{\nu_1\bar{x}_i+\nu_2 x_i(\tau)\} = \bar{\alpha}\sum_i{}^* c_{ij}\{\nu_1\bar{x}_i+\nu_2 x_i(\tau+1)\}, \qquad j = 1, ..., n. \tag{25}$$

As $\bar{x}_i$s are all positive, and $x_i(\tau)$s are bounded, we may choose ν_1 and ν_2 such that, for all $i = 1, ..., m^*$,

$$\nu_1\bar{x}_i+\nu_2 x_i(\tau) \geqq 0 \qquad \tau = 0, 1, ..., \sigma_1.$$

It is obvious that a *compound* process τ using $\sum_i{}^* c_{ij}\{\nu_1\bar{x}_i+\nu_2 x_i(\tau)\}$ amounts of goods as inputs produces $\sum_i{}^* b_{ij}\{\nu_1\bar{x}_i+\nu_2 x_i(\tau)\}$ amounts of goods. Equations (25) imply that the compound process τ operating at unit intensity produces outputs that are enough to start the compound process $\tau+1$ at intensity $\bar{\alpha}$. Since $\sigma_1 = 2\pi/\theta_1$, we have from (24),

$$\nu_1\bar{x}_i+\nu_2 x_i(0) = \nu_1\bar{x}_i+\nu_2 x_i(\sigma_1) \qquad i = 1, ..., m^*.$$

Therefore, there are σ_1 compound processes such that the outputs produced by the first compound process operating at unit intensity are

[1] Note that these characteristic solutions are, in general, complex numbers.

used as inputs of the second at intensity $\bar{\alpha}$, whose outputs are in turn used as inputs of the third at intensity $\bar{\alpha}^2$, and so on, until the σ_1th compound process at intensity $\bar{\alpha}^{\sigma_1-1}$ produces enough outputs to be used as inputs of the first compound process operating at intensity $\bar{\alpha}^{\sigma_1}$. Since for any τ

$$\nu_1\bar{x}_i+\nu_2x_i(\tau) \neq \nu_1\bar{x}_i+\nu_2x_i(\tau+1) \qquad i = 1, ..., m^*,$$

there is no balanced growth in any single period; but the initial inputs and final outputs of the compound period consisting of σ_1 single periods are proportional to one another. Thus the DOSSO path traces out, throughout its 'middle' stretch, a spiral which winds around σ_1 different states; the period of the oscillation is σ_1 and the amplitude discounted at the Turnpike rate remains constant.

If, on the other hand, $2\pi/\theta_1$ does not equal an integer but $\sigma_1 < 2\pi/\theta_1 < \sigma_1+1$ for some integer σ_1, then the period of the sinusoidal oscillation is not a multiple of the production period. It is greater than σ_1 but less than σ_1+1. A cycle starting at the beginning of period 0 is completed at a point of time in the σ_1th production period; a new cycle with a phase angle $\phi_1 = (\sigma_1+1)\theta_1-2\pi$ starts when the (σ_1+1)th production period begins. There is no change in our main conclusion that assumption (v) cannot be dispensed with in order to rule out oscillatory paths.

Finally, an example, substantially the same as the one given in my former book,[1] will serve to illustrate that a system may generate oscillatory DOSSO paths if it does not satisfy the critical assumption (v). Suppose an economy has two processes to produce three goods. Suppose the material-input matrix, the output matrix, the vector of labour-input coefficients and the vector of consumption of goods per worker are

	Process 1		Process 2		Consumption per worker
	Input	*Output*	*Input*	*Output*	
Good 1	1	3	2	3	1
Good 2	1	2	1	3	1
Good 3	1	$2\sqrt{(1{\cdot}5)}$	$2\sqrt{(1{\cdot}5)}-1$	3	1
Labour	1	—	1	—	—

respectively. These give the augmented-input coefficient matrix as

$$C = \begin{pmatrix} 2 & 2 & 2 \\ 3 & 2 & 2\sqrt{(1{\cdot}5)} \end{pmatrix}.$$

We find that the Turnpike solution is:

$$\bar{\alpha} = \sqrt{(1{\cdot}5)}, \quad (\bar{y}_1, \bar{y}_2, \bar{y}_3) = (1, \sqrt{(1{\cdot}5)}, \sqrt{(1{\cdot}5)}), \quad (\bar{x}_1, \bar{x}_2) = (\sqrt{(1{\cdot}5)}, 1).$$

[1] See *Equilibrium, Stability, and Growth*, p. 173.

Let us now classify goods such that goods 1 and 2 are members of the difference equation of (17) and good 3 is the sole member of (18). Then the characteristic equation (19) has two roots: $\sqrt{(1{\cdot}5)}$ and $-\sqrt{(1{\cdot}5)}$, where the latter is associated with the characteristic solution,

$$(q_{12}, q_{22}) = (-\sqrt{(1{\cdot}5)}, 1).$$

This satisfies, with $\lambda_2 = -\sqrt{(1{\cdot}5)}$, the equation for good 3,

$$b_{13}q_{12}+b_{23}q_{22} = \lambda_2(c_{13}q_{12}+c_{23}q_{22}),$$

so that assumption (v) does not hold true for the present miniature model.

Let us now take the starting point and the terminal composition of processes as

$$(q_1(-1), q_2(-1)) = (1, 1) \text{ and } (q_1{}^*, q_2{}^*) = (0{\cdot}5, 0{\cdot}5).$$[1]

If $T-1$ is odd, the DOSSO path, $q(t)$, will be

t	0	1	2	3	...	$T-1$
$q_1(t)$	$1{\cdot}5$	$1{\cdot}5$	$1{\cdot}5^2$	$1{\cdot}5^2$	...	$1{\cdot}5^{T/2}$
$q_2(t)$	1	$1{\cdot}5$	$1{\cdot}5$	$1{\cdot}5^2$	...	$1{\cdot}5^{T/2}$

If $T-1$ is even, it will be[2]

t	0	1	2	3	...	$T-1$
$q_1(t)$	$1{\cdot}2$	$1{\cdot}2\times1{\cdot}5$	$1{\cdot}2\times1{\cdot}5$	$1{\cdot}2\times1{\cdot}5^2$	...	$1{\cdot}2\times1{\cdot}5^{(T-1)/2}$
$q_2(t)$	$1{\cdot}2$	$1{\cdot}2$	$1{\cdot}2\times1{\cdot}5$	$1{\cdot}2\times1{\cdot}5$	...	$1{\cdot}2\times1{\cdot}5^{(T-1)/2}$

It is clearly seen from the tables that $q_1(t)/q_2(t)$ does not converge to the Turnpike intensity ratio $\sqrt{(1{\cdot}5)}$, however large T is taken; we have undamped oscillations of the DOSSO relative intensities around the Turnpike.

7. The Turnpike Theorem, which has so far been discussed for its own sake, now serves as a lemma for establishing the convergence (to the Turnpike) of the Hicks–Malinvaud full equilibrium path that will be

[1] Note that here the starting point and the terminal composition are specified in terms of intensities. In terms of stocks of goods, they are

$$(b_1(0), b_2(0), b_3(0)) = (6, 5, 3+2\sqrt{(1{\cdot}5)})$$

and

$$(b_1{}^*, b_2{}^*, b_3{}^*) = (3, 2{\cdot}5, 1{\cdot}5+\sqrt{(1{\cdot}5)}.)$$

[2] My book, *Equilibrium, Stability, and Growth*, contains a slip in calculating the DOSSO intensities, $q_1(t)$ and $q_2(t)$, in the case of T being *odd*. In the second table on p. 173 of that book the figure 2/3 should be replaced by 1 and all the figures for $t \geqq 1$ should be multiplied by $1{\cdot}2$.

obtained, without any guidance from the planning authorities, in a competitive economy when entrepreneurs can foresee all affairs in the future. For this purpose we strengthen one of the assumptions of the Turnpike Theorem as follows:

(iv′) The economy can move from a point on the Turnpike to *any* point with an arbitrary stock composition b^*, within a *fixed* number of periods $\bar{T}_1$.

We then get an inequality similar to (15) but with $\bar{T}_1$ in place of T_1, which determines, independently of the prescribed terminal stock structure, the maximum difference δ between the Turnpike rate and the Nth smallest rate of growth along a DOSSO path. Hence, if we can show that the Hicks–Malinvaud path from $b(0)$ to $b(T)$ is a DOSSO path of order T with the same terminal stock structure, then we may regard δ as a negligible small number by taking N sufficiently large. We may take, as before, N as the nearest integer to $\varepsilon\sqrt{T}$ (ε is an arbitrary small positive number); when T is very large, N would be large enough to make δ negligible. But, as the ratio of N to T becomes very small for very large T, we have a long period during which the economy grows, along the Hicks–Malinvaud path, at some rate which may vary from period to period but remains close to the Turnpike rate of growth. It now follows that a long Hicks–Malinvaud path has a long stretch throughout which difference equations (17) and (18) hold approximately. The second and third stages of the proof of the Turnpike Theorem will *mutatis mutandis* apply to our present problem too, so that the Hicks–Malinvaud path is guaranteed to converge to the Golden Equilibrium.

Therefore, we need to show that any Hicks–Malinvaud path is efficient in the sense of DOSSO; that is to say, we shall observe that it is a DOSSO path with a suitably prescribed final composition of stocks. With this aim in mind we remind the reader of section 1 of this chapter where we have compared these two paths with each other. It was found there that, provided with a number of assumptions including that of the infinite elasticity of the supply of labour at the Golden Equilibrium real-wage rate, the only difference between the DOSSO and the Hicks–Malinvaud path is that the 'terminal ray' of the former is (arbitrarily) specified by the planning authorities, whereas the latter is guided by entrepreneurs' expectations of prices. This implies that when the DOSSO terminal ray is given so as to coincide with the ray on which the final state of the Hicks–Malinvaud path is located, these two paths are found to be identical with each other.

We may therefore conclude our long investigation into stability of the Golden Equilibrium by stating that an economy which works according to the principle of competition approaches the state of Golden Equilibrium and remains within its vicinity during most periods. This is a happy conclusion we wanted to obtain, but it must be noticed that it is merely a tentative conclusion subject to a number of restrictive assumptions. As soon as some of them are removed, the Hicks–Malinvaud path will no longer be convergent; we aim to show this in the next chapter.

XI

OSCILLATIONS DUE TO CONSUMER'S CHOICE

1. In Chapter VI we introduced consumer's choice into the conventional framework of economic growth originated by J. von Neumann. We assumed that consumers are classified into two broad groups of persons, within each of which differences in tastes may be ignored. Both giant consumers, the Worker and the Capitalist, have their own, exogenously given propensities to save and they spend all the rest of their income (after subtracting savings) on current consumption. The total amount of expenditure of a Consumer is distributed among goods so as to maximize his utility function subject to his budget constraint. Clearly, the competitive equilibria of the Lindahl–Hicks–Malinvaud type discussed in Chapter VIII as well as the solutions of the balanced growth equilibrium of the Cassel–von Neumann variety in Chapter VII depend on the derived consumption functions.

In Chapter IX we observed that a balanced growth equilibrium obtained when only the Worker consumes and only the Capitalist saves is distinguished as the 'best' one from all other possible states of balanced growth and is, therefore, referred to as the Golden Equilibrium. Attention was then concentrated in Chapter X upon a particular economy where the Capitalist is thrifty enough to carry out no consumption of goods at all while the Worker is well paid so that he can buy goods in the Golden Equilibrium amounts. Such a specification enabled us to establish convergence to the Turnpike.

This summarizes our previous treatment of consumption of goods. Clearly, the history should not end here, because the hypothesis, that the Worker consumes goods in any non-equilibrium state exactly in the same amounts as in the Golden Equilibrium, is true only when his tastes for goods can be described by a family of L-shaped indifference curves. In other more natural cases his demand for consumption goods would be such as to allow substitution in response to price changes. When the current position of an economy is off the Golden Equilibrium path, prices of goods will generally change, and the Worker will adjust his consumption so as to maintain his maximum satisfaction from goods. The following question is then naturally asked: is the Golden Equilibrium still stable when the assumption of rigid consumption is replaced by the more realistic one that the Worker's demand for consumption goods depends on prices and the wage income?

In association with the assumption of rigid consumption, in Chapter X we made another powerful assumption that there is no shortage at all in the supply of labour, that is to say, even if there is a shortage at some point of time, immigrants rush in from outside the economy and the excess demand for labour will disappear at once; therefore, entrepreneurs can at all times employ as much labour as they want. In the following, we get rid of this assumption and consider an economy where the labour force grows at a constant rate which is exogenously determined. The Worker, who is assumed to be the sole consumer in the economy, is confronted with prices $P_1(t), ..., P_n(t)$ and the wage rate $w(t)$ which may vary from period to period but they are determined in every period t by the market. It is assumed that he spends all his income; he will determine his demands for goods, $e_1(t), ..., e_n(t)$, so as to maximize his utility function $U^w(e_1(t)/N(t), ..., e_n(t)/N(t))$ subject to

$$e_1(t)P_1(t)+...+e_n(t)P_n(t) = N(t)w(t)$$

where $N(t)$ is the Worker's supply of labour, which grows at a constant rate $\rho-1$. Taking it for granted that the utility function is homogeneous of degree zero in $e_1, ..., e_n$ and N (this rather restrictive condition would be fulfilled if individual workers constituting the giant 'Worker' have similar tastes), we can write the demand functions as

$$e_j(t) = g_j(y_1(t), ..., y_n(t), \Omega(t))N(t), \qquad j = 1, ..., n,$$

where $y_h(t)$ is the normalized price of good h in period t, i.e., the price $P_h(t)$ divided by $\sum_j P_j(t)$, and as before the real-wage rate $\Omega(t)$ is defined as $w(t)$ divided by $\sum_j P_j(t)$.

It was found that a state of balanced growth is compatible with such a flexible demand schedule. In that state, the demand for consumption goods will grow steadily in proportion to the supply of labour (although potentially it may be affected by price changes), since prices and the real-wage rate remain unaltered through time. If, however, the economy starts from an initial position that is off the Golden Equilibrium path and by any chance prices and the real-wage rate oscillate around their equilibrium values, then the consumption demand for goods will also oscillate. Therefore, the 'book of blue prints' of processes (if they are described in terms of augmented input coefficients) are 'periodical', and the one issued in some period is different from that of the preceding period. Naturally, we suspect that the flexible demand for consumption goods is an additional cause of the cyclic behaviour of the Hicks–Malinvaud competitive equilibrium path and the DOSSO efficient growth path.

2. We first deal with the Hicks–Malinvaud path. In order to have oscillations, it is necessary for the economy to be provided with a catalogue of

processes which generates cycles of prices, wage rate and interest factor. Let $\{P_1(t), ..., P_n(t), w(t), \beta(t)\}$ be a set of prices, the wage rate and the interest factor. They are fixed according to the principle of competitive full-cost pricing: All processes are evaluated at the prevailing price-wage-interest set; the prices in the following period are determined in such a way that the value of outputs of each process does not exceed the corresponding value of inputs including interest charges; and finally, the prices are set at zero in period t if the corresponding goods are offered in excess of the demand for them in that period. We postulate that prices thus determined can return after several periods to those with which the sequence began. That is to say, we suppose that prices, wage rate, and interest factor which are determined by the price-cost inequalities,

$$\sum_j b_{ij}P_j(t+1) \leqq \beta(t)\{\sum_j a_{ij}P_j(t)+l_i w(t)\}, \tag{1}$$
$$i = 1, ..., m;\ t = 0, 1, ..., \textit{ad inf.},$$

take on the values in some period, which they initially took.[1] If t_0 ($t_0 \geqq 2$) is the first of such points of time, then it is evident that prices, wage rate and interest factor beginning with $\{P_1(0), ..., P_n(0), w(0), \beta(0)\}$ trace out cycles with period t_0.

To each price-wage set there corresponds a set of consumption coefficients. The consumption of good j per unit of labour in period t, $e_j(t)/N(t)$, depends upon prices and the wage rate in that period. On the assumption of flexible demand for consumption goods, periodic movements of prices and the wage rate will be reflected in the consumption coefficients. A cycle with period t_0 is generated for each augmented input coefficient, c_{ij}, because it is defined as the material input coefficient a_{ij}, added to the consumption coefficient $e_j(t)/N(t)$ multiplied by the labour-input coefficient l_i. In terms of augmented input coefficients, the economy may be regarded as if it were provided with a different 'book of blue prints' for each period $t = 0, 1, ..., t_0-1$ and in period t_0 it returns for the first time to the original book of period 0. This fact may be symbolized in the following way:

$$C(t) \rightarrow B \text{ with } C(kt_0+h) = C(h) \text{ for any integer } k,$$

where B denotes, as before, the output coefficient matrix which remains unchanged through time and $C(t)$ the augmented input coefficient matrix which depends on prices and the wage rate in period t.

Granted that the Capitalist does not consume at all and devotes all his income to accumulation, the total (production and consumption) demand

[1] As before, b_{ij} denotes the output coefficient (the quantity of good j produced per unit level of operation of process i), a_{ij} the material-input coefficient (the quantity of good j used per unit level of operation of process i), and l_i the labour-input coefficient of process i.

for a good, say j, in period 0 is $\sum_i c_{ij}(0)q_i(0)$, which cannot exceed the availability of that good inherited from the past; we have

$$\sum_i b_{ij}q_i(-1) \geqq \sum_i c_{ij}(0)q_i(0) \qquad j = 1, ..., n,$$

In period 1 when the economy is provided with $\sum_i b_{ij}q_i(0)$ amounts of goods $i = 1, ..., n$, there prevails a price-wage-interest system which is different from that in period 0, so that in terms of the augmented input coefficients the book of blue prints is 'revised'. The coefficients applied to the determination of the total demands are now $c_{ij}(1)$s instead of $c_{ij}(0)$s; the supply-demand inequalities are written as

$$\sum_i b_{ij}q_i(0) \geqq \sum_i c_{ij}(1)q_i(1) \qquad i = 1, ..., n. \tag{2}$$

We have similar inequalities for all other ts up to $T-1$:

$$\sum_i b_{ij}q_i(t-1) \geqq \sum_i c_{ij}(t)q_i(t) \qquad j = 1, ..., n.$$

It would be rather surprising to find that even though each issue of the book of blue prints, $\{B, C(t)\}$, $t = 0, 1, ..., t_0-1$, satisfies the critical condition (v) which excludes cyclic exceptions to the Turnpike Theorem,[1] it is still possible that the whole 'volume' consisting of these t_0 issues allows the intensities of operating the processes, $q_i(t)$, $i = 1, ..., m$, to oscillate. As an illustration in the next section shows, if the initial intensities $q_i(-1)$ are suitably given, the intensity vector $q(t)$ may return in period t_0 to a multiple of the vector $q(0)$ of period 0. Once we have $q_i(t_0) = \alpha q_i(0)$, $i = 1, ..., m$ for a positive number α equal to ρ^{t_0}, where ρ is one plus the rate of growth of the labour force, then the supply-demand inequalities for period t_0+1 would be the same as those in period 1 if both sides of the inequalities are divided by α. That is to say, we have the inequalities (2) again in period t_0+1. The motion generated in the first t_0 periods will repeat itself in the second t_0 periods but it will be amplified by a common factor α; similarly until the period $T-1$.

Even though each $q_i(t)$ fluctuates, the sum of $q_i(t)$s with weights l_is can grow at a constant rate, so that we may conceive of a cyclic path or a zigzag meeting the condition for a steady increase in the employment of labour:

$$\rho^t\bar{N} = \sum_i l_i q_i(t) \qquad \text{for all } t.$$

We can also choose $q_i(t)$ so as to fulfil the Rule of Profitability; that is to say, $q_i(t)$ is set at zero if process i is unprofitable in period t. Finally, when

[1] See p. 191 above.

prices, the wage rate and the interest factor trace out oscillations for the coming T periods, entrepreneurs will naturally expect the same prices to prevail in period T (i.e., in the $(T+1)$th period) as those which prevailed in period 0, when $T = kt_0$. Then the conditions for expectations will be satisfied.

It is easy to see that the path characterized by all these conditions may be referred to as a Hicks–Malinvaud path of order T. First, the prices are determined by the full cost principle, and entrepreneurs correctly predict prices of period T. Second, the supply-demand condition holds for each commodity and labour in each period. Finally, under the rules of profitability and competitive pricing, the condition requiring that investment be as much as savings in every period is automatically satisfied. Hence it is confirmed that the Hicks–Malinvaud conditions for competitive equilibrium of order T are all met.

The above consideration leads to the conclusion that consumer's choice is a possible cause of a cyclic Hicks–Malinvaud path; and its existence will really be confirmed by the numerical example presented below.

3. Let us consider an economy with two processes to produce two commodities. Input and output coefficients are given so that oscillations in prices and the wage rate can be generated; for example:

	Process 1		Process 2	
	Input	*Output*	*Input*	*Output*
Good 1	1	4·5	2	4·5
Good 2	1	3·0	1	4·5
Labour	1	—	1	—

Suppose the labour force increases at a constant rate of 50 per cent per period; the interest rate is kept, not only in the state of balanced growth equilibrium but also in all other states, equal to the rate of growth of the labour force, so that the interest factor (1 plus the interest rate) is pegged at 1·5. When prices of the two goods and the wage rate are given as 1/5, 2/5, and 1, respectively, in a certain period, say 0, then the equations of full cost pricing are established for both processes at the prices 2/5 and 1/5 of the two goods in the next period. If the wage rate is set at 4/5 in period 1, it, together with the prices just determined, gives us the prices in period 2 as 1/5 and 2/5; an association of the wage rate 1 with these prices would cause the same price-wage system to prevail in period 3 as that in period 1; and so on until period $T-1$. The price equations (1) are written as

$$\begin{pmatrix} 4\cdot5 & 3 \\ 4\cdot5 & 4\cdot5 \end{pmatrix}\begin{pmatrix} 2/5 \\ 1/5 \end{pmatrix} = 1\cdot5\left[\begin{pmatrix} 1 & 1 \\ 2 & 1 \end{pmatrix}\begin{pmatrix} 1/5 \\ 2/5 \end{pmatrix} + 1\begin{pmatrix} 1 \\ 1 \end{pmatrix}\right] \qquad \text{for } t = 0, 2, 4, \ldots$$

$$\begin{pmatrix} 4\cdot5 & 3 \\ 4\cdot5 & 4\cdot5 \end{pmatrix}\begin{pmatrix} 1/5 \\ 2/5 \end{pmatrix} = 1\cdot5\left[\begin{pmatrix} 1 & 1 \\ 2 & 1 \end{pmatrix}\begin{pmatrix} 2/5 \\ 1/5 \end{pmatrix} + 4/5\begin{pmatrix} 1 \\ 1 \end{pmatrix}\right] \qquad \text{for } t = 1, 3, 5, \ldots .$$

Next, we assume that the Worker's choice is such that he would buy 2 units of good 1 and 1·5 units of good 2 at the price-wage system $(P_1, P_2, w) = (1/5, 2/5, 1)$, and 1·5 units of good 1 and 1 unit of good 2 at (2/5, 1/5, 4/5). Such points of subjective equilibrium are referred to as a and b, respectively, in Fig. 6 depicting the indifference map of the Worker based on his revealed preferences. The budget constraint is satisfied at these points, a and b. The augmented input coefficients will be:

$$C(t) = \begin{pmatrix} 3 & 2\cdot5 \\ 4 & 2\cdot5 \end{pmatrix} \qquad \text{in period } t = 0, 2, 4, \ldots,$$

$$C(t) = \begin{pmatrix} 2\cdot5 & 2 \\ 3\cdot5 & 2 \end{pmatrix} \qquad \text{in period } t = 1, 3, 5, \ldots .$$

If goods 1 and 2 are available in the respective amounts 4·5 and 3·75 at the beginning of period 0, then processes 1 and 2 are operated in period 0 at intensities 1·5 and 0, respectively, so that 6·75 and 4·5 amounts of these goods are available at the beginning of period 1. In that period, the second type of the matrix of augmented input coefficients is applied, and the stocks of goods are enough to operate every process at the same intensity, 1·125. The economy will then be provided with 10·125 amounts of good 1 and 8·4375 amounts of good 2 at the beginning of period 2, which are $(1\cdot5)^2$ times the amounts, 4·5 and 3·75, available at the start. It is clear that in period 2 when the same augmented input coefficients are employed as those in period 0, the intensities are $(1\cdot5)^2$ times greater than those in period 0; similarly in period 3. Thus it is found that the intensities of the two processes go in a zigzag as depicted in Fig. 7. Also the demand for labour increases at a steady rate that is equal to the growth rate of the labour force (so full employment will persist once it is established in period 0), but the consumption of goods will have a 'jagged' growth.

The Hicks–Malinvaud path so far discussed is now compared with the

Golden Equilibrium path. It was found in the last chapter that even though consumption coefficients do not respond to changes in prices and the wage rate, the Hicks–Malinvaud and the DOSSO path might, in a

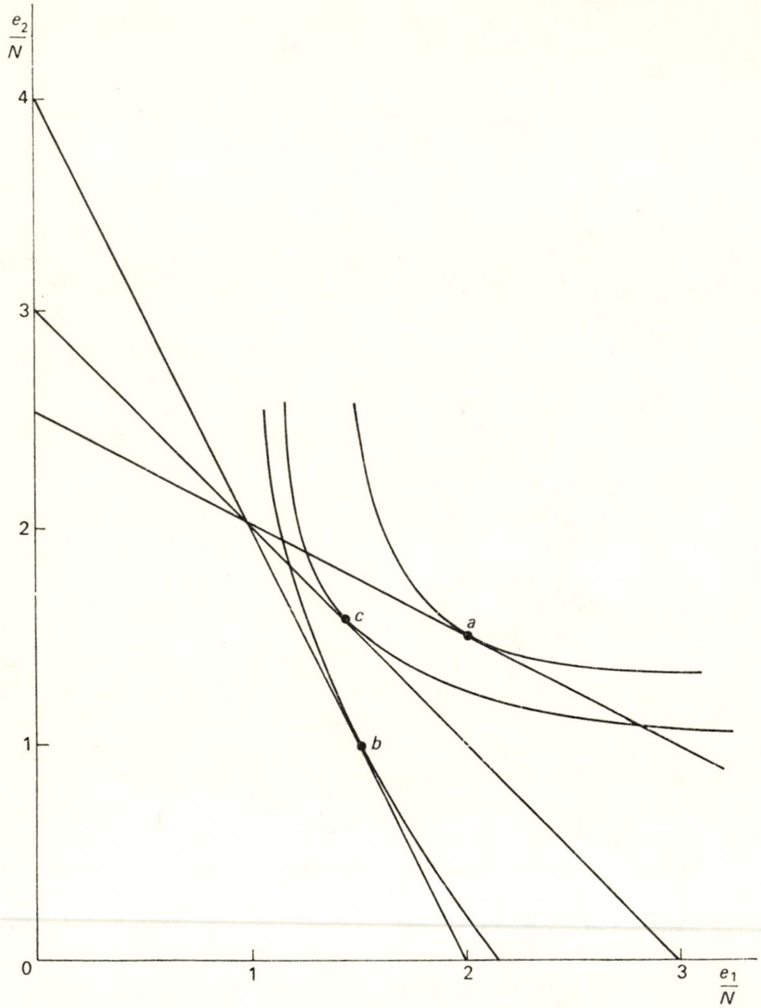

FIG. 6

certain class of exceptional cases, trace out cycles around the Golden Equilibrium ray; we have never found any persistent cycles of such paths centring around any other ray. In contrast with this, it would be surprising to find that when consumption coefficients are flexible, the cyclic Hicks–

Malinvaud path may run in a direction different from that of the Golden Equilibrium path.

We assume the same input and output coefficients as before and solve the price equations with respect to stationary prices and wage rate. The Golden Equilibrium is established when the normalized prices, $\bar{y}_1$ and $\bar{y}_2$, are both 0·5 and the real wage rate $\bar{\Omega}$ is 1·5. The interest factor $\bar{\beta}$ (which equals the growth factor $\bar{\alpha}$ since the Capitalist is assumed to consume nothing at all) is computed as 1·5.

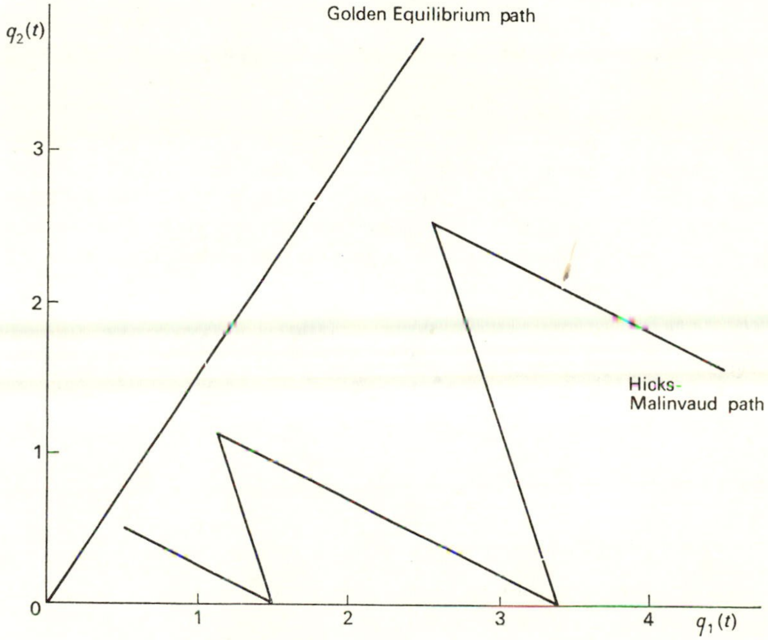

FIG. 7

Let us now suppose that the Worker chooses the point c in Fig. 6 when the Golden Equilibrium price-wage set prevails; that is to say, he buys 1·4 units of good 1 and 1·6 units of good 2 when their prices are both 0·5 and he is paid at the wage rate 1·5. The Golden Equilibrium intensities are then obtained as $\bar{q}_1 = 0{\cdot}4$ and $\bar{q}_2 = 0{\cdot}6$ by solving the equations

$$(\bar{q}_1, \bar{q}_2)\begin{pmatrix} 4{\cdot}5 & 3 \\ 4{\cdot}5 & 4{\cdot}5 \end{pmatrix} = (\bar{q}_1, \bar{q}_2)(1{\cdot}5)\left[\begin{pmatrix} 1 & 1 \\ 2 & 1 \end{pmatrix} + \begin{pmatrix} 1{\cdot}4 & 1{\cdot}6 \\ 1{\cdot}4 & 1{\cdot}6 \end{pmatrix}\right].$$

As is shown in Fig. 7, the Golden Equilibrium ray does not, in this particular case, go through the Hicks–Malinvaud zigzag. However, if the

Worker chooses a different basket containing, say, 1·6 units of good 1 and 1·4 units of good 2, then the input-output equations would yield a set of $\bar{q}_1$ and $\bar{q}_2$ such that the Golden Equilibrium path would cross the zigzag, as $\bar{q}_1 = 0{\cdot}6$ and $\bar{q}_2 = 0{\cdot}4$.

4. We now turn to the DOSSO problem. In its usual formulation all of the variables are classified into two families; intensities of processes are variables of the 'primal' DOSSO problem, whereas prices appear only in the 'dual' problem. Our present treatment of the consumption of goods as depending upon prices and the wage rate necessitates a new formulation of the problem that is distinguished from the conventional one in including prices among those variables which directly enter the primal problem.

Let us suppose, as before, the stocks of goods that the economy intends to leave at the end of the programming period for the future generations are specified in their proportions (but not in absolute levels) by the planning authorities. The object of the programming of the DOSSO type is to find an efficient path that starts from the historically given present initial point and attains the aim as much as possible. A feasible path is required to satisfy supply-demand inequalities

$$\sum_i b_{ij}q_i(t-1) \geqq \sum_i [a_{ij}+g_j(y(t),\ \Omega(t))l_i]q_i(t), \tag{3}$$

$$\sum b_{ij}q_i(T-1) \geqq b_j{}^*u, \tag{4}$$

$$\rho^t\bar{N} \geqq \sum_i l_iq_i(t), \tag{5}$$

for all $j = 1, ..., n$, and $t = 0, 1, ..., T-1$, where the consumption coefficients $g_j(y, \Omega)$ depending on the normalized prices $y_1, ..., y_n$ and the real wage rate Ω satisfy the identity

$$\sum_j g_j(y(t),\ \Omega(t))y_j(t) = \Omega(t). \tag{6}$$

The final stock vector $(b_1{}^*, ..., b_n{}^*)$ gives the proportions prescribed by the authorities. As the Worker's consumption demands are flexible, the price variables, $y_1, ..., y_n$, and Ω have to be controlled in such a way that u takes on a maximum value.

This non-linear programming problem may be solved by the familiar Kuhn–Tucker method, with the assistance of the Farkas multipliers.[1] Let $\lambda(t)$, $\lambda(T)$, $\mu(t)$, and $\nu(t)$ be the Farkas multipliers associated with inequalities (3), (4), (5), and (6), respectively. The Kuhn–Tucker criteria

[1] Cf. Chapter IX, sections 4 and 5 above.

for $\{q^0(t), y^0(t), \Omega^0(t), u^0\}$ to give a maximum can be written as

$$\sum_j \{a_{ij}+g_j(t)l_i\}\lambda_j(t)+l_i\mu(t) \begin{cases} = \sum_j b_{ij}\lambda_j(t+1) & \text{if} \quad q_i^0(t) > 0, \\ \geqq \sum_j b_{ij}\lambda_j(t+1) & \text{if} \quad q_i^0(t) = 0, \end{cases} \tag{7}$$

$$\sum_j b_j^*\lambda_j(T) \begin{cases} = 1 & \text{if} \quad u^0 > 0, \\ \geqq 1 & \text{if} \quad u^0 = 0, \end{cases} \tag{8}$$

$$\{\sum_i l_i q_i^0(t)\}\left\{\sum_j \frac{\partial g_j(t)}{\partial y_k(t)}\lambda_j(t)\right\} = v(t)\left\{\sum_j \frac{\partial g_j(t)}{\partial y_k(t)} y_j^0(t)+g_k^0(t)\right\}, \tag{9}$$

$$\{\sum_i l_i q_i^0(t)\}\left\{\sum_j \frac{\partial g_j(t)}{\partial \Omega(t)}\lambda_j(t)\right\} = v(t)\left\{\sum_j \frac{\partial g_j(t)}{\partial \Omega(t)} y_j^0(t)-1\right\}, \tag{10}$$

where we designate $g_j(y(t), \Omega(t))$ by $g_j(t)$. The consumption coefficients $g_j(t)$ and their derivatives $\partial g_j(t)/\partial y_k(t)$ and $\partial g_j(t)/\partial \Omega(t)$ are evaluated at the point of maximum; (7) should hold for $i = 1, ..., m$ and $t = 0, 1, ..., T-1$, (9) for $k = 1, ..., n$ and $t = 0, ..., T-1$, and (10) for $t = 0, ..., T-1$.

The familiar Slutsky equation,

$$\frac{\partial g_j(t)}{\partial y_k(t)} = -g_k(t)\frac{\partial g_j(t)}{\partial \Omega(t)} + X_{jk}(t),$$

($X_{jk}(t)$ stands for the so-called substitution effect[1]) enables us to reduce (9) and (10) to the following n equations:

$$\{\sum_i l_i q_i^0(t)\}\{\sum_j X_{jk}^0(t)\lambda_j(t)\} = v(t)\{\sum_j X_{jk}^0(t) y_j^0(t)\} \qquad k = 1, ..., n.$$

Applying the third Hicksian rule about the substitution terms,[2] we find that the part in the braces on the right-hand side vanishes for any values of prices, $y_1(t), ..., y_n(t)$. This implies that the part in the second braces on the left-hand side should also vanish, because the employment of labour, $\sum_i l_i q_i(t)$, is necessarily positive along an efficient path. Hence, the Farkas multipliers $\lambda_1(t), ..., \lambda_n(t)$ are proportional to $y_1^0(t), ..., y_n^0(t)$[3] and therefore may be interpreted as optimum prices.

[1] See, for example, J. R. Hicks, *Value and Capital*, p. 309.

[2] See op. cit.

[3] Note that the substitution term matrix (X_{jk}) generated from a 'regular' indifference map is of rank $n-1$.

Let us consider the following linear programming problem: Find $\lambda_j(t)$ and $\mu(t)$ such that

$$\sum_i \sum_j b_{ij} q_i(-1)\lambda_j(0) + \sum_{t=0}^{T-1} \rho^t \bar{N} \mu(t) \tag{11}$$

is as small as possible, subject to the requirements

$$\sum_j b_{ij}\lambda_j(t+1) \leqq \sum_j [a_{ij}+g_j(y^0(t), \Omega^0(t))l_i]\lambda_i(t)+l_i\mu(t), \tag{12}$$

$$1 \leqq \sum_j b_j{}^*\lambda_j(T). \tag{13}$$

With the Farkas multipliers $q_i(t)$, the Kuhn–Tucker conditions to this minimizing problem can be written as

$$\sum [a_{ij}+g_j(y^0(t), \Omega^0(t))l_i]q_i(t) \begin{cases} = \sum_i b_{ij}q_i(t-1) & \text{if} \quad \lambda_j{}^0(t) > 0, \\ \leqq \sum_i b_{ij}q_i(t-1) & \text{if} \quad \lambda_j{}^0(t) = 0; \end{cases} \tag{14}$$

$$b_j{}^* u \begin{cases} = \sum_i b_{ij}q_i(T-1) & \text{if} \quad \lambda_j{}^0(t) > 0, \\ \leqq \sum_i b_{ij}q_i(T-1) & \text{if} \quad \lambda_j{}^0(T) = 0; \end{cases} \tag{15}$$

$$\sum_i l_i q_i(t) \begin{cases} = \rho^t \bar{N} & \text{if} \quad \mu^0(t) > 0, \\ \leqq \rho^t \bar{N} & \text{if} \quad \mu^0(t) = 0; \end{cases} \tag{16}$$

$j = 1, \ldots, n$, and $t = 0, 1, \ldots, T-1$. From the dual Kuhn–Tucker conditions (7)–(8) and (14)–(16), it follows that the maximum value of the objective function u of the 'primal' problem is equated with the minimum value of the objective function (11) of the 'dual' problem (the Duality Theorem).[1]

We then find that a maximum of u is achieved when (and only when) all $\mu(t)$s vanish. (This is so because if $\mu^0(t) > 0$ at a certain price-wage set $\{y^0(t), \Omega^0(t)\}$ for some t, then $\mu^0(t)$—hence the value of (11)—can be diminished by increasing $\Omega^0(t)$.) This fact, together with the proportionality of $\lambda^0(t)$ to $y^0(t)$, i.e., $\lambda_j{}^0(t) = \gamma(t)y_j{}^0(t)$, $j = 1, \ldots, n$, enables us to put the conditions for the DOSSO efficiency, (7), (14), and (15), in the following forms:

$$\beta(t)\sum_j [a_{ij}+g_j(y^0(t), \Omega^0(t))l_i]y_j{}^0(t) \begin{cases} = \sum_j b_{ij}y_j{}^0(t+1) & \text{if} \quad q_i{}^0(t) > 0, \\ \geqq \sum_j b_{ij}y_j{}^0(t+1) & \text{if} \quad q_i{}^0(t) = 0; \end{cases} \tag{7'}$$

[1] To get this result multiply the constraints (3), (4), (5) of the primal problem by $\lambda_j(t)$, $\lambda_j(T)$, $\mu(t)$ respectively, and add them. Then consider the switching rules stated in (7)–(8) and (14)–(16).

$$\sum_i [a_{ij}+g_j(y^0(t),\ \Omega^0(t))l_i]q_i^0(t)\begin{cases} = \sum_i b_{ij}q_i^0(t-1) & \text{if} \quad y_j^0(t) > 0, \\ \leqq \sum_i b_{ij}q_j^0(t-1) & \text{if} \quad y_j^0(t) = 0; \end{cases} \tag{14$'$}$$

$$b_j{}^*u\begin{cases} = \sum_i b_{ij}q_i^0(T-1) & \text{if} \quad y_j^0(T) > 0, \\ \leqq \sum_i b_{ij}q_i^0(T-1) & \text{if} \quad y_j^0(T) = 0; \end{cases} \tag{15$'$}$$

where $\beta(t) = \gamma(t)/\gamma(t+1)$, $t = 0, 1, ..., T-1$.

We are now able to compare the DOSSO path with the Hicks–Malinvaud competitive equilibrium path whose behaviour through time has been discussed extensively in the preceding sections. An interpretation of $\beta(t)$ as the interest factor allows us to consider the left-hand side of (7′) as the total (material and wage) costs including interest charges. Condition (7′) requires that processes be chosen according to the Rule of Profitability, so that unprofitable processes are eliminated from the list of efficient processes. On the other hand, condition (14′) implies that the Rule of Competitive Pricing (or the Rule of Free Goods) should prevail; that is to say, the price of a good whose supply exceeds the demand for it must be set at zero.

These conditions are common between the Hicks–Malinvaud and the DOSSO path. But the last condition for DOSSO efficiency (15′) is completely different from the remaining condition for the Hicks–Malinvaud competitive equilibrium. The latter requires that entrepreneurs correctly predict the prices of period T while the former implies that goods are free if the production targets for them are exceeded.

5. This final section is devoted to constructing a numerical example which shows that flexible consumer's choice might be a cause of an oscillating DOSSO path. We continue to assume the same input and output coefficients as before. We specify the terminal ray at which the economy aims as:

$$(b_1{}^*, b_2{}^*) = (4{\cdot}5, 3).$$

Fig. 8 describes the Worker's indifference map we are now assuming. It is like Fig. 6, except that the Golden Equilibrium point of consumption c is shifted and a new point d is laid down in the map. The point is given in Fig. 8 such that the Worker buys 1·8 units of good 1 and 1·2 units of good 2 when the Golden Equilibrium price-wage system, $(\bar{y}_1, \bar{y}_2, \bar{\Omega}) = (0{\cdot}5, 0{\cdot}5, 1{\cdot}5)$ prevails. The point d stating that the Worker would buy 1·5 units of both goods at the price-wage system (0·4, 0·16, 0·84) is a point which might, as will be seen below, be chosen in an early stage of a DOSSO programme.

As points a and b in Fig. 8 are identical with those in Fig. 6, the same initial endowments as in the example in section 3 generates the same

Hicks–Malinvaud paths. Intensity of process 1, $q_1(t)$, would be $(1{\cdot}0)\times(1{\cdot}5)^{t+1}$ when t is 0 or an even number, and $(0{\cdot}5)\times(1{\cdot}5)^{t+1}$ when t is an odd number, whereas intensity $q_2(t)$ would be 0 for $t = 0$ or an even number,

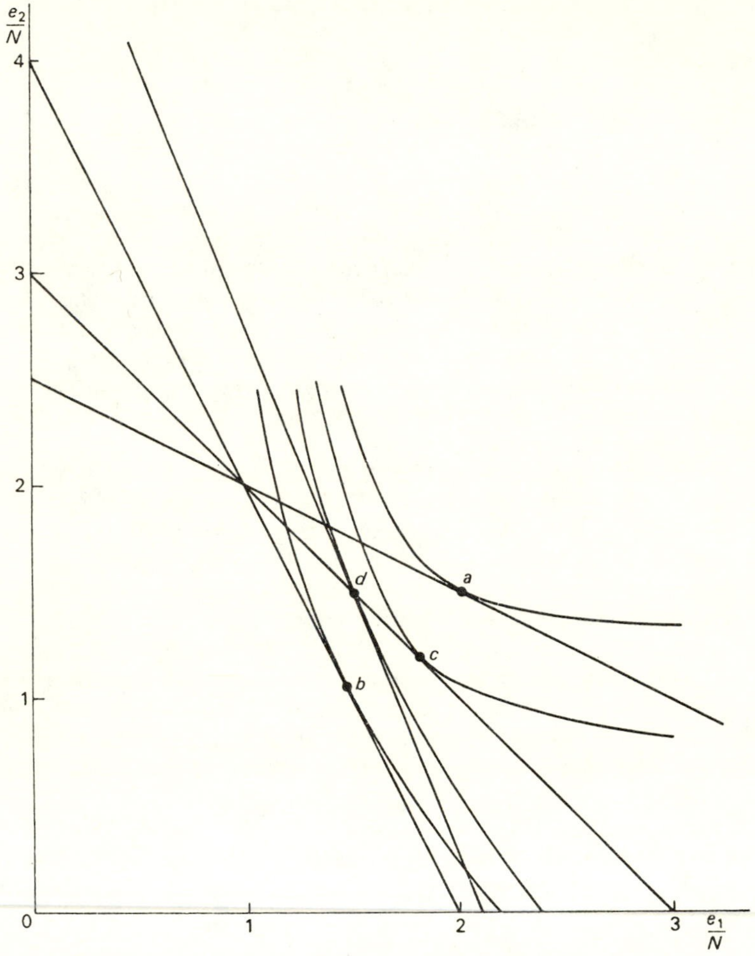

FIG. 8

and $(0{\cdot}5)\times(1{\cdot}5)^{t+1}$ for odd t. If the order of the path is odd so that $T-1$ is even, the corresponding Hicks–Malinvaud growth programme offers, at the beginning of period T, $b_1(T) = (4{\cdot}5)\times(1{\cdot}5)^T$ and $b_2(T) = 3\times(1{\cdot}5)^T$ amounts of goods, which fulfil with equality the final stock conditions

(15′) of the DOSSO programme. Hence the Hicks–Malinvaud path would, in that case, be efficient in the sense of DOSSO.

However, when T is even, at the end of the Hicks–Malinvaud path $b_1(T) = (4{\cdot}5)\times(1{\cdot}5)^T$ and $b_2(T) = (3{\cdot}75)\times(1{\cdot}5)^T$ amounts of goods would result, so that the target of good 2 would be exceeded. From the DOSSO pricing rule (15′) it follows that this Hicks–Malinvaud path cannot be a DOSSO path unless the price of good 2 is fixed at zero in period T. But the calculations in section 3 tell us that *both* goods have *positive* prices in that period.

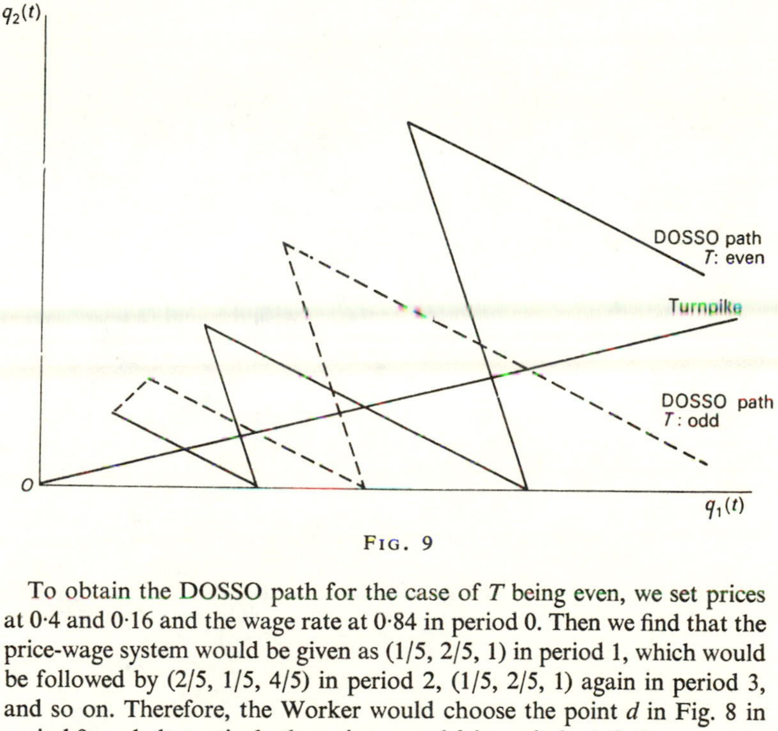

FIG. 9

To obtain the DOSSO path for the case of T being even, we set prices at 0·4 and 0·16 and the wage rate at 0·84 in period 0. Then we find that the price-wage system would be given as (1/5, 2/5, 1) in period 1, which would be followed by (2/5, 1/5, 4/5) in period 2, (1/5, 2/5, 1) again in period 3, and so on. Therefore, the Worker would choose the point d in Fig. 8 in period 0, and alternatively the points a and b in periods, 1, 2, 3, ...

The augmented-input coefficients are then given as:

$$\begin{pmatrix} 2{\cdot}5 & 2{\cdot}5 \\ 3{\cdot}5 & 2{\cdot}5 \end{pmatrix} \quad \text{in period 0;}$$

$$\begin{pmatrix} 3{\cdot}0 & 2{\cdot}5 \\ 4{\cdot}0 & 2{\cdot}5 \end{pmatrix} \quad \text{in periods 1, 3, 5, ... ;}$$

$$\begin{pmatrix} 2{\cdot}5 & 2{\cdot}0 \\ 3{\cdot}5 & 2{\cdot}0 \end{pmatrix} \quad \text{in periods 2, 4, 6, ...}$$

Using them, we compute intensities $q_1(t)$ and $q_2(t)$:

t	0	1	2	...	$T-1$
$q_1(t)$	0·75	2·25	1·6875	...	$(1.0)\times(1\cdot5)^T$
$q_2(t)$	0·75	0	1·6875	...	0

The final stock conditions (15′) are now fulfilled with equality. Moreover, all other conditions for the DOSSO efficiency are also met. From these it follows that the path just derived is the DOSSO path for even T.

We have thus obtained DOSSO zigzags, regardless of T being odd or even. As Fig. 9 clearly shows, our example is enough for illustrating that DOSSO paths do not necessarily converge to the Turnpike (or the Golden Equilibrium path), however large T is taken; they may oscillate for ever.

XII

DYNAMIC UTILITY FUNCTIONS PROPOSED

1. We have so far confined ourselves to the case where the Worker, the sole consumer in the economy, maximizes his 'instantaneous utility function' in each period subject to the condition that all his income is spent, without any time-lag, on current consumption of goods. He is a momentalist and does not see his demands for goods in various periods in their proper perspective. He has no dynamic utility function setting goods at different points of time against one another. The budget equation is satisfied period-wise with savings identically zero.

It is evident that if he were paid as well as ordinary workers in civilized countries are, he would more or less be able to abstain from current consumption of goods for their future use. He could calculate enjoyments and sacrifices at different times and find a consumption plan that gives the maximum satisfaction over time. The optimum schedule has to be balanced in the sense that the present (or capitalized) value of the stream of the Worker's expected incomes equals the present value of the stream of his expected expenditures;[1] but he is no longer required to arrange for income and consumption to be equal in each period. He would take full advantage of being allowed to making transient borrowing and lending. In fact, if preferable, he would lend some of his income to someone (say an entrepreneur) in some period on the understanding that it is returned in a later period.

Evidently, the possibility of saving and dissaving provides the consumer with a wider range of options; the best choice from this range will be an improvement on his previous choice when he is forced to live on his current income in each period. Although the DOSSO path may be recommended to the dictator or the Chairman of the economy as he is only interested in the scale of production in the 'final' period, it would not give an optimum path. The DOSSO programme is not designed to maximize the utilities of the citizens during the course *en route* to the final state; the unhappiest woman (I dare to use the superlative) would be the wife of a man who stakes his whole life on happiness and glory in his last moments.

2. In order to find an optimum growth programme we thus require a dynamic utility function which can serve as a criterion for judging welfare

[1] The length of the streams depends on the perspective of the schedule.

over time. On the assumption that savings of the present generation are not selfishly consumed by subsequent generations, the problem of optimum saving was first formulated by Ramsey as a problem of maximizing a dynamic utility function subject to a budget constraint over time.[1] He also made various simplifying assumptions, among which the following seems most important for the present argument. That is to say, he assumed that utilities at different points of time could be calculated independently and added.

An idea similar to this basic assumption of Ramsey was later proposed by Frisch.[2] Having been stimulated by Sir Roy Harrod's lecture at the University of Oslo, he was led to investigate the relationships that hold among the long-term interest rate, the long-term growth rate in the economy, and the flexibility of the marginal utility of income. He then made a Cardinalist Manifesto to the effect that the idea that cardinal utility should be avoided in economic theory was derived from the static part of economic theory but is completely sterile in many other domains. He concluded that cardinal utility is indispensable in dynamic analysis. In a study of a similar nature Strotz also appeared as a cardinalist.[3] He stated that the dynamic theory of utility maximization should assume that the utility function is determined up to a linear transformation, since it deals with the consumer as if he maximized a (weighted) sum of instantaneous utilities arising at different times.

Unfortunately, however, Professor Frisch did not succeed in giving an example from dynamic economic theory, showing 'it is absolutely *necessary* to consider the concept of cardinal utility if we want to develop a sensible sort of analysis' (italics by Frisch). A basic assumption involved in his argument is that the utility of income[4] in a current period, t, is independent of the incomes of the past periods, ..., $t-2$, $t-1$, as well as of the future, $t+1$, $t+2$, ... ; thus, the utility over two periods, t and $t+1$, is given by the sum of the respective current utilities $f_t(Y_t)$ and $f_{t+1}(Y_{t+1})$, where $f_t(Y_t)$ is the utility function and Y_t is income in period t. It may be true that when the length of period is sufficiently long, so that people in period t do not survive until period $t+1$, the 'instantaneous' utility function of income in period t, f_t, is independent of income in any other period. But the long-run utility function that is relevant when we ask how much of her

[1] F. P. Ramsey, loc. cit.

[2] R. Frisch, 'Dynamic utility', *Econometrica*, Vol. XXXII (1964), pp. 418–24.

[3] R. H. Strotz, 'Myopia and inconsistency in dynamic utility maximization', *Review of Economic Studies*, Vol. XXIII (1955–6), pp. 165–80.

[4] We follow Frisch in using the term 'income' where we intend 'consumption'. Thus the utility function is defined in terms of income. This device is justified by assuming that income is devoted entirely to consumption, as Frisch did implicitly. When there is saving out of current income, Frisch introduces the concept of 'actual income', defined as the amount of income exceeding saving (i.e. consumption), and gives utility as a function of 'actual' income.

income a country (say, U.S.A.) should save is obtained by consolidating the instantaneous utility functions of the representative men from George Washington to R. M. Nixon into

$$u = U(\dots, f_{t-1}(Y_{t-1}), f_t(Y_t), f_{t+1}(Y_{t+1}), \dots),$$

which makes the long-run marginal utility of Y_t depend upon Ys in other periods. Frisch's assumption amounts to specifying the form of the function U above in the additive form $\sum_t f_t(Y_t)$. However, there is no gain in choosing such a special utility function, because Frisch was concerned with optimum growth over a *finite* number of periods but not with that of infinite duration. Moreover, we need not assume cardinality for the total utility function. Any arbitrary function $F(U)$ with $F'(U) > 0$ may serve as a utility function; Frisch's results are all derived from the ordinalist's apparatus without being affected by a monotonic transformation of the general utility function U.[1]

Thus, so far as we are confined to growth programmes of *finite* duration, neither cardinality nor any other specification of U makes any contribution to dynamic economics; what we need in establishing a dynamic theorem is simply the ordinality of U, i.e., the indifference relationship between income streams. However, when we are concerned with a 'very-long-run' growth problem of choosing one from among possible growth paths of *infinite* order, it is necessary to describe the utility function over infinitely many periods as the limit of the utility function over T periods as T tends to infinity. This necessitates specifying the utility function such that it obtains a limit; we have, as one of such possible functions, the utility function of the form:

$$u(T) = U\left(\sum_{t=0}^{T-1} \frac{1}{\theta^t} f(Y_t)\right),$$

where $u(T)$ denotes utility acquired over T periods, $U(x)$ is an arbitrary increasing function of x, and θ is a constant playing the role of a discount factor.

In the following we make a number of assumptions which imply that the utility function is of the above form. It is of course true that our argument based on such a specification of the utility function cannot claim to be generally applicable. But it must be emphasized that it is completely

[1] See my 'Should dynamic utility be cardinal?', *Econometrica*, Vol. XXXIII (1965), pp. 869–71.

independent of the cardinality of the utility function. We assume a special internal structure of the dynamic utility function, but remain ordinalists.[1]

3. In order to get a utility function of the desired form, we make use of the powerful idea of 'separability' which was first introduced by Sono.[2] Like Slutsky's celebrated article, Sono's work originally published in Japanese in the midst of World War II remained unknown for a long time without attracting attention from English-speaking economists until it was translated into English in 1961. Four years after the publication of Sono's original paper, Leontief discussed the same problem completely independently, and recent contributions to the subject include those by Hicks, Strotz, Gorman, Miss Rajaoja, Pearce, Debreu, and others.[3] Strotz and Miss Rajaoja gave two definitions of a separable utility function, which they called the weak and the strong definition.[4] According to the former, a utility function

$$u = U(x_1, x_2, ..., x_n) \tag{1}$$

is said to be separable into groups $(1, ..., a)$, $(a+1, ..., b)$, ..., $(m+1, ..., n)$ if for any two goods belonging to a given group, the marginal rate of substitution between them is independent of the quantity of any commodity not in that group. On the other hand, the strong definition states that a function (1) is separable into groups if the quantity of any good in a given group cannot affect the marginal rate of substitution between any goods not in that group. It has been observed by those writers mentioned above that a utility function that is separable in the sense of the weak definition can be written as

$$u = U(f_A(x_1, ..., x_a), f_B(x_{a+1}, ..., x_b), ..., f_N(x_{m+1}, ..., x_n)),$$

[1] Let $x_1, x_2, ..., x_n$ be the amounts of the respective commodities an individual buys at a certain point of time. Suppose his (static) utility function can be put in the Gossen–Jevons–Walras form:

$$U = f_1(x_1)+f_2(x_2)+...+f_n(x_n).$$

It is evident that U could be replaced with any monotonically increasing function of itself, but the replacement of $f_i(x_i)$ with a monotonically increasing (non-linear) function of itself would affect the equilibrium and the stability conditions for the individual. It is clear that nobody should conclude from this fact the cardinality of the total utility function U, although earlier writers wrongly inferred from the cardinality of each part $f_i(x_i)$ that of the whole.

[2] M. Sono, 'The effect of price change on the demand and supply of separable goods', *International Economic Review*, Vol. II (1961), pp. 239–71 (translation of a paper first published in Japanese in 1943).

[3] Detailed references are found in my short survey of separability theories, 'A historical note on Professor Sono's theory of separability', *International Economic Review*, Vol. II (1961), pp. 272–5.

[4] Cf. R. H. Strotz, 'The utility tree—a correction and further appraisal', *Econometrica*, Vol. 27 (1959), pp. 482–8, and Vieno Rajaoja, *A Study in the Theory of Demand Functions and Price Indexes*, Commentationes Physico-Mathematicae XXI 1, Societas Scientiarum Fennica (Helsinki: Academic Bookstore, 1958).

whereas if it is separable in the strong sense, it can be written as

$$u = U(f_A(x_1, ..., x_a)+f_B(x_{a+1}, ..., x_b)+\cdots+f_N(x_{m+1}, ..., x_n)).$$

These results are applied to our present problem in the following way. Let $u(T)$ be the total utility which the Worker (the sole consumer in the economy) acquires over T periods. It depends on the quantities of goods that he buys in periods 0, 1, ..., $T-1$; that relationship is referred to as the dynamic utility function of order T which is written in our customary notation as

$$u(T) = U(e_1(0), ..., e_n(0); e_1(1), ..., e_n(1); ...; e_1(T-1), ..., e_n(T-1)),$$

where $e_j(t)$ represents the quantity of good j consumed in period t.

Let us group commodities period-wise. Following Koopmans, suppose the dynamic utility function is strongly as well as weakly separable into T groups thus defined.[1] The weak definition implies that the marginal rate of substitution between any two goods planned to be consumed in a given period is independent of the consumption of goods in other periods. On the other hand, it follows from the strong definition that the marginal rate of substitution between two commodities planned to be consumed in two different periods is independent of the consumption of goods in any other period.

It is clear that the separability of the utility function is very unrealistic when the period of unit length is very short. All Japanese know that the marginal rate of substitution between *norimaki* (rice cakes rolled in seaweed) and *sukiyaki* on 2 January would be greatly affected by the amount of *zoni* (rice cakes boiled with vegetables) taken at the New Year breakfast. An alcoholic who is forced to abstain from all alcoholic drinks for the whole of a certain day would increase the amount of liquor he consumes on the next day in substitution for liquor in the remote future. Thus, strictly speaking, the dynamic utility cannot be separable period-wise in both the weak and strong senses. Even if the length of the period taken is very long, it seems that the same conclusion will follow. The fact that children of dons in Oxford usually prefer Cambridge to Oxford and vice versa would serve as evidence.

Nevertheless, it is true that the marginal rate of substitution between two commodities depends on the contemporary variables much more

[1] T. C. Koopmans, 'Stationary ordinal utility and impatience', *Econometrica*, Vol. XXVIII (1960), pp. 287–309. He has presented a set of assumptions which would leave only the possibility that the dynamic utility function of *infinite* order is, in our present notation, of the form,

$$U^{(\infty)}(e(0), e(1), ...) = \sum_{t=0}^{\infty} \frac{1}{\theta^t} f(e(t)),$$

with a constant discount factor θ. The following is no more than a *finite* version of his argument.

than the consumption of goods in other periods. We may, therefore, legitimately assume, as a first approximation to reality, that the dynamic utility function is strongly separable. We can then write

$$u(T) = U^{(T)}[f_0^{(T)}(e_1(0), ..., e_n(0)) + f_1^{(T)}(e_1(1), ..., e_n(1)) + \\ + \cdots + f_{T-1}^{(T)}(e_1(T-1), ..., e_n(T-1))], \quad (2)$$

where the function $U^{(T)}$ can be replaced with any monotonically increasing function of itself, while each f is unique up to a linear transformation.

It is evident from the definition that the notion of strong separability can be applied only to those dynamic utility functions which are of order T not less than 3. The utility function of order two can at most be separable only in the weak sense, so that it cannot be put in an additive form unless some additional assumptions are made. We thus have a series of dynamic utility functions of various orders,

$$u(1) = U^{(1)}(e_1(0), ..., e_n(0)),$$

$$u(2) = U^{(2)}[f_0^{(2)}(e_1(0), ..., e_n(0)), f_1^{(2)}(e_1(1), ..., e_n(1))],$$

$$u(3) = U^{(3)}[\sum_{t=0}^{2} f_t^{(3)}(e_1(t), ..., e_n(t))],$$

$$u(4) = U^{(4)}[\sum_{t=0}^{3} f_t^{(4)}(e_1(t), ..., e_n(t))],$$

and so on.

4. To get a series of well specified utility functions we require two additional assumptions. First, we assume that the preferences of any order T are *consistent* with those of any higher order T^* in the sense that between any two consumption streams of order T^* which offer identical quantities of goods in periods $T, T+1, ..., T^*-1$, we prefer one $(e(0), ..., e(T-1); e(T), ..., e(T^*-1))$ say, to the other $(e'(0), ..., e'(T-1); e(T), ..., e(T^*-1))$ if and only if we prefer $(e(0), ..., e(T-1))$ to $(e'(0), ..., e'(T-1))$ according to the utility function of order T. Note that $e(t) = (e_1(t), ..., e_n(t))$. Second, we assume that the preferences of order T are *stationary* in the sense that between any two consumption streams of order T which have in common the same consumption of goods in period 0, we prefer $(e(0); e(1), ..., e(T-1))$ to $(e(0); e'(1), ..., e'(T-1))$ if and only if we prefer $(e(1), ..., e(T-1))$ to $(e'(1), ..., e'(T-1))$ according to the utility function of order $T-1$. These two, together with the weak- and strong-separability assumptions, lead to the following conclusions.

(i) As the preferences of order three are stationary, the inequality

$$U^{(3)}(e(0); e(1), e(2)) > U^{(3)}(e(0); e'(1), e'(2))$$

holds for any consumption of goods $e(0) = (e_1(0), ..., e_n(0))$ in period 0 if and only if

$$U^{(2)}(e(1), e(2)) > U^{(2)}(e'(1), e'(2)),$$

where $U^{(2)}$ denotes the utility function of order 2. Because of the strong separability of $U^{(3)}$ and the weak separability of $U^{(2)}$, this implies that

$$f_1^{(3)}(e(1))+f_2^{(3)}(e(2)) > f_1^{(3)}(e'(1))+f_2^{(3)}(e'(2))$$

if and only if

$$U^{(2)}[f_0^{(2)}(e(1)), f_1^{(2)}(e(2))] > U^{(2)}[f_0^{(2)}(e'(1)), f_1^{(2)}(e'(2))].$$

Hence we find that there exists an increasing function $G(u)$ such that

$$f_1^{(3)}(e(1))+f_2^{(3)}(e(2)) = G[U^{(2)}[f_0^{(2)}(e(1)), f_1^{(2)}(e(2))]],$$

for all $e(1)$ and $e(2)$. It is evident that the inverse of this function gives

$$U^{(2)}(f_0^{(2)}, f_1^{(2)}) = H(f_1^{(3)}+f_2^{(3)}), \qquad H'(f) > 0; \tag{3}$$

that is to say, the dynamic utility function of order 2 which has so far been merely weakly separable is now strongly (or additively) separable.

(ii) Since the preferences of order two are consistent, we have, for any $e(2)$,

$$U^{(3)}[f_0^{(3)}(e(0))+f_1^{(3)}(e(1))+f_2^{(3)}(e(2))]$$
$$> U^{(3)}[f_0^{(3)}(e'(0))+f_1^{(3)}(e'(1))+f_2^{(3)}(e(2))]$$

if and only if

$$U^{(2)}(e(0), e(1)) > U^{(2)}(e'(0), e'(1)).$$

From (3) we find that this implies the inequality,

$$f_0^{(3)}(e(0))+f_1^{(3)}(e(1)) > f_0^{(3)}(e'(0))+f_1^{(3)}(e'(1)),$$

which holds if and only if

$$H[f_1^{(3)}(e(0))+f_2^{(3)}(e(1))] > H[f_1^{(3)}(e'(0))+f_2^{(3)}(e'(1))],$$

Therefore, we can write

$$f_0^{(3)}(e(0))+f_1^{(3)}(e(1)) = J[H[f_1^{(3)}(e(0))+f_2^{(3)}(e(1))]]. \tag{4}$$

Let us now differentiate this with respect to $e_j(0)$ and $e_j(1)$; we then get

$$\frac{\partial f_0^{(3)}(e(0))}{\partial e_j(0)} = J'H' \frac{\partial f_1^{(3)}(e(0))}{\partial e_j(0)},$$

$$\frac{\partial f_1^{(3)}(e(1))}{\partial e_j(1)} = J'H' \frac{\partial f_2^{(3)}(e(1))}{\partial e_j(1)}.$$

From the former it is found that $J'H'$ is independent of $e(1)$ and from the latter it is independent of $e(0)$; we can then write

$$f_0^{(3)}(e(0))+f_1^{(3)}(e(1)) = \theta_0\{f_1^{(3)}(e(0))+f_2^{(3)}(e(1))\}+\zeta_0, \tag{5}$$

where θ_0 and ζ_0 are constant.

It now follows immediately from (5) that $f_0^{(3)}(e(0))$ is a linear function of $f_1^{(3)}(e(0))$, while $f_1^{(3)}(e(1))$ is of $f_2^{(3)}(e(1))$; or conversely, $f_1^{(3)}(e(0))$ and $f_2^{(3)}(e(1))$ are linear functions of $f_0^{(3)}(e(0))$ and $f_1^{(3)}(e(1))$, respectively. Furthermore, both functions have the same slope, $1/\theta_0$. It is then verified that $f_2^{(3)}(e(1))$ is a linear function of $f_0^{(3)}(e(1))$ with slope, $1/\theta_0^2$. Therefore, we may conclude that the (additively separable) dynamic utility function of order three can finally be put in the form,

$$u(3) = V^{(3)}\left(f_0^{(3)}(e(0))+\frac{1}{\theta_0}f_0^{(3)}(e(1))+\frac{1}{\theta_0^2}f_0^{(3)}(e(2))\right).$$

(iii) By applying the same reasoning that we have done in the derivation of (4), we obtain, from the consistency of the utility function of order four with that of order two, a functional relationship,

$$f_0^{(4)}(e(0))+f_1^{(4)}(e(1)) = K[H[f_1^{(3)}(e(0))+f_2^{(3)}(e(1))]]. \tag{4'}$$

From this we can find that $K'H'$ is a constant completely independent of $e(0)$ and $e(1)$. We have, therefore, a linear expression

$$f_0^{(4)}(e(0))+f_1^{(4)}(e(1)) = \theta_1\{f_1^{(3)}(e(0))+f_2^{(3)}(e(1))\}+\zeta_1. \tag{5'}$$

On the other hand, the stationariness of the preferences of order four implies the inequality,

$$U^{(4)}[f_0^{(4)}(e(0))+\sum_{t=1}^{3}f_t^{(4)}(e(t))] > U^{(4)}[f_0^{(4)}(e(0))+\sum_{t=1}^{3}f_t^{(4)}(e'(t))],$$

that holds for any consumption of goods $e(0)$ in period 0, when and only when the consumption stream $(e(1), e(2), e(3))$ is preferred to $(e'(1), e'(2), e'(3))$ according to the utility function of order 3. We then have

$$\sum_{t=1}^{3}f_t^{(4)}(e(t)) = L\left[V^{(3)}\left(f_0^{(3)}(e(1))+\frac{1}{\theta_0}f_0^{(3)}(e(2))+\frac{1}{\theta_0^2}f_0^{(3)}(e(3))\right)\right] \tag{6}$$

in terms of the $V^{(3)}$-expression of the utility function of order three. By differentiating this equation with respect to $e(1)$, $e(2)$, and $e(3)$, we find, in the same way as we found that $J'H'$ is constant, that $L'V^{(3)'}$ is constant. Hence it is a linear relationship with slope, θ_2 say, so that $f_1^{(4)}(e(1))$ is expressed as a linear function of $f_0^{(3)}(e(1))$ with the same slope coefficient, i.e.

$$f_1^{(4)}(e(1)) = \theta_2\{f_0^{(3)}(e(1))\}+\zeta_2.$$

It is seen from (5′) that $f_1^{(4)}$ is a linear function of $f_2^{(3)}$ with the slope, θ_1. We have also seen in (ii) that $f_2^{(3)}$ is a linear function of $f_0^{(3)}$ with the slope $1/\theta_0^2$. These findings lead to the result that $\theta_2 = \theta_1/\theta_0^2$. Since $L'V^{(3)\prime} = \theta_2$, the function (6) may be written as

$$\sum_{t=1}^{3} f_t^{(4)}(e(t)) = \frac{\theta_1}{\theta_0}\left\{\sum_{t=1}^{3} \frac{1}{\theta_0^t} f_0^{(3)}(e(t))\right\} + \text{constant}.$$

This, together with

$$f_0^{(4)}(e(0)) = \theta_1\{f_1^{(3)}(e(0))\} + \text{constant} = \frac{\theta_1}{\theta_0}\{f_0^{(3)}(e(0))\} + \text{constant}$$

that follows from (5′), enables us to write the utility function of order four as

$$u(4) = U^{(4)}\left(\sum_{t=0}^{3} f_t^{(4)}(e(t))\right) = V^{(4)}\left(\sum_{t=0}^{3} \frac{1}{\theta_0^t} f_0^{(3)}(e(t))\right).$$

Similarly, the utility function of any order $T \geqq 3$ can be put in the following form:

$$u(T) = V^{(T)}\left(\sum_{t=0}^{T-1} \frac{1}{\theta^t} f(e(t))\right), \tag{7}$$

where for the sake of simplicity we designate θ_0 and $f_0^{(3)}$ by θ and f, respectively.

5. The V-formula relating the utility level $u(T)$ to consumption of order T, $(e(0), e(1), ..., e(T-1))$, has been derived by assuming the existence of a particular family of dynamic utility functions $(U^{(1)}, U^{(2)}, U^{(3)}, ...)$. Remember, however, that these functions are given in the ordinal sense, i.e., $U^{(T)}$ may be replaced by any arbitrary function which orders consumption in the same way as $U^{(T)}$. As the function $f(e)$ and the discount factor θ in the V-expression are unaffected by any monotonic transformation of $U^{(1)}, U^{(2)}, ...$, we may take a particular utility function such that

$$u(T) = \sum_{t=0}^{T-1} \frac{1}{\theta^t} f(e(t)), \tag{7′}$$

and the optimum consumption stream does not depend on the absolute level of $u(T)$.

Suppose now that $\Phi^{(1)}, \Phi^{(2)}, ...$ give an alternative family of dynamic utility functions. Provided with the assumptions of consistency and stationariness of the preferences of various orders as well as those of weak and strong separability, $\Phi^{(T)}$ can be put in a new V-form:

$$\phi(T) = \Psi^{(T)}\left(\sum_{t=0}^{T-1} \frac{1}{\zeta^t} h(e(t))\right). \tag{8}$$

Taking account of the fact that (7) and (8) are different but equivalent representations of the same indifference map, we find that the marginal rates of substitution derived from them must be equal to each other. Calculating the marginal rate of substitution of a good j in period t for the same good in another period t' at a point where $e_k(t) = e_k(t')$ for all $k = 1, ..., n$, we find from (7) that it is $\theta^{t'-t}$, while from (8) that it is $\zeta^{t'-t}$; hence we obtain $\theta = \zeta$. Thus the factor θ measuring the degree of preference for advanced timing of satisfaction (i.e. the 'impatience' in the sense of Irving Fisher[1]) remains invariant with respect to the replacement of utility functions $U^{(1)}, U^{(2)}, ...$ by $\Phi^{(1)}, \Phi^{(2)}, ...$.

Next, let us compare the marginal rate of substitution between two contemporary goods $e_j(t)$ and $e_k(t)$ obtained from (7) with that from (8). The equation between them is written as

$$\frac{\partial f(e(t))}{\partial e_j(t)} \Big/ \frac{\partial f(e(t))}{\partial e_k(t)} = \frac{\partial h(e(t))}{\partial e_j(t)} \Big/ \frac{\partial h(e(t))}{\partial e_k(t)},$$

which must hold for any pair of goods, j and k, and for all values of $e(t)$. Therefore, h can be expressed as a monotonic increasing function of f.

Let $h = \eta(f)$ be such a function. Then the intertemporal marginal rate of substitution of $e_j(t)$ for $e_j(t')$ is computed as

$$\theta^{t'-t} \frac{\partial f(e(t))}{\partial e_j(t)} \Big/ \frac{\partial f(e(t'))}{\partial e_j(t')}$$

from (7), and as

$$\theta^{t'-t} \frac{d\eta[f(e(t))]}{df} \frac{\partial f(e(t))}{\partial e_j(t)} \Big/ \frac{d\eta[f(e(t'))]}{df} \frac{\partial f(e(t'))}{\partial e_j(t')}$$

from (8) after substituting θ and $\eta(f)$ for ζ and h, respectively. They should be identical; so we must have

$$\frac{d\eta[f(e(t))]}{df} = \frac{d\eta[f(e(t'))]}{df}$$

for all values of $e(t)$ and $e(t')$. This implies that the function f should be unique up to a linear transformation. We can, therefore, write (8) as

$$\phi(T) = \Lambda^{(T)}\left(\sum_{t=0}^{T-1} \frac{1}{\theta^t} f(e(t))\right);$$

hence $\phi(T) = F(u(T))$, F being a monotonic increasing function of u. It has thus been shown that any function which can serve as a utility function is reducible to the standard form (7′) by applying a suitable monotonic transformation to it. Our discussion of optimum growth in the next chapter

[1] Irving Fisher, *The Theory of Interest* (New York: Macmillan, 1930), Chapter IV.

will be made in terms of the standard utility function (7′) obtained in this way. Although I use the same type of objective function that Ramsey, Frisch, Strotz, and many other 'cardinalists' used, the whole argument above permits me to declare myself an ordinalist.

The final but important specification is made of the dynamic utility function by introducing an assumption which limits the flexibility of the marginal rate of substitution between two goods of different periods. The marginal rate of substitution of good j in period t for the same good in another period t' is given by the utility function (7′) as

$$\theta^{t'-t} f_j(e(t))/f_j(e(t')),$$

where the subscript j applied to f denotes partial differentiation. As before, it reduces to $\theta^{t'-t}$ when $e_k(t) = e_k(t')$ for all $k = 1, ..., n$, but may take on different values when $e_k(t) \neq e_k(t')$ for some k. Such flexibility of the marginal rate of intertemporal substitution will, in the next chapter on the Consumption Turnpike Theorem, be lost to a considerable degree by assuming that the rate is fixed at $\theta^{t'-t}$ not only when $e(t')$ equals $e(t)$ but also when $e(t')$ is proportional to $e(t)$. This amounts to assuming that

$$f_j(e(t)) = f_j(\lambda e(t)) \qquad j = 1, ..., n,$$

for all $\lambda > 0$, that is to say, the partial derivatives of f are homogeneous of degree *zero* in variables $e_1(t), ..., e_n(t)$. Accordingly, f is homogeneous of degree *one* in the same variables, or in other words, f changes in proportion to the number of persons if the per capita consumption of each good remains unchanged. We may, therefore, put (7′) in the form,

$$u(T) = \sum_{t=0}^{T-1} \frac{N(t)}{\theta^t} f(\zeta(t)),$$

where $N(t)$ is the population in period t and $\zeta_j(t)$ the per capita consumption of good j in period t.[1] It is of course true that the introduced inflexibility of the marginal rate of substitution is a very restrictive assumption to be avoided if possible. Unfortunately, it seems to me that it is indispensable for a theory of optimum balanced growth.

6. One of the basic assumptions made throughout the discussion so far is the assumption of (weak) separability which requires that the marginal rate

[1] Though I do not like to smell any scent of 'cardinalism', some others might, as they often do, call $f(\xi(t))$ the instantaneous utility derived from the consumption *per capita*, $\xi(t)$. They might paraphrase the total utility over T periods as the sum of the *per capita* instantaneous utilities multiplied by the weighted populations, $N(t)/\theta^t$.

of substitution between any two contemporary goods is independent of consumption in any other period. That is to say, the partial derivatives

$$\frac{\partial}{\partial e_k(t')}\left(\frac{\partial U^{(T)}}{\partial e_i(t)}\bigg/\frac{\partial U^{(T)}}{\partial e_j(t)}\right) \qquad k = 1, \ldots, n,$$

vanish for all t' when $t' \neq t$, whereas those with respect to contemporary variables may (as they usually do) take on positive or negative values. This drastic asymmetry between intertemporary and contemporary variables in their effects on the marginal rates of substitution is responsible for the derivation of the utility function of the form (7′). It must be remembered that it is a very restrictive assumption, so that it shuts out many important cases.

Let the marginal rate of substitution between i and j in the same period t be denoted by

$$\frac{\partial U^{(T)}}{\partial e_i(t)}\bigg/\frac{\partial U^{(T)}}{\partial e_j(t)} = R_{ij,t}{}^{(T)}.$$

Among the various cases which we have left undiscussed, one which is easily manageable but still most important is the case of $\dfrac{\partial R_{ij,t}{}^{(T)}}{\partial e_k(t')}$, $t' = 0, 1, \ldots, T-1$, having the same sign as $\dfrac{\partial R_{ij,t}{}^{(T)}}{\partial e_k(t)}$. A highlighting of this case may be warranted because the same goods in different periods, $e_k(0)$, $e_k(1), \ldots, e_k(T-1)$, would be more or less in competition with one another. We are, in the following, concerned with a more special case where the effects of $e_k(0), e_k(1), \ldots, e_k(T-1)$ on the marginal rate of substitution between i and j in the same period, diminish at a constant rate θ that is independent of all i, j, and k; i.e., we assume, for all triads (i, j, k),

$$\frac{\partial R_{ij,t}{}^{(T)}}{\partial e_k(0)} : \frac{\partial R_{ij,t}{}^{(T)}}{\partial e_k(1)} : \ldots : \frac{\partial R_{ij,t}{}^{(T)}}{\partial e_k(T-1)} = 1 : \frac{1}{\theta} : \ldots : \frac{1}{\theta^{T-1}}.$$

It then follows that $R_{ij,t}{}^{(T)}$ remains unchanged as long as there is no change in the sum of $e_k(0)$, $\frac{1}{\theta}e_k(1), \ldots, \frac{1}{\theta^{T-1}}e_k(T-1)$. Therefore, we find that

$$R_{ij,t}{}^{(T)} = F_{ij,t}{}^{(T)}(x_1, x_2, \ldots, x_n), \tag{9}$$

where

$$x_j = e_j(0) + \frac{1}{\theta}e_j(1) + \cdots + \frac{1}{\theta^{T-1}}e_j(T-1).$$

As (9) holds for all pairs (i, j) and all t, $u(T)$ may be written as

$$u(T) = U^{(T)}(x_1, x_2, ..., x_n).$$

In words, the consumer has a subjective time-preference factor θ and aggregates the consumption of good j during different periods as a discounted sum x_j; he is supposed to choose among totals $x_1, ..., x_n$ disregarding their time-distribution. This type of the dynamic utility function will also be used in the discussion of optimum growth in Chapter XVI.

XIII

CONSUMPTION EN ROUTE: THE SECOND TURNPIKE THEOREM

1. In Chapter X, we were concerned with the Final State Turnpike Theorem on the assumptions that consumption of each good per worker is fixed throughout the planning period and that the authorities try to maximize the stocks of goods which they can bestow, at the horizon, upon the future citizens. Such a partial optimization for the sake of the future should more properly be superseded by a general mutual optimization, so that the benefits from the properties initially available are shared between the people living in the planning period and those after that. This would inevitably confront us with one of the hardest problems of economics, the interpersonal and intertemporal comparisons of utilities.

Attempts to solve the crux of the problem have to be abandoned. We content ourselves by running to the other extreme. In this chapter, we derive the conditions for Ramsey optimality as distinct from DOSSO-efficiency, that is to say, we optimize in favour of the people in the planning period; the satisfaction of the future residents is pegged at a certain level that the present residents approve of. Among all feasible programmes that leave, at the end of the planning period, necessary amounts of goods for the future residents, will the people living choose a single one which is most preferable from their own point of view. There is a switch-over of ideology from abstinence for the future to satisfaction in the transient life.

People of the coming generation yet to be born have no chance to reveal to their seniors their own preferences; they can only give the planning authorities a *carte blanche*. Let k_j be the stock of good j per man which is available when the planning period closes at the end of period $T-1$. It may directly be consumed by the future residents of the society or may be combined with the stock of other goods for further production of goods. As attorney for the future generation, the planning authorities partition all possible combinations of goods $(k_1, k_2, ..., k_n)$ into classes such that any two belonging to the same class are equally useful. To each class is attached a number in such a way that a class consisting of combinations of goods that are more useful than a combination of goods of another class has a number that is greater than the number of the second class. Such a function is referred to as the posterity utility function which describes the preference preordering of the stocks of goods that the planning authorities set on behalf of the coming generation. It is denoted by

$$\gamma = \Gamma(k_1, k_2, ..., k_n); \tag{1}$$

it is determined only up to an increasing (monotonic) transformation, because the utility function is not cardinal but merely ordinal; any other function will serve if it orders combinations of stocks of goods in the same way. The underlying indifference map (like the one of the usual theory of consumer's choice) obeys the law of diminishing marginal rate of substitution. It is noted that the function (1) includes the extreme case of L-shaped indifference curves, where the desired proportions of the stocks of commodities at the 'final' date are exogenously fixed by the planning authorities before they make a growth programme—the case we were concerned with in the previous discussion of the Turnpike Theorem.

There may be a struggle between the living and the coming generation. The former with the utility function of the form (XII. 7′) is confronted by the latter with the utility function (1) above. The indifference curves of the living generation (as well as those of the coming one) may have, in the limit, 'squared' corners. When both are L-shaped and the game is one-sidedly in favour of the coming generation (sponsored by the authorities), we obtain the Final State Turnpike Theorem; desired proportions of the final stocks of goods and consumption coefficients of the living workers are fixed, and the utility of the coming generation (1) is maximized subject to the technical requirements of feasibility and given consumption coefficients. On the contrary, when the present generation dominates over the coming one in Parliament, the utility of the latter will be repressed at a certain level, say $\bar{y}$, whereas the utility of the former will be maximized subject to a number of requirements. In this formulation of the Ramsey optimum growth, the present members of the society do not necessarily consume all their income at once; they will save from period to period, but enjoyment from consumption en route is still maximized over time.

2. We can now conceive of a Ramsey optimality problem of order T, where a level $\bar{y}$ of the posterity utility is specified by the planning authorities and the utility function of the living generation

$$u(T) = \sum_{t=0}^{T-1} \frac{1}{\theta^t} f(e(t)) \tag{2}$$

is maximized subject to constraints of technical feasibility. We compare paths or growth programmes beginning with historically given stocks of goods, $b_1(-1)$, $b_2(-1)$, ..., $b_n(-1)$, available at the beginning of period 0 and bestowing k_1N_T, ..., k_nN_T amounts of goods upon the future generation at the beginning of period T, where N_T represents the number of persons (workers) living in period T. On the assumption that the rate of growth of the population is constant over time, feasibility requires the following inequalities to be fulfilled in every period $t = 0, 1, ..., T-1$:[1]

$$\sum_{i=1}^{m} b_{ij}q_i(t-1) \geqq \sum_{i=1}^{m} a_{ij}q_i(t)+e_j(t), \tag{3}$$

$$\rho^t\bar{N} \geqq \sum_{i=1}^{m} l_i q_i(t), \tag{4}$$

where $j = 1, ..., n$; as before, bs denote output coefficients, as material-input coefficients, ls labour-input coefficients, $q(t)$s the activity levels in period t, $\bar{N}$ the population in period 0, and ρ one plus the rate of growth of the population. Through the present government the future citizens claim the stocks of goods $k_1\rho^T\bar{N}, ..., k_n\rho^T\bar{N}$, which ought to be reserved for them, such that

$$\sum_{i=1}^{m} b_{ij}q_i(T-1) \geqq k_j\rho^T\bar{N}, \qquad j = 1, ..., n, \tag{5}$$

$$\bar{\gamma} = \Gamma(k_1, k_2, ..., k_n). \tag{6}$$

The Ramsey optimum path would of course be obtained by maximizing the utility function (2) subject to (3)–(6). Before proceeding to that business, for a while we must concentrate our attention on the following two paths each of which will play the role of the norm (or the standard of reference) in the discussion of the long-run convergence of optimum growth paths. The first of them is the Maximum or Golden Balanced Growth path, which is defined in the following way. Let us consider balanced growth paths growing at the common rate $\rho-1$. Choose, from among them, a particular one associated with the relative intensities of the processes, $q_1(-1), ..., q_m(-1)$, that are kept unchanged forever. Then the citizens are able to consume goods in the amounts

$$h_j(t) = \rho^t\{\sum_{i=1}^{m} b_{ij}q_i(-1)-\rho\sum_{i=1}^{m} a_{ij}q_i(-1)\} = \rho^t h_j(0), \quad j = 1, ..., n,$$

in period $t = 0, 1, ..., T-1$; the enjoyment the citizens can derive from them over T periods will be

$$u(T) = \sum_{t=0}^{T-1} \frac{1}{\theta^t} f(\rho^t h(0)). \tag{7}$$

If the economy were provided with different amounts of goods and advanced along a different path of balanced growth, they would enjoy a different level of satisfaction. All such possible and imaginable states of balanced growth are examined for the purpose of singling out a state

[1] Remember, in (3) for $t = 0$, the definitional relationship: $b_j(-1) = \sum_{i=1}^{m} b_{ij}q_i(-1)$.

which maximizes $u(T)$; and the one thus selected is referred to as the *maximum balanced growth path* of order T. We find that the maximum balanced growth path is unique and independent of the discount factor θ and the order of maximization T, because ρ is common to all paths and the function f is homogeneous of degree one in variables $h_1(t)$, ..., $h_n(t)$, so that for any given value of T, $u(T)$ records the greatest possible value when $f(h(0))$ is maximized subject to the constraints

$$h_j(0) = \sum_i b_{ij}q_i(-1) - \rho \sum_i a_{ij}q_i(-1) \geqq 0$$

which are independent of θ and T.[1] Furthermore, the Maximum Balanced Growth path thus obtained will satisfy the Golden Rule of Accumulation. In fact it can be verified that at the shadow prices and wage rate associated with that state the wage income is exactly equal to the total consumption. A sufficient condition for this equality is that there is no savings by the workers and no consumption by the capitalists. Obviously the Golden Balanced Growth path is no more than the Turnpike already discussed.

The second norm is obtained by examining whether Ramsey paths are balanced. For given initial intensities, $q_1(-1)$, ..., $q_m(-1)$, we have an array of stocks of goods per capita $k_1(0)$, ..., $k_n(0)$, where $k_j(0) = \sum_{i=1}^{m} b_{ij}q_i(-1)/\bar{N}$. Let $\bar{\gamma}$ be that level of utility which the future citizens would enjoy if each of them were provided with the same amounts of goods at the beginning of period T as the present generation had *per capita* at the beginning of period 0; $\bar{\gamma}$ is then given as $\bar{\gamma} = \Gamma(k_1(0), ..., k_n(0))$. For $\bar{\gamma}$ thus specified, let us consider a Ramsey optimum growth path of order T starting with given $q_1(-1)$, ..., $q_m(-1)$. It is evident that for general initial intensities the optimum growth is not always steady, and relative intensities may fluctuate. However, so long as the subjective time-preference factor θ is set within an admissible range, there is a particular starting point $\{q_1(-1), ..., q_m(-1)\}$—relative to θ—which generates the Ramsey optimum path that coincides with the balanced growth path from that point. If a Ramsey optimum path is a *balanced* growth path for some T, then it is so for any t greater than T; so that the optimality of the balanced growth path is independent of the order of the path. We shall take such a balanced optimum path as the second norm and call it the *Consumption Turnpike* and its existence will later be discussed more rigorously under certain additional assumptions.

Let the utility (7) realized by a balanced growth of order T from a given initial point $\{q_1(-1), ..., q_m(-1)\}$ be denoted simply by

$$u_B(T, q(-1)).$$

[1] In the maximization, $q_1(-1)$, ..., $q_m(-1)$, as well as $h_1(0)$, ..., $h_n(0)$, are treated as variables.

Similarly, $u_R(T, q(-1))$ symbolizes the total utility of a Ramsey optimum growth path of order T that starts from $q(-1)$. Let a particular point q_G be on the Golden Balanced Growth path and q_C on the Consumption Turnpike. The definitions given above imply the following relationships: First, $u_B(T, q(-1))$ is maximized at q_G; that is to say,

$$u_B(T, q_G) \geqq u_B(T, q(-1)), \text{ for all } q(-1) \text{ and all } T. \tag{8}$$

Second, a Ramsey optimum path generally surpasses the corresponding balanced growth path; in other words, we have

$$u_R(T, q(-1)) \geqq u_B(T, q(-1)), \text{ for all } q(-1) \text{ and all } T. \tag{9}$$

Third, this weak equality is replaced by the strict inequality unless $q(-1) = q_C$; and at the exceptional point q_C, we have the equation,

$$u_R(T, q_C) = u_B(T, q_C) \qquad \text{for all } T. \tag{10}$$

We then get

$$u_B(T, q_G) \geqq u_R(T, q_C)$$

from (8) and (10), while

$$u_R(T, q_G) \geqq u_B(T, q_G)$$

from (9). When q_G and q_C are distinct, these inequalities would obviously become strict inequalities implying, respectively, that the Consumption Turnpike does not obey the Golden Rule of economic growth and that the Golden Balanced Growth path cannot be a Ramsey optimum path.

3. A rigorous proof of existence of the Consumption Turnpike should be given before we ask in what circumstances it swerves from the genuine Turnpike.[1] For this purpose we classify possible combinations of goods left to the future generation into two classes: one consists of all combinations for which a proportional expansion (at the rate $\rho-1$) of all productive activities is possible, while the other includes only those which cannot generate such an expansion. We assume, throughout the following discussion, that the planning authorities are not wilful as the spokesman of the coming generation; so that they attach, on behalf of the coming generation, the same index of usefulness to two different combinations of goods belonging to the first class if and only if the *present* generation can enjoy the same level of satisfaction from these two sets of the stocks of goods (after subtracting the necessary inputs for maintaining the stocks of goods per capita). This implies that for two different sets, $(k_1, \ldots, k_n)$

[1] The Golden Balanced Growth path or the genuine Turnpike that has played the role of the norm for development in the Final State Turnpike Theorem will be referred to as the Production Turnpike.

and $(k_1', ..., k_n')$, we have the same value of posterity utility index γ if and only if $f(e)$ takes on the same largest value in a region where

$$k_j = \sum_i b_{ij} q_i, \qquad j = 1, ..., n, \tag{11.1}$$

$$1 = \sum_i l_i q_i, \tag{11.2}$$

$$e_j = \sum_i b_{ij} q_i - \rho \sum_i a_{ij} q_i \geqq 0, \qquad j = 1, ..., n, \tag{11.3}$$

as in another region defined by similar equations with k_j' in place of k_j.[1] Thus $\Gamma(k)$ is a function of the maximum of $f(e)$ subject to (11.1)–(11.3) with given $k_1, ..., k_n$, provided $(k_1, ..., k_n)$ belongs to the first class. Hence partial derivatives of Γ with respect to $k_1, ..., k_n$ (the marginal posterity utilities) are proportional to $\dfrac{\partial \max f}{\partial k_1}, ..., \dfrac{\partial \max f}{\partial k_n}$, where $\max f$ represents the maximum of $f(e)$ subject to the above three sets of conditions.

Let π_j and τ be the Farkas–Lagrange multipliers associated with (11.1) and (11.2). The conditions for a maximum of f subject to (11.1)–(11.3) may be written as

$$\sum_j f_j(b_{ij} - \rho a_{ij}) \begin{cases} \leqq \sum_j b_{ij}\pi_j + \tau l_i & \text{if } q_i = 0, \\ = \sum_j b_{ij}\pi_j + \tau l_i & \text{if } q_i > 0, \end{cases} \tag{12}$$

where f_j represents the partial derivative of f with respect to e_j. We also find that[2]

$$\frac{\partial \max f}{\partial k_j} = \pi_j \qquad j = 1, ..., n.$$

[1] We are here assuming that the authorities compare the usefulness of the sets of the stocks of goods obtained at the end of the planning period, in terms of the utilities which posterity will enjoy when the economy grows in balance with the respective stock sets. This means that the authorities are not so kind to the unborn as to take possibilities of unbalanced growth into account.

[2] Differentiate (11.1)–(11.3) with respect to one of the k_js, the other k_js remaining unchanged. As

$$\frac{\partial f}{\partial k_j} = \sum_r f_r \frac{\partial e_r}{\partial k_j} = \sum_r \sum_i f_r(b_{ir} - \rho a_{ir}) \frac{\partial q_i}{\partial k_j}$$

and $\dfrac{\partial q_i}{\partial k_j} = 0$ if (12) holds with strict inequality, we get

$$\frac{\partial f}{\partial k_j} = \sum_r \sum_i b_{ir} \frac{\partial q_j}{\partial k_j} \pi_r + \tau \sum_i l_i \frac{\partial q_i}{\partial k_j}$$

which equals π_j because of restrictions (11.1) and (11.2).

In view of the proportionality postulated above, we obtain from (12)

$$\sum_j f_j(b_{ij}-\rho a_{ij})-\tau l_i \begin{cases} \leqq \xi \sum_j b_{ij}\Gamma_j & \text{if } q_i = 0, \\ = \xi \sum_j b_{ij}\Gamma_j & \text{if } q_i > 0, \end{cases} \tag{12'}$$

for a positive number ξ. Obviously, the multipliers π_j and τ can as usual be interpreted as shadow prices and the shadow wage rate.

Provided with this construction of the posterity utility function we at once find that there is no set of final stocks of goods which is different from the Production Turnpike set but is at least as desirable, because this set (which is no more than the Golden Balanced Growth set of stocks of goods) maximizes the value of max f. This means that the indifference curve of the coming generation is undefined at the Production Turnpike point; the degeneracy of the indifference curve to a point occurs for that curve which would pass through the Production Turnpike point. Then the differential calculus (or the marginal substitution approach) is not applicable to Γ when the society decides to give stocks of goods of the Production Turnpike configuration to the future citizens at the end of the planning period. Such a case must be discussed separately and can be ruled out (as will later be demonstrated) if we make the additional assumption that the discount factor θ is not equal to the natural growth factor ρ.

Let us now assume that the planning authorities peg the posterity utility function at the particular level of satisfaction $\bar{y}$ which the coming generation would expect to enjoy if they were provided with the same amounts of goods per capita as the present generation had at the beginning of period 0. Among possible programmes securing the coming generation the stocks of goods which are rated as high as the existing stocks, the authorities choose the one that maximizes the level of satisfaction (2) of the living people subject to the conditions for feasibility, (3) and (4). Let the Farkas–Lagrange multipliers associated with constraints (3), (4), (5), and (6) be denoted by $\lambda_j(t)$, $\mu(t)$, ν_j, and κ, respectively, to which the familiar shadow-price interpretation can be given. The Kuhn–Tucker conditions for optimality can then be written as follows:

$$\frac{1}{\theta^t} f_j(e(t)) \begin{cases} \leqq \lambda_j(t) & \text{if } e_j(t) = 0, \\ = \lambda_j(t) & \text{if } e_j(t) > 0, \end{cases} \tag{13}$$

for $t = 0, 1, ..., T-1$;

$$\sum_j b_{ij}\lambda_j(t+1) \begin{cases} \leqq \sum_j a_{ij}\lambda_j(t)+l_i\mu(t) & \text{if } q_i(t) = 0, \\ = \sum_j a_{ij}\lambda_j(t)+l_i\mu(t) & \text{if } q_i(t) > 0, \end{cases} \tag{14}$$

for $t = 0, 1, \ldots, T-2$;

$$\sum_j b_{ij}v_j \begin{cases} \leqq \sum_j a_{ij}\lambda_j(T-1) + l_i\mu(T-1), & \text{if } q_i(T-1) = 0, \\ = \sum_j a_{ij}\lambda_j(T-1) + l_i\mu(T-1), & \text{if } q_i(T-1) > 0; \end{cases} \tag{15}$$

and

$$\kappa\Gamma_j(k_1, \ldots, k_n) \begin{cases} \leqq \rho^T \bar{N} v_j, & \text{if } k_j = 0, \\ = \rho^T \bar{N} v_j, & \text{if } k_j > 0. \end{cases} \tag{16}$$

These are conditions for a Ramsey optimum that remain valid regardless of whether the optimum path is a path of proportional growth or not. As the Consumption Turnpike we are interested in is a balanced growth path, $q(T-1)$ must be an intensity set which can generate a further balanced growth; so at $q(T-1)$ (12′) must hold, which together with (16) enables us to put (15) in the form:

$$\sum_j (b_{ij} - \rho a_{ij})\lambda_j(T) - \theta^{-T}\tau l_i/\sigma \begin{cases} \leqq \sum_j a_{ij}\lambda_j(T-1) + l_i\mu(T-1), \\ \qquad\qquad \text{if } q_i(T-1) = 0, \\ = \sum_j a_{ij}\lambda_j(T-1) + l_i\mu(T-1), \\ \qquad\qquad \text{if } q_i(T-1) > 0, \end{cases} \tag{15′}$$

where

$$\sigma = \left(\frac{\rho}{\theta}\right)^T \frac{\xi\bar{N}}{\kappa},$$

and $\lambda_j(T)$s are defined as

$$\lambda_j(T) = f_j(e(T))\theta^{-T}/\sigma, \qquad j = 1, \ldots, n, \tag{17}$$

with f_j evaluated at $e(T)$ such that

$$\sum_i b_{ij}q_i(T-1) = \rho \sum_i a_{ij}q_i(T-1) + e_j(T), \qquad i = 1, \ldots, n.$$

It is evident that with $q(-1)$ historically (or arbitrarily) given the Ramsey optimum programme characterized by the above inequalities does not usually allow the whole economy to grow at a uniform rate of expansion. But, if there exists a particular initial position denoted by $q_C = (q_{1,C}, \ldots, q_{m,C})$ that generates a balanced optimum growth, there flows along the path a steady stream of consumption, $e(t)$, $t = 0, 1, \ldots, T$, which grows at the rate, $\rho - 1$, common to all commodities. We have

$$e_j(t) = \rho^t e_{j,C} \qquad = 1, \ldots, n \tag{18}$$

where $e_{j,C}$s are the balanced growth consumption proportions which satisfy

$$\sum_i b_{ij}q_{i,C} \geqq \rho \sum_i a_{ij}q_{i,C}+e_{j,C} \qquad j = 1, ..., n. \tag{19}$$

Remembering that all f_js are homogeneous of degree zero in their arguments, we see that they should remain unchanged along the balanced growth path, and hence from (13) and (17) we have

$$f_j(ec) = \lambda_{j,C} = \begin{cases} \theta^t \lambda_j(t) & t = 0, 1, ..., T-1, \\ \sigma\theta^T \lambda_j(T). \end{cases} \tag{20}$$

Substituting for $\lambda_j(t)$ and $\lambda_j(t+1)$ from (20), (14) gives $\mu(t) = \theta^{-t}\mu_C$ for $t = 0, 1, ..., T-2$, and all the $T-1$ inequalities (14) are reduced to

$$\sum_j b_{ij}\lambda_{j,C} \begin{cases} \leqq \theta(\sum_j a_{ij}\lambda_{j,C}+l_i\mu_C) & \text{if } q_{i,C} = 0, \\ = \theta(\sum_j a_{ij}\lambda_{j,C}+l_i\mu_C) & \text{if } q_{i,C} > 0, \end{cases} \tag{21}$$

while (15′) is reduced to

$$\sum_j b_{ij}\lambda_{j,C} \begin{cases} \leqq \theta\left[\sum_j a_{ij}\lambda_{j,C}\left(\sigma+\frac{\rho}{\theta}\right)+l_i\{\sigma\mu(T-1)\theta^{T-1}+\tau/\theta\}\right], \\ \qquad \text{if } q_{i,C} = 0, \\ = \theta\left[\sum_j a_{ij}\lambda_{j,C}\left(\sigma+\frac{\rho}{\theta}\right)+l_i\{\sigma\mu(T-1)\theta^{T-1}+\tau/\theta\}\right], \\ \qquad \text{if } q_{i,C} > 0. \end{cases} \tag{21′}$$

Let us now give attention to the fact that our 'catalogue of processes' includes a number of 'fictitious' processes that are introduced for standardizing processes of different production duration. A famous and conventional example of pluri-period production is that of wine or that of cultured pearls. A fifteen-year production process of wine is 'synchronized' with the one-year production process of orange juice by breaking up the whole production process of wine into fifteen standardized processes consisting of the prime process converting initial inputs of commodities (grapes and others) and labour into one-year wine, the second process converting one-year wine into two-year wine (with no input of labour), and so on until the final one converting fourteen-year wine into fifteen-year wine. Thus, unless we are concerned with a 'dry' economy, we might safely assume that there are a number of processes which are operated at positive intensities $q_{i,C} > 0$ and whose labour coefficients are zero, $l_i = 0$. For them, we have from (21) and (21′)

$$\sigma + \frac{\rho}{\theta} = 1 \qquad \text{or} \qquad \sigma = \frac{\theta - \rho}{\theta},^{1} \tag{22}$$

which, in turn, yields

$$\mu_C = \sigma\mu(T-1)\theta^{T-1} + \tau/\theta \qquad \text{or} \qquad \mu(T-1) = \theta^{-T}(\mu_C\theta - \tau)/\sigma \tag{22′}$$

As is seen from the definition of σ it should be positive and hence the discount factor θ should be greater than the growth factor ρ; this means that if θ is less than ρ, there is no initial point which generates a balanced Ramsey optimum growth,[2] or a Consumption Turnpike. Therefore, we assume $\theta > \rho$ throughout the rest of this section.

In the state of balanced growth where σ and $\mu(T-1)$ fulfil (22) and (22′), the optimality condition (21′), originally given in the form of (15) and (16), is reduced to (21). Thus, as long as we confine ourselves to discussing the existence of a *balanced* Ramsey optimum growth, we may work with a handy system consisting of three sets of inequalities, (19), (20), and (21), instead of dealing with the entire Kuhn–Tucker conditions (13)–(16) and (19).

As the population in period t is $\rho^t \bar{N}$, the per capita consumption of good j is given (from (18)) as $\hat{e}_{j,C} = e_{j,C}/\bar{N}$ on the balanced growth path. This, together with the fact that the balanced growth intensities $q_{i,C}$ are normalized so that

$$\bar{N} = \rho \sum_i l_i q_{i,C}, \tag{23}$$

enables us to write (19) in the form

$$\sum_i b_{ij} q_{i,C} \geqq \rho\left(\sum_i a_{ij} q_{i,C} + e_j \sum_i l_i q_{i,C}\right) \qquad j = 1, ..., n. \tag{19′}$$

On the other hand, all the f_js are homogeneous of degree zero; hence we can replace the balanced growth consumption e_C in (20) by the balanced growth consumption *per capita* $\hat{e}_C$. Thus we obtain n expressions, each equating $f_j(\hat{e}_C)$ with $\lambda_{j,C}$. Because of the homogeneity of the f_js they are functionally dependent (and their Jacobian vanishes everywhere); so the consumption *per capita* of each good is not determined absolutely but as a function of relative Farkas–Lagrange multipliers. Therefore,

$$\hat{e}_j = \eta g_j(\tilde{\lambda}_{1,C}, ..., \tilde{\lambda}_{n,C}), \tag{24}$$

[1] The same result follows in more general circumstances; i.e., even if $l_i > 0$ for all $q_{i,C} > 0$, we get (22) except in the singular case when the capital intensities (evaluated at 'shadow prices' $\lambda_{i,C}$) of all active processes are equal to each other.

[2] Note that we assume $\rho \neq \theta$. The case of $\rho = \theta$ will be discussed later.

where, in the following also, the tilde denotes normalization (i.e., the sum of $\tilde{\lambda}_{1,C}, \ldots, \tilde{\lambda}_{n,C}$ is equal to unity) and η stands for the undetermined scale factor defined such that $\eta = \sum_j \hat{e}_j \tilde{\lambda}_{j,C}$; hence

$$\sum_j g_j(\tilde{\lambda}_{1,C}, \ldots, \tilde{\lambda}_{n,C}) \tilde{\lambda}_{j,C} = 1 \tag{25}$$

is an identity.

In Chapter VII we used the concepts of 'net outputs' and 'augmented labour-inputs' in establishing the existence of the long-run growth equilibrium. From similar definitions we obtain

$$m_{ij}(q) = \frac{1}{\rho} b_{ij} - \frac{\theta}{\rho} a_{ij} + \frac{\theta - \rho}{\rho} l_i \frac{\sum_k a_{kj} q_k}{\sum_k l_k q_k}$$

and

$$n_{ij}(\tilde{\lambda}) = l_i g_j(\tilde{\lambda}).$$

In fact, the former may be regarded as a variant of the 'net output coefficient' while the latter as a variant of the 'augmented labour-input coefficient', since they reduce to the m_{ij} and n_{ij} (respectively) originally defined when the discount factor equals the natural growth factor, provided that capitalists only save and workers only consume.

Let us now seek those values of $q_{1,C}, \ldots, q_{m,C}, \tilde{\lambda}_{1,C}, \ldots, \tilde{\lambda}_{n,C}$ and η which establish the two sets of inequalities,

$$\sum_i m_{ij}(q_C) q_{i,C} \geqq \eta \sum_i n_{ij}(\tilde{\lambda}_C) q_{i,C} \qquad j = 1, \ldots, n, \tag{26}$$

$$\sum_j m_{ij}(q_C) \tilde{\lambda}_{j,C} \leqq \eta \sum_j n_{ij}(\tilde{\lambda}_C) \tilde{\lambda}_{j,C} \qquad i = 1, \ldots, m. \tag{27}$$

In view of (24) we find that (26) is no more than an alternative and equivalent expression of (19′). Putting

$$\mu_C = \frac{\rho - \theta}{\theta} \frac{\sum_i \sum_j a_{ij} \tilde{\lambda}_{j,C} q_{i,C}}{\sum_i l_i q_{i,C}} + \frac{\rho}{\theta} \eta \tag{28}$$

and taking (25) into account, we find that (27) is equivalent to (21). Thus the existence proof boils down to a game-theoretic problem of solving inequalities (26) and (27).

These differ from the similar inequalities (1′) and (3′) in Chapter VII[1] in having, as the adjuster of the value of the 'game', the level of consumption per capita η in place of the real wage rate Ω and also in having net output coefficients which are affected by activity levels q_C, whereas in the

[1] See p. 119 above.

previous model they fluctuated in response to changes in shadow prices. In spite of these differences, however, the same proof *mutatis mutandis* establishes the existence of solutions to (26) and (27). That is to say, we may as before conceive of a Game between the 'Entrepreneur' and the 'Market' who regulate activity levels, q_C, and shadow prices, $\tilde{\lambda}_C$, respectively. Let us set q_i^*s and $\tilde{\lambda}_j^*$s at any non-negative values which satisfy (23) and $\Sigma\, \tilde{\lambda}_j^* = 1$, respectively. It follows from the definition of $n_{ij}(\tilde{\lambda})$ that if $n_{i,j}(\tilde{\lambda}^*)$ is positive for some i' with $l_{i'} > 0$, then $n_{i''j}(\tilde{\lambda}^*)$ is positive for any i'' with $l_{i''} > 0$. This particular sign pattern of the matrix of the augmented labour-input coefficients implies, as we have seen before, that for a fair game with pay-off matrix $M(q^*)-\eta N(\tilde{\lambda}^*)$ the level of consumption *per capita* η is unique.[1] With given q^* and $\tilde{\lambda}^*$, the inequalities (26) and (27) are fulfilled at optimum strategies q^0 and $\tilde{\lambda}^0$ by the fair level of consumption η^0. The mapping $(q^*, \tilde{\lambda}^*) \to (q^0, \tilde{\lambda}^0)$ thus obtained satisfies the requirements for the fixed point theorem by Kakutani; so there is a set of solutions, $(q_C, \tilde{\lambda}_C, \eta_C)$, to the inequalities (26) and (27).[2] The absolute level of λ_C is determined by (20).

4. In this section we make a slight digression and elucidate an implication of the Consumption Turnpike property (28). Interpreting λ_C and μ_C as the shadow prices and the shadow wage rate associated with the state of balanced Ramsey-optimum growth, we find from (21) that there prevails in that state a rate of profits which equals the discount rate, $\theta-1$. The total profits,

$$(\theta-1)\rho^t\Big(\sum_i \sum_j a_{ij}\lambda_{j,C}q_{i,C} + \mu_C \sum_i l_i q_{i,C}\Big), \tag{29}$$

are available for spending in period t.[3] They are combined with the wages, $\mu_C \rho^{t+1} \sum_i l_i q_{i,C}$, that the workers receive in that period, to give the total income which in turn gives the total savings after subtracting the total consumption, $\eta_C \rho^{t-1} \sum_i l_i q_{i,C}$. The total savings thus obtained along the Consumption Turnpike are then compared with the total profits (29). The ratio of the former to the latter might legitimately be called the optimum savings-profits ratio and is in view of (28)

$$s = \frac{\rho-1}{\theta-1} \qquad \text{in any period.}$$

[1] Cf. p. 123 above.

[2] The theorem whose proof is outlined above is no more than a special case of a more general theorem discussed by G. L. Thompson and myself for a game with pay-off coefficients, $m_{ij}(q,\lambda)-\eta n_{ij}(q,\lambda)$, both m_{ij} and n_{ij} depend on q and λ. See M. Morishima and G. L. Thompson, 'Balanced growth of firms in a competitive situation with external economies', *International Economic Review*, Vol. I (1960), pp. 129–42.

[3] They were earned from the activities in the previous period.

In other words, the optimum savings-profits ratio must equal the rate of growth divided by the rate of profits. It approaches unity in the limit as the discount factor (hence one plus the rate of profits) tends to the growth factor. Thus we get a rule of optimum saving referred to as the Silvery Rule of Accumulation, which may be regarded as an extension of the famous Golden Rule to the case where the subjective time-preference factor is greater than one.

As I have previously established, for an economy consisting of workers who consume their *entire* income and capitalists who save a constant proportion of their income, there exists an equilibrium balanced growth rate that is equal to the capitalists' propensity to save times the equilibrium rate of profits.[1] This state evidently obeys the above Silvery Rule, so that Ramsey optimality is ensured provided the future is appropriately discounted. Note, however, that the converse of this proposition is not true; that is to say, in a state obeying the Silvery Rule it is not necessarily true that the workers do not save at all, while the capitalists save a part of their income. But as we will show below, the Consumption Turnpike is the Pasinetti equilibrium which in the long run would be established under less restrictive conditions on the propensities to save.

Let us concentrate our attention upon an economy consisting of those capitalists who save at a positive savings ratio, s_c, and those workers who are also allowed to save at a positive ratio, s_w, which is less than s_c. Let W denote the total wages, E_w the profits accruing to the workers, and E_c the profits accruing to the capitalists. Next, take the discount rate $\theta-1$ equal to $\rho-1$ divided by the capitalist's propensity to save, and consider the Consumption Turnpike corresponding to the discount ratio thus specified. When the Silvery Rule of Accumulation prevails, it is clear from the definition of the optimum savings-profits ratio s that total savings equal that ratio multiplied by the total profits. As the total savings are the total income, $W+E_w+E_c$, *minus* the total consumption, $c_w(W+E_w)+c_cE_c$, where c_w and c_c represent the workers' and the capitalists' average propensity to consume, $1-s_w$ and $1-s_c$, respectively, we have

$$\frac{W+E_w+E_c-c_w(W+E_w)-c_cE_c}{E_w+E_c} = s.$$

Since the discount factor is taken such that $s_c = s$, we obtain from the above equation

$$\frac{s_w(W+E_w)}{E_w} = \frac{s_cE_c}{E_c},$$

[1] See M. Morishima, *Equilibrium, Stability, and Growth*, pp. 131–53. See also M. Morishima, 'Economic expansion and the interest rate in generalized von Neumann models', *Econometrica*, Vol. XXVIII (1960), pp. 352–63.

which implies that in the state of balanced Ramsey optimum growth the total profits are distributed, among capitalists and workers, in proportion to their ownership of capital (the Pasinetti distribution of income). Thus we may say that a Pasinetti equilibrium gives a Ramsey optimum, and vice versa, so long as the capitalists save with a savings ratio that is appropriately connected with the rate of 'impatience' at which consumption streams are discounted. This conclusion is clearly a generalization of the so-called 'Neo-classical Theorem'.[1]

5. The argument has so far proceeded on the assumption that the discount factor differs from the growth factor. However, when people at different times are treated as if they were contemporaries, that is to say, when we do not discount later citizens in comparison with earlier ones, future outcomes must be discounted by the population growth rate. We are now concerned with the case of $\theta = \rho$ which was ruled out of the discussion in the previous section and shall show that a balanced Ramsey-optimum growth path can start from a Golden Equilibrium point.

Consider an economy where the capital stocks are available in the Golden Equilibrium proportions. The authorities, on behalf of the coming generation not living during the planning period, will want to equip them with the stocks of goods that are at least as desirable as the Golden Equilibrium stocks. Evaluation of the future stocks is made in terms of the utility which they command when they are used so that the stocks of goods per capita are maintained for ever. We assume that the future generation has the same tastes as the living one. Since it follows from the definition of Golden Equilibrium that there is no set of capital stocks which is comparable with the Golden Equilibrium one, the authorities would definitely decide to bestow on the coming people the stocks of goods in the Golden Equilibrium amounts. Therefore, the economy starting from a point on the Golden Balanced Growth path will return, after the lapse of T periods, to a point on the same path. We thus find that the authorities would maximize the sum of $\frac{1}{\rho^t} f(e(t))$ over T periods,[2] $t = 0, 1, \ldots, T-1$, subject to

$$\sum_i b_{ij} q_i(t-1) \geqq \sum_i a_{ij} q_i(t) + e_j(t),$$

$$t = 0, 1, \ldots, T-1,$$

$$\rho^t \bar{N} \geqq \sum_i l_i q_i(t)$$

[1] Cf. Joan Robinson, 'A neo-classical theorem', *Review of Economic Studies*, Vol. XXIX (1962), pp. 219–26.

[2] Note that fs are now discounted by ρ instead of θ as previously.

where $q(-1)$ is set at q_G and $q(T-1)$ at $\rho^T q_G$ with the Golden intensities, $q_G = (q_{1,G}, ..., q_{m,G})$, such that $\bar{N} = \rho \sum_i l_i q_{i,G}$; other $q(t)$s, as well as all $e(t)$s, are regarded as variables of the plan.

Let $\lambda_j(t)$ and $\mu(t)$ denote the Farkas–Lagrange multipliers as before; the Kuhn–Tucker conditions are then given as

$$\frac{1}{\rho^t} f_j(e(t)) \begin{cases} \leqq \lambda_j(t) & \text{if} \quad e_j(t) = 0, \\ = \lambda_j(t) & \text{if} \quad e_j(t) > 0, \end{cases} \tag{30}$$

for $t = 0, 1, ..., T-1$; and

$$\sum_j b_{ij}\lambda_j(t+1) \begin{cases} \leqq \sum_j a_{ij}\lambda_j(t) + l_i\mu(t) & \text{if} \quad q_i(t) = 0, \\ = \sum_j a_{ij}\lambda_j(t) + l_i\mu(t) & \text{if} \quad q_i(t) > 0, \end{cases} \tag{31}$$

for $t = 0, 1, ..., T-2$. On the other hand, q_G is defined as a point at which $f(e)$ takes on a maximum subject to

$$\sum_i b_{ij} q_i \geqq \rho \sum_i a_{ij} q_i + e_j,$$

$$\bar{N} = \rho \sum_i l_i q_i;$$

this implies that the shadow prices and the shadow wage rate associated with the Golden Balanced Growth must satisfy the inequalities:

$$f_j(e) \begin{cases} \leqq \lambda_{j,G} & \text{if} \quad e_j = 0 \\ = \lambda_{j,G} & \text{if} \quad e_j > 0, \end{cases} \tag{30'}$$

and

$$\sum_j b_{ij}\lambda_{j,G} \begin{cases} \leqq \rho(\sum_j a_{ij}\lambda_{j,G} + l_i\mu_G) & \text{if} \quad q_i = 0 \\ = \rho(\sum_j a_{ij}\lambda_{j,G} + l_i\mu_G) & \text{if} \quad q_i > 0. \end{cases} \tag{31'}$$

Comparing (30) and (31) with (30′) and (31′), and taking the homogeneity (of degree zero) of the derivatives f_js into account, we find that the balanced growth with the initial intensities $q_{1,G}, ..., q_{m,G}$ satisfies the optimality conditions (30) and (31) with discounted prices, $\lambda_j(t) = \rho^{-t}\lambda_{j,G}$, and discounted wage rates, $\mu(t) = \rho^{-t}\mu_G$. Hence we may conclude by saying that the Golden Equilibrium (or the Turnpike) is the balanced optimum growth path (or the Consumption Turnpike) that is obtained when θ is set at ρ.

6. We are now in a position to pass on to the problem of convergence to the Consumption Turnpike. It is a problem that is still attracting attention of mathematically inclined, contemporary economists. The classical model of a stationary labour force, no time preference and a single aggregate commodity (that can serve both as capital and consumption goods) which Frank Ramsey first (in 1928) examined for optimality, has been further explored by Samuelson[1] so as to establish the proposition that is now called the Consumption Turnpike Theorem:

If a sufficiently long programming period is taken, any Ramsey optimal path spends most of its time in a small neighbourhood of the Consumption Turnpike.[2]

This prototype of the theorem was later extended in various directions; for example, in the direction of introducing technical progress and uncertainty about the future (Mirrlees and Weizsäcker), in the direction of introducing autonomous growth of the labour force at a constant rate (Atsumi, Cass, Koopmans, Tsukui), in the direction of introducing the discount factor of future utilities (Cass, Koopmans), and in the direction of introducing multiple commodities and alternative production processes (Gale, McKenzie, Samuelson and Solow, Tsukui).[3] The model we will discuss below is very similar to the one studied by McKenzie[4] but is more general than that in dealing with the case where the discount factor is different from the population rate of growth also.

It is rather ironic to observe that the case of the discount factor not exceeding the growth factor is more easily handled in the stability discussion than the other one, whereas it has required delicate treatment in establishing the existence of optimal growth programmes. It is always the best way of approach to begin with the easiest case, so that our Turnpike business first proceeds on the assumption that $\rho \geqq \theta$. In the other case of $\rho < \theta$ (left to section 7) the theorem is subject to certain important exceptions and cannot claim so general validity as in the case we are concerned with immediately below.

[1] F. P. Ramsey, loc. cit.; P. A. Samuelson, 'A catenary Turnpike Theorem involving consumption and the Golden Rule', *American Economic Review*, Vol. LV (1965), pp. 486–96.

[2] By virtue of Samuelson's assumption of the absence of time preference, his model obtains the special property that the Production Turnpike and the Consumption Turnpike lie one upon another.

[3] Most references are found in recent issues of *Review of Economic Studies*. See also T. C. Koopmans, 'On the concept of optimal growth', in *Semaine d'Etude sur le Role de l'Analyse Econometrique dans la Formulation de Plans de Developpement*, Pontificiae Academiae Scientiarum Scripta Varia, 28 I (1965), pp. 225–87; L. W. McKenzie, 'Accumulation programs of maximum utility and the von Neumann facet', in J. N. Wolfe (ed.) *Value, Capital, and Growth, Papers in honour of Sir John Hicks* (Edinburgh: Edinburgh University Press, 1968); P. A. Samuelson and R. M. Solow, 'A complete capital model involving heterogeneous capital goods', *Quarterly Journal of Economics*, Vol. LXX (1956), pp. 538–62.

[4] See McKenzie, loc. cit.

When $\rho = \theta$, the Consumption Turnpike coincides with the Production Turnpike, while though we have no Consumption Turnpike at all when $\rho > \theta$ there would still prevail a strong tendency for optimum paths to lead to Production Turnpike. The proof of this is similar in its essence to that for the Final State Turnpike Theorem. Roughly speaking, we first show that any infinite Ramsey-optimum path—a path that is obtained as the limiting path of Ramsey-optimum paths when the programming period T tends to infinity—does not often use those processes which become unprofitable at the Turnpike prices and wage rate. It will then be seen that there is a long period during which only 'top' processes (that is to say, the processes which are profitable at the Turnpike prices and wage rate) are adopted. And the final part of the proof will be devoted to demonstrating that all infinite Ramsey-optimum paths approach nearer and nearer to the Turnpike with the lapse of time during the long period.

We assume that indifference curves between goods generated by the function $f(e)$ slope downwards and are convex to the origin of the commodity space. This property, often referred to as the (strict) quasi-concavity of $f(e)$,[1] is combined with the homogeneity of degree one of $f(e)$ to yield the following basic inequality:

$$f(e)-f(e^*) \leqq \sum_j f_j(e^*)(e_j-e_j^*),$$

where $f_j(e^*)$ is the partial derivative at e^* with respect to the jth element of e. The inequality holds for all e and e^*. If we take e^* as the Production Turnpike or the Golden Equilibrium consumption in period t (denoted below by $\bar{e}(t)$), each $f_j(\bar{e}(t))$ equals the (stationary) Turnpike price, $\bar{\lambda}_j$, of good j; whence we get, for all t,

$$f(e(t))-f(\bar{e}(t)) \leqq \sum_j \bar{\lambda}_j\{e_j(t)-\bar{e}_j(t)\}.$$

As consumption $e(t)$ should be feasible, we have

$$\sum_j \bar{\lambda}_j e_j(t) \leqq \sum_j \bar{\lambda}_j\{\sum_i b_{ij}q_i(t-1)-\sum_i a_{ij}q_i(t)\}, \tag{32}$$

the right-hand side of which can further be put in the form:

$$K(t)-\frac{1}{\rho}K(t+1)+\bar{\mu}\sum_i l_i q_i(t)+\sum_i\left[\frac{1}{\rho}\sum_j b_{ij}\bar{\lambda}_j-\sum_j a_{ij}\bar{\lambda}_j-\bar{\mu}l_i\right]q_i(t),$$

where in defining the stock index, $K(t)$, the stocks of goods available at the beginning of period t, $\sum_i b_{ij}q_i(t-1)$, are evaluated at the Turnpike prices. The value of the part in the square brackets (denoted by $-D_i$

[1] For the definition of the quasi-concavity see, for example, my *Equilibrium, Stability, and Growth*, p. 43.

hereafter) is zero for top processes and negative for all others. As for the Turnpike consumption $\bar{e}(t)$, (32) holds with equality with the Turnpike activity levels $\bar{q}(t-1)$ and $\bar{q}(t)$; and the right-hand side of the equation thus obtained is also equal to $\bar{\mu} \sum_i l_i \bar{q}_i(t)$. Along any optimum path, labour should always be fully employed and the Turnpike consumption must equal the full employment wages; hence we finally get

$$f(e(t)) - f(\bar{e}(t)) \leqq K(t) - \frac{1}{\rho} K(t+1) - \sum_i D_i q_i(t). \tag{33}$$

In particular, when some non-top processes operate at least at intensity $\rho^t \varepsilon$ in period t, the last term of (33) will be at least as large as $\rho^t D\varepsilon$, where D is the minimum of $D_1, \ldots, D_m$. Such a period will be called *perverse*. We have from (33), for a series beginning with any particular period t_0, the inequality:

$$\sum_{t=t_0}^{\infty} \frac{1}{\rho^t} [f(e(t)) - f(\bar{e}(t))] \leqq \rho^{-t_0} K(t_0) - \lim_{t \to \infty} \rho^{-t} K(t) - n(t_0) D\varepsilon, \tag{34}$$

where $n(t_0)$ represents the total number of perverse periods after t_0.

Let us now designate the left-hand side of (34) by $S(t_0)$. Since $\rho \geqq \theta$, the present value of the infinite stream of differences, $f(e(t)) - f(\bar{e}(t))$, $t = 0, 1, \ldots$ discounted by the factor θ can be expressed as the sum of $S(t_0)$, $t_0 = 0, 1, 2, \ldots$, ad infinitum, with appropriate non-negative weights, $1, v_1, v_2, \ldots$. On the other hand, if there were infinitely many perverse periods, the right-hand side of (34) would be $-\infty$ for each t_0; this evidently implies that $u(\infty)$ would *definitely* be below $\bar{u}(\infty)$, i.e. the value of $u(\infty)$ along the particular feasible path (called the bottom path in Chapter X) that starts with the historically given endowments, arrives at a point on the Turnpike in a certain period and drives along it forever after that.[1] Thus the infinite path we are examining for a Ramsey optimum can not pass the test unless the number of the perverse periods is finite. By taking ε arbitrarily small, we get a very long period, throughout which along any endless Ramsey-optimum path non-top processes will be utilized at negligible intensity. Similarly, the number of periods in which the difference between the right-hand and the left-hand side of (33) is at least as great as δ (a positive, very small constant) should be finite. Hence there is a long period throughout which the equation

$$f(e(t)) + \frac{1}{\rho} K(t+1) - K(t) = f(\bar{e}(t)) \tag{35}$$

approximately holds.

[1] Note that $u(\infty)$ and $\bar{u}(\infty)$ denote $\sum_{t=0}^{\infty} \frac{1}{\theta^t} f(e(t))$ and $\sum_{t=0}^{\infty} \frac{1}{\theta^t} f(\bar{e}(t))$, respectively.

Let us designate, the per capita (or normalized) intensity of process i in the previous period, $q_i(t-1)/\sum_i l_i q_i(t-1)$, by ϕ_i; the per capita intensity of process i in the current period, $q_i(t)/\sum_i l_i q_i(t)$, by ϕ_i'; the per capita consumption of good j in the current period, $e_j(t)/\sum_i l_i q_i(t)$, by ζ_j and the per capita consumption of good j in the state of Golden Equilibrium by $\bar{\zeta}_j$. In view of the definition of the stock index, (35) after normalization can be written as

$$\rho u + \sum_j \bar{\lambda}_j b_j - \sum_j \bar{\lambda}_j a_j = \rho \bar{u}, \tag{35'}$$

where $u = f(\zeta)$, $\bar{u} = f(\bar{\zeta})$, $a_j = \sum_i b_{ij}\phi_i$, and $b_j = \sum_i b_{ij}\phi_i'$. Then any point $(u, b_1, ..., b_n, a_1, ..., a_n)$ satisfying (35′) lies in a $2n$-dimensional plane. It is true that the number of such points can be greater than $2n+1$, but the maximum number, m^*, of independent points that lie in the plane (35′) cannot exceed $2n+1$. We may choose m^* linearly independent $(2n+1)$-dimensional vectors,

$$(u^r, b_1^r, ..., b_n^r, a_1^r, ..., a_n^r), \qquad r = 1, ..., m^*, \tag{36}$$

lying in the plane (35′) and may express any other point in the same plane as a linear combination of them. Hence, for $a_j(t)$ and $b_j(t)$ in period t of the long period, we may write

$$a_j(t) = \sum_{r=1}^{m^*} a_j^r \psi_r(t) \text{ and } b_j(t) = \sum_{r=1}^{m^*} b_j^r \psi_r(t), \qquad j = 1, ..., n, \tag{37}$$

where $\psi_r(t)$ $(r = 1, ..., m^*)$ are real (positive or negative) numbers whose sum is unity.

From the definitions of $a_j(t)$ and $b_j(t)$ as $\{\sum_i b_{ij} q_i(t-1)\}/\{\sum_i l_i q_i(t-1)\}$ and $\{\sum_i b_{ij} q_i(t)\}/\{\sum_i l_i q_i(t)\}$, respectively, we have n identities $a_j(t+1) = b_j(t)$, which together with (37) give us the following difference equations with constant coefficients, a_j^r and b_j^r:

$$\sum_{r=1}^{m^*} b_j^r \psi_r(t) = \sum_{r=1}^{m^*} a_j^r \psi_r(t+1) \qquad j = 1, ..., n. \tag{38}$$

We also have

$$\sum_{r=1}^{m^*} \psi_r(t) = \sum_{r=1}^{m^*} \psi_r(t+1), \tag{39}$$

because the sum of $\psi_r(t)$ is unity for all t. Equations (38) and (39) are discussed by classifying possibilities into the case of $m^* > n+1$ and the case of $m^* \leqq n+1$.

Let us now assume that the Production Turnpike is *unique* and that every top process operates at some *positive* intensity along the Turnpike. If m^* (the number of unknown functions $\psi_r(t)$) is greater than $n+1$ (the number of equations (38) and (39)), there are infinitely many stationary solutions to (38) and (39), among which there are found those which are meaningful in the sense that they give non-negative intensities of processes, $q_1(t), ..., q_m(t)$.[1] All such solutions generate the balanced growth of all $q_i(t)$ at the rate $\rho-1$ and give the 'utility' $f(e(t))$ which is as high as the Turnpike utility $f(\bar{e}(t))$. It is clear that each of them is a solution which gives a Production Turnpike, so that the assumption of the uniqueness of the Production Turnpike is violated. The case of $m^* > n+1$ is thus ruled out.

On the other hand if $m^* \leqq n+1$, equations (38) and (39), like similar equations in Chapter X, may be grouped into two sets. One set consists of (39) and the following m^*-1 equations:

$$\sum_{r=1}^{m^*} b_j{}^r \psi_r(t) = \sum_{r=1}^{m^*} a_j{}^r \psi_r(t+1), \qquad j = 1, ..., m^*-1, \tag{40}$$

while the other set contains the remaining $n+1-m^*$ equations:

$$\sum_{r=1}^{m^*} b_k{}^r \psi_r(t) = \sum_{r=1}^{m^*} a_k{}^r \psi_r(t+1), \qquad k = m^*, ..., n. \tag{41}$$

It is evident that the second set is empty when $m^* = n+1$.

These equations are compared with (X.17) and (X.18), respectively. The solutions to difference equations (39) and (40) are given in terms of their associated characteristic roots (m^* at most): Each $\psi_r(t)$ is expressed as a sum of the tth powers of the characteristic roots weighted by constants depending upon the coefficients $a_j{}^r$ and $b_j{}^r$ and upon the 'initial' conditions (i.e., the values of $\psi_r(t)$s at the beginning of the long period). We can show that one of the characteristic roots is unity, because in the state of Golden Equilibrium the stocks of goods per capita remain unchanged, so that there are non-zero stationary solutions, $\psi_1{}^0, ..., \psi_{m^*}{}^0$, to equations (39)–(41).

We have taken $\phi_i'^1, \phi_i'^2, ..., \phi_i'^{m^*}$ as basic independent intensities (*per capita*) of top process i, hence the intensity (*per capita*) of process i in any period t can be obtained by summing each product of $\phi_i'^r$ and the corresponding $\psi^r(t)$. We have, for each top process i and in each period t,

$$\frac{q_i(t)}{\sum_k l_k q_k(t)} = \sum_{r=1}^{m^*} \phi_i'^r \psi_r(t). \tag{42}$$

[1] There is a set of stationary solutions ($\psi_1{}^0, \psi_2{}^0, ..., \psi_{m^*}{}^0$) which gives the Production Turnpike. Let ($\psi_1{}^1, \psi_2{}^1, ..., \psi_{m^*}{}^1$) be another set of stationary solutions to (38) and (39). We may get a third one by mixing these two sets. If the weight of the first set in the mixture is made great enough, the third set is also meaningful; that is to say, the $q_i(t)$s that the third set gives are all non-negative.

Therefore, we get

$$\sum_i^* l_i\{\sum_{r=1}^{m^*} \phi_i'^r \psi_r(t)\} = 1, \tag{43}$$

where Σ^* denotes the summation over top processes. Equation (43) implies that the weights associated with those characteristic roots which are greater than one in modulus should be of negligible magnitude in $\psi_r(t)$, or such components of $\psi_r(t)$ should offset each other in the expression (42). In fact, if they were neither negligible nor counterbalancing and $\psi_r(t)$ grew steadily or cyclically in an amplifying way, then it would be impossible for intensities of all processes to remain non-negative throughout the long period, because otherwise (43) would be violated sooner or later.[1] Consequently, characteristic roots that can appear with significant weights in *meaningful* solutions to (39) and (40) must have moduli not exceeding one, and among the characteristic solutions thus selected those which conflict with the additional equations (41) should further be ruled out or enter the meaningful solutions with weights of negligible magnitude since we seek a path approximately fulfilling all equations (39)–(41).

Hence we may conclude by saying that any infinite path remains, throughout a long stretch of it, within a very small neighbourhood of the Turnpike, provided that there is no, negative or complex, characteristic root which has a modulus of one; or more exactly, it behaves so, provided that coefficients a_j^r and b_j^r satisfy an assumption similar to assumption (v) in Chapter X.

This is the Consumption Turnpike Theorem we want to establish. It asserts, with a proviso, that the distance from a point in period t on a Ramsey-optimum path of order T to a corresponding point on the Turnpike approaches zero for most values of t as the length of programming period T increases indefinitely. If the proviso, however, is not satisfied, that is, if there are, in addition to the Golden Equilibrium characteristic root, a number of characteristic roots, imaginary or real (negative) with an absolute value of one, then the Ramsey optimum paths may trace out oscillations around the Turnpike, which would not be dominated by the particular solution of the Golden steady growth, however long the programming period T is taken. It is worth mentioning, particularly in relation to cyclic exceptions obtained in the case of the discount factor being greater than the growth factor ($\theta > \rho$) (discussed in the following section), that though we cannot rule out oscillatory exceptions in the present case, oscillations can take place only between top processes; that is to say, processes that reveal themselves unprofitable at the Turnpike prices and wage rate cannot repeatedly be adopted in the state of Ramsey optimum

[1] This means that the economy would in the long run suffer from deficiency of labour.

growth. This general tendency towards the 'von Neumann facet' (in McKenzie's terminology) will not, however, prevail in the remaining case, that is, when the future events are discounted at a rate greater than the growth rate of the labour force.

7. When the discount factor θ is greater than the growth factor ρ, the Consumption Turnpike departs from the Production Turnpike; it then follows that the stocks of goods available at the beginning of each period have to appear in the stock index $K(t)$ in terms of the corresponding Consumption Turnpike prices instead of the Production Turnpike prices. An argument similar to that used for deriving (34) is applicable *mutatis mutandis*; we get

$$\sum_{t=0}^{\infty} \frac{1}{\theta^t} [f(e(t)) - f(\bar{e}(t))] \leq K(0) - \lim_{t\to\infty} K(t) - \sum_{t=0}^{\infty} \sum_i D_i(t) q_i(t), \tag{44}$$

where the vector $\bar{e}(t)$ denotes the quantities of goods which would be consumed in period t when the economy expands along the Consumption Turnpike; the index $K(t)$ is defined as

$$K(t) = \sum_i \sum_j b_{ij} q_i(t-1) \bar{\lambda}_j(t), \qquad \text{with} \qquad \bar{\lambda}_j(t) = \frac{1}{\theta^t} f_j(\bar{e}(t));$$

and operation of process i at unit intensity would yield a loss of the amount

$$D_i(t) = \sum_j a_{ij} \bar{\lambda}_j(t) + l_i \bar{\mu}(t) - \sum_j b_{ij} \bar{\lambda}_j(t+1),$$

when the Consumption Turnpike prices prevail in periods t and $t+1$.

Let us now assume that the technology is indecomposable, that is to say, any process even if it does not directly employ labour cannot operate at an intensity exceeding some bound which is determined by the availability of the labour force; otherwise that process would fail in getting some indispensable materials for the production of which labour is required directly or indirectly. Therefore, no intensity variables $q_i(t)$ can increase in the long run at a rate greater than $\rho-1$. On the other hand, all the Consumption Turnpike prices decrease at a rate, $\theta-1$, greater than $\rho-1$. Hence it follows that both series, $\{K(t)\}$ and $\{\sum_i D_i(t) q_i(t)\}$ are *convergent*.

We are now able to compare a Ramsey-optimum path starting from a given initial position with a feasible path starting from the same point, reaching the Consumption Turnpike at the end of a certain period T_0 and then running along it forever after that date. Call the latter 'a feasible path joining the Consumption Turnpike in period T_0+1', which would generate a consumption stream $\{e^*(t)\}$ such that $e^*(t) = \bar{e}(t)$ for all $t = T_0+1, T_0+2, \ldots,$ *ad infinitum*. As $\lim_{t\to\infty} K(t) = 0$, it is then observed from (44) that between the optimum path of infinite order (whose consumption and intensity-of-production streams are denoted by $\{e(t)\}$ and $\{q(t)\}$, respectively) and any feasible path joining the Consumption Turnpike will be established the following inequality:

$$\sum_{t=0}^{\infty} \frac{1}{\theta^t} f(e(t)) - \sum_{t=0}^{\infty} \frac{1}{\theta^t} f(e^*(t)) \leqq K(0) + \sum_{t=0}^{T_0} \frac{1}{\theta^t} f(\bar{e}(t))$$

$$- \sum_{t=0}^{T_0} \frac{1}{\theta^t} f(e^*(t)) - \sum_{t=0}^{\infty} \sum_i D_i(t) q_i(t).$$

As $\{\sum_i D_i(t) q_i(t)\}$ converges, it is possible for the right-hand side to remain positive for all feasible paths joining the Consumption Turnpike in some period T_0; so that it is possible, although less probable, for the left-hand side also to take on positive values for all such paths. If this should happen, any path which sooner or later joins the Consumption Turnpike cannot be Ramsey-optimal. In other words, we cannot get rid of a certain class of exceptional cases where the optimum path will remain remote from the Consumption Turnpike throughout a large fraction of the very long planning period. It would not be a surprise to find that the Theorem might be violated when the future citizens are discounted at a rate greater than the growth rate. If there is a strong time preference in favour of the present and near future it would in fact be possible that the gain received by running along the Consumption Turnpike in later periods could not compensate the loss suffered in earlier periods by shifting towards the direction of the Consumption Turnpike.

The same fact can be viewed from another angle. Since the 'book of blueprints' is assumed to be indecomposable it is impossible for the intensities of production to grow along an infinite feasible path at a greater rate than the given (natural) growth rate of the labour force, $\rho - 1$. Therefore, the discounted intensities along an infinite Ramsey-optimum path, $q_1(t)/\rho^t, \ldots, q_m(t)/\rho^t$, would remain in a bounded region in m-dimensional Euclidean space; it then follows from the familiar Bolzano–Weierstrass theorem that there is in the region an accumulation point of the sequence $\{q(t)/\rho^t\}$. If there is only one accumulation point, it does lie on the Consumption Turnpike. This is so because once an infinite Ramsey-optimum path approaches sufficiently near the accumulation point, it continues to be in a small vicinity of it in later periods; in fact, if the path did not behave so and departed from the accumulation point after the path arrived at that point, it should behave in the same way when it reached that point for the second time; it is clear that there could be another accumulation point, but its existence would evidently violate the assumed uniqueness of the accumulation point. Hence we find that if the economy initially starts from the accumulation point, it will perpetually remain there (that is, all $q_1(t), ..., q_m(t)$ will grow in balance at the common rate, $\rho-1$) so long as the economy advances in a manner consistent with Ramsey optimality. Thus the accumulation point, if it is unique, would give a path of balanced Ramsey-optimum growth, that is to say, the Consumption Turnpike. Thus the uniqueness of the accumulation point yields the Consumption Turnpike Theorem, whereas the multiplicity implies that the infinite Ramsey-optimum path oscillates between accumulation points without reducing the amplitude.

8. The argument is perfected by giving an example of cyclic Ramsey-optimum growth. Consider an economy producing two goods only, to which is available a book of blueprints of three pages. Processes are normalized so that each of them employs one unit of labour; other input and output coefficients might be given as follows.

	Process 1		Process 2		Process 3	
	Input	*Output*	*Input*	*Output*	*Input*	*Output*
Good 1	0·4	2·0	0·9	1·0	1·0	1·0
Good 2	1·8	2·0	0·8	4·0	0·7	4·0

Next we assume that the labour force increases at the rate 0·5 per period, while the subjective rate of time preference is set at 1·0. We then have $\rho = 1{\cdot}5$ and $\theta = 2{\cdot}0$. As to the valuation function $f(e_1, e_2)$, we assume, in addition to the general properties of strict quasi-concavity and homogeneity of degree one, that its partial derivatives with respect to consumption of goods take on the following values at four particular values of the consumption ratio which will play important roles in the discussion below.

Consumption ratio e_2/e_1	Partial derivatives of the valuation function $f_1(e_2/e_1)$	$f_2(e_2/e_1)$
3·25	1·00	0·25
2·00	0·70	0·35
1·90	0·50	0·50
1·23	0·40	1·00

According to the assumed valuation function of the final stocks of goods future generations are indifferent between receiving two units of both goods and receiving one unit of good 1 and four units of good 2, as bequests from the present generation. In addition to this we also assume that the marginal rate of substitution of good 1 for good 2 is one in the first state, while it is four in the second state. (Note that neither of these states can generate a balanced growth path; so they do not satisfy the proportionality conditions (12′).) Finally we set the initial position (i.e. the intensities of production and the labour force in period -1) at $(q_1, q_2, q_3, N) = (1, 0, 0, 1)$.

We then calculate the Consumption Turnpike prices and wage rate to be $\bar{\lambda}_1 = 0{\cdot}70$, $\bar{\lambda}_2 = 0{\cdot}35$, and $\bar{\mu} = 0{\cdot}14$, respectively, at which processes 1 and 2 are profitable, but process 3 is not. Along the Consumption Turnpike, process 3 will never be adopted; in fact intensities and consumptions in that state are

$$\bar{q}_1(t) = 0{\cdot}5(1{\cdot}5)^t, \qquad \bar{q}_2(t) = 0{\cdot}5(1{\cdot}5)^t, \qquad \bar{q}_3(t) = 0,$$
$$\bar{e}_1(t) = 0{\cdot}525(1{\cdot}5)^t, \qquad \bar{e}_2(t) = 1{\cdot}05(1{\cdot}5)^t.$$

Let us now shift our attention to Ramsey-optimum growth from the given initial point. At the beginning of period 0 two units of both goods and 1·5 units of labour are available. The planning authorities want to bequeath the future generations stocks of goods which are at least as desirable as the initial ones. Consider the following path:

t	-1	0	1	2	...	$T-1$
q_1	1	0	$(1{\cdot}5)^2$	0	...	$\delta_T(1{\cdot}5)^{T-1}$
q_2	0	0	0	0	...	0
q_3	0	1·5	0	$(1{\cdot}5)^3$	...	$(1-\delta_T)\,(1{\cdot}5)^{T-1}$

where δ_T is 0 if T is odd and 1 if it is even. With the given input-output coefficients it is a feasible path offering the following consumption stream:

t	0	1	2	...	$T-1$
e_1	0·50	0·60	$(1{\cdot}5)^2 0{\cdot}50$	...	(*)
e_2	0·95	1·95	$(1{\cdot}5)^2 0{\cdot}95$	...	(**)

where (*) and (**) are $(1{\cdot}5)^{T-1}$ times 0·50 and $(1{\cdot}5)^{T-1}$ times 0·95 if T is odd, and $(1{\cdot}5)^{T-1}$ times 0·60 and $(1{\cdot}5)^{T-1}$ times 1·95 if it is even. At the end of the path in period T the coming generation will receive $(1{\cdot}5)^{T-1}$ and $4(1{\cdot}5)^{T-1}$ amounts of goods 1 and 2, respectively, if T is odd, or $2(1{\cdot}5)^{T-1}$ amounts of both goods if T is even. Therefore, according to the assumed posterity utility function $\Gamma(k_1, k_2)$, the utility derived from the final stocks of goods per capita, regardless of the length of the programming period T, is the same as that from the initial stocks.

Since the consumption ratio is 1·9 in periods 0, 2, 4, ... and 3·25 in periods 1, 3, 5, ..., the partial derivatives of f are $f_1 = f_2 = 0{\cdot}5$ in even periods, but $f_1 = 1$ and $f_2 = 0{\cdot}25$ in odd periods. With prices and the wage rate,

$$\lambda_1(t) = \frac{0{\cdot}5}{2{\cdot}0^t}, \quad \lambda_2(t) = \frac{0{\cdot}5}{2{\cdot}0^t}, \quad \mu(t) = \frac{0{\cdot}15}{2{\cdot}0^t} \qquad \text{for} \qquad t = 0, 2, 4, \ldots$$

and

$$\lambda_1(t) = \frac{1}{2{\cdot}0^t}, \quad \lambda_2(t) = \frac{0{\cdot}25}{2{\cdot}0^t}, \quad \mu(t) = \frac{0{\cdot}15}{2{\cdot}0^t} \qquad \text{for} \qquad t = 1, 3, 5, \ldots,$$

process 3 and process 1 are profitable in even and odd periods, respectively. Finally, the optimality conditions (15) and (16) are fulfilled in the last period, $T-1$, irrespective of the value of T.

Thus the proposed feasible path satisfies the requirements for Ramsey optimality of any order. It obviously oscillates around the Consumption Turnpike without showing any tendency to converge to it. Process 3 which is unprofitable at the Consumption Turnpike prices and wage rate repeatedly appears in every even period; so that there is not observed any convergence towards the Consumption Turnpike facet of the technological frontier, either. Thus, when the future outcomes are discounted at a rate $\theta-1$ greater than the rate of growth of the population $\rho-1$, we obtain a powerful counter-example violating the Consumption Turnpike Theorem in spite of the fact that its general validity was asserted for neo-classical macro-economic models by Koopmans, Cass, and others, not only in the former case of θ but exceeding ρ but also in the present case of θ exceeding ρ.

To avoid such exceptions we must make some restrictive assumptions about technology. Alternatively, we must assume that the society more or less averts fluctuations in the sense that a more stable stream of consumption is preferred to those with fluctuations. An optimum will then be regarded as a state where the objective of maximizing the utility from consumption of goods is compatible with the other objective of stabilizing the consumption stream.

When the society's fluctuation-aversion is very strong, all Ramsey-optimum consumption streams will sooner or later join the Consumption Turnpike stream as the planning period becomes longer. As will be discussed more explicitly later, we may even in this case have fluctuations in *outputs* around the Consumption Turnpike. But it is very natural to have such phenomena because people will be prepared to accept fluctuations in outputs if they are technically required for an optimal steady stream of consumption. We may therefore conclude our long investigation by saying that the introduction of the device of very strong fluctuation-aversion will eliminate cycles of the per capita consumption of goods, but not those of per capita outputs; we still cannot rid the Theorem of cyclic exceptions.

PART IV

A FURTHER DEVELOPMENT

XIV

FLEXIBLE POPULATION AND AVOIDANCE OF MALTHUSIAN POVERTY

1. WE HAVE so far been concerned with an economy where the labour force increases, independently of the real wage rate and other economic factors, at a given constant rate. As we can easily discern by inspecting historical experiences, the rate of growth of the population has not been stationary in many countries, but has been influenced *inter alia* by the level of income per man, the level of capital per man (the number of hospitals, the number of rooms per man, etc.), the level of some specific economic activities (the production of medicines, etc.), and so on. These influences would certainly be very complicated ones; we begin this part by taking only the effect of the real-wage rate upon the growth rate of population into account.[1]

The following parable due to Volterra would be valid in a closed economy at the crudest stage.[2] In an isolated region there live two types of animals, say, giraffes and lions. We assume that grasses upon which giraffes feed are always available in sufficient amounts; lions exclusively feed upon giraffes. If only a few lions live in the region, the number of giraffes will continually increase; there will be no food problem for lions, so that they will grow at a rapid rate. Sooner or later the number of giraffes will then begin to diminish; therefore many lions will starve and giraffes will again be able to propagate themselves.

This cyclical poverty of lions results from the following two basic assumptions. (i) The rate of growth of giraffes that clearly takes on a positive value in the absence of lions will become smaller as the number of lions becomes larger and will remain negative for very large numbers of lions. (ii) The rate of growth of lions, on the other hand, is evidently negative in the absence of giraffes but will increase with the enlargement

[1] An argument similar to the one developed in this chapter can *mutatis mutandis* be applied to a more general situation where the growth rate of the labour force depends not only on the real-wage rate but also on other normalized prices. Also note that we need not assume the constancy of capitalists' average propensity to save (or to consume), although in the following we really continue to assume it. It may be a general, continuous function of the rate of interest, the real-wage rate, and the normalized prices. It will be seen that our method of proof establishes existence of the long-run growth equilibrium in a system of very general character.

[2] A. A. Andronow, and C. E. Chaikin, *Theory of Oscillations* (Princeton, N. J.: Princeton University Press, 1949), pp. 99–101.

of the species of giraffes until it finally takes on an enormous value when the number of giraffes which lions can eat becomes infinitely many.[1] Malthus' theory of population may be regarded as a variation of the Volterra fantasia which is obtained when the rate of growth of food (or giraffes) is assumed to be independent of the number of people (or lions). In fact, if we replace assumption (i) by a more rigid one to the effect that the time series of the numbers of giraffes forms a geometric progression with a small common ratio or an arithmetic progression with a constant common difference, then the society of lions obeying the law of population (ii) will eventually fall into secular Malthusian misery, the number of lions becoming larger and larger in spite of their food *per capita* becoming smaller and smaller.[2]

In more advanced communities flexible population growth has a dual diverse effect: In the first place, an increase in the population gives rise to an increase in the supply of labour. If it grows at a rapid rate, there will not be sufficient machines to equip all of the workers; some of the workers will be left without any machines to operate or will be equipped with almost obsolete machines which are very unproductive. If, on the other hand, the population increases at a very small rate or decreases, we do not have enough increase in the demand for consumption goods; a deficiency of 'effective demand' brought about in this way might result in a portion of the stocks of capital goods being unemployed, so that it would lead to a decline in the investment demand for goods. Thus we are put in a dilemma in which we find ourselves between the Malthusian Scylla and the Keynesian Charybdis.

2. Our object in this last part of the book is to find an optimum growth path of the population on which we can avoid both these dangers. We begin with a model which is a slight modification of the one we have so far been concerned with throughout the last two Parts. With the exceptions of the assumption about the population growth and the assumption about the propensity to save of workers, all the other assumptions made in Chapter VI are retained. The only alterations we make are as follows: First, for the sake of simplicity we assume that workers devote their entire income to consumption,[3] whereas we still assume that capitalists save a constant fraction s_c of their income. Second, the assumption of the

[1] Note that the rate of growth of lions is, in the text, assumed to be a function of the total number of giraffes, although it might more adequately be regarded as depending on the number of giraffes per lion.

[2] For a case where the population growth terminates at a stationary equilibrium level, see, for example, P. A. Samuelson, *Foundations of Economic Analysis* (Cambridge: Harvard University Press, 1947), pp. 296–99.

[3] We make this assumption to avoid excessive complications; because of it we need not be bothered with the classification of growth equilibrium into the Pasinetti and the anti-Pasinetti type.

constant rate of growth of the population we have so far been accustomed to is replaced by our old assumption of flexible population growth in Part I. In particular, we assume that:

(IIIa) The rate of growth, $\rho-1$, of the working population is a continuous function of the real wage rate, Ω, such that it is negative (but ρ is still positive) for very low levels of Ω, and zero for the subsistence level of Ω, and positive (but less than some finite number) for Ω exceeding the subsistence level.

We also assume, in place of assumption (III) in Chapter VI, that:

(IIIb) To any non-negative rate of real wages Ω, there corresponds a rate of growth of the labour force, $\rho(\Omega)-1$, that is so low that there is a non-negative intensity vector $(x_1, x_2, ..., x_m)$ such that for all goods $j = 1, ..., n$,

$$\sum_i b_{ij}x_i > \rho(\Omega) \left(\sum_i a_{ij}x_i \right),$$

where a_{ij} and b_{ij} are the input and the output coefficients of process i.

We require this assumption to hold for all Ω, hence at first sight, it may look very restrictive. But (IIIb) is weaker than the previous productivity assumption (III) asserting the existence of an intensity vector such that

$$\sum_i b_{ij}x_i > \frac{\rho-c_c}{s_c} \left(\sum_i a_{ij}x_i\right), \quad j = 1, ..., n.$$

This is so because ρ in this expression is greater than one and the capitalists' propensity to save s_c equals $1-c_c$ by definition (c_c is the capitalist' propensity to consume), so that we have $(\rho-c_c)/s_c > \rho$; hence if (III) holds for the least upper bound of $\rho(\Omega)$, then (IIIb) *a fortiori* holds for all possible values of the real wage rate.

The only change in the entire set of conditions for growth equilibrium, which is caused by this shifting from the rigid to the flexible population growth, is a replacement of the rigid natural rate of growth in the equation between the warranted and the natural rate of growth by the flexible natural growth-rate function. We must then find a real wage rate that equates both rates of growth with each other. An ordinary way of finding it would be to trace out on a (ρ, Ω) plane the natural growth rate curve $\rho(\Omega)$ and the Silvery Equilibrium wage rate graph, and to find their intersection. In fact, the argument in Chapter VII claims that to any natural rate of growth there corresponds at least one Silvery Equilibrium rate of real wages (and hence a non-empty set $\Omega_G(\rho)$ of Silvery Equilibrium real-wage rates) at which all the conditions for growth equilibrium are satisfied. But even so, we cannot yet conclude that it does have an intersection with the natural growth rate curve unless some other requisites (say the convexity of the set $\Omega_G(\rho)$ for all ρ) are shown to be fulfilled. It is very difficult to verify them; hence, as Fig. 10 illustrates, we cannot exclude the possibility of perverse cases so long as we proceed with this approach.

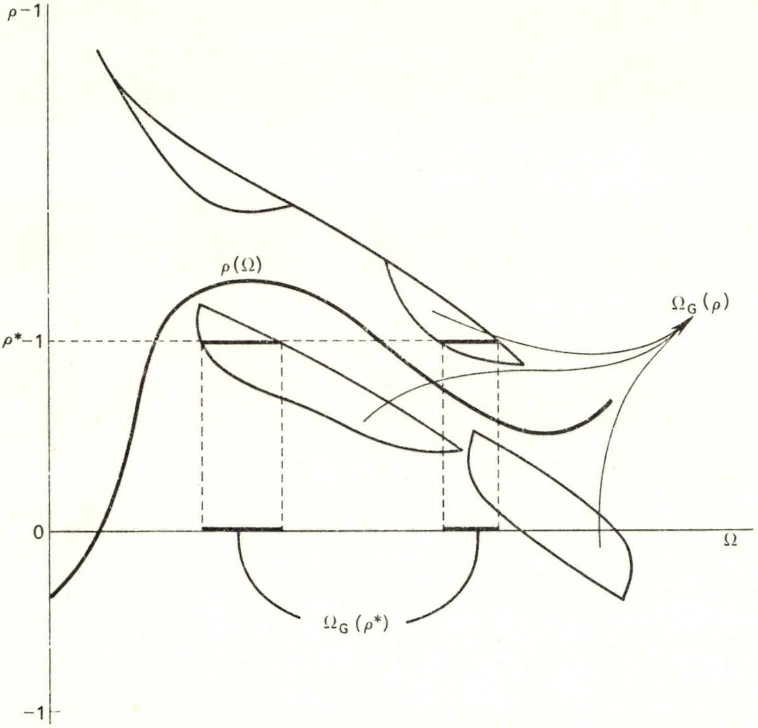

FIG. 10

An alternative way is our old procedure of reducing the system consisting of the following conditions (in matrix terms) to a 'game' between the Entrepreneur and the Market:[1]

$$By \leqq \beta(Ay+\Omega L), \tag{1}$$

$$xBy = \beta x(Ay+\Omega L), \tag{2}$$

$$xB \geqq \alpha\{xA+\Omega xLg(y)\} + (\beta-1)(xAy+\Omega xL)f(y), \tag{3}$$

$$xBy = (\alpha+(\beta-1)c_c)(xAy+\Omega xL), \tag{4}$$

$$xBy > 0, \tag{5}$$

$$\alpha = \rho(\Omega), \tag{6}$$

[1] For derivation and implications of them, see Chapter VI above. Putting $s_w = 0$, we find that (3′) in that chapter is reduced to (3) in the text.

where B is the output coefficient matrix, A the material-input coefficient matrix, L the labour-input coefficient vector, x the normalized intensity vector, y the normalized price vector, α the warranted growth factor, β the interest factor, $f(y)$ the capitalists' Engel-coefficient vector, and $g(y)$ the workers' Engel-coefficient vector.

Let us choose an arbitrary set y^* of normalized prices, and a non-negative real-wage rate Ω^*. The former determines the Engel coefficients, $f(y)$ and $g(y)$, while the latter the natural rate of growth, which in turn determines the equilibrium rate of interest since conditions (1)–(6) imply that the rate of interest $\beta-1$ equals the rate of growth $\rho(\Omega)-1$ divided by the capitalists' propensity to save s_c.[1]

In the above we have tacitly assumed, as in Chapter VI, that workers have identical tastes. Throughout the following, however, we are concerned with a more general case in which the workers operating process i (say stevedores) may have different tastes from those operating a different process i' (say pilots); we use the notation $g_{ij}(y)$ to distinguish from others the Engel coefficients for good j of workers employed in process i. We may then write the 'net-output coefficients' and the 'augmented labour-input coefficients' as

$$m_{ij}(y^*, \Omega^*) = \frac{1}{\rho(\Omega^*)} b_{ij} - a_{ij} - \frac{1}{\rho(\Omega^*)} [\{\beta(\Omega^*)-1\} \sum_k a_{ik} y_k^*] f_j(y^*)$$

and

$$n_{ij}(y^*, \Omega^*) = l_i g_{ij}(y^*) + \frac{\beta(\Omega^*)-1}{\rho(\Omega^*)} l_i f_j(y^*),$$

respectively. Then the inequalities (1) and (3) which are of fundamental importance among the conditions for growth equilibrium (1)–(6) can be reduced to the following two sets of inequalities which define the 'game':

$$\sum_j m_{ij}(y^*, \Omega^*) y_j \leqq \Omega \sum_j n_{ij}(y^*, \Omega^*) y_j, \qquad i = 1, ..., m, \qquad (1^*)$$

$$\sum_i m_{ij}(y^*, \Omega^*) x_i \geqq \Omega \sum_i n_{ij}(y^*, \Omega^*) x_i, \qquad j = 1, ..., n. \qquad (3^*)$$

As we have seen in Chapter VII, these inequalities give the fair wage rate Ω, the optimum strategies y of the Market and the optimum strategies x of the Entrepreneur. Let $T(y^*, \Omega^*)$ be the set of all possible pairs of the fair wage rate Ω and the optimum price set y in association with the pay-off matrix, $M(y^*, \Omega^*) - \Omega N(y^*, \Omega^*)$. Evidently, any y belonging to

[1] It is shown, however, that when $\rho(\Omega^*) < 1$, the profits are negative, so that the capitalists do not consume at all. Hence the capitalists' average propensity to save is unity; we have: $\beta-1 = \rho-1$, in equilibrium. (See my *Equilibrium, Stability, and Growth*, pp. 144–5.) Corresponding to this, the last term of each 'net-output coefficient' and that of each 'augmented labour-input coefficient' disappear when $\rho(\Omega^*) < 1$. The switching occurs only at those points where $\rho-1$ vanishes. Hence, it cannot be a cause of discontinuity.

$T(y^*, \Omega^*)$ is an n-dimensional non-negative vector with unit sum and any Ω in $T(y^*, \Omega^*)$ is between two finite numbers.[1] This holds for any (y^*, Ω^*). Therefore, we obtain the boundedness of the fair wage rates for *all* (y^*, Ω^*): that is to say, there are two finite numbers, Ω_0 and Ω_1, such that any Ω belonging to $T(y^*, \Omega^*)$ is not less than Ω_1, nor is it greater than Ω_0, for all (y^*, Ω^*).

Ω_1 may be negative, while Ω_0 can be shown to be definitely positive. If some fair wage rates are negative, the correspondence $(y^*, \Omega^*)\rightarrow T(y^*, \Omega^*)$ is *not* a transformation from the non-negative set

$$S = \{(y, \Omega) \mid y_j \geqq 0, \sum_j y_j = 1, \Omega \geqq 0\}$$

into itself; that is, there exists some (y, Ω) in $T(y^*, \Omega^*)$ which does not belong to S, although the point (y^*, Ω^*) does. Accordingly, we cannot directly apply any kind of fixed-point theorem because all the fixed-point theorems now available to us do not deal with a transformation from one set into a different set. We must set up scaffolding before we begin to build our house.

Suppose Ω_1 is negative, and define the set S_0 as

$$S_0 = \{(y, \Omega) \mid y_j \geqq 0, \sum_j y_j = 1, \Omega_0 \geqq \Omega \geqq \Omega_1\}.$$

It is clear that $T(y^*, \Omega^*)$ belongs to S_0 if (y^*, Ω^*) belongs to S. Next, we make an extension of the natural growth rate function $\rho(\Omega)$ such that $\rho(\Omega) = \rho(0)$ for all negative Ω not less than Ω_1. We then find that if $\Omega_1 \leqq \Omega^* \leqq 0$, the sets $T(y^*, \Omega^*)$ and $T(y^*, 0)$ coincide; hence, $T(y^*, \Omega^*)$ belongs to S_0 for negative Ω^* also. We thus find that $(y^*, \Omega^*)\rightarrow T(y^*, \Omega^*)$ is a transformation from S_0 into itself.

It will lighten the reader's burden and will help him see far ahead into the problem to tell him now the tool which plays a most significant role in a later stage of the argument. It is the fixed-point theorem due to Eilenberg and Montgomery,[2] a generalization of Kakutani's fixed-point theorem which was used in Chapter VII for establishing the existence of a growth equilibrium. In its most general form, it may be stated as follows:

Let Q be a non-empty, closed, bounded, convex subset of a Euclidean space. (i) *If a multi-valued correspondence $z\rightarrow R(z)$ from Q into Q is upper semicontinuous, and* (ii) *if the set $R(z)$ is contractible for all z in Q, then R has a fixed point, i.e., there is a point $\bar{z}$ which is in $R(\bar{z})$.*

[1] Because the system preserves, in particular, assumption (Ic) of Chapter VI which means that labour is indispensable for the reproduction of all commodities, and assumption (IIIb) plays the part of (III) in Chapter VI, the argument in Chapter VII, section 2 can *mutatis mutandis* be applied in order to verify the boundedness of 'fair' wage rates.

[2] S. Eilenberg and D. Montgomery, 'Fixed point theorems for multi-valued transformations', *American Journal of Mathematics*, Vol. LXVIII (1946), pp. 214–22.

In our present application, $Q = S_0$, $z = (y, \Omega)$ and $R(z) = T(y, \Omega)$. Clearly, S_0 is a product of the simplex, $y_j \geqq 0$, $\Sigma y_j = 1$, and the line segment, $\Omega_0 \geqq \Omega \geqq \Omega_1$, so that it is a non-empty, closed, bounded, convex subset of Euclidean $(n+1)$-dimensional space as the Theorem requires. Moreover, the correspondence $(y, \Omega) \rightarrow T(y, \Omega)$ is a transformation from S_0 into S_0. Hence, if we succeed in establishing the contractibility of the set $T(y, \Omega)$ for all (y, Ω) in S_0, as well as the upper semicontinuity of that correspondence, then we can immediately apply the Eilenberg–Montgomery theorem to find a fixed point $(\bar{y}, \bar{\Omega})$. The next section is devoted to verifying these properties of an exclusively mathematical character.

3. Let us first consider upper semicontinuity. Let (y^{*k}, Ω^{*k}) and (y^k, Ω^k) ($k = 1, 2, ...,$ *ad infinitum*) be any sequences of points in S_0 that converge to (y^*, Ω^*) and (y, Ω), respectively. Suppose each (y^k, Ω^k) is in the set $T(y^{*k}, \Omega^{*k})$. By definition, the correspondence T is upper semicontinuous at the limit point (y^*, Ω^*) of the sequence (y^{*k}, Ω^{*k}), if the limit of the image sequence (y^k, Ω^k) belongs to the image-set $T(y^*, \Omega^*)$ of the limit point (y^*, Ω^*).

As (y^k, Ω^k) is taken as a member of $T(y^{*k}, \Omega^{*k})$, we have

$$\sum m_{ij}(y^{*k}, \Omega^{*k}) y_j{}^k \leqq \Omega^k \sum_j n_{ij}(y^{*k}, \Omega^{*k}) y_j{}^k, \qquad (1, k)$$

$$i = 1, ..., m,$$

for each k. As Ω^k is a fair wage rate corresponding to (y^{*k}, Ω^{*k}), there is a non-negative vector x^k (with unit sum) such that

$$\sum m_{ij}(y^{*k}, \Omega^{*k}) x_i{}^k \geqq \Omega^k \sum_i n_{ij}(y^{*k}, \Omega^{*k}) x_i{}^k, \qquad (3, k)$$

$$j = 1, ..., n.$$

Let x be a limit point of the sequence $\{x^k\}$ ($k = 1, 2, ...,$ *ad infinitum*). The continuity of Engel coefficients and the extended natural growth-rate function implies that the net-output and the augmented labour-input coefficients are continuous at every point (y, Ω) in S_0; consequently, $(1, k)$ and $(3, k)$, which hold for every k, must hold with the limits x, y, and Ω at the limit point (y^*, Ω^*) also. That is to say, we have (1^*) and (3^*) in the limit. These inequalities imply the fairness of the limit Ω; and the limit y fulfills the requirements to be an element of $T(y^*, \Omega^*)$. Therefore, (y, Ω) belongs to $T(y^*, \Omega^*)$. This implies that the correspondence T is upper semicontinuous at the point (y^*, Ω^*) arbitrarily taken.

Let us now turn to the contractibility of the set $T(y, \Omega)$. A set H of points is said to *contract* or *deform* to a point h^0, if there is a continuous transformation $G(h, \mu)$ such that, for any h in H, $G(h, \mu)$ is h when $\mu = 0$, while it is h^0 at $\mu = 1$, and $G(h, \mu)$ always belongs to the set H for all values of μ in the interval [0, 1]. From this definition it is at once seen that convex sets are contractible; but as the following ideographical paradox illustrates, the converse is not generally true.

Please permit me to teach you a piece of Chinology. The Chinese ideograph meaning 'convexity' is the T-shape turned upside down as is seen in Fig. 11. From the point of view of mathematics, it does not correctly symbolize the state of being 'convex', because convex combinations of points h and h' in the shape may lie outside of it. Thus Chinese people might look, at a glance, unmathematical; but in point of fact, the reverse would be the case. We might say that they were really highly advanced mathematicians; they already knew in the ancient times when they

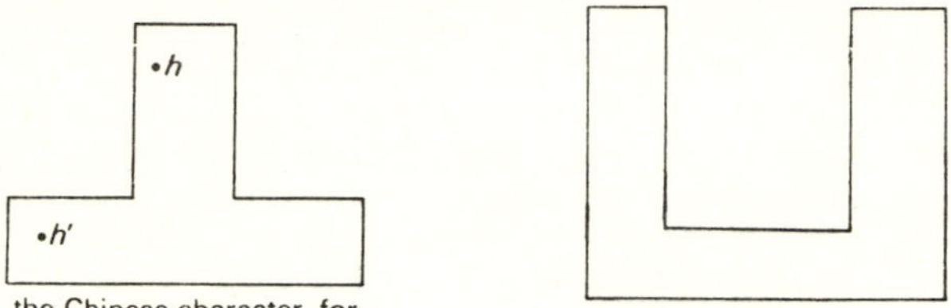

the Chinese character for 'convex'

the Chinese character for 'concave'

FIG. 11

created their characters that contractibility is a concept of topology that is more basic and more general than the concept of convexity, so that they invented an ideograph whose shape is contractible!

In advance of establishing the contractibility of the set $T(y, \Omega)$, we first show that it is not a convex set, as a general rule,[1] but of the same type as the Chinese character for 'convex'. Consider an economy to which there are available two processes producing two commodities. Suppose, for simplicity, that capitalists do not consume at all, while workers do not save; that is, $c_c = 0$ and $c_w = 1$, so that $f_1(y)$ and $f_2(y)$ vanish, while the sum of $g_{i1}(y)y_1$ and $g_{i2}(y)y_2$ is unity for each i. Suppose the input and output coefficients are:

$$A = \begin{pmatrix} 1 & 1 \\ 1 & 1 \end{pmatrix}, \quad B = \begin{pmatrix} 2{\cdot}2 & 2{\cdot}2 \\ 2{\cdot}2 & 0 \end{pmatrix}, \quad L = \begin{pmatrix} 4 \\ 1 \end{pmatrix},$$

[1] If all workers have identical tastes, i.e., $g_{1j}(y^*) = g_{2j}(y^*) = \ldots = g_{mj}(y^*)$ for each $j = 1, \ldots, n$, the fair wage rate is unique, as we have seen in Chapter VII. It then follows that the set $T(y^*, \Omega^*)$ is a convex set; this dispenses with the Eilenberg–Montgomery theorem for finding a fixed point, and we may effectively use the Kakutani theorem. But, when $g_{ij}(y^*) \neq g_{kj}(y^*)$ for some j we *must* use the former, instead of the latter, as the following example in the text shows.

while the rate of growth of the labour force and the Engel coefficients of workers are:

$$\rho(\Omega^*)-1 = 0{\cdot}1, \qquad \begin{pmatrix} g_{11}(y^*) & g_{12}(y^*) \\ g_{21}(y^*) & g_{22}(y^*) \end{pmatrix} = \begin{pmatrix} \frac{1}{2} & \frac{1}{2} \\ 1 & 0 \end{pmatrix}.$$

Then

$$M(y^*, \Omega^*) = \begin{pmatrix} 1 & 1 \\ 1 & 0 \end{pmatrix}, \quad N(y^*, \Omega^*) = \begin{pmatrix} 2 & 2 \\ 1 & 0 \end{pmatrix}.$$

Solving (1*) and (3*) with these coefficients, we find that the critical values of the fair wage rates Ω' and Ω'' are 1 and $\frac{1}{2}$ respectively; we also find that any Ω between these two critical values is fair. Moreover, we can see that when $\frac{1}{2} \leqq \Omega < 1$, $(y_1, y_2) = (0, 1)$ is the only optimal price set associated with it, whereas when $\Omega = 1$, any price set (y_1, y_2) such that $y_1+y_2 = 1$ is optimal. Consequently, the set $T(y^*, \Omega^*)$ is not convex but of the same shape as the left half of the Chinese character for 'convex', as illustrated in Fig. 12.

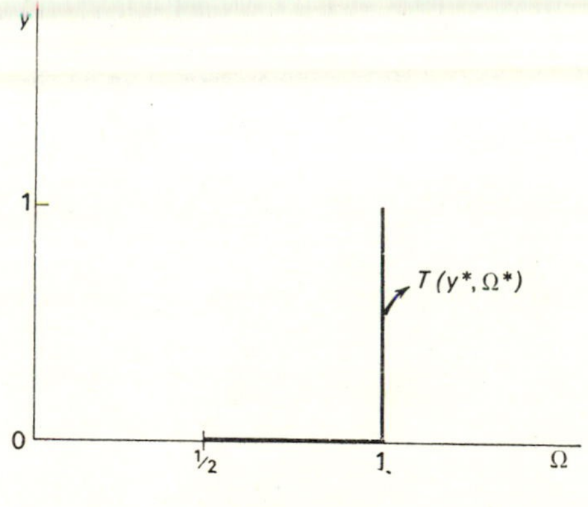

FIG. 12

The same argument as Lemma 1 in Chapter V of my *Equilibrium, Stability and Growth* is now applied in order to show the contractibility of the set $T(y, \Omega)$. Let Ω' and Ω'' be the largest and the smallest fair real-wage rate when prices and the real-wage rate are fixed at y^* and Ω^*. Let y'' be an optimum price set associated with Ω'', so that (y'', Ω'') is a member of $T(y^*, \Omega^*)$. We shall show that for any (y, Ω) belonging to $T(y^*, \Omega^*)$ and for any non-negative μ not exceeding unity, convex combinations $\{(1-\mu)y+\mu y'', (1-\mu)\Omega+\mu\Omega'\}$ belong to $T(y^*, \Omega^*)$. Then it at once follows from the definition of contractibility that $T(y^*, \Omega^*)$ contracts to the point (y'', Ω') which is also a point in $T(y^*, \Omega^*)$.[1]

We first show that for any $(y, \Omega) \in T(y^*, \Omega^*)$,

$$(y, (1-\mu)\Omega+\mu\Omega') \in T(y^*, \Omega^*) \qquad \text{for all } \mu \text{ in } [0, 1]. \tag{7}$$

As Ω' is fair, there is a non-negative vector x' (with unit sum) such that

$$\sum_i m_{ij}(y^*, \Omega^*)x_i' \geqq \Omega' \sum_i n_{ij}(y^*, \Omega^*)x_i', \qquad j = 1, ..., n.$$

As the augmented labour-input coefficients are non-negative, these inequalities hold *a fortiori* with the same x', even though we replace Ω' by ψ which is greater than Ω but less than Ω'. On the other hand, we have

$$\sum_j m_{ij}(y^*, \Omega^*)y_j \leqq \Omega \sum_j n_{ij}(y^*, \Omega^*)y_j, \qquad i = 1, ..., m,$$

because (y, Ω) is an element of the set $T(y^*, \Omega^*)$. It is evident that substitution of any ψ between Ω and Ω' for the Ω on the right-hand side of the above inequalities does not disturb the sense of the inequalities at all. Thus, the triplet (x', y, ψ) satisfies (1*) and (3*). This implies that any optimum price set y associated with a fair wage rate Ω remains optimal if it appears in combination with any ψ between Ω and Ω'. Hence, (7) has been proved.

As a trivial corollary of the above argument, we get, for any optimum price set y'' associated with the minimum fair wage rate Ω'', the relationship:

$$\{y'', (1-\mu)\Omega+\mu\Omega'\} \in T(y^*, \Omega^*) \qquad \text{for all } \mu \text{ in } [0, 1].$$

Since y (an optimum price set associated with Ω) and y'' are two optimum price sets which are associated with any fair wage rate ψ between Ω and Ω', their convex combinations would also be optimum, so long as the wage rate takes on a fair value between Ω and Ω'. It now follows that

$$\{(1-\mu)y+\mu y'', \psi\} \in T(y^*, \Omega^*) \qquad \text{for all } \mu \text{ in } [0, 1].$$

As ψ may be any number between Ω and Ω', it may, of course, be $(1-\mu)\Omega+\mu\Omega'$. Hence, for any non-negative μ not exceeding unity, we have

$$\{(1-\mu)y+\mu y'', (1-\mu)\Omega+\mu\Omega'\} \in T(y^*, \Omega^*).$$

Furthermore, the convex combination reduces to (y, Ω) when μ is zero, and (y'', Ω') when μ is unity. Thus the contractibility of the set $T(y^*, \Omega^*)$ has been verified.

[1] Put, in the definition above, $H = T(y^*, \Omega^*)$, $h^0 = (y'', \Omega')$, $h = (y, \Omega)$, and
$$G(h, \mu) = ((1-\mu)y+\mu y'', (1-\mu)\Omega+\mu\Omega').$$

We are finally in a position to apply the Eilenberg–Montgomery fixed-point theorem ensuring the existence of an equilibrium point $(\bar{y}, \bar{\Omega})$ such that

$$\sum_j m_{ij}(\bar{y}, \bar{\Omega})\bar{y}_j \leqq \bar{\Omega} \sum_j n_{ij}(\bar{y}, \bar{\Omega})\bar{y}_j, \qquad i = 1, ..., m, \tag{1'}$$

$$\sum_i m_{ij}(\bar{y}, \bar{\Omega})\bar{x}_i \geqq \bar{\Omega} \sum_i n_{ij}(\bar{y}, \bar{\Omega})\bar{x}_i, \qquad j = 1, ..., n, \tag{3'}$$

where $\bar{x}$ and $\bar{y}$ are non-negative vectors with unit sums, and $\bar{\Omega}$ is in the closed interval $[\Omega_0, \Omega_1]$. These inequalities can be converted into the alternative forms (1) and (3) in terms of outputs, material inputs, labour inputs, capitalists' and workers' consumption. Clearly, (6) holds at $\bar{\Omega}$; (1′), together with (3′), implies both (2) and (4), as in the case of the rigid population growth discussed in Chapter VII. Thus all inequalities other than (5) are satisfied at $(\bar{x}, \bar{y}, \bar{\Omega})$.

4. It remains to show that a positive value of output is produced at $(\bar{x}, \bar{y}, \bar{\Omega})$, as well as to show that the equilibrium real-wage rate $\bar{\Omega}$ is strictly positive. These problems are closely related to each other; in fact, as we have seen in Chapter VII, the first problem is merely a direct consequence of the second problem.

Let us suppose the contrary, namely, that $\bar{\Omega}$ is negative or zero. As, for all negative $\Omega \geqq \Omega_0$, $\rho(\Omega)$ is set equal to $\rho(0)$, it follows from assumption (IIIb) that $\bar{\Omega}$ has a non-negative intensity vector x (with unit sum) such that for all goods $j = 1, ..., n$,

$$\sum_i b_{ij}x_i > \rho(\bar{\Omega})(\sum_i a_{ij}x_i). \tag{8}$$

As $\rho(\bar{\Omega}) = \rho(0) < 1$, the equilibrium rate of profits is negative, so that by our switching rule capitalists do not consume at all. This implies that

$$m_{ij}(\bar{y}, \bar{\Omega}) = \frac{1}{\rho(\bar{\Omega})} b_{ij} - a_{ij}.$$

Therefore, we obtain from (1′) and (8)

$$\bar{\Omega} \sum_i \sum_j n_{ij}(\bar{y}, \bar{\Omega})x_i\bar{y}_j \geqq \sum_i \sum_j m_{ij}(\bar{y}, \bar{\Omega})x_i\bar{y}_j > 0.$$

Since the augmented labour-input coefficients $n_{ij}(\bar{y}, \bar{\Omega})$ are non-negative, it now follows that the real-wage rate $\bar{\Omega}$ is strictly positive, but this is a contradiction. Hence $\bar{\Omega}$ must be positive.

Let us now consider the first problem. Equation (2) which has already been established states that the value of the equilibrium outputs equals the total value of inputs (including the wages). As a growth equilibrium is a state of expanding (or decaying) reproduction, labour is indispensable for 'reproduction' (assumption (Ic) in Chapter VI). We also have just seen that the real-wage rate is positive. Therefore, the wage payments (and hence the value of outputs) are positive and the inequality (5) is verified.

5. In a model where the working population is assumed to grow at a given positive rate irrespective of the level of the real wages, the economy really expands when it proceeds along the Silvery Equilibrium path. In the flexible-population growth model, however, the Silvery real-wage rate may be too low to reach the subsistence level and the Silvery Growth Equilibrium may be a decaying state or a stationary state. This rather unfavourable conclusion is a natural outcome of our very weak condition (IIIb) on the productivity of available processes. In order to get a true Silvery *Growth* solution, we must make further specifications about biology and technology.

We have so far assumed that the workers' Engel coefficients $g_{ij}(y)$ depend on prices $y_1, ..., y_n$ only and are independent of the real-wage rate Ω (assumption (IIc) in Chapter VI).

Alternatively we may assume that:

(IIc′) The workers' Engel coefficients are continuous functions of both prices and the real-wage rate satisfying the identity, $\Sigma g_{ij}(y, \Omega)y_j = 1$; furthermore, they are not very sensitive to price changes, and are constant or almost constant (for biological reasons) when the real-wage rate is not greater than the subsistence level.

It is not difficult to confirm that in spite of this change in the assumptions, the whole argument in this chapter still holds true *mutatis mutandis*.

When the real-wage rate is not greater than the subsistence level there will be an associated non-positive rate of population growth. Accordingly, the equilibrium rate of profits will be non-positive, so that the capitalists will not consume; their Engel coefficients do not appear in $m_{ij}(y^*, \Omega^*)$ and $n_{ij}(y^*, \Omega^*)$. We have

$$\begin{aligned} m_{ij}(y^*, \Omega^*) &= \frac{1}{\rho(\Omega^*)} b_{ij} - a_{ij} \\ n_{ij}(y^*, \Omega^*) &= l_i g_{ij}(y^*, \Omega^*). \end{aligned} \tag{9}$$

The reader should note that the workers' coefficients $g_{ij}(y^*, \Omega^*)$ are constant, or almost constant, by assumption (IIc′) just made.

Attention may now be paid to our old idea of the greatest technically permissible real-wage rate.[1] It is defined, in the flexible population growth model, as the maximum of those Ω which satisfy input-output inequalities (3*) with non-negative (not all zero) activity levels $(x_1, x_2, ..., x_m)$. Since

[1] See above, Chapter VII.

the net-output and the augmented labour-input coefficients generally depend on prices y^*, the real-wage rate Ω^* and the rate of population growth $\rho-1$ (the last depending, in turn, upon the real-wage rate Ω^*), the greatest technically permissible real-wage rate depends on them and may be denoted by $\Omega_T(y^*, \Omega^*)$. If the wage rate Ω^* is low, then the rate of growth of the population and hence the equilibrium profit rate will also be low; it follows from the definitions of the net-output and the augmented labour-input coefficients (9) that they will respectively move upwards and downwards, if at all, when ρ decreases. Hence, $\Omega_T(y^*, \Omega^*)$ is high for low Ω^*, as it should be.

Let us now take (IIc′) into account. We then find that when the preassigned wage rate Ω^* does not exceed the subsistence level, the greatest technically permissible real-wage rate $\Omega_T(y^*, \Omega^*)$ is completely, or almost, independent of prices y^*. It seems that it is not unrealistic to specify technology such that:

(IIIc) At any prices y^*, the greatest technically permissible real-wage rate $\Omega_T(y^*, \Omega^*)$ is greater than the preassigned value of the real-wage rate Ω^*, if Ω^* is fixed at a very low value that is not greater than the subsistence level; that is, $\Omega_T(y^*, \Omega^*) > \Omega^*$, irrespective of y^*, for all Ω^* not exceeding the subsistence wage rate.

We are now very near our goal. First, in spite of these alterations and specifications, it can be verified, as before, that in growth equilibrium, the actual rate of real wages $\bar{\Omega}$ is equated with the greatest technically permissible real-wage rate $\Omega_T(\bar{y}, \bar{\Omega})$. Then it follows as a direct consequence of assumption (IIIc) that the equilibrium rate of real wages $\bar{\Omega}$ should be greater than the subsistence rate. By assumption (IIIa), there corresponds to $\bar{\Omega}$ a *positive* growth rate of the population. Every output grows at the same positive rate. Thus we finally obtain a true growth equilibrium of population and outputs.

XV

AN ALTERNATIVE APPROACH: REMODELLING AND REFINEMENTS

1. THE argument developed in the previous chapter was based on the tacit assumption that the production of goods by means of goods and labour is independent of the feeding of labour. It was described in terms of the matrices of input and output coefficients and the vector of labour-input coefficients, all of which were considered as technologically given constants. As a matter of fact, however, it is difficult to obtain precise figures of these coefficients, especially the figures of the labour-input coefficients, without knowing how and at what level people are fed. The productivity of labour depends not only on technology in the narrowest sense but also on the workers' state of health, their living and working conditions and so on, as well as on domestic troubles between them and their wives, which will often occur when they are paid poor wages. We must furthermore remember the historical fact that in a slave economy, with the wages fixed at a subsistence level, the productivity of labour was low, so that it was replaced by a more productive system, the capitalist economy. It is not surprising to see that outputs of goods might increase, even though the allocation of available goods among industries and families became unfavourable for the former; in fact, the positive indirect effect on outputs of a transfer of goods from industries to families causing an improvement in the welfare of the workers might be so strong as to overcome the negative direct effect on outputs of the decrease in industrial inputs. Thus the production of goods and the feeding of men should be treated as an inseparable process.

We now convert our notation into an entirely new one. Let $x_i(t)$ be the amount of good i available at the beginning of period t, and $m(t)$ the number of people living in the economy at the same point of time. $x_i(t)$ is allocated among industries and families for the production of goods and for the production (or feeding) of men, respectively; the former part is denoted by $x_i^I(t)$, the latter part by $x_i^F(t)$. Obviously, they add up to $x_i(t)$,

$$x_i(t) = x_i^I(t)+x_i^F(t),$$

unless some of good i is exposed to the wind and rain without being used by any of the industries and families. There are n kinds of goods. $x(t)$ denotes the n-dimensional vector $(x_1(t), x_2(t), ..., x_n(t))$; similarly, $x^I(t)$ and $x^F(t)$ represent $(x_1^I(t), x_2^I(t), ..., x_n^I(t))$ and $(x_1^F(t), x_2^F(t), ..., x_n^F(t))$, respectively.

The number of people at the end of period t, $l(t)$, depends on the feeding $x^F(t)$ in that period, in addition to the number of people at the beginning. If good i is perishable, the families have no stock of that good at the end of the period, but if it is durable, they will enter the next period with certain amounts of the used good i. To avoid unnecessary complications, we assume, throughout the rest of this part, that goods are all perishable when they are delivered to households, but may be durable if they are used by industries. Therefore, the families have no outfit of goods at the end of the period. We may write a biologically feasible transformation of goods and men as follows:

$$(x^F(t), m(t)) \rightarrow l(t).$$

It is evident that the amounts of goods 1, ..., n produced in period t are determined *primarily* by the industrial inputs $x^I(t)$ and the number of workers employed $m(t)$; so that we might have a technologically feasible transformation:

$$(x^I(t), m(T)) \rightarrow y(t),$$

where $y(t)$ is the vector of the quantities of goods which the industries will have at the end of period t; a component of $y(t)$, say $y_i(t)$, stands for the total quantity of good i newly produced during the period. The same good i that the industries will have at the end of period t in the form of fixed capital after using $x_i^I(t)$ for one period for production is treated as a different good, as we did in Chapter VI. But, as we have seen, there can be no definite input-output relationship that is *purely* technological; the amounts of goods produced, $y(t)$, depend not only on the industrial inputs, $x^I(t)$, and the employment of labour, $m(t)$, but also on how workers are fed in period t. Thus the set of all possible transformations of industrial inputs $x^I(t)$ and $m(t)$ into industrial outputs $y(t)$ will not be well defined, even though there is no change in technology, unless the level of the welfare the workers are enjoying is specified. The argument cannot conveniently run in terms of the set of the 'purely technological possibilities'.

We consider instead the set Π of all possible transformations of social inputs $(x(t), m(t))$ into social outputs $(y(t), l(t))$. In these transformations $y(t)$ depends not only on $x^I(t)$ and $m(t)$ but also on $x^F(t)$. This means that many different final states, $(y(t), l(t))$, can correspond to the same initial states, $(x(t), m(t))$. We assume that the set Π of such set-to-point correspondences remains constant. This is an assumption which is true so long as there is no change in biological factors and technology.

2. Throughout the following, each process which converts the social inputs $(x(t), m(t))$ into the social outputs $(y(t), l(t))$ will be referred to as an 'aggregate' production process. Let $(x, m) \rightarrow (y, l)$ and $(x_*, m_*) \rightarrow (y_*, l_*)$

be any two aggregate processes.[1] The former consists of a labour feeding process, $(x^F, m) \rightarrow l$, and an industrial production process, $(x^I, m; x^F) \rightarrow y$.[2] Similarly, the latter aggregate process is analyzed as two processes $(x_*{}^F, m_*) \rightarrow l_*$ and $(x_*{}^I, m_*; x_*{}^F) \rightarrow y_*$. Obviously, x^I and x^F in the former process add up to x, while $x_*{}^I$ and $x_*{}^F$ in the latter add up to x_*.

Let us consider an economy in which an outfit of goods, $x+x_*$, is available to $m+m_*$ workers. We can give the bundle of goods x^F to m workers, and $x_*{}^F$ to m_* workers; then the numbers of workers will grow at the rate l/m and l_*/m_*, respectively, so that at the end of the period there will be $l+l_*$ people in the economy. After having fed workers, $x+x_*-x^F-x_*{}^F$ amounts of goods are available for production processes. There is enough to be allocated among workers, so that m of them, being fed with x^F, can use x^I to produce y, while the remaining m_* workers fed with $x_*{}^F$ can convert $x_*{}^I$ into y_*. It is therefore always possible for the economy to close the period with goods $y+y_*$. This fact may be paraphrased as:

(i) If two aggregate production processes $(x, m) \rightarrow (y, l)$ and $(x_*, m_*) \rightarrow (y_*, l_*)$ are feasible, then a third aggregate process, $(x+x_*, m+m_*) \rightarrow (y+y_*, l+l_*)$, formed by operating the two simultaneously, is also feasible.

By taking $x = x_*$, $m = m_*$, $y = y_*$, and $l = l_*$, it clearly follows from (i) that if $(x, m) \rightarrow (y, l)$ is a feasible process, then $(\lambda x, \lambda m) \rightarrow (\lambda y, \lambda l)$ is also feasible for any positive *integer* λ. But (i) does not imply that the same relationship holds for *any non-negative number* λ. We must have another assumption of the divisibility of aggregate processes, in order to obtain the law of constant returns to scale, not only for discrete changes but also for continuous changes in scale:

(ii) If all the social inputs (x, m) to an aggregate process are multiplied by any (non-negative) number λ, then the social outputs (y, l) are multiplied by the same λ.

Although it would be extremely difficult to decide empirically whether the aggregate production possibility set Π contains all its boundary points (or whether it is closed or not), it is true that much analytical advantage is gained by assuming it. Moreover, it is not implausible or unreasonable to assume that the set Π is closed if it is put in the following equivalent form (iii). There would be no reason to reject it; indeed, we have just accepted a similar mathematical condition—that is, the divisibility of the aggregate

[1] In denoting the input and the output vectors we omit t if the dating of them is clear from the context.

[2] We introduce x^F to make explicit the dependence of the industrial process on the welfare of workers.

production process for the purpose of analytical convenience. We thus have:

(iii) If a transformation $(x, m) \rightarrow (y, l)$ is not feasible, then all transformations differing from it only infinitesimally are also infeasible.

Together with (i) and (ii), condition (iii) implies that the production possibility set Π is a closed convex cone in $2(n+1)$-dimensional Euclidean space.

By putting $\lambda = 0$ in (ii), we find that nothing can produce nothing; that is, an aggregate process of transforming (0, 0) into (0, 0) is feasible. This, however, does not mean that the converse is also true. Without some additional assumptions, the above three conditions do not logically rule out the possibility that something is produced from nothing. But as a matter of fact it is universally true that when $x = 0$, workers have nothing to eat and nothing to use for production, and hence we would have $y = 0$ and $l = 0$. On the other hand, it is also obviously true that vipers are bred only by vipers, so that if $m = 0$, then $l = 0$. We thus postulate the following:

(iv) If an aggregate process $(x, m) \rightarrow (y, l)$ is feasible with $x = 0$, then $y = 0$ and $l = 0$; and if $m = 0$, then $l = 0$.

The next assumption we impose is that which is usually referred to as the assumption of free disposal of goods. It asserts that any goods can be disposed of without any additional inputs. Under this assumption, by disposing of $x_* - x$, we can transform (x_*, m) into (x, m), which in turn is transformed into social outputs (y, l) by an aggregate production process, and hence we finally obtain (y_*, l) by once more disposing of $y - y_*$ without additional inputs. We, therefore, find that:

(v) If an aggregate process $(x, m) \rightarrow (y, l)$ is feasible, then any other process $(x_*, m) \rightarrow (y_*, l)$ such that $x_* \geqq x$ and $y_* \leqq y$ is also feasible.

On the other hand, the free disposal of labour is possible only in a shameless world like a slave society, but never in any modern society, of course. I am very sorry to confess that in our hypothetical economy, however, persons of no use can be eliminated in the following way. Suppose there are m_* workers living in an economy where goods are available in the amounts x. Suppose also that m workers out of m_* can transform x into (y, l). In such a situation, we may group the m_* workers into two classes consisting of m and $m_* - m$ members, respectively. We may then employ m workers so as to transform x into (y, l), and leave $m_* - m$ workers without food. It follows from (i) that by operating two processes $(x, m) \rightarrow (y, l)$ and $(0, m_* - m) \rightarrow (0, 0)$ simultaneously, the initial state (x, m_*) can be transformed into (y, l). Thus, if $(x, m) \rightarrow (y, l)$ is feasible, then

$(x, m_*) \rightarrow (y, l)$ is feasible for any m_* which is not less than m. Workers can be freely disposed of since they will die of starvation. (People have to work in order to live.) It is, of course, an extremely immoral rule, but a logical consequence of assumptions (i) and (iv).[1]

Let us now make two further restrictions on the aggregate production processes. One of them allows the possibility of growth and may be stated as follows:

(vi) Among feasible aggregate processes there is at least one such that $y > x$ and $l > m$.

The other is that which ensures the system is indecomposable. Suppose $m > 0$, and arrange goods in two mutually exclusive groups, G_1 and G_2. A set of goods G_1 is said to be *independent* of G_2 if those goods can be produced from themselves, that is, without consuming any goods in G_2. We assume that:

(vii) The system is indecomposable (or irreducible) in the sense that there are no proper independent subgroups of goods.

This hypothesis implies that if $m > 0$ and $y_i > 0$ for all goods in the group G_1, then there are some goods j in G_2 with $x_j > 0$. It is a restrictive and even unrealistic assumption, for it is not difficult to find exceptions to it.[2] From any actual Input-Output tables so far obtained, however, we may observe that nation-wide economies are likely to be indecomposable if individual goods are aggregated into 'composite' goods whose number is of a manageable size.[3]

The final assumption we require has some relation to the famous (or notorious) Malthusian law of population. Let $(x, m) \rightarrow (y, l)$ be a feasible production process; define the rate of growth of the 'gross' production of the economy, g, as the smallest among the n rates of growth of outputs such that

$$g+1 = \min (y_1/x_1, ..., y_n/x_n).$$

With a free, but recapitulating interpretation, the Malthusian law may be formulated as a 'law' requiring that for *each* feasible process the rate of growth of the 'gross' production is less than the corresponding rate of growth of population, $l/m-1$. (An additional assumption that is implicit

[1] But the free disposal of the workers available at the *end* of the period (assassination of them) does not follow from any of the assumptions made. I am not so immoral as to make an additional assumption that implies it; but to be proud of that is a case of 'the pot calling the kettle black' since we have accepted the free disposal of the m^*-m workers at the *beginning* of the period.

[2] Group all goods other than 'land' into the second class G_2; it is obvious that land produces land without using the goods in G_2. This shows the independency of land. (Note that outputs of durable goods are measured in terms of their stocks.)

[3] Our system (like Leontief's) ignores land.

in the Malthusian economy is that the rate of growth of agriculture (food) is the smallest among the n growth rates.) This is a strong assumption; but if it is weakened as in (viii) below, it will be accepted even in a contemporary, highly advanced society with a low actual (but not maximum) rate of growth of the population:

(viii) The highest feasible value of the rate of growth of the population is greater than that of 'gross' production.

In fact, since we assume that there are no technical improvements, it will not be far from reality to assume that human beings can grow at a rate faster than the maximum growth rate of the gross production, although it is true that they cannot grow as fast as Sony or Honda.

3. As for the capitalists' demand for consumption goods, we accept all the assumptions in Chapter VI. First, all capitalists have identical tastes, and the 'Capitalist' consumes a constant fraction of his income. Secondly, his demand for consumption remains unchanged when we have a proportional change in all prices and income. Moreover, it is assumed that the Capitalist's Engel-coefficients are independent of the level of his income; that is to say, the income elasticity of his consumption demand for each good is unity. Therefore, we have

$$d_j = f_j(p_1, p_2, ..., p_n)e \qquad j = 1, ..., n,$$

where d_j is the Capitalist's demand for the consumption good j, p_is are normalized prices, and e represents the Capitalist's normalized income (profits). Since at any prices a constant proportion of e is devoted to consumption, we have, as before,

$$\sum_j f_j(p_1, p_2, ..., p_n)p_j = c \qquad \text{for all } p_i\text{s},$$

where c is the Capitalist's average propensity to consume.

The state of Silvery Equilibrium which has been discussed at length for the case of the von Neumann 'polyhedral' technology, can now be defined in terms of the following five sets of inequalities. Let α_j be the growth factor (i.e., 1+the rate of growth) of the total (industrial and labour-feeding) inputs of good j. As the amount $y_j - f_j(p)e$ of good j which is left after deducting the Capitalist's consumption $f_j(p)e$ from the output y_j, is available for the production in the next period, the total input of j can expand at the rate $\alpha_j - 1$ such that

$$y_j - f_j(p)e \geqq \alpha_j x_j.$$

As for labour, the total number of workers available at the beginning of the next period is l, which should not fall short of α_{n+1} (the growth factor of the employment of labour) times the total number of employed workers m in the present period; thus,

$$l \geqq \alpha_{n+1} m.$$

At the state of balanced growth, the α_js are obviously equal to each other, so that we obtain

$$\bar{y}_j - f_j(\bar{p})\bar{e} \geqq \bar{\alpha}\bar{x}_j \qquad i = 1, \ldots, n \tag{1}$$

$$\bar{l} \geqq \bar{\alpha}\bar{m}, \tag{1'}$$

where $\bar{\alpha}$ is the common rate of growth, $\bar{p}$ the equilibrium price vector, $(\bar{x}, \bar{m}) \rightarrow (\bar{y}, \bar{l})$ the Silvery Equilibrium process and $\bar{e}$ the profits that accrue to capitalists.

The prices of goods are determined by the rule of competition. If there is an excess demand for a good, the price of that good is increased, while if there is an excess supply, it will be decreased. It follows from this rule that the prices of those goods that are overproduced in the state of Silvery Equilibrium cannot remain stationary unless they have already fallen to the bottom. Thus, the price equilibrium is only established when zero prices are charged for those goods that fulfil inequalities (1) with strict inequality. We have, therefore,

$$\sum_j \bar{p}_j \bar{y}_j - \{\sum_j \bar{p}_j f_j(\bar{p})\}\bar{e} = \bar{\alpha} \sum_j \bar{p}_j \bar{x}_j. \tag{2}$$

A similar rule is often applied to the labour market. As has been criticized by Keynes, however, there is a positive lower bound on the wage rate at which there may exist involuntary unemployment that will persist over a very long period. From the realistic point of view wages are not subject to the neoclassical rule of competitive pricing. An alternative assumption—that the wage rate is fixed at a level such that the workers can just buy the necessaries of life by spending all of their wages—would more nearly approximate reality than the traditional one; and this observation leads to the equation,

$$\bar{w}\bar{m} = \Sigma \bar{p}_j \bar{x}_j^F, \tag{2'}$$

where $\bar{w}$ is the wage rate per worker, and $\bar{x}_j^F$ the amount of good j consumed by the workers in the state of Silvery Equilibrium.[1]

The third set of inequalities insists that the principle of maximizing the rate of profit holds good in Silvery Equilibrium. It may be put into two different (but equivalent) forms, according to how we define the costs of production. Let us choose one from among feasible aggregate production processes $(x, m) \rightarrow (y, l)$ such that the labour force will grow at a rate at

[1] This means that persons involuntarily unemployed will starve to death in one period. Note that (2′) holds, irrespective of whether (1′) holds with equality or inequality.

least as high as the silvery rate, i.e., $l \geqq \bar{\alpha}m$. For the society as a whole, the total costs of that process and the profits accruing from it are

$$\Sigma \bar{p}_j(x_j{}^I + x_j{}^F) \qquad \text{and} \qquad \Sigma \bar{p}_j y_j - \Sigma \bar{p}_j(x_j{}^I + x_j{}^F)$$

respectively, at the equilibrium prices. Its rate of profit (i.e., the ratio of the profits to the total costs) will not exceed the silvery rate of profit, $\bar{\beta}-1$, realized along the path of balanced growth since the profit rate is maximized on that path; in fact, it requires that no feasible aggregate process can yield profits at a rate greater than the silvery rate unless the reproduction of the labour force is sacrificed. Hence, for all feasible processes $(x, m) \rightarrow (y, l)$ such that $l \geqq \bar{\alpha}m$, we

$$\Sigma \bar{p}_j y_j \leqq \bar{\beta}\{\Sigma \bar{p}_j(x_j{}^I + x_j{}^F)\}. \tag{3}$$

On the other hand, from the firms' point of view it is clear that the costs of production should not be defined as $\sum_j p_j(x_j{}^I + x_j{}^F)$ but $\sum_j p_j x_j{}^I + wm$. It is, of course, true that goods are consumed in the amounts $x_1{}^I + x_1{}^F$, ..., $x_n{}^I + x_n{}^F$ by the *aggregate* production process. If the excess of $\sum_j p_j x_j{}^F$ over wm is positive it is charged to the workers and if it is negative it is added to their net worth. The firms are unconcerned about the workers' family finances and will choose a process that yields the maximum rate of profits over costs in the sense of the second definition. As the equality of the workers' income and their expenditure does not necessarily follow, the two definitions of the costs of production are not identical. Thus, the principle of maximizing the rate of profit may not hold in one sense, even though it holds in the other sense. But under the assumption that the workers are always paid just enough wages for purchasing the necessities of life, we have the equality, $wm = \sum_j p_j x_j{}^F$, not only for $(\bar{x}^F, \bar{m})$, but also for all other feasible feeding processes (x^F, m). In particular, when the equilibrium prices prevail, the wage rate must satisfy

$$wm = \sum_j \bar{p}_j x_j{}^F. \tag{2''}$$

Then there is no discrepancy between the two definitions of the production costs. The principle of maximizing the rate of profit requires that

$$\sum_j \bar{p}_j y_j \leqq \bar{\beta}\left(\sum_j \bar{p}_j x_j{}^I + wm\right) \tag{3'}$$

for all feasible processes subject to the qualification, $l \geqq \bar{\alpha}m$;[1] (3′) immediately follows from (2″) and (3).

[1] If the reproduction of the labour force could be sacrificed, we may neglect the wages in the costs of production by making $x_1{}^F$, ..., $x_n{}^F$ arbitrarily small. At such poor wage rates, the rate of profits might be greater than the silvery rate, $\bar{\beta}-1$.

Since the rate of profit must be maximized in the state of Silvery Equilibrium, the above inequalities, (3) and (3′), hold with equality at $(\bar{x}^I, \bar{x}^F, \bar{m}, \bar{y})$. We thus have

$$\sum_j \bar{p}_j \bar{y}_j = \bar{\beta} \sum_j \bar{p}_j(\bar{x}_j{}^I + \bar{x}_j{}^F) = \bar{\beta}(\sum_j \bar{p}_j \bar{x}_j{}^I + \bar{w}\bar{m}), \tag{4}$$

the right-hand side of which is the sum of $\bar{e}$ (the normalized total profits) and the costs (social and private) of production.

The final inequality is required so that the Silvery Equilibrium is economically non-trivial. It means that all goods produced in that state should not be free; i.e., the sum of equilibrium outputs $\bar{y}_1, ..., \bar{y}_n$ evaluated at prices $\bar{p}_1, ..., \bar{p}_n$ is positive:

$$\sum_j \bar{p}_j \bar{y}_j > 0. \tag{5}$$

4. The whole argument for establishing the existence of a Silvery Equilibrium is highly mathematical, but is familiar, in its essential character, to those who have read Chapters II, VII, and XIV of this book; so we may dispense with a detailed exposition and may just prove it in mathematical terms.

We begin with transforming (1), the inequality most fundamental for the definition of balanced growth, into a form which is more convenient. In considering $\Sigma \bar{p}_j f_j(\bar{p}) = c$, and defining s as $1-c$, we obtain from (2), (2′), and (4) the familiar relationship between the rate of profits (or interest) and the rate of growth:

$$\bar{\beta}-1 = (\bar{\alpha}-1)/s \qquad \text{or} \qquad \bar{\beta} = (\bar{\alpha}-c)/(1-c); \tag{6}$$

in words, if an equilibrium path of balanced growth exists for the system (1)–(5), the equilibrium rate of profit, $\bar{\beta}-1$, must equal the balanced rate of growth, $\bar{\alpha}-1$, divided by the capitalists' average propensity to save, s. Using (6) and (2′) we eliminate $\bar{\beta}$ and $\bar{w}\bar{m}$ from (4) and the result is substituted into (1); we then find that for each j the value which

$$u_j(p;\, x, y) = y_j + \frac{f_j(p)}{s} \sum_i p_i x_i,$$

takes on at $(\bar{p}, \bar{x}, \bar{y})$ must be at least as large as $\bar{\alpha}$ times the value of

$$v_j(p;\, x) = x_j + \frac{f_j(p)}{s} \sum_i p_i x_i.$$

at $(\bar{p}, \bar{x})$.

In order to find a Silvery Equilibrium satisfying such inequalities we begin by neglecting effects of prices on the capitalists' consumption of goods. We fix prices at arbitrary non-negative values, $p_1^*, ..., p_n^*$, and consider the system:

$$\begin{aligned} u_j(p^*; x, y) &\geqq \alpha v_j(p^*; x) \qquad j = 1, ..., n, \\ l &\geqq \alpha m. \end{aligned} \tag{1*}$$

For any given $(x, m) \neq 0$, we may define α^* as the largest value of α fulfilling (1*), and call α^*-1 the 'quasi-equilibrium expansion rate' associated with p^*. It is clear that for any $(x, m) \neq 0$, α^* exists and is non-negative.

Next, let $\bar{\Pi}$ be the set of all feasible aggregate processes $(x, m) \rightarrow (y, l)$ such that

$$\sum_j x_j + m + \sum_j y_j + l = 1.$$

It follows from (i'') that there is no process belonging to $\bar{\Pi}$ such that $(x, m) = 0$ because (y, l) would also be zero. Therefore α^* is well defined on $\bar{\Pi}$. As α^* is continuous at every point of $\bar{\Pi}$ and $\bar{\Pi}$ is closed by the assumption, α^* attains a maximum $\bar{\alpha}^*$ on $\bar{\Pi}$. Let an aggregate process associated with $\bar{\alpha}^*$ be denoted by $(\bar{x}^*, \bar{m}^*) \rightarrow (\bar{y}^*, \bar{l}^*)$; call it a 'quasi-equilibrium process' as it would give a balanced growth if the capitalists' consumption did not respond to price changes. With any given set of prices there is associated one quasi-equilibrium process. Assumption (vi) implies $\bar{\alpha}^* > 1$.

To any arbitrarily fixed price set $p^* = (p_1^*, ..., p_n^*)$ there corresponds a non-negative, non-zero set of prices, $\bar{p}_1^*, ..., \bar{p}_n^*, \bar{p}_{n+1}^*$ (called 'quasi-equilibrium prices' and 'quasi-equilibrium wage rate'), such that

$$\sum_j \bar{p}_j^* u_j(p^*; \bar{x}^*, \bar{y}^*) + \bar{p}_{n+1}^* \bar{l}^* = \bar{\alpha}^* \{\sum_j \bar{p}_j^* v_j(p^*, \bar{x}^*) + \bar{p}_{n+1}^* \bar{m}^*\} \tag{7}$$

at the quasi-equilibrium values $\bar{x}_i^*$s and $\bar{y}_i^*$s and

$$\sum_j \bar{p}_j^* u_j(p^*; x, y) + \bar{p}_{n+1}^* l \leqq \bar{\alpha}^* \{\sum_j \bar{p}_j^* v_j(p^*; x) + \bar{p}_{n+1}^* m\} \tag{8}$$

for all other feasible processes $(x, m) \rightarrow (y, l)$. This assertion is verified by applying a theorem due to Gale, which states that:[1]

If a cone C in the $(n+1)$-dimensional space contains no vector c such that $c_i < 0$ for all $i = 1, ..., n+1$, then there is a non-negative, non-vanishing set $(\bar{p}_1^*, ..., \bar{p}_{n+1}^*)$ such that

$$\sum_i^{n+1} \bar{p}_i^* c_i \geqq 0$$

for all c in C.

[1] The theorem follows from the classical properties of linear subspaces. See Gale, 'Convex polyhedral cones and linear inequalities', in T. C. Koopmans (ed.), *Activity Analysis of Production and Allocation* (New York: Wiley, 1951), p. 294. Also see my *Equilibrium, Stability, and Growth*, pp. 183–4.

Let

$$c_i = \bar{\alpha}^* v_i(p^*; x) - u_i(p^*; x, y) \qquad \text{and} \qquad c_{n+1} = \alpha^* m - l.$$

We then have a point $c = (c_1, ..., c_{n+1})$ (in the $(n+1)$-dimensional Euclidean space) associated with each feasible aggregate process. All of such points form a closed convex cone C in $(n+1)$-space. It is clear from the definition of $\bar{\alpha}^*$ that there is no feasible process with which a point $c < 0$ associates; hence (8) is a direct result from Gale's theorem.

To establish (7), we suppose the contrary, i.e., that the right-hand side of (7) is larger than the left-hand side. As $(\bar{x}^*, \bar{m}^*, \bar{y}^*, \bar{l}^*)$ and $\bar{\alpha}^*$ satisfy (1*), the relationship we are supposing clearly contradicts the inequality that follows from (1*) and the non-negativity of the $\bar{p}_i^*$s. Hence, we get (7) from which it follows that $\bar{p}_i^*$ (or $\bar{p}_{n+1}^*$) is zero if good i (or labour) is free at the quasi-equilibrium point $(\bar{\alpha}^*, \bar{x}^*, \bar{m}^*, \bar{y}^*, \bar{l}^*)$.

Since $\bar{\alpha}^* > 1$, we may eliminate the terms, $\{f_j(p^*) \sum_i p_i^* \bar{x}_i^*\}/s$ and $\bar{\alpha}^*\{f_j(p^*) \sum_i p_i^* \bar{x}_i^*\}/s$, from both sides of (1*) respectively, to obtain

$$\bar{y}_j^* \geqq \bar{\alpha}^* \bar{x}_j^* \qquad j = 1, ..., n;$$

so that the rate of growth of the 'gross' production defined as $\min_i(\bar{y}_i^*/\bar{x}_i^*) - 1$ is at least as large as the growth rate, $\bar{\alpha}^* - 1$, along the quasi-equilibrium path. From (viii) there is a feasible aggregate process, say $(x', m') \rightarrow (y', l')$, producing a population growth at a rate greater than $\bar{\alpha}^* - 1$. Accordingly, if the $\bar{p}_i^*$s vanished for all $i = 1, ..., n$, and hence $\bar{p}_{n+1}^*$ did not vanish, we would have for $(x', m') \rightarrow (y', l')$,

$$\bar{p}_{n+1}^* l' > \bar{\alpha}^* \bar{p}_{n+1}^* m'.$$

This contradicts (8). Therefore, some of the $\bar{p}_i^*$s $(i = 1, ..., n)$ should be positive, so that $\bar{p}_1^*, ..., \bar{p}_{n+1}^*$ may be normalized such that the sum of the first n quasi-equilibrium prices $\bar{p}_i^*$ $(i = 1, ..., n)$ is unity. In the following, our argument is confined to such normalized prices; for the sake of simplicity, we write $\bar{p}^* = (\bar{p}_1^*, ..., \bar{p}_n^*)$ and refer to it as a quasi-equilibrium price vector.[1]

5. We have found so far that to any given price vector p^* there corresponds at least one quasi-equilibrium price vector $\bar{p}^*$. But its uniqueness does not follow from that argument; it is possible that a number of quasi-equilibrium price vectors may coexist for the same (arbitrarily given) price vector p^*. Define $R(p^*)$ as a set of all quasi-equilibrium price vectors that are obtained when prices are preassigned at p^*. We have a

[1] Notice that $\bar{p}^*$ is not $(n+1)$-dimensional but n-dimensional; quasi-equilibrium wage rate P_{n+1}^* is not a component of it.

multi-valued (possibly a single-valued) correspondence, $p^* \to R(p^*)$, from the simplex $S = \{p \mid p_j \geqq 0, \sum_j^n p_j = 1\}$ into S.

In order to show that the correspondence has a fixed point (i.e., a point $\bar{p}$ such that $\bar{p} \in R(\bar{p})$), we shall apply Kakutani's fixed-point theorem, in place of which the Eilenberg–Montgomery theorem was used in the previous chapter for a similar purpose. It requires that the set $R(p)$ is non-empty and convex for all p in S, and that the correspondence is upper semi-continuous.[1] $R(p)$ is a non-empty set as we have established its existence, above, and the convexity of $R(p)$ is shown as follows. Let both $\bar{p}^*$ and $\bar{p}'$ belong to $R(p^*)$. We have (7) and (8) for $(\bar{p}^*, \bar{p}_{n+1}^*)$, and we also have a similar relationship with $(\bar{p}', \bar{p}_{n+1}')$ in place of $(\bar{p}^*, \bar{p}_{n+1}^*)$. Hence, it is clear that for any (p, p_{n+1}) such that $p_i = \lambda \bar{p}_i^* + (1-\lambda)\bar{p}_i'$ $(i = 1, \ldots, n+1)$, where $0 \leqq \lambda \leqq 1$, we have

$$\sum_j p_j u_j(p^*; \bar{x}^*, \bar{y}^*) + p_{n+1}\bar{l}^* = \bar{\alpha}^*\{\sum_j p_j v_j(p^*; \bar{x}^*) + p_{n+1}\bar{m}^*\},$$

$$\sum_j p_j u_j(p^*; x, y) + p_{n+1} l \leqq \bar{\alpha}^*\{\sum_j p_j v_j(p^*; x) + p_{n+1} m\}.$$

Note that this last inequality, as well as (8), holds for all feasible aggregate processes. Thus p is a quasi-equilibrium price set. Hence $R(p^*)$ contains p as an element; consequently it is a convex set.

Let us now turn to verifying the upper semicontinuity of the correspondence. Let $p^{(k)} = (p_1^{(k)}, \ldots, p_n^{(k)})$ $(k = 1, 2, \ldots, \textit{ad infinitum})$ be any sequence of normalized prices converging to p^*. Corresponding to each $p^{(k)}$, we have a quasi-equilibrium $(\bar{\alpha}^{(k)}, \bar{x}^{(k)}, \bar{m}^{(k)}, \bar{y}^{(k)}, \bar{l}^{(k)}, \bar{p}^{(k)}, \bar{p}_{n+1}^{(k)}$, so that

$$\bar{u}_j^{(k)} \geqq \bar{\alpha}^{(k)}\bar{v}_j^{(k)} \quad \text{for each } j, \text{ and} \quad \bar{l}^{(k)} \geqq \bar{\alpha}^{(k)}\bar{m}^{(k)}, \tag{1^k}$$

$$\sum_j \bar{p}_j^{(k)}\bar{u}_j^{(k)} + \bar{p}_{n+1}^{(k)}\bar{l}^{(k)} = \bar{\alpha}^{(k)}\{\sum_j \bar{p}_j^{(k)}\bar{v}_j^{(k)} + \bar{p}_{n+1}^{(k)}\bar{m}^{(k)}\}, \tag{7^k}$$

$$\sum_j \bar{p}_j^{(k)} u_j(p^{(k)}; x, y) + \bar{p}_{n+1}^{(k)} l \leqq \bar{\alpha}^{(k)}[\sum_j \bar{p}_j^{(k)} v_j(p^{(k)}; x) + \bar{p}_{n+1}^{(k)} m], \tag{8^k}$$

where $\bar{u}_j^{(k)}$ stands for $u_j^{(k)}$ $(p^{(k)}; \bar{x}^{(k)}, \bar{y}^{(k)})$ and $\bar{v}_j^{(k)}$ for $v_j(p^{(k)}; \bar{x}^{(k)})$; and inequality (8^k) holds for all feasible aggregate production processes. Let $(\bar{\alpha}^*, \bar{x}^*, \bar{m}^*, \bar{y}^*, \bar{l}^*, \bar{p}^*, \bar{p}_{n+1}^*)$ be a limit point of $(\bar{\alpha}^{(k)}, \bar{x}^{(k)}, \bar{m}^{(k)}, \bar{y}^{(k)}, \bar{l}^{(k)}, \bar{p}_{n+1}^{(k)})$ when k tends to infinity. As (1^k), (7^k), and (8^k) hold for every k, and the Engel-coefficients, $f_j(p)$, $j = 1, \ldots, n$, are assumed to be continuous with respect to prices, we have in the limit similar inequalities with asterisk * in place of each superscript k, which are referred to as (1^*), (7^*), and (8^*).

[1] For the definition of upper semicontinuity, see p. 13 and for Kakutani's fixed-point theorem, see p. 125.

Since by (iii) the aggregate production possibility set $\bar{\Pi}$ is closed, the limiting process $(x^*, m^*)\to(y^*, l^*)$ is feasible. Moreover, the indecomposability assumption (vii) implies that there is no feasible process $(x', m')\to(y', l')$ such that

$$\alpha' > \bar{\alpha}^*, \tag{9}$$

$$u_j(p^*; x', y') \geqq \alpha' v_j(p^*; x'), \quad l' \geqq \alpha' m', \quad j = 1, ..., n. \tag{10}$$

This is verified in the following way. If there existed such a feasible process, we would have for it:

$$\sum_j \bar{p}^* u_j(p^*; x', y') + \bar{p}_{n+1}{}^* l' \geqq \alpha' \{\sum_j \bar{p}^* v_j(p^*; x') + \bar{p}_{n+1}{}^* m'\}. \tag{11}$$

As $\alpha' > \bar{\alpha}^*$, this would contradict (8*) unless the part in the braces on the right-hand side of (11) is zero. Suppose now $y_i' > 0$ for $i = 1, ..., h$, and $y_i' = 0$ for $i = h+1, ..., n$. Then by (vii) there is a good j ($> h$) for which $x_j' > 0$. For such j, (10) may be written as

$$\frac{f_j(p^*)}{s} \sum_i p_i{}^* x_i' \geqq \alpha' \left(x_j' + \frac{f_j(p^*)}{s} \sum_i p_i{}^* x_i' \right),$$

from which we get $\alpha' \leqq 1$. As $\bar{\alpha}^* \geqq 1$, we have a contradiction to (9).[1] Accordingly, $y_i' > 0$ for all $i = 1, ..., n$. Therefore, the left-hand side of (11) is positive. It now follows from (8*) that the part in the square brackets on the right-hand side (that is the same as the corresponding part of (11)) is also positive. This is a contradiction because we have seen that the right-hand side of (11) is zero. Hence, there should be no feasible process satisfying (9) and (10).

Thus α attains a maximum $\bar{\alpha}^*$ at $(\bar{x}^*, \bar{m}^*, \bar{y}^*, l^*)$ when prices are fixed at p^*. We may, therefore, conclude that $(\bar{\alpha}^*, \bar{x}^*, \bar{m}^*, \bar{y}^*, l^*, \bar{p}^*, \bar{p}_{n+1}{}^*)$ is a quasi-equilibrium, so that $\bar{p}^* \in R(p^*)$. This establishes the upper semi-continuity of the correspondence $p\to R(p)$.

6. We are now in a position to apply the Kakutani theorem to ensure the existence of a fixed point $\bar{p} \in R(\bar{p})$. It is clear from the construction of the mapping that at the fixed point inequalities (1′) and $u_j(\bar{p}; \bar{x}, \bar{y}) \geqq \bar{\alpha} v_j(\bar{p}; \bar{x})$ (the latter is referred to as (1″)) are satisfied in addition to the conditions,

$$\sum_j \bar{p}_j u_j(\bar{p}; \bar{x}, \bar{y}) + \bar{p}_{n+1} \bar{l} = \bar{\alpha}\{\sum_j \bar{p}_j v_j(\bar{p}; \bar{x}) + \bar{p}_{n+1} \bar{m}\}, \tag{12}$$

$$\sum_j \bar{p}_j u_j(\bar{p}; x, y) + \bar{p}_{n+1} l \leqq \bar{\alpha}\{\sum_j \bar{p}_j v_j(\bar{p}; x) + \bar{p}_{n+1} m\}, \tag{13}$$

[1] Since $\bar{\alpha}(^k) > 1$ for all k, we have $\bar{\alpha}^* \geqq 1$ in the limit.

where the last inequality must hold for all feasible processes. The equilibrium wage rate $\bar{w}$ is now determined from (2′).[1] Then, in view of the definitions of u_j and v_j, (13) may be put, with $\bar{\beta}$ fixed by (6), in the form of (3) which holds for all feasible processes such that $l \geqq \bar{\alpha}m$. As the efficiency price $\bar{p}_{n+1}$ is zero if labour is free (i.e., if $l > \bar{\alpha}\bar{m}$), we have $\bar{p}_{n+1}l = \bar{\alpha}\bar{p}_{n+1}\bar{m}$ for all possible values of $\bar{p}_{n+1}$. As $\bar{w}$ and $\bar{\beta}$ are determined so as to satisfy (2′) and (6) respectively, we obtain (4) from (12). We now find that (1″) and (12) can be converted into (1) and (2) respectively.

Finally, since $\bar{\alpha}^* \geqq 1$ for any preassigned price set $\bar{p}^*$, we have $\bar{\alpha} \geqq 1$; therefore, $\bar{y}_j > 0$ for some goods. Let us rearrange goods so that the outputs of the first h goods are positive. Suppose now h is less than n. By the powerful indecomposability assumption (vii), there is at least one commodity i ($i > h$) such that $\bar{x}_i > 0$. It then follows from (1) that $\bar{y}_i$ is positive for that commodity i. This is a contradiction; hence, $h = n$, that is, $\bar{y}_i > 0$ for all $j = 1, \ldots, n$. We can now immediately verify (5).

The existence proof is now concluded since all the conditions for Silvery Equilibrium are satisfied at the fixed point. However, it should be noticed that in the above nothing definite has been said about the scarcity of labour. In a Silvery Equilibrium it may be free; $\bar{\alpha}\bar{m}$ persons out of l are employed, while the rest are unemployed and starved to death unless a powerful social security system is put in force or birth control is effectively practiced. If the equilibrium wage rate is set at $\bar{w}$ it would differ from the efficiency price of labour $\bar{p}_{n+1}$ which is set at zero. In contrast with such a Keynesian or Malthusian Silvery Equilibrium bringing about involuntary unemployment, we may also have a balanced growth equilibrium with persistent full employment of labour; along that path outputs per man remain constant, so that in spite of the weak Malthusian assumption (viii), we may avoid the Malthusian poverty and enjoy plenty in the midst of plenty.

7. Let us now turn to the efficiency and optimality aspects of the growth equilibrium. There are two important differences between the model that is being discussed in this chapter and that which was examined for efficiency and optimality in Parts II and III. First, unlike the capitalists but like horses, the workers in the former are not allowed to choose goods so as to maximize their own utility indices, but can only eat the bread and wear the clothes distributed by the public authorities, or by the capitalists or someone else; on the other hand, those in the model in the previous parts cannot be distinguished from the capitalists in their principles of consumption decisions, although they may have different Engel-coefficients

[1] There is no necessity for $\bar{w}$ to equal $\bar{p}_{n+1}$. Under the living-cost principle of wage determination, workers may be paid at a rate different from the efficiency price of labour $\bar{p}_{n+1}$. $\bar{w}$ may remain positive, while $\bar{p}_{n+1}$ is set at zero. This is an interpretation (or a variation) of Keynes's famous proposition of the downward rigidity of the wage rate.

and average propensities to consume. The workers in the present model are no better than farm animals, and the capitalists are the only persons who can choose goods. Just as national consumption does not include consumption by cows, hens, rabbits, and so on, we may be advised, when we accept such treatment of workers, to define the consumable output of a commodity as that portion of the commodity produced which is received by the capitalists after deducting the part fed to the workers as well as that consumed during the process of production. The distribution among the capitalists of the consumable outputs thus defined is first examined for Pareto optimality and then in the next chapter the feeding of the workers is examined for Ramsey optimality.

Secondly, the present model treats the growth of the labour force as an exogenous phenomenon; the working population can increase at different rates, depending on the workers' welfare. Although the case with a flexible labour force has already been discussed in Part I and Chapter XIV, the models which have been examined there for dynamic efficiency and optimality are those in which the working population grows at an exogenously determined fixed rate. As will be seen later, the efficiency of Silvery Equilibrium greatly depends on whether the population growth is exogenous or not. In a model with a flexible labour force it is possible to find a path of order 2, say, along which in the first period the workers are so poorly fed, clothed, and housed that they cannot produce much consumable output, but in the second period they are well paid so that the actual population growth path will catch up with its Silvery Growth path. It is true that the value of the consumable outputs in the second period is less than the maximum that could be attained when the working population grows at a slower rate; but by choosing processes appropriately, it may be possible to make as much consumable output in period 2 as the corresponding amounts on the Silvery Equilibrium growth path, thus violating the (weak) efficiency of the Silvery Equilibrium of order 2. Such an intertemporal substitution between the consumable outputs and the labour force is impossible if we are confined to the evaluation of the shortest paths of order one. In the next section we shall observe that the Silvery Equilibrium is a state of instantaneous efficiency bringing about a temporary Pareto optimum; in section 9 we shall see that its intertemporal efficiency and Pareto optimality do *not* necessarily follow as they did in the previous model with exogenous population growth.

8. Let $y_j(0)$ be the amount of good j available in the economy at the beginning of period 1, and $l(0)$ the number of workers available at the same point of time. Suppose $y_1(0)$, ..., $y_n(0)$, and $l(0)$ are given such that

$$y_j(0) \geqq \mu \bar{y}_j \qquad j = 1, ..., n, \tag{14}$$

$$l(0) = \mu l \tag{14'}$$

for some positive μ; and assume $\mu = 1$ for the sake of simplicity. It is then possible for the economy to have a balanced growth, $(\bar{\alpha}\bar{x}, \bar{\alpha}\bar{m}) \rightarrow (\bar{\alpha}\bar{y}, \bar{\alpha}l)$ from the given initial capital-labour endowments $\{y(0), l(0)\}$ by putting $\bar{\alpha}\bar{x}$ of $y(0)$ and $\bar{\alpha}\bar{m}$ of $l(0)$ into the production process. The total value of the consumable quantities of goods[1] during the period amounts to

$$\sum_j \bar{p}_j\{y_j(0) - \bar{\alpha}\bar{x}_j\}, \tag{15}$$

if it is evaluated at the equilibrium prices $\bar{p}_1, \ldots, \bar{p}_n$. The economy leaves the future people the means of production of the discounted value,

$$\sum_j \bar{\beta}^{-1}\bar{p}_j\bar{\alpha}\bar{y}_j + \bar{\beta}^{-1}\bar{p}_{n+1}\bar{\alpha}l, \tag{16}$$

where the stocks of goods at the end of the period $\bar{\alpha}\bar{y}_1, \ldots, \bar{\alpha}\bar{y}_n$ are evaluated at the discounted equilibrium prices $\bar{\beta}^{-1}\bar{p}_1, \ldots, \bar{\beta}^{-1}\bar{p}_n$, respectively, and the labour force, $\bar{\alpha}l$, at the discounted efficiency price of labour, $\bar{\beta}^{-1}\bar{p}_{n+1}$, but not at the discounted equilibrium wage rate, $\bar{\beta}^{-1}\bar{w}$.

Let us now compare such a temporary Silvery Equilibrium in period 1 with any other feasible state. Let $x_i(1)$ be the amount of good i consumed in period 1 for production of goods and men: $x_1(1), \ldots, x_n(1)$ are distributed among industries and families so that for each good j the sum of $x_j^I(1)$ and $x_j^F(1)$ is equal to $x_j(1)$. $m(1)$ denotes the number of workers employed in period 1, and $y_1(1), \ldots, y_n(1)$ and $l(1)$ the outputs of goods and men that are available at the end of the period. The feasibility of the process $(x(1), m(1)) \rightarrow (y(1), l(1))$ implies that each element of $(x(1), m(1))$ does not exceed the corresponding element of $(y(0), l(0))$. Evaluated at the equilibrium prices, the total value of the consumable amounts is

$$\sum_j \bar{p}_j(y_j(0) - x_j(1)), \tag{17}$$

and the economy is endowed in the second period with goods and labour force of the discounted value,

$$\sum_j \bar{\beta}^{-1}\bar{p}_j y_j(1) + \bar{\beta}^{-1}\bar{p}_{n+1}l(1). \tag{18}$$

It is now easy to show that the Silvery Equilibrium is an efficient state. In accordance with the definition of efficiency that we gave before, we say that the temporary Silvery Equilibrium is strongly efficient (of order 1) if there is no other feasible path for which the sum of (17) and (18) (that is, the total value of consumable amounts during the period *plus* the discounted value of the stocks of goods and the labour force at the end of

[1] Consumable for the capitalists.

the period) exceeds the corresponding sum, (15) plus (16), at the Silvery Equilibrium. In view of the relationships,

$$\sum_j \bar{p}_j \bar{y}_j + \bar{p}_{n+1} \bar{l} = \bar{\beta} \sum_j \bar{p}_j \bar{x}_j + \bar{\alpha} \bar{p}_{n+1} \bar{m}, \tag{12'}$$

$$\sum_j \bar{p}_j y_j(1) + \bar{p}_{n+1} l(1) \leqq \bar{\beta} \sum_j \bar{p}_j x_j(1) + \bar{\alpha} \bar{p}_{n+1} m(1), \tag{13'}$$

following from the rule of competitive pricing,[1] we find that the sum of (15) and (16) can exceed the sum of (17) and (18) by $\bar{\alpha}\bar{\beta}^{-1}\bar{p}_{n+1}\{\bar{\alpha}\bar{m} - m(1)\}$ at most. The last quantity is non-negative, because $\bar{p}_{n+1}\bar{\alpha}\bar{m}$ equals $\bar{p}_{n+1}\bar{l}$ for all cases, $m(1)$ does not exceed $l(0)$ and $l(0)$ is set at $\bar{l}$ by (14′). Hence the sum of (17) and (18) cannot be greater than the sum of (15) and (16). Thus, there is no feasible path of order one which is superior to the Silvery Equilibrium path; along any feasible path that provides us with net outputs whose total value is greater than the corresponding value in the Silvery Equilibrium, the economy can only leave for future production a smaller amount of some good (or labour) than it would leave in the other state.

The Pareto optimality of the temporary Silvery Equilibrium follows as a simple corollary to its efficiency. It is evident that the total value of consumable outputs, (17), from a feasible process $(x(1), m(1)) \to (y(1), l(1))$ is distributed among capitalists, while the discounted value of the end-of-period stocks of goods and labour force, (18), of that process is distributed among the future persons. Similarly, in the state of Silvery Equilibrium, the values (15) and (16) are distributed among the capitalists and the future citizens, respectively. As we have seen, the sum of (17) and (18) cannot be greater than the sum of (15) and (16). This means that if a shift from the equilibrium process $(\bar{\alpha}\bar{x}, \bar{\alpha}\bar{m}) \to (\bar{\alpha}\bar{y}, \bar{\alpha}\bar{l})$ to $(x(1), m(1)) \to (y(1), l(1))$ leads a capitalist to a preferred position (as a consumer), then it necessarily leaves someone else (another capitalist or a future person) worse off than before. Thus, in so far as we confine our prospects to one period, the state of balanced growth is a Pareto optimum; but it may not be a Pareto optimum if we consider growth paths extending over two or more periods. That is to say, the optimality established for the Silvery Equilibrium is merely temporary or instantaneous, or of order one.

9. Let us now present a rather surprising discovery: A Silvery Equilibrium of order more than one in a system with a flexible labour force may be a

[1] Because of the definitions of $u(p; x, y)$ and $v(p; x)$, the relation (6) between α and β, and the identity, $\Sigma p_j f_j(p) = c$, we can rewrite (12) and (13) as (12′) and (13′), respectively.

state which is not necessarily efficient or optimal (strong or weak). We will illustrate this by using a numerical example.

We assume, for the sake of simplicity, that the technology is independent of the labour-feeding activities. Suppose there are four basic technological processes with the following input and output coefficients:

	Process 1		Process 2		Process 3		Process 4	
	Input	*Output*	*Input*	*Output*	*Input*	*Output*	*Input*	*Output*
Good 1	2	5	1	4	1·7	4	2·15	6
Good 2	2	4	2	5	2	5	2·7	6
Labour	0·5	0	1·5	0	5/6	0	1·2	0

The technology may then be described as before in terms of the input-coefficient matrix A, the output-coefficient matrix B, and the labour-input-coefficient vector L with goods being arranged in columns and processes in rows.

Next, suppose that the labour force grows at the rate θ if goods are given to the existing m workers in the amounts:

$$x_i^F = (0{\cdot}6\theta + 0{\cdot}2)m, \qquad (i = 1, 2) \quad \text{for} \quad 0 \leqq \theta \leqq 0{\cdot}5$$

$$x_i^F = \theta m, \qquad (i = 1, 2) \quad \text{for} \quad \theta \geqq 0{\cdot}5.$$

If the capitalists' average propensity to save is 0·5, and their Engel-coefficients (at the prices $p_1 = 0{\cdot}5$ and $p_2 = 0{\cdot}5$) are 2/3 for good 1, and 1/3 for good 2, then a Silvery Equilibrium is obtained at

$$\bar{p} = \begin{bmatrix} 1/2 \\ 1/2 \end{bmatrix}, \quad \bar{w} = 1/2, \quad \bar{v} = (1, 1, 0, 0),$$

$$\bar{m} = 2, \quad \bar{l} = 3, \quad \bar{\alpha} = 1{\cdot}5, \quad \bar{\beta} = 2,$$

where $\bar{v}$ is the intensity vector (i.e., $\bar{x}$ in Chapter XIV), whose ith component denotes the intensity at which the ith process operates in the state of Silvery Equilibrium.

This is verified in the following way. As the labour force grows at the rate 0·5 and $\bar{m}$ is 2, we have: $\bar{x}^F = (1, 1)$, so that $\bar{x} = \bar{v}A + \bar{x}^F = (4, 5)$. We also have $\bar{y} = \bar{v}B = (9, 9)$, and $\bar{e} = (\bar{\beta} - 1)(\bar{v}A\bar{p} + \bar{w}\bar{m}) = 4{\cdot}5$. Hence, the balanced growth conditions (1) and (1′) in the previous section are fulfilled. On the other hand, since

$$\sum \bar{p}_j y_j = vB\bar{p} = (v_1, v_2, v_3)\begin{bmatrix} 4{\cdot}5 \\ 4{\cdot}5 \\ 4{\cdot}5 \end{bmatrix},$$

$$\sum \bar{p}_j x_j^F = vA\bar{p} = (v_1, v_2, v_3)\begin{bmatrix} 2 \\ 1{\cdot}5 \\ 1{\cdot}85 \\ 2{\cdot}425 \end{bmatrix},$$

$$m = vL \;\; = (v_1, v_2, v_3)\begin{bmatrix} 0{\cdot}5 \\ 1{\cdot}5 \\ 5/6 \\ 1{\cdot}2 \end{bmatrix},$$

and $$\sum_j \bar{p}_j x_j^F = \theta m \qquad \text{for} \quad \theta \geqq 0{\cdot}5,$$

inequality (3) holds for all $\theta \geqq 0{\cdot}5$, with equality at $\bar{v} = (1, 1, 0, 0)$ and $\theta = 0{\cdot}5$. Finally, (2), (2′), and (5) are all satisfied.

Let us now consider paths starting from the initial position given by

$$y(0) = (9, 9) \qquad \text{and} \qquad l(0) = 3.$$

Along the Silvery Equilibrium path the consumable outputs of the two goods are 3 and 1·5 in period 1, and 4·5 and 2·25 in period 2. The amounts of goods and labour left to the future persons at the end of period 2 are: $\{y_1(2), y_2(2), l(2)\} = (20{\cdot}25, 20{\cdot}25, 6{\cdot}75)$.

An alternative path with the same starting point is to choose process 4 in period 1, and to choose processes 1 and 3 in period 2; the workers are fed such that the growth rate of the working population θ will be zero in period 1, and 1·25 in period 2. As $l(0) = 3$ and the labour-input coefficient is 1·2, process 4 can operate at intensity 2·5. Then

$$x^I = (5{\cdot}375, 6{\cdot}75).$$

On the other hand, substituting $m = 3$ and $\theta = 0$, we have

$$x^F = (0{\cdot}6, 0{\cdot}6).$$

By subtracting x^I and x^F from $y(0) = (9, 9)$, we find that the consumable outputs in period 1 are 3·025 for good 1 and 1·65 for good 2.

At the beginning of period 2, 15 units of each good and 3 units of the working population are available (because, in period 1, process 4 operates at the intensity 2·5 and only the subsistence wages are paid to the workers).[1]

[1] Comparing this state at the beginning of period 2 with the corresponding state along the Silvery Equilibrium, we find that in the former state more of both goods are available than in the latter.

Both processes 1 and 3 can now operate at the common intensity 2·25, and the workers can draw large salaries so that their numbers will increase at the rate $\theta = 1{\cdot}25$. Such activities in period 2 yield 4·5 and 2·25 of consumable outputs of goods 1 and 2, respectively, and the final state at the end of period 2 is exactly the same as that reached by the Silvery Growth path.

Comparing the consumable outputs along this path with those along the Silvery Growth path, we at once find that the latter is not efficient even in the weak sense. If it is not weakly efficient, it is clear that it cannot be a Pareto optimum (of order 2) because it is always possible to satisfy the preferences of some capitalists better without leaving other capitalists worse off than they are in the state of Silvery Equilibrium.

10. Rather surprising exceptions of this kind are based on the discrepancy between the equilibrium rate of interest $\bar{\beta}-1$ and the rate of balanced growth $\bar{\alpha}-1$, and will disappear when $\bar{\alpha} = \bar{\beta}$, viz. when $s = 1$, or in other words, in the state of Golden Equilibrium. Suppose that the capitalists do not consume and reinvest all their income automatically. Then they are disqualified from being treated as 'men', and are nothing but 'self-service stands of capital'. The sole person (or the sole group of people) in the economy is the 'future'. The waggoner cries 'Accumulation, accumulation!' and the horses gallop with all their might.

As before, $x_j^I(t)$ and $x_j^F(t)$ denote industrial and feeding inputs of good j in period t, and $y_j(t)$ output of good j at the end of period t (and hence available at the beginning of period $t+1$). $m(t)$ and $l(t)$ denote the amount of labour used in period t and the number of people living at the beginning of period $t+1$, respectively. As the capitalists do not consume, the so-called 'consumable outputs',

$$h_j(t) = y_j(t-1) - x_j^I(t) - x_j^F(t), \qquad j = 1, \ldots, n, \tag{19}$$

are now better called 'surplus outputs' which may be devoted as offerings to Gods who live outside the society of workers and capitalists or may be accumulated for, say, military purposes. We define the total (discounted) value of the 'net' outputs of order T, $V(T)$, as the sum of the total discounted values of the surplus outputs from period 1 to period T and the discounted value of the final stocks of goods and the final labour force at the end of period T:

$$V(T) = \sum_{t=1}^{T} \sum_{j} \bar{\beta}^{-(t-1)} \bar{p}_j h_j(t) + \bar{\beta}^{-T} \bar{p}_j y_j(T) + \bar{\beta}^{-T} \bar{p}_{n+1} l(T),$$

the evaluation being made at the equilibrium prices and the efficiency price of labour.

Let us compare the value of the net outputs $V(T)$ of any feasible path of order T with the corresponding value $\bar{V}(T)$ along the Golden Equilibrium path. We suppose, as in the case of order 1 previously discussed, $y_j(0) \geqq \bar{y}_j$, $j = 1, ..., n$, and $l(0) = \bar{l}$. In view of definition (19), inequality (13′) (which holds not only for $t = 1$, but also for all t) and the Golden Rule $\bar{\alpha} = \bar{\beta}$, we get

$$V(T) \leqq \sum_j \bar{p}_j y_j(0) + \sum_{t=1}^{T} \bar{\beta}^{-(t-1)} \bar{p}_{n+1} m(t) - \sum_{t=1}^{T-1} \bar{\beta}^{-t} \bar{p}_{n+1} l(t).$$

On the other hand, the feasibility of the path implies

$$m(t) \leqq l(t-1) \qquad t = 1, ..., T.$$

We have $l(0) = \bar{l}$ also. Hence we finally get

$$V(T) \leqq \sum_j \bar{p}_j y_j(0) + \bar{p}_{n+1} \bar{l}.$$

Since (12′) is obtained, we find that this weak inequality holds with equality in the state of Golden Equilibrium; accordingly,

$$V(T) \leqq \bar{V}(T).$$

This inequality implies the (strong) efficiency of the Golden Equilibrium of any order T, and hence the intertemporal Pareto optimality is established.

As we shall see in the next chapter, the Golden Growth path is a particular path along which there is no votive offering to the Gods. Therefore, the wealth of the 'future' human beings is maximized and the tributes to the Gods are minimized when the economy advances according to the Golden programme of economic growth. The unreligious future citizens will definitely prefer the Golden Growth path to any other feasible path, even though the Gods are made better off along it. The living citizens have no part in this struggle between the Gods and unborn persons. Someone may feel it is tragic that the long-run efficiency of the equilibrium has been secured on the 'no-man' assumption, although it is not absurdly far from reality as it might look since no man—or no bourgeois—is allowed to live in a 'pure gold' communist society.

XVI

SIMULTANEOUS OPTIMIZATION OF POPULATION AND CAPITAL

1. How much of its income should a nation save? This problem of optimum savings has been discussed by Ramsey on the assumption of a constant population and later by a number of economists on the more general assumption that the labour force expands at a constant rate exogenously fixed. Different rates of population growth lead to different solutions; that is to say, the path of optimum capital accumulation is relative to the population growth.

On the other hand, Meade and others have been concerned with the problem of optimum population, assuming among other things that at any given time the economy is provided with a given rate of savings as well as a given stock of capital equipment to be used.[1] It follows that the path of optimum population is relative to capital accumulation. In fact a population growth that is optimal in some circumstances would be too fast in other circumstances—say, when capital is accumulated at a very low rate.

It is evident that these two partial optimizations procedures should be synthesized so as to give a genuine supreme path which is an optimum with respect to both capital and population. We devote this final chapter to a generalization of the Ramsey-Meade problem in that direction and show that two kinds of long-run paths—efficient and optimum paths—will under some conditions converge to the Golden Growth path when the time-horizon of the paths becomes infinite. Efficiency is defined in terms of the 'final' outcomes of paths, while optimality takes into account not only the final states but also intermediate states en route. Two long-run tendencies we shall derive may be regarded as extensions of those discussed in the chapters entitled First and Second Turnpike Theorems.

2. In the previous chapter, the Silvery or Golden Equilibrium has been compared, for efficiency and Pareto Optimality, with feasible paths starting from an initial position from which the economy can grow in equilibrium without discarding any labour but possibly discarding some goods.[2] It is

[1] See, for example, J. E. Meade, *Trade and Welfare: The Theory of International Economic Policy*, Vol. 2 (Oxford University Press, 1955), pp. 80–101.

[2] Note that paths discussed in Chapter XV satisfy inequalities (XV. 14) and (XV. 14′) at the beginning.

not necessarily true, however, that labour is always a limiting factor; it may be superfluous (as it is in many underdeveloped countries) and some goods which are indispensable for equilibrium growth may be exhausted before labour is fully employed. By replacing the equality in the restriction (XV. 14′) on the starting point by inequality '$\geqq$', we are able to examine a more general case: all goods and labour are provided at the beginning in positive amounts without the limiting factor being specified. Under this more general assumption, we shall show that the Final State Turnpike Theorem is obtained in the sense that all of the long-run efficient paths—efficiency is defined in terms of the final states—will converge (in the broad sense, to be defined exactly below) to the Golden Equilibrium path.

The Golden Equilibrium would be a norm of economic growth for a communist economy where, with no bourgeosie, all the available stocks of goods are automatically reinvested for reproduction of goods and men. Similarly, the Silvery Equilibrium would be a norm for a capitalistic economy, where the capitalists spend on industrial investment the remainder of their income after deducting from it the part devoted to their private consumption. We begin by observing that the rate of growth at the former type of equilibrium is *ceteris paribus* greater than the growth rate at the latter. Let $\bar{p}$ and $\bar{\bar{p}}$ be the Golden and Silvery Equilibrium price vectors in the communist and capitalist economies, respectively.[1] We assume that the capitalists consume some goods which would be valuable in the communist economy; more exactly, for some goods with positive communist prices $\bar{p}_j$, the capitalists have positive propensity to consume so that their Engel-coefficients $f_j(\bar{\bar{p}})$ are positive. As we have

$$\bar{\bar{y}}_j - f_j(\bar{\bar{p}})\bar{\bar{e}} \geqq \bar{\bar{\alpha}}\bar{\bar{x}}_j, \qquad j = 1, \ldots, n,$$
$$\bar{\bar{l}} \geqq \bar{\bar{\alpha}}\bar{\bar{m}}$$

in the state of capitalist Silvery Equilibrium, we have *a fortiori*

$$\bar{\bar{y}}_j \geqq \bar{\bar{\alpha}}\bar{\bar{x}}_j, \quad \bar{\bar{l}} \geqq \bar{\bar{\alpha}}\bar{\bar{m}}, \qquad j = 1, \ldots, n.$$

The assumption just made implies that the capitalists' consumption, $\Sigma\, \bar{p}_j f_j(\bar{\bar{p}})\bar{\bar{e}}$, is taken to be positive at the communist prices; therefore we have

$$\Sigma\, \bar{p}_j \bar{\bar{y}}_j > \bar{\bar{\alpha}} \Sigma\, \bar{p}_j \bar{\bar{x}}_j.$$

If $\bar{\bar{\alpha}}$ were the Golden Equilibrium growth factor associated with the Golden Equilibrium price vector $\bar{p}$, then $\bar{\bar{\alpha}} = \bar{\alpha} = \bar{\beta}$; so that it follows from (XV.3) that the total value of outputs (the left-hand side of the above inequality) would not exceed the total value of inputs (the right-hand side). The above inequality contradicts this Rule of Competitive

[1] Similarly, Golden and Silvery Equilibrium values of other quantities are distinguished from each other by putting, respectively, '—' and '=' above the symbols.

Pricing. Hence $\bar{\bar{\alpha}}$ cannot be the growth factor of the Golden Equilibrium. On the other hand, the Golden Equilibrium growth factor $\bar{\alpha}$ is the largest value of α fulfilling

$$y_j \geqq \alpha x_j, \quad l \geqq \alpha m, \qquad j = 1, ..., n.^1$$

Therefore, we obtain $\bar{\alpha} > \bar{\bar{\alpha}}$. Thus, the Golden Growth path, which is efficient and optimal not only in the short run but also in the long run, is the true Turnpike with the fastest rate of growth, and its convergence will be examined below.

3. Let us now assume the Turnpike is positive and unique; that is, there is only one Golden Equilibrium aggregate process $(\bar{x}, \bar{m}) \to (\bar{y}, \bar{l})$, and $(\bar{x}, \bar{m})$ is a strictly positive vector. Consider a sequence of feasible aggregate processes $(x(t), m(t)) \to (y(t), l(t))$ such that $y(t-1) \geqq x(t)$ and $l(t-1) \geqq m(t)$ $(t = 1, 2, ..., T)$, and call it, as before, a feasible path of order T. All feasible paths of the same order T may be compared with each other with respect to their final outcomes $(y(T), l(T))$ disregarding all the intermediate outcomes $(y(t), l(t))$ $(t = 1, ..., T-1)$ which may be considered as 'goods in process' developing into 'final product' in period T. We call a feasible path of order T, $(x(t), m(t)) \to (y(t), l(t))$, $t = 1, ..., T$, an (weakly) efficient path of order T if there is no other feasible path of the same order, $(x'(t), m'(t)) \to (y'(t), l'(t))$, $t = 1, ..., T$, such that inequalities $y_j'(T) \geqq y_j(T)$ and $l'(T) \geqq l(T)$ hold with at least one strict inequality, while $x_j'(1) \leqq x_j(1)$ and $m'(1) \leqq m(1)$ for all $j = 1, ..., n$. We first show that all efficient paths thus defined in terms of the final states converge on the Turnpike in the broad (or average) sense that the average output per man (discounted by the Turnpike growth factor $\bar{\alpha}$) over T periods of each good j,

$$\frac{\dfrac{y_j(1)}{\bar{\alpha}} + \dfrac{y_j(2)}{\bar{\alpha}^2} + \ldots + \dfrac{y_j(T)}{\bar{\alpha}^T}}{\dfrac{l(1)}{\bar{\alpha}} + \dfrac{l(2)}{\bar{\alpha}^2} + \ldots + \dfrac{l(T)}{\bar{\alpha}^T}}, \qquad j = 1, ..., n, \tag{1}$$

approximates the Turnpike output per man $\bar{y}_j/\bar{l}$ when T tends to infinity. It is, of course, true that this convergence does not necessarily imply the convergence of unaveraged output per man $y_j(t)/l(t)$ to $\bar{y}_j/\bar{l}$ which is asserted by the usual Turnpike Theorem; but it still implies that all efficient paths

[1] This is seen *reductio ad absurdum*. If there were a feasible aggregate production process such that

$$y_j > \bar{\alpha} x_j, \quad l > \bar{\alpha} m, \quad j = 1, ..., n,$$

then we would have

$$\Sigma \bar{p}_j y_j + \bar{p}_{n+1} l > \bar{\alpha} \Sigma \bar{p}_j x_j + \bar{\alpha} \bar{p}_{n+1} m.$$

This is a contradiction to (XV. 13′), because $\bar{\alpha} = \bar{\beta}$ in the Golden Equilibrium.

cannot depart from the Turnpike in the sense that if they are averaged, the averages are close to the Turnpike output per man, $\bar{y}_j/\bar{l}$, although $y_j(t)/l(t)$ may fluctuate regularly or irregularly around the Turnpike output per man.

The following argument is a proof of the weak (or average) Turnpike Theorem. It is assumed that the amounts of goods available in the economy at the beginning of period 0, $y_1(0)$, $y_2(0)$, ..., $y_n(0)$, and the number of workers at the same point of time, $l(0)$, are given so as to fulfill inequalities

$$y_j(0) \geqq \mu \bar{y}_j, \qquad j = 1, ..., n \quad \text{and} \quad l(0) \geqq \mu \bar{l}$$

for a positive number μ. (We assume without loss of generality $\mu = 1$.) It then follows from the costless disposal of labour and goods implied by assumptions (i), (iv), and (v) in the previous chapter that we can drive on the Turnpike for t periods since we enter it by disposing of goods and labour in the amounts $y_j(0)-\bar{y}_j$ ($j = 1, ..., n$) and $l(0)-\bar{l}$ at the beginning of period 1. If the Turnpike social outputs $\bar{\alpha}^t\bar{y}_j$ ($j = 1, ..., n$) and $\bar{\alpha}^t\bar{l}$ in some period t are greater than the corresponding social outputs $y_j(t)$ ($j = 1, ..., n$) and $l(t)$ of an efficient path, then we may find a positive number ν such that

$$\bar{\alpha}^t\bar{y}_j \geqq y_j(t)+\nu\bar{\alpha}^t\bar{y}_j, \qquad j = 1, ..., n,$$
$$\bar{\alpha}^t\bar{l} \geqq l(t)+\nu\bar{\alpha}^t\bar{l}.$$

It is evident that costless disposal of goods and labour in appropriate amounts at the beginning of period $t+1$ enables us to move from the Turnpike onto a hybrid path obtained by superimposing the original efficient path on the Turnpike. We thus find a feasible path of order T which starts from the same initial position ($y(0)$, $l(0)$) as that of the original efficient path, and arrives at a better terminus ($y(T)+\nu\bar{\alpha}^T\bar{y}$, $l(T)+\nu\bar{\alpha}^t\bar{l}$) than that of the latter. This is an apparent contradiction, for the efficiency of a path requires that there is no feasible path superior to it. Hence, we find that for each t either there is at least one good j_t such that its output along the efficient path is at worst as great as the Turnpike output

$$y_{j_t}(t) \geqq \bar{\alpha}^t\bar{y}_{j_t}, \tag{2}$$

or a similar inequality is obtained for the labour force,

$$l(t) \geqq \bar{\alpha}^t\bar{l}. \tag{2'}$$

Let us now write $k = \min(\bar{y}_1, \bar{y}_2, ..., \bar{y}_n, \bar{l})$ which is positive by assumption. It follows from (2) and (2′) that either the discounted output of some good j, $y_j(t)/\bar{\alpha}^t$, or the discounted number of workers, $l(t)/\bar{\alpha}^t$, is at least as great as k. Taking account of the fact that $y_j(t)$ and $l(t)$ are non-negative, we may *a fortiori* say that the contemporary sum, $\sum y_j(t)/\bar{\alpha}^t+l(t)/\bar{\alpha}^t$, can never be less than k. Taking the total sum of the sums over T periods, and writing

$$w(T) = \sum_{1}^{T} \sum_{j} \frac{y_j(t)}{\bar{\alpha}^t} + \sum_{1}^{T} \frac{l(t)}{\bar{\alpha}^t},$$

we get $w(T) \geqq Tk$. Consequently, $w(T)$ becomes larger and larger when T tends to infinity, and this result will play a most important role in the following discussion of the weak convergence of efficient paths.

As aggregate processes are subject to constant returns to scale, we find from the feasibility of the original undiscounted processes that the following discounted processes are also feasible:

$$\left(\frac{x(t)}{\bar{\alpha}^t}, \frac{m(t)}{\bar{\alpha}^t}\right) \rightarrow \left(\frac{y(t)}{\bar{\alpha}^t}, \frac{l(t)}{\bar{\alpha}^t}\right) \qquad t = 1, ..., T.$$

By operating these T processes jointly (the composition or 'super-addition' of processes is ensured by assumption (i) in Chapter XV), we have a feasible process,

$$(X(T), M(T)) \rightarrow (Y(T), L(T)),$$

where $X(T)$ denotes the sum of $x(t)/\bar{\alpha}^t$ over T periods; $M(T)$, $Y(T)$ and $L(T)$ are defined in the same way. Taking $y(t-1) \geqq x(t)$ and $l(t-1) \geqq m(t)$ $(t = 1, ..., T)$ into account, we have

$$X(T) \leqq \frac{x(1)}{\bar{\alpha}} + \frac{Y(T)}{\bar{\alpha}} - \frac{y(T)}{\bar{\alpha}^{T+1}}, \quad \text{and} \quad M(T) \leqq \frac{m(1)}{\bar{\alpha}} + \frac{L(T)}{\bar{\alpha}} - \frac{l(T)}{\bar{\alpha}^{T+1}}.$$

Besides, as goods and labour are freely disposable and aggregate processes are subject to constant returns to scale, we find that the following process is feasible:

$$\left(\frac{x(1)}{\bar{\alpha}w(T)} + \frac{Y(T)}{\bar{\alpha}w(T)}, \frac{m(1)}{\bar{\alpha}w(T)} + \frac{L(T)}{\bar{\alpha}w(T)}\right) \rightarrow \left(\frac{Y(T)}{w(T)}, \frac{L(T)}{w(T)}\right). \qquad (3)$$

From the definition of $w(T)$ it is seen that $\left(\frac{Y(T)}{w(T)}, \frac{L(T)}{w(T)}\right)$ belongs to a bounded, closed region $\{(y, l) \mid y_j \geqq 0,\ l \geqq 0,\ \sum_j y_j + l = 1\}$, so that it has a limit point (y^*, l^*) as T tends to infinity. Furthermore, $w(T)$, which is at least as large as Tk, becomes very large when T is large enough; we may therefore safely neglect $x(1)/\{\bar{\alpha}w(T)\}$ and $m(1)/\{\bar{\alpha}w(T)\}$. We thus have from (3) a limiting feasible process,

$$\left(\frac{y^*}{\bar{\alpha}}, \frac{l^*}{\bar{\alpha}}\right) \rightarrow (y^*, l^*) \qquad \text{or} \qquad (y^*, l^*) \rightarrow (\bar{\alpha}y^*, \bar{\alpha}l^*),$$

which gives a balanced growth at the Golden Equilibrium rate. We get $y^* = \bar{y}$, and $l^* = \bar{l}$ from the assumed uniqueness of the Turnpike. We have thus shown that there is a long-run tendency for the average discounted output per man (1) to approximate the Turnpike output per man; the weak convergence of efficient paths is established.[1]

4. It must be admitted, however, that the above argument does not ensure the strong or proper convergence (i.e., convergence of each $y_j(t)/l(t)$ to $\bar{y}_j/\bar{l}$) which is usually asserted by the Turnpike Theorem; to get it we need some additional assumptions, say the assumption of 'strong super-additivity' discussed below, whose empirical foundation is flimsier than those of the other assumptions. Thus, the strong Turnpike Theorem is not so generally accepted as the weak one, but it is still important and of much interest to see how the system works when it is strongly super-additive.

Consider any two feasible processes. By super-adding them—i.e., by operating them jointly—we can form a third process in which the output for any commodity is not less than the sum of the corresponding outputs for that commodity in the two given processes, and a similar relationship holds for labour as well. If the output of some good (or the number of workers as an output) from the third process is greater than the sum of the corresponding outputs (or the sum of the corresponding numbers of workers) from the two processes (i.e., if the composition of the two processes makes a positive contribution to productivity), then we say that the two feasible processes are strongly super-additive. A sufficient condition for the strong Turnpike property may be stated as follows:

(ix) Any feasible process is strongly super-additive to the Golden Equilibrium process.

In order to verify the sufficiency of the condition, we need a rather long prelude. We have already assumed the uniqueness of the Turnpike, from which it follows that each of the Golden Equilibrium conditions,

$$\bar{y}_j \geqq \bar{\alpha}\bar{x}, \qquad \bar{l} \geqq \bar{\alpha}\bar{m}, \qquad j = 1, ..., n,$$

must hold with equality. (Otherwise the costless disposal of goods and labour would imply that there is another feasible aggregate process satisfying the above conditions; this is a clear contradiction to the uniqueness.) Therefore, in the state of Golden Equilibrium all goods and labour are fully used; that is to say, there is no free good so that all efficiency prices

[1] It must be emphasized that convergence is obtained with respect to all efficient paths, so that efficient paths leading from a given initial point to a point on the prescribed terminal ray will *a fortiori* converge (in the weak sense) to the Turnpike when the programming period T increases indefinitely. Dorfman, Samuelson, and Solow specified the terminal ray but it is unnecessary for the weak convergence. (Cf. their *Linear Programming and Economic Activity*, pp. 329–35.)

$\bar{p}_1, ..., \bar{p}_n$, and the efficiency wage rate $\bar{p}_{n+1}$ associated with the Golden Equilibrium are positive.

Let us now evaluate outputs and inputs (including those of labour) at the efficiency prices. The rule of competitive pricing implies that the value of outputs cannot grow at a rate greater than the Turnpike rate $\bar{\alpha}-1$; we have

$$\Sigma \bar{p}_j y_j + \bar{p}_{n+1} l \leqq \bar{\alpha}(\Sigma \bar{p}_j x_j + \bar{p}_{n+1} m) \tag{4}$$

for any feasible aggregate process; and, as will be shown below, if a non-Golden process is *strongly* super-additive to the Golden process, relationship (4) holds with strict inequality for it.

Suppose the contrary, i.e., that (4) is an equality for some non-trivial feasible process which is not proportional to the Golden Equilibrium process. They are super-added to form a third process, $(\bar{x}+x, \bar{m}+m) \rightarrow (y', l')$ such that

$$y_j' \geqq \bar{y}_j + y_j, \qquad l' \geqq \bar{l}+l, \qquad j = 1, ..., n,$$

where at least one of them holds with strict inequality by virtue of the assumed strong super-additivity. For the Golden Equilibrium process, (4) holds with equality. Since all the prices are positive and (4) holds, by supposition, with equality for the feasible process we are dealing with, it follows from the strong super-additivity that

$$\sum_j \bar{p}_j y_j' + \bar{p}_{n+1} l' > \bar{\alpha}\{\sum_j \bar{p}_j(\bar{x}_j + x_j) + \bar{p}_{n+1}(\bar{m}+m)\}$$

for the third process; this, however, contradicts the Rule of Competitive Pricing requiring that inequality (4) is valid for the third process also. Thus, under the strong assumption (ix), (4) holds with strict inequality for all non-Golden processes.

Let us take a feasible process which is outside a given neighbourhood of the Golden Equilibrium process, i.e., a process $(x, m) \rightarrow (y, l)$, whose distance from $(\bar{x}, \bar{m}) \rightarrow (\bar{y}, \bar{l})$ is at least as great as a given number θ. For any such process, consider the output-input ratio,

$$(\sum_j \bar{p}_j y_j + \bar{p}_{n+1} l)/(\sum_j \bar{p}_j x_j + \bar{p}_{n+1} m), \tag{5}$$

which is less than $\bar{\alpha}$ because of the strict inequality (4) which follows from the assumption of strong super-additivity.

The maximum value of the ratio (5) cannot exceed $\bar{\alpha}$. If it were equal to $\bar{\alpha}$, the process $(x, m) \rightarrow (y, l)$ which attains that value of the ratio should be the Golden Equilibrium process, because the strong super-additivity implies that the latter is the only process associated with $\bar{\alpha}$. But we are maximizing (5) outside a given neighbourhood of the Golden Equilibrium process; hence, the maximum, say $\bar{\alpha}^0$, is less than $\bar{\alpha}$. And the difference, $\bar{\alpha}-\alpha^0$, depends on the distance, θ, to the Turnpike. We have thus obtained

Radner's property, which is famous among Turnpike theorists: given a neighbourhood of the Golden Equilibrium process, there is a positive constant α^0 (less than $\bar{\alpha}$ and depending on the size of the neighbourhood) such that

$$\sum_j \bar{p}_j y_j + \bar{p}_{n+1} l < \alpha^0 (\sum_j \bar{p}_j x_j + \bar{p}_{n+1} m)$$

for all feasible processes outside the neighbourhood.

The prelude immediately leads to the finale. Consider a feasible path $(x(t), m(t)) \rightarrow (y(t), l(t))$, $t = 1, 2, \ldots$. We have

$$\sum_j \bar{p}_j y_j(t) + \bar{p}_{n+1} l(t) < \alpha^0 \{\sum_j \bar{p}_j x_j(t) + \bar{p}_{n+1} m(t)\} \tag{6}$$

in those periods in which the path runs outside the prescribed neighbourhood of the Golden Equilibrium path, and

$$\sum_j \bar{p}_j y_j(t) + \bar{p}_{n+1} l(t) \leqq \bar{\alpha} \{\sum_j \bar{p}_j x_j(t) + \bar{p}_{n+1} m(t)\} \tag{7}$$

in the other periods. Discounting both sides of (6) or (7) by the factor $\bar{\alpha}^t$ and adding them up over periods $t = 1, \ldots, T$, we have

$$\sum_j \bar{p}_j Y_j(T) + \bar{p}_{n+1} L(T) \leqq \alpha_T \{\sum_j \bar{p}_j X_j(T) + \bar{p}_{n+1} M(T)\}, \tag{8}$$

where α_T is a number less than $\bar{\alpha}$ if the path runs outside the neighbourhood in some periods. When T tends to infinity, we have a similar inequality with α^* in place of α_T, where α^* is the limit (or the supremum) of α_T. α^* will be less than $\bar{\alpha}$ when the percentage of the number of those periods in which the path remains within the prescribed neighbourhood to the total number of periods is significantly less than 100 per cent. If $\alpha^* < \bar{\alpha}$, we have, from the limiting inequality of (8), $Y_j(T)/w(T) < \bar{\alpha} X_j(T)/w(T)$ for some j or $L(T)/w(T) < \bar{\alpha} M(T)/w(T)$, when T is taken very large.[1] On the other hand, (3) implies that the senses of these inequalities should be reversed for very large T. It is evidently a contradiction. Hence $\alpha^* = \bar{\alpha}$. We therefore conclude that the longer the length T of the efficient path, the greater (not only in the absolute but also in the relative sense) becomes the number of periods in which the path remains within the neighbourhood and the percentage finally approaches 100 per cent. The strong convergence of efficient paths to the Golden Equilibrium path is thus established.

5. If the assumption of strong super-additivity is rejected, we must seek another assumption which is sufficient for generating strong convergence to the Turnpike. This is the line of approach that was taken in the previous discussion of the same problem in Chapter X. We shall later make an

[1] The existence of a limiting production process is ensured by the weak Turnpike Theorem.

assumption that will play a crucial role in eliminating 'cyclic' exceptions to the Turnpike Theorem; but preceding the discussion on strong convergence, we first consider a general rule which is independent of that specific assumption.

We group aggregate production processes into two classes. As in Chapter X, a process is classified as a *top* process if the discounted value of outputs (including, as output of men, the labour force at the end of the process), evaluated at the Golden Equilibrium prices and discount factor, does compensate for the value of inputs. On the other hand, *non-top* processes are unprofitable when the Golden Equilibrium prices and discount factor prevail. Under this classification top processes satisfy the profitability condition (4) with equality, while for non-stop processes (4) is a strict inequality.[1] A linear combination of two different top processes is also a top process; we call the set of all top processes the top facet (or the von Neumann facet, in McKenzie's terminology) of the aggregate-production-possibility set. It is evident that the Golden Equilibrium process belongs to this facet.

The Radner inequality (6) is revised so as to be true only for all non-top processes which lie outside a given neighbourhood of the *top facet*. Thus, as we have (6) in those periods during which the economy chooses processes not belonging to the prescribed neighbourhood of the top facet, while (7) in other periods, the argument at the end of the last section holds *mutatis mutandis*. We find that the ratio of the number of the periods, in which the path remains within the prescribed neighbourhood, to the total number of periods comes nearer and nearer to unity when the length of the efficient path becomes longer and longer. By taking the neighbourhood to be sufficiently small, we get a 'long period', throughout which the efficient path can be regarded as staying almost on the top facet.

Let us now introduce the assumption that there are a finite number, say n^*, of basic (or linearly independent) top processes which can be combined linearly with appropriate weights to produce any other top process. Basic top processes are denoted by

$$(x_{1i}, \ldots, x_{ni}\ m_i) \to (y_{1i}, \ldots, y_{ni}, l_i), \qquad i = 1, \ldots, n^*.$$

By hypothesis, for any top process, $(x, m) \to (y, l)$, there is a non-negative vector $q = (q_1, \ldots, q_{n^*})$ such that

$$x_j = \sum_i^{n^*} x_{ji} q_i, \qquad m = \sum_i^{n^*} m_i q_i, \qquad i = 1, \ldots, n,$$

$$y_j = \sum_i^{n^*} y_{ji} q_i, \qquad l = \sum_i^{n^*} l_i q_i, \qquad j = 1, \ldots, n.$$

[1] When the strong super-additivity prevails, the Golden Equilibrium process is the one and only top process.

Since the input-output equations, $y(t-1) = x(t)$ and $l(t) = m(t)$, are approximately fulfilled throughout the long period,[1] we obtain the set of difference equations:

$$\sum_{i}^{n^*} y_{ji}q_i(t-1) = \sum_{i}^{n^*} x_{ji}q_i(t), \qquad j = 1, ..., n,$$
$$\sum_{i}^{n^*} l_i q_i(t-1) = \sum_{i}^{n^*} l_i q_i(t), \tag{9}$$

for t in the long period. Notice that the particular vector q that gives the Golden Equilibrium process satisfies these equations with $q(t-1) = \bar{q}$ and $q(t) = \bar{\alpha}\bar{q}$.

We are now confronted with the same problem we met in the proof of the Turnpike Theorem in Chapter X. The argument may advance in exactly the same way. In fact, if the system of difference equations (9) satisfies an assumption that is equivalent to the assumption on critical characteristic roots (v) in Chapter X, the efficient path remains for most of the long period within the prescribed (very small) neighbourhood of the Golden Growth path. Also we can show that unless we have such an assumption, we generally cannot get rid of cycles around the Golden Growth path. The winning trick is that assumption, but the trump is not always in our hands.

6. Before concluding the discussion of the Final State Turnpike Theorem, we make a supplementary analysis which supplies interesting additional information about convergence of efficient paths to the Turnpike. So far we have been concerned with the convergence of the proportions between the outputs $y_1(t)$, ..., $y_n(t)$, $l(t)$ in the case of the strong theorem (or between the discounted total outputs $Y_1(T)$, ..., $Y_n(T)$, $L(T)$ in the case of the weak theorem) to the Turnpike proportions. But convergence of the level of the passing state $(y(t), l(t))$ or of the average state $\left(\frac{Y(T)}{T}, \frac{L(T)}{T}\right)$ has been left untouched. We can show that when the proportions are strongly convergent, the level of $(y(t), l(t))$ will grow for most of the programming period T at a rate approximately equal to $\bar{\alpha}-1$; that is, when T is sufficiently long, we have for most t,

$$\frac{y_j(t)}{\bar{\alpha}^t} \simeq q\bar{y}, \qquad \frac{l(t)}{\bar{\alpha}^t} \simeq q\bar{l}, \qquad j = 1, ..., n,$$

[1] If $y_j(t-1)$ (or $l(t-1)$) exceeds $x_j(t)$ for some j (or $m(t)$) by a significant amount, we shall lose nothing in later periods by replacing $(x(t-1), m(t-1)) \to (y(t-1), l(t-1))$ by $(x(t-1), m(t-1)) \to (x(t), m(t))$ which is also feasible because excessive outputs and labour can be disposed of freely. This new process is a non-top process lying outside the prescribed neighbourhood of the top facet; this is a contradiction, because such a non-top process can never appear during the long period if the path is to be efficient.

where the common constant scalar q depends on the starting point $(y(0), l(0))$ of the path but is independent of the length of the programming period T.

Convergence of the level (discounted by $\bar{\alpha}$) of $(y(t), l(t))$ may be verified in the following way: As (7) holds in each period and feasibility requires that each element of $(x(t), m(t))$ should not exceed the corresponding element of $(y(t-1), l(t-1))$, we find that

$$\sum_j \bar{p}_j y_j(t) + \bar{p}_{n+1} l(t) \leqq \bar{\alpha}^t \{\sum_j \bar{p}_j y_j(0) + \bar{p}_{n+1} l(0)\}.$$

Together with the fact that all $\bar{p}_1, \ldots, \bar{p}_{n+1}$ are positive, this means that $y_j(t)/\bar{\alpha}^t$ and $l(t)/\bar{\alpha}^t$ cannot tend to infinity. Consider two efficient paths $(y_j(t), l(t))$ and $(y_j'(t), l'(t))$ of different programming periods T and T', respectively (both being sufficiently long), such that for most t,

$$\frac{y_j(t)}{\bar{\alpha}^t} \doteqdot q\bar{y}_j, \qquad \frac{l(t)}{\bar{\alpha}^t} \doteqdot q\bar{l}, \qquad j = 1, \ldots, n$$

and

$$\frac{y_j'(t)}{\bar{\alpha}^t} \doteqdot q'\bar{y}_j, \qquad \frac{l'(t)}{\bar{\alpha}^t} \doteqdot q'\bar{l}, \qquad j = 1, \ldots, n.$$

Suppose these two sets of approximate equalities hold for t_1 and t_2, respectively. We may assume without loss of generality that $t_1 < t_2$ and $q \geqq q'$.

The discounted level of the efficient path of order T is almost as high as q at time t_1, and its proportions approximate the Turnpike proportions. We may switch the path onto the Golden Equilibrium path at a negligible cost, and may proceed along it until period t_2. Hence, there is a feasible path of greater order t_2 with Turnpike proportions of about the same discounted level q. If $q > q'$, it is clear that it dominates the efficient path of order T' at t_2. This disproves the efficiency of the path $(y'(t), l'(t))$. Thus, q and q' must be equal to each other as far as efficient paths are concerned.

On the other hand, when we have only the weak Turnpike property, there may be a number of long-run efficient paths converging to the same Turnpike at different average levels. In fact, as is illustrated below, we can construct a model in which the same initial position generates different long-run efficient paths with different average levels. Thus, the convergence implications of the weak theorem are poor; it does not rule out various cases, say 'cyclic' cases, which are considered as exceptions to the strong theorem. In order to strengthen the former into the latter we must introduce some additional condition or set of conditions. The strong super-additivity and the 'critical' assumption about the characteristic roots are sufficient conditions, but their reality is dubious; and even the original von Neumann model without consumption may not fulfil either of them. Unless we have the strong theorem that is based on more realistic sufficient conditions, it is nothing but an abortive flower, however ample its implications are.

The final paragraphs are devoted to giving a numerical example which shows that efficiency in terms of the final state does not imply the convergence of the level of the average state $\left(\frac{Y(T)}{T}, \frac{L(T)}{T}\right)$. Let us consider a two-sector economy where a single kind of commodity (or a composite commodity consisting of various kinds of commodities) is produced by means of labour, and itself and is consumed by labour. Assume that only three basic aggregate processes are available in the economy. They might emerge as follows.

	Process 1		Process 2		Process 3	
	Input	*Output*	*Input*	*Output*	*Input*	*Output*
Commodity	1	4	2	2	1	$2\frac{1}{3}$
Labour	2	2	1	4	2	$2\frac{5}{6}$

The good and labour are arranged so that the first elements of the input and output vectors stand for the input x and the output y of the commodity, while the second elements for the labour forces, m and l, at the beginning and end of a period, respectively. It can be verified that the production possibilities generated by these processes give the Golden Equilibrium rate of growth of unity (that is to say, $\bar{\alpha} = 2$), and the Golden Equilibrium process is formed by super-adding the first and second processes; $(\bar{x}, \bar{m}) \rightarrow (\bar{y}, \bar{l})$ is $(3, 3) \rightarrow (6, 6)$.

Now suppose one unit of the commodity and two units of labour are available at the beginning of period 1. They are enough for the first process to operate at unit intensity; therefore, at the end of the period we get four units of the commodity and two units of labour, which may be used up by the second process in period 2. Such alternate operations of the first and second processes will generate the path shown in Table 1.

TABLE 1

t	0	1	2	3	4	...
$y(t)$	1	4	4	16	16	...
$l(t)$	2	2	8	8	32	...

On the other hand, the same initial amounts of the commodity and labour are sufficient for operating the first and third processes at respective intensities, 0.2 and 0.8. This combination of the processes will yield the commodity and labour in the same amount, $2\frac{2}{3}$, at the end of period 1, so that we may use the first and second processes in period 2 and thereafter get a balanced growth at the rate $\bar{\alpha}-1$. We thus have an alternative path given in Table 2.

TABLE 2

t	0	1	2	3	4	...
$y(t)$	1	$2\frac{2}{3}$	$5\frac{1}{3}$	$10\frac{2}{3}$	$21\frac{1}{3}$	...
$l(t)$	2	$2\frac{2}{3}$	$5\frac{1}{3}$	$10\frac{2}{3}$	$21\frac{1}{3}$	...

These two paths have efficiency of any order. As $\lim_{T\to\infty} Y(T)/T = \lim_{T\to\infty} L(T)/T = 1.5$ for the first path, while they are $1\frac{1}{3}$ for the second path, we find that there are two kinds of efficient paths which have different asymptotic discounted average levels. It may be worth pointing out that one of the two paths (the first one) traces out cycles around the Turnpike; it seems that the non-convergence of the average level is closely related to the cyclic phenomena in the Turnpike problem.

7. The criterion we have so far applied to choosing efficient paths is given in terms of the final states. This procedure may be justified if it is our object to bequeath as much as we can to the 'future'. But if children and grandchildren are not to be sacrificed in the interest of great grandchildren, their consumption should also be the desiderata in making the long-run growth programme. Not only the final state but also intermediate states on the way must be evaluated according to some principle of welfare judgment.

In Chapter XV and the preceding sections of this chapter, the workers' consumption of goods has been discussed in terms of the aggregate process of producing goods and manpower, but not in terms of the utility it brings them. It is nevertheless true that even a meal for a dog may be criticized by a veterinary surgeon (and by the dog himself), so we may introduce, with more justification, a utility (or welfare) function which describes the preference ordering (by the workers or planning authorities) of various labour-feeding activities.

Let $y_j(t-1)$ be the amount of good j available at the beginning of period t, and $x_j^I(t)$ the amount of good j used as industrial input in the same period. It is evident that the workers' consumption $x_j^F(t)$ in period t cannot exceed the remainder of the stock $y_j(t-1)$ after subtracting the input $x_j^I(t)$. For each good we have a stream of the workers' consumption,

$$x_j^F(1),\ x_j^F(2),\ \ldots,\ x_j^F(T),\ y_j(T), \qquad j = 1, \ldots, n,$$

of order $T+1$, ending with $y_j(T)$; $x_j^F(t)$ is consumed by $m(t)$ or by $l(t-1)$ workers, while the disposal of $y_j(T)$ is in the hands of the $l(T)$ 'future' people. We could assume as before that the dynamic utility function is of the popular form,

$$u(T) = \sum_{t=1}^{T} \frac{1}{\theta^{t-1}} f(x^F(t)),$$

but instead we assume, throughout the rest of this chapter, that it is of the alternative form that has been discussed at the end of Chapter XII.

Now suppose society has a subjective time-preference factor θ such that $\alpha \geqq \theta \geqq 1$[1] and aggregate the consumption of good j at different dates as the discounted average:

$$C_j(T) = \frac{x_j^F(1) + \dfrac{x_j^F(2)}{\theta} + \ldots + \dfrac{x_j^F(T)}{\theta^{T-1}} + \dfrac{y_j(T)}{\theta^T}}{T+1}, \qquad j = 1, \ldots, n.$$

Similarly, we have the discounted average of the time stream of the number of workers:

$$N(T) = \frac{m(1) + \dfrac{m(2)}{\theta} + \ldots + \dfrac{m(T)}{\theta^{T-1}} + \dfrac{l(T)}{\theta^T}}{T+1}.$$

When a Golden Equilibrium path starts from a point $(\bar{x}, \bar{m})$ in the balanced proportions at the beginning of period 1, the amounts of goods consumed by the workers and the size of the labour force grow according to the formulae,

$$x^F(t) = \bar{\alpha}^{t-1}\bar{x}^F \quad \text{and} \quad m(t) = \bar{\alpha}^{t-1}\bar{m}, \qquad j = 1, \ldots, n,$$

respectively, and we have at the end of period T goods and labour in the amounts

$$\bar{\alpha}^{T-1}\bar{y}_j \qquad \text{and} \qquad \bar{\alpha}^{T-1}\bar{l}, \qquad j = 1, \ldots, n.$$

They are discounted to give

$$\bar{C}_j(T) = \frac{\left\{1 + \dfrac{\bar{\alpha}}{\theta} + \ldots + \left(\dfrac{\bar{\alpha}}{\theta}\right)^{T-1}\right\}\bar{x}_j^F + \dfrac{\bar{\alpha}^{T-1}\bar{y}_j}{\theta^T}}{T+1},$$

$$\bar{N}(T) = \frac{\left\{1 + \dfrac{\bar{\alpha}}{\theta} + \ldots + \left(\dfrac{\bar{\alpha}}{\theta}\right)^{T-1}\right\}\bar{m} + \dfrac{\bar{\alpha}^{T-1}\bar{l}}{\theta^T}}{T+1}.$$

[1] That is to say, the subjective rate of time-preference cannot be greater than the Golden Equilibrium rate of growth. As in Chapter XIII, the case of $\theta > \bar{\alpha}$ is subject to important exceptions of the Consumption Turnpike Theorem and is not considered in the subsequent discussion int he text.

where $j = 1, ..., n$. The preference ordering (of the workers or the authorities) between the Golden average state $(\bar{C}(T), \bar{N}(T))$ and any feasible $(C(T), N(T))$, is described by a utility function $U(C(T), N(T))$, which in addition to the usual properties of U such as continuity, diminishing marginal rates of substitution between goods etc., has the following two properties:

(a) quasi-homogeneity in the sense that

$$U(C(T), N(T)) \geqq U(\bar{C}(T), \bar{N}(T)) \quad \text{if and only if}$$
$$U(\lambda C(T), \lambda N(T)) \geqq U(\lambda \bar{C}(T), \lambda \bar{N}(T)) \quad \text{for any} \quad \lambda > 0,$$

and

(b) the positive utility of the Golden Equilibrium in the sense that

$$U(\bar{C}(T), \bar{N}(T)) > U(a_1, ..., a_{n+1}) \quad \text{for all sufficiently small positive numbers } a_1, ..., a_{n+1}.$$

We then see from the former that if $N(T) = \bar{N}(T)$, then

$$U(C(T), N(T)) \geqq U(\bar{C}(T), \bar{N}(T))$$

implies $U(C(T)/N(T), 1) \geqq U(\bar{C}(T)/\bar{N}(T), 1)$ and vice versa; that is to say no matter how large the population is, a path with the same discounted average number of persons as that of the Golden Equilibrium can consistently be compared with the Golden Equilibrium in terms of the average consumption per man, $C(T)/N(T)$ and $\bar{C}(T)/\bar{N}(T)$; while property (b) implies that the Golden Equilibrium is preferred to the 'desert', with very little fruits, water only at oases, ..., and a few inhabitants. Assumption (a) is rather restrictive, but (b) is very realistic in spite of rejection of it by such odd people as Zen Buddists who would enjoy a state of nothing.

Let us assume, as in the previous section, the uniqueness of the Turnpike; that is to say, there are no two different Golden Equilibrium processes which remain different after normalization; after normalization they become the same process $(\bar{x}, \bar{m}) \rightarrow (\bar{y}, \bar{l})$. We also assume that goods and labour are available in positive amounts at the starting point, i.e., $(y(0), l(0)) > 0$. Being armed with these assumptions, we can establish a weak (or average) Consumption Turnpike Theorem which states that when the programming period T is taken long, any Ramsey optimal path maximizing the utility $U(C(T), N(T))$ converges to the Turnpike in the weak or average sense, that is, each $Y_j(T)/L(T)$ tends to $\bar{y}_j/\bar{l}$ as T tends to infinity.

Prior to launching into the proof of the theorem, we pay attention to the following fundamental relationship. When goods available in the future are discounted at a rate of subjective time-preference that is not greater than the Turnpike rate of growth, the Turnpike (that is a balanced growth path with the maximum rate) gives the maximum of U among all possible balanced growth paths. To show this we compare any balanced growth path whose growth rate is $\alpha-1$ (say), with the Turnpike which has growth rate $\bar{\alpha}-1$. Let

$$\gamma = \frac{1+\dfrac{\alpha}{\theta}+\left(\dfrac{\alpha}{\theta}\right)^2+\ldots+\left(\dfrac{\alpha}{\theta}\right)^{T-1}}{T+1} \quad \text{and} \quad \delta = \frac{\dfrac{\alpha^{T-1}}{\theta^T}}{T+1}.$$

Replacing α by $\bar{\alpha}$ in these formulas, we obtain $\bar{\gamma}$ and $\bar{\delta}$. From the definitions of $C(T)$ and $N(T)$, it is evident that the first path brings about the utility

$$u(T) = U(\gamma x^F(1)+\delta y(1),\ \gamma m(1)+\delta l(1)),$$

while the second brings about

$$\bar{u}(T) = U(\bar{\gamma}\bar{x}^F+\bar{\delta}\bar{y},\ \bar{\gamma}\bar{m}+\bar{\delta}\bar{l}).$$

As $\bar{\alpha}-1$ is the unique maximum among all possible rates of balanced growth, we have $\alpha < \bar{\alpha}$. This, together with $\theta \leqq \bar{\alpha}$, leads to the following long-run properties:

$$\lim_{T\to\infty} \frac{\gamma}{\bar{\gamma}} = 0 \quad \text{and} \quad \lim_{T\to\infty} \frac{\delta}{\bar{\gamma}} = 0,$$

which result in the finding that $\bar{u}(T)$ is definitely greater than $u(T)$ as T becomes very large. This is so because, by the quasi-homogeneity (a), we may compare the two utilities in terms of $U\left(\dfrac{\gamma}{\bar{\gamma}}x^F(1)+\dfrac{\delta}{\bar{\gamma}}y(1),\ \dfrac{\gamma}{\bar{\gamma}}m(1)+\dfrac{\delta}{\bar{\gamma}}l(1)\right)$ and $U\left(\bar{x}^F+\dfrac{\bar{\delta}}{\bar{\gamma}}\,\bar{y},\ m+\dfrac{\bar{\delta}}{\bar{\gamma}}\,l\right)$, the latter being greater than the former for large T because of the above long-run properties and assumption (b). The identity of the Turnpike with the best one among possible paths of balanced growth is thus established.

8. The proof of the Consumption Turnpike Theorem is not different in its essence from that of the Final State Turnpike Theorem. We have already seen that super-additivity and the constant returns to scale of aggregate processes imply, together with costless disposal of goods and labour, the feasibility of the following process:

$$\left(\frac{x(1)}{\bar{\alpha}w(T)}+\frac{Y(T)}{\bar{\alpha}w(T)},\ \frac{m(1)}{\bar{\alpha}w(T)}+\frac{L(T)}{\bar{\alpha}w(T)}\right) \to \left(\frac{Y(T)}{w(T)},\ \frac{L(T)}{w(T)}\right), \tag{3}$$

where $w(T)$ is the sum of all $Y_j(T)$ and $L(T)$, as before.

To show that $\lim_{T\to\infty} w(T) = \infty$, we normalize the Golden process $(\bar{x}, \bar{m})$ such that

$$y(0) \geqq \bar{x} \quad \text{and} \quad l(0) \geqq \bar{m}. \tag{10}$$

We first observe that if $C(T)$ and $N(T)$ are the discounted averages generated by a Ramsey optimal path, then there is a positive constant k such that

$$\lim_{T\to\infty}\left(\sum_j \frac{C_j(T)}{\bar{N}(T)}+\frac{N(T)}{\bar{N}(T)}\right) \geqq k. \tag{11}$$

This is shown in the following way. If the contrary were true we would have

$$\lim_{T\to\infty} U\left(\frac{C(T)}{\bar{N}(T)}, \frac{N(T)}{\bar{N}(T)}\right) = U(0, 0),$$

which under property (b) is less than $U(\bar{C}(T)/\bar{N}(T), 1)$.[1] Hence, $U(C(T), N(T))$ is less than $U(\bar{C}(T), \bar{N}(T))$ by the quasi-homogeneity property (a). On the other hand, (10) means that the Golden Equilibrium growth is feasible for the given initial state. Therefore, the inequality just derived contradicts the Ramsey optimality of the path $(x(1), m(1))$, $(x(2), m(2))$, ..., $(y(T), l(T))$, so that (11) holds.

Let us now suppose the contrary of the conclusion to be obtained, i.e., that $w(T)$ converges as T tends to infinity. Then, from the definition of $w(T)$, it follows that $y_j(t)$ and $l(t)$ grow at rates less than $\bar{\alpha}-1$. As $x_j^F(t)$ and $m(t)$ are bounded above by $y_j(t-1)$ and $l(t-1)$, it follows that they must also grow at rates less than $\bar{\alpha}-1$. Accordingly, in view of the definitions of $C_j(T)$, $N(T)$ and $\bar{N}(T)$, as well as the hypothesis that $\bar{\alpha}/\theta$ is greater than unity, we find that $\bar{N}(T)$ diverges as T tends to infinity at a greater rate than $C_j(T)$ and $N(T)$ do. This implies that $C_j(T)/\bar{N}(T)$ and $N(T)/\bar{N}(T)$ converge to zero. On the other hand (11) is valid; an obvious contradiction.

Once the divergence of $w(T)$ is established, the argument proceeds just as it did in a previous section. In (3), $x(1)/w(T)$ and $m(1)/w(T)$ become negligible, while $Y(T)/w(T)$ and $L(T)/w(T)$ approach the limits y^* and l^*, respectively. It is obvious that a feasible process $\left(\frac{y^*}{\bar{\alpha}}, \frac{l^*}{\bar{\alpha}}\right) \to (y^*, l^*)$ thus obtained as a limiting process gives a balanced growth at the rate $\bar{\alpha}-1$. It follows from the uniqueness assumption that it must be normalized as $(\bar{x}, \bar{m}) \to (\bar{y}, \bar{l})$. Hence, the weak (or average) Turnpike property is verified for Ramsey optimal paths; namely, along a very long-run path of Ramsey optimal growth the discounted average output per man (defined as (1)) of each good is approximately equal to its Golden Equilibrium value.

9. Like the weak Final State Turnpike Theorem, the Consumption Turnpike Theorem does not assert anything about the convergence of time components $x_j^F(t)/m(t)$ and $y_j(t)/l(t)$, $j = 1, ..., n$, of the discounted

[1] Note that $U(\bar{C}(T)/\bar{N}(T), 1)$ is independent of T.

averages $C_j(T)/N(T)$ and $Y_j(T)/L(T)$, $j = 1, \ldots, n$, to the Turnpike, if it is formulated in the present manner. What additional condition (or set of conditions) is sufficient for ensuring strong convergence? The one which at once comes to mind is that of strong super-additivity used in the proof of the Final State Theorem. It is confirmed that a parallel argument can be made in the present case, but as has been mentioned the assumption of strong super-additivity lacks firm realistic foundations.

However, as for the Consumption Turnpike Theorem we have an interesting case worth discussing. So far, it has been supposed that society maximizes the utility which depends upon the discounted averages of consumption streams and the population stream, $C_j(T)$ and $N(T)$, $j = 1, \ldots, n$. This implies that there is no preference between two paths which give the same averages; it is highly probable, however, that society will more or less avoid fluctuations in the sense that a more stabilized stream of consumption of goods is preferred to those with fluctuations.[1]

Let S_j be the average of deviations of the per capita consumption of good j from its equilibrium value; i.e.,

$$S_j(T) = \left(\left| \frac{x_j^F(1)}{m(1)} - \frac{\bar{x}_j^F}{\bar{m}} \right| + \ldots + \left| \frac{x_j^F(T)}{m(T)} - \frac{\bar{x}_j^F}{\bar{m}} \right| + \left| \frac{y_j(T)}{l(T)} - \frac{\bar{y}_j}{\bar{l}} \right| \right) \Big/ (T+1).$$

It is clear that the discounted average consumption per man $C(T)/N(T)$ strongly converges to the Golden value if and only if $\lim_{T\to\infty} S_j(T) = 0$. We now assume that the planning authorities maximize the utility depending not only on $C(T)$ and $N(T)$ but also on $S(T)$:

$$U = U(C(T), N(T), S(T)), \qquad \text{where } S = (S_1, \ldots, S_n),$$

which preserves properties (a) and (b) with respect to $C(T)$ and $N(T)$; i.e.,

(a′) $U(C(T), N(T), S(T)) \geqq U(\bar{C}(T), \bar{N}(T), 0)$ if and only if $U(\lambda C(T), \lambda N(T), S(T)) \geqq U(\lambda \bar{C}(T), \lambda \bar{N}(T), 0)$ for any $\lambda > 0$,

(b′) $U(\bar{C}(T), \bar{N}(T), 0) > U(a_1, \ldots, a_{n+1}, 0)$ for all sufficiently small positive numbers, $a_1, \ldots, a_{n+1}$.

For establishing the strong convergence we make the additional assumption of 'fluctuation aversion':

(c) U is a decreasing function of S.

Let us now suppose that $x_j^F(t)/m(t)$ does not tend strongly towards the equilibrium value $\bar{x}_j^F/\bar{m}$; then $S_j(T)$ will remain positive, however large

[1] From the individual's point of view it is often said that the time-pattern of consumption would not be steady as a general rule. Remember, however, that the Consumption Turnpike Theorem is concerned with comparison between consumption streams of the society over a number of generations.

T may be. On the other hand, it follows from the free disposal of goods and labour, and the uniqueness of the Turnpike, that goods and labour are not free at the state of Golden Equilibrium; this in turn implies that along any feasible path $y_j(t)$, $x_j^F(t)$, $m(t)$ and $l(t)$ cannot grow at a long-run rate greater than $\bar{\alpha}-1$. Hence, $C(T)/\bar{N}(T)$, and $N(T)/\bar{N}(T)$ are bounded above. By putting $\lambda = 1/\bar{N}(T)$ in (a′), we have

$$U\left(\frac{C(T)}{\bar{N}(T)}, \frac{N(T)}{\bar{N}(T)}, S(T)\right) \geqq U\left(\frac{\bar{C}(T)}{\bar{N}(T)}, 1, 0\right)$$

for a Ramsey optimal path. The negative effect of $S(T)$ on U and the boundedness of $C(T)/\bar{N}(T)$ and $N(T)/\bar{N}(T)$ imply that there should be an S^* such that the above expression does hold only for those $S(T)$ which do not exceed S^*. It is evident that when the negative effect of $S(T)$ on U is very strong, that is to say, when people have very strong fluctuation-aversion, S^* is nearly equal to zero; hence $S_j(T) \simeq 0$ for each j. We obtain the strong convergence of $x_j^F(t)/m(t)$ to $\bar{x}_j^F/\bar{m}$, $j = 1, ..., n$.

A sharp eye will not fail to find that strong convergence of the consumption per man, $x_j^F(t)/m(t)$, does not imply that of the output per man, $y_j(t)/l(t)$ to $\bar{y}_j/\bar{l}$, and that it is the latter property which the strong Turnpike Theorem asserts. A simple device to get it would be to assume, instead of the aversion to fluctuation in per capita consumption of goods, that the people or the authorities prefer a more balanced growth of outputs to a growth at the same long-run rate but with fluctuations. Such aversion to fluctuation in outputs would easily be incorporated into the present model by re-defining $S_j(T)$ only as

$$S_j(T) = \left(\left|\frac{y_j(1)}{l(1)} - \frac{\bar{y}_j}{\bar{l}}\right| + \left|\frac{y_j(2)}{l(2)} - \frac{\bar{y}_j}{\bar{l}}\right| + \ldots + \left|\frac{y_j(T)}{l(T)} - \frac{\bar{y}_j}{\bar{l}}\right|\right)\Big/ T.$$

But such a simple, formal revision will be criticized on the grounds that there is no justification in avoiding output fluctuations; in fact, people will be prepared to accept cycles of outputs if they are technically required for a Ramsey optimal growth. We may, therefore, conclude by saying that the introduction of the device of very strong fluctuation-aversion could eliminate cycles of the per capita consumption of goods, but not those of the per capita outputs; we still cannot get rid of cyclic exceptions from the Turnpike Theorem.[1]

[1] As for the discounted level of the average state $\left(\frac{Y(T)}{T}, \frac{L(T)}{T}\right)$ it has been shown that if the long-run *efficient* paths are strongly convergent, their average states approach an asymptotic discounted level depending on the initial position. We have a similar observation with respect to Ramsey optimal paths; that is to say, if Ramsey optimal paths are strongly convergent, their average states approach an asymptotic discounted level. But it seems to be difficult to make any general statement concerning the convergence of the levels of Ramsey optimal paths that are merely weakly convergent.

APPENDIX

EXISTENCE OF THE VON NEUMANN EQUILIBRIUM

1. THIS appendix aims at facilitating a clearer comprehension of Chapters VI and VII. A large literature is already available on existence of the von Neumann balanced-growth equilibrium. Nevertheless, an additional exposition will be welcomed, because most of the previous writings are highly sophisticated and average economic students still find them difficult to read.[1]

For the sake of simplicity we confine ourselves to examination of the *original* von Neumann system fulfilling, among other things, the following assumptions: (a) capitalists do not consume and automatically invest their whole income; (b) workers cannot save and are prohibited from consumer choice; and (c) the system is 'indecomposable' so that every good is involved, either as input (in the 'augmented' sense) or as output, in every process. As much as possible, we shall stick to the notation that was used in the text: A denotes the input-coefficient matrix, B the output-coefficient matrix, L the labour-input-coefficient vector, x the intensity vector, y the normalized price vector, α one plus the rate of growth, and β one plus the rate of profits.

In the market there is only one kind of 'basket' which workers can buy. Each basket contains commodities in the fixed amounts, $e_j, j = 1, \ldots, n$, and e denotes the n-dimensional row vector $(e_1, \ldots, e_n)$. Suppose now each worker buys h baskets. In a state of balanced growth, αxL workers

[1] The original proof by von Neumann uses a fixed-point theorem; the proof by Kakutani uses a more general (and more difficult) fixed-point theorem; the proofs by Georgescu–Roegen and Gale use the theorem of the separating hyperplane; the proof by Kemeny, Morgenstern and Thompson uses theorems of game theory; the proof by Howe uses a duality theorem derived by Tucker. See J. von Neumann, 'A Model of General Economic Equilibrium,' *Review of Economic Studies*, Vol. 13 (1945–46); S. Kakutani, 'A Generalization of Brouwer's Fixed Point Theorem,' *Duke Mathematical Journal*, Vol. 8 (1941); N. Georgescu-Roegen, 'The Aggregate Linear Production Function and its Applications to von Neumann's Economic Model,' *Activity Analysis of Production and Allocation*, ed. by T. C. Koopmans (1951); D. Gale, 'The Closed Linear Model of Production,' *Linear Inequalities and Related Systems*, ed. by H. W. Kuhn and A. W. Tucker (1956); J. G. Kemeny, O. Morgenstern and G. L. Thompson, 'A Generalization of the von Neumann Model of an Expanding Economy,' *Econometrica*, Vol. 24 (1956); Charles W. Howe, 'An Alternative Proof of the Existence of General Equilibrium in a von Neumann Model,' *Econometrica*, Vol. 28 (1960). The following is a variation of elementary proof devised by Gale who proved the key lemma by mathematical induction. There is a similar elementary proof by Loomis. See D. Gale, *The Theory of Linear Economic Models* (McGraw-Hill, 1960); L. H. Loomis, 'On a Theorem of von Neumann,' *Proceedings of National Academy of Sciences, U.S.A.*, Vol. 32 (1946).

are employed, so that after subtracting their consumption from the outputs, xB, having resulted from the activities in the previous period, there remain goods of the amounts, $xB - \alpha xhLe$. The feasibility requires that these be not exceeded by the current inputs, αxA. Thus we have

$$\alpha xC(h) \leqq xB, \qquad x \in X, \tag{1}$$

where $C(h)$ represents $A + hLe$ and X is the set of all nonnegative x which are normalized such that the sum of the elements of each x is unity.

Regarding α and x as variable but h as given, we consider a problem to maximize α subject to (1). It is evident that the maximum value of α depends on the value of h specified:

$$\alpha = \alpha(h), \text{ or } g = \alpha - 1 = g(h).$$

This traces out the curve which was called the Optimum Transformation Frontier by M. Bruno.[1] Since h and g reflect the level of consumption and the level of investment, respectively, the curve gives the frontier of consumption and investment.

Next, let w be the wage rate which prevails when the prices y are normalized such that the sum of the elements of y equals unity. (We define Y as the set of all such nonnegative y's.) By spending w, one can buy ω baskets so that $w = \omega ey$. The augmented-input-coefficient matrix is then defined as $C(\omega) = A + \omega Le$, which is a function of ω, a kind of the real wage rate. Obviously, $C(\omega)y = Ay + wL$; so that the price-cost inequalities can be written as

$$\beta C(\omega)y \geqq By, \qquad y \in Y. \tag{2}$$

Regarding ω as given and y as variable, we minimize β subject to (2). The minimum value is a function of ω,

$$\beta = \beta(\omega), \text{ or } r = \beta - 1 = r(\omega),$$

which gives the outer envelope of the factor-price frontiers.

Let us now assume:

Assumption 1. For any $\omega \geqq 0$, every row of $C(\omega)$ has at least one positive entry.

Assumption 2. Every column of B has at least one positive entry.

Assumption 3. $B + C(\omega) > 0$ for all $\omega \geqq 0$.

Assumptions 1 and 2 were introduced by Kemeny, Morgenstern, and Thompson, whilst Assumption 3 was made by von Neumann himself for assuring the indecomposability of the system. By Assumption 1, $xC(h) \neq 0$ for all $x \in X$, so that $\alpha(h)$, the maximum of α, is finite. Next, let $y > 0$. By Assumption 1, $C(\omega)y > 0$, so that (2) holds for some finite β for

[1] M. Bruno, 'Fundamental Duality Relations in the Pure Theory of Capital and Growth,' *Review of Economic Studies*, Vol. XXXVI (1969).

[2] See pp. 93–94 above.

$y > 0$. Therefore, $\beta(\omega)$, the minimum of β, should be finite. Moreover, it can be shown that $\alpha(h)$ and $\beta(\omega)$ are monotonic decreasing functions, because as $Le \geqq 0$, an increase in ω gives rise to a monotonic increase of $C(\omega)$.

Now, let $x(h)$ be an x at which α is maximized subject to (1), and let $y(\omega)$ be a y at which β is minimized subject to (2). In the original von Neumann model, because of the assumption that workers cannot save, every worker has to consume ω baskets, so that $h = \omega$. Therefore, we obtain

$$\alpha(\omega)x(\omega)C(\omega) \leqq x(\omega)B, \tag{1'}$$

$$\beta(\omega)C(\omega)y(\omega) \geqq By(\omega). \tag{2'}$$

In view of the nonnegativity of $x(\omega)$ and $y(\omega)$, we have from these

$$\alpha(\omega)x(\omega)C(\omega)y(\omega) \leqq x(\omega)By(\omega) \leqq \beta(\omega)x(\omega)C(\omega)y(\omega).$$

Furthermore, by virtue of Lemma 2 to be proved in Section 2 below, $\alpha(\omega)$ is at least as large as $\beta(\omega)$; therefore, the extreme right-hand side of the above expression does not exceed its extreme left-hand side. This implies that the above expression must hold with equality; hence

$$\alpha(\omega)x(\omega)C(\omega)y(\omega) = x(\omega)By(\omega), \tag{3}$$

$$\beta(\omega)x(\omega)C(\omega)y(\omega) = x(\omega)By(\omega). \tag{4}$$

Let us confine our examination to the case of indecomposability.[1] From Assumption 3 we have $x(\omega)[B + C(\omega)]y(\omega) > 0$, so that either $x(\omega)By(\omega)$ or $x(\omega)C(\omega)y(\omega)$ (or both) must be positive. Suppose now $x(\omega)C(\omega)y(\omega)$ is positive and $x(\omega)By(\omega)$ is zero. Then from (3), $\alpha(\omega)$ should be zero. But this contradicts Assumption 2, because it implies that $xB > 0$ for all $x > 0$, so that the maximum, $\alpha(\omega)$, has to be positive. Hence,

$$x(\omega)By(\omega) > 0. \tag{5}$$

Obviously, (1′), (2′), (3), (4), (5) establish the von Neumann equilibrium. Therefore, $\alpha(\omega)$, $\beta(\omega)$, $x(\omega)$, $y(\omega)$ are solutions. It follows from (3), (4) and (5) that $\alpha(\omega)$ equals $\beta(\omega)$. This result is valid for any $\omega \geqq 0$, provided that the system is indecomposable. Thus we obtain the conclusion which Bruno called the fundamental duality theorem; that is to say, the optimum transformation frontier is mathematically identical with the outer envelope of the factor-price frontiers. It must, however, be emphasized that the theorem is no longer true when the system is decomposable, as I have seen in the paper just mentioned.

[1] My article, 'Consumption-Investment Frontier, Wage-Profit Frontier and the von Neumann Growth Equilibrium,' *Zeitschrift für Nationalökonomie*, 1971, deals with a more general case where Assumption 3 does not necessarily hold.

2. Now we have to prove necessary lemmas.

Lemma 1. *Let Z be an $m \times n$ matrix. If there is no $y \in Y$ such that $Zy \leqq 0$, then $xZ > 0$ for some $x \in X$.*

Proof. The lemma is true when $n = 1$. Let us show that it is true for n if it is so for $n - 1$.

Let z_i be the i-th column of Z. Let $Z(\lambda)$ be the $m \times (n - 1)$ matrix defined as

$$Z(\lambda) = [z_1, \ldots, z_{n-2}, \lambda z_{n-1} + (1 - \lambda)z_n].$$

Then for any λ_0 in the interval [0, 1] there is no nonnegative, non-zero, $(n - 1)$-dimensional vector η such that $Z(\lambda_0)\eta \leqq 0$, because, by hypothesis, there is no $y \in Y$ such that $Zy \leqq 0$. As the lemma is true for $n - 1$, there is an $x \in X$ such that $xZ(\lambda_0) > 0$.

Let $\zeta(\lambda_0) = x[\lambda_0 z_{n-1} + (1 - \lambda_0)z_n]$ be maximized at $x = x(\lambda_0)$ subject to $xZ(\lambda_0) \geqq 0$ and $x \in X$. Of course, max $\zeta(\lambda_0) > 0$, so that either $x(\lambda_0)z_{n-1}$ or $x(\lambda_0)z_n$ (or both) is positive. When $\lambda_0 = 0$, we have max $\zeta(0) = x(0)z_n > 0$; when $\lambda_0 = 1$, $x(1)z_{n-1} > 0$.

Suppose now $x(0)z_{n-1} \leqq 0$. Both $x(\lambda)z_{n-1}$ and $x(\lambda)z_n$ are continuous functions of λ, and the latter is positive so long as the former is non-positive. Hence there is a λ, say λ^*, such that

$$x(\lambda^*)z_{n-1} > 0 \qquad \text{and} \qquad x(\lambda^*)z_n > 0. \tag{6}$$

Otherwise, we would have $x(1)z_{n-1} \leqq 0$, a contradiction.

On the other hand, if $x(0)z_{n-1} > 0$, then it is evident that we have (6) at $\lambda^* = 0$. Thus, in any case, we have a λ^* at which the two inequalities of (6) hold.

With respect to other elements we only have

$$x(\lambda^*)z_i \geqq 0, \qquad i = 1, \ldots, n - 2.$$

But we have seen that $xZ(\lambda^*) > 0$ for some $x \in X$. Hence, for a sufficiently small positive number μ, we obtain $[\mu x + (1 - \mu)x(\lambda^*)]Z > 0$. Clearly, $\mu x + (1 - \mu)x(\lambda^*) \in X$. Q.E.D.

Lemma 2. $\alpha(\omega) \geqq \beta(\omega)$.

Proof. Suppose the contrary, i.e., $\alpha(\omega) < \beta(\omega)$. Lemma 1 can be applied to $Z = B - \alpha(\omega)C(\omega)$. Since $\beta(\omega)$ is the minimum of β subject to (2) and $\alpha(\omega)$ is less than $\beta(\omega)$, there is no $y \in Y$ such that $Zy \leqq 0$. Hence, by Lemma 1, there is an x such that

$$xZ = x[B - \alpha(\omega)C(\omega)] > 0,$$

which implies that $\alpha(\omega)$ is not the maximum of α subject to (1), a contradiction. Q.E.D.

INDEX